THE NATIONAL CCF 1932-61

WALTER D. YOUNG

University of Toronto Press

1002740256

© University of Toronto Press 1969
Reprinted 1971
Printed in the United States of America
for University of Toronto Press
Toronto and Buffalo
ISBN 0-8020-5221-5 (cloth)
ISBN 0-8020-6117-6 (paper)
LC 73-460705

Michael Brook 1973.

THE ANATOMY OF A PARTY

THE ANATOMY OF A PARTY:

For
R. J. B.
teacher and friend

PREFACE

Although the Co-operative Commonwealth Federation ceased to exist formally in 1961 when it joined with the Canadian Labour Congress to found the New Democratic Party, it disappeared in name only. The same people, essentially the same goals, and the same belief in the cause of socialism continue to form the solid core of the NDP. Although its establishment was more carefully planned and directed by party politicians than was the case with the CCF, the NDP nevertheless retains many aspects of the movement of deeply concerned persons that brought the CCF into being. Like the CCF, the NDP is able to call upon its members for services and support in terms of time and money that evokes the envy of Liberal and Conservative organizers. And, unlike these two parties, it is based on mass membership.

In this book what is attempted is an analysis of the CCF as a movement and a party in order to shed some light on its success and failure in the Canadian polity. Hartzian analysis notwithstanding, the character of the CCF as a movement operating within the context of a parliamentary federal system served to preserve as a unique North American phenomenon a socialist party that did not die, that exerted a significant influence on the shape of Canadian politics and public policy far in excess of what its size and electoral strength would warrant, and that, with some modifications, formed the government of Manitoba in 1969 while remaining the official opposition in two other western provinces.

Research for this study began as a doctoral dissertation and benefitted much at that stage from the advice and encouragement of Professors C. B. Macpherson, Paul Fox and, particularly, Alex Brady. Throughout its preparation I had the full co-operation of the CCF and NDP National Offices and the several provincial headquarters across the country. In this respect the assistance of Carl Hamilton and Terry Grier was invaluable.

I would like to acknowledge the generosity of Frank Scott and George Grube, who gave me full access to their papers and the benefit of their personal knowledge of the CCF. The Hon. M. J. Coldwell made all his papers available and generously submitted to extensive interviews. His co-operation and enthusiasm added a great deal to whatever is worthwhile in this book. Many others in the CCF offered whatever help they could. I would like particularly to acknowledge the help of Frank Underhill, Stanley Knowles, Douglas Fisher, David Lewis, Henry Spencer, the late Angus MacInnis, the late William Irvine, and Mrs. Grace MacInnis, MP. My friends and colleagues, Ivan Avakumovic and Kenneth McNaught, read drafts of the manuscript and gave me much sound advice and criticism. Peter Shapiro helped with some of the research and proofreading. Miss Jean Wilson of the University of Toronto Press was a painstaking editor and I am grateful for that. My wife Beryl, a thorough and patient critic, was a constant source of encouragement. What value there is in this book is the product of this help; the errors and weaknesses are mine.

Research was assisted at various points by Canada Council grants, as well as by the Centennial Publications Fund. The book has been published with the help of a grant from the Social Science Research Council, using funds provided by the Canada Council, and with the assistance of the Publications Fund of the University of Toronto Press.

Burgoyne Bay, July 1969   WY

CONTENTS

PREFACE vii

ONE / Introduction 2

TWO / The Radical Background 12

THREE / The Regina Manifesto 38

FOUR / Movement into Party, 1933–40 68

FIVE / Success and Failure, 1940–60 102

SIX / Organization and Structure 138

SEVEN / The CCF and the Voter 176

EIGHT / The CCF in Parliament 218

NINE / The CCF and the Communist Party 254

TEN / Conclusion 286

APPENDIX A 303

APPENDIX B 318

INDEX 321

THE ANATOMY OF A PARTY

INTRODUCTION

But the department store cannot be defined in terms of its brands and a party cannot be defined in terms of its principles. A party is a group whose members propose to act in concert in the competitive struggle for political power.

JOSEPH SCHUMPETER
Capitalism, Socialism and Democracy

Socialists belong to movements, capitalists support parties. From beginning to end, the Co-operative Commonwealth Federation (CCF) was referred to as a movement by its leaders and members. To them it was much more than a political party although, of necessity, it had to compete in the party battle. And, like its counterpart and mentor, the British Labour party, it struggled to prevent the demands of the party from overwhelming the ethic of the movement.[1] Belonging to a movement placed the members of the CCF somehow outside and above the party struggle; it meant that they stood for something more than the mere winning of power for its own sake. By contrast, it makes little sense to talk about membership in the Liberal or Progressive Conservative movements. People who are members of these parties have never considered themselves to be part of a movement or associated with a "cause." The distinction between a party and a movement is an important one to establish in discussing the CCF.

The analysis of a political party in a democracy must begin with one fundamental question: how successful was it in attracting popular support? All other questions are secondary because the purpose of a political party is winning elections in order to control the government.[2] Parties do perform other functions, but these are secondary and often incidental. Any body which does not function or at least attempt to function as an electoral machine is not a political party. And by the same token, the success of a party is best measured by the number of elections it wins. In 1935 Social Credit, for example, swept into power in Alberta largely on the strength of its appeal as a movement, but it quickly made the necessary adaptation to the party role. The Progressives, on the other hand, after their sudden success in the federal election of 1921, were unable to rationalize the goals of the movement with the requirements of party life and their failure to do so contributed significantly to their rapid decline.

Whereas the "pure" party seeks electoral victory, the movement seeks some major social change or reform. The program the party presents to the electorate is designed as a means to

1 / See, for example, "We, We Only, Are Left," *Times Literary Supplement*, March 31, 1966, 268, where the reviewer comments, "these young activists are keeping the soul of Labour alive, by preventing the *movement* from degenerating into just another party." Emphasis in original.

2 / "A political party is first of all an organized attempt to get power." E. E. Schattschneider, *Party Government* (New York 1942), 35. "The party is thus a loosely formed group of men who cooperate chiefly in an effort to get some of their number elected to office." A. Downs, *An Economic Theory of Democracy* (New York 1957), 25. And see J. R. Mallory, "Social Credit: Party or Movement," *Canadian Forum*, xxxv (June 1955), 52.

victory. The program of the movement is an expression of its
ultimate ideals and goals. Success for a party necessarily includes
success at the polls; for a movement the same is not true in that
its goals may be achieved by another agency stimulated by the
mere existence of the movement. Movements are similar to parties
in that they employ organization to achieve their objectives and
they usually extend beyond a single community in scope. Their
structure may be less clearly defined than a party's, but this is
not a major difference, for a definable and articulated structure
is a fairly recent phenomenon in Canadian parties. The major
distinction is one of goals. A movement is "a group venture
extending beyond a local community or a single event and involving a systematic effort to inaugurate changes in thought,
behaviour, and social relationships."[3] A movement seeks fundamental change and may or may not use political means to achieve
it; a party seeks power for its leaders through electoral success.
Its leaders may or may not then use this power to achieve goals
similar in nature to those sought by a movement; and it is
customary for party leaders to use their power in such a way as
to ensure their continuance in office, even if this means ignoring
or perverting their goals.

One of the characteristics of a movement is the dogged determination with which it clings to its ideals. Political parties are
often subject to pressures which call for, and produce, rapid and
occasionally radical alteration of their policies or doctrine. Political movements are subject to pressures to avoid any shift or
dilution of their principles. Because they are organizations of
like-minded people dedicated to a cause that is predicated on
what are seen as high moral values, movements have a vitality
and a tenacity which parties lack. They continue to exist in the
face of setbacks which would reduce a party to a shadow. Where
support given to a party may often shift to its opponents, members and supporters of movements are astonishingly faithful. It
is the dedication to an extra-personal cause that accounts for
this devotion. It is difficult to "believe in" winning elections;
belief in the rightness and inevitability of a co-operative commonwealth is easy by comparison. Losing an election shakes a
party, for this is the measure of its validity, its criterion of excellence. The validity of a movement, however, is contained in
its ideology. Failure to make converts does not alter or diminish

3 / Wendell King, *Social Movements in the United States* (New York
1956), 27. See also Rudolf Heberle, *Social Movements* (New York 1951),
6–11; W. B. Cameron, *Modern Social Movements* (New York 1966),
1–13; and H. Blumer, "Collective Behaviour," in R. E. Park, ed., *An
Outline of the Principles of Sociology* (New York 1939), 255.

the rightness of the cause: it merely demonstrates the need for more determined effort. Movements are affected by more subtle and complex social changes than parties, which are subject to the coarse and clear decisions of elections.

Movements with broad, inclusive goals requiring a major change in social values characteristically develop when demands for reform, that is, normative change, are frustrated; and when traditional avenues of access to the centres of power are blocked.[4] The Progressive movement represented a desire to reform the system in a manner more consistent with the farmers' notions of individualism and democracy. The changes sought were essentially normative, that is, they did not involve any radical alteration of the dominant values of Canadian society. The frustration of many farmers with the apparent failure of their demands for reform and the developing frustration of many urban intellectuals and supporters of the various labour parties meant that grievances then came to be stated in terms of values: production for use, not for profit; co-operation instead of competition, and so on. The *Manitoba Free Press*, reporting a meeting of the United Farmers of Canada (Saskatchewan Section) in 1931, pointed to a "rapidly dividing gulf developing between the business and professional classes in the towns and cities and the farming population, a division based upon the economic issues. Laissez-faire is no longer adequate as an economic doctrine in the rural area."[5] The same attitude was evident at a meeting of the Conference of Western Labour Political Parties the same year: "Delegates took the stand that the unemployed are not responsible personally for unemployment ... "[6] The demands for normative change or reform were focused in the Progressive movement and then gave way to demands for more fundamental change that were focused in the CCF.

The CCF was formed from the confederation of a number of different movements, both urban and rural, that had a common desire to change the system by changing the values on which it was based. All fell, more or less, into the category of social movements in the sense defined above. Smelser points out that value-oriented movements are common among politically disinherited people such as immigrants, the colonially dominated, persecuted minorities, people faced with seemingly inflexible political structures, and people in a situation where government by the established political parties seem to have failed them.[7] In

4 / A more elaborate statement of this argument may be seen in Neil J. Smelser, *Theory of Collective Behavior* (New York 1963), esp. chs. 9 and 10.
5 / *Manitoba Free Press*, July 8, 1931, and see W. L. Morton, *The Progressive Party in Canada* (Toronto 1950), 201. 6 / *Ibid.*, July 18, 1931.

short, where part of the population is faced with social or
economic disorder and with a political system which seems un-
responsive and which, like the social and economic system, has
not met their expectations, their reaction is to postulate a change
in the values of the system and to organize to bring about that
change.

In the CCF, the avenue of change utilized was the political
system. The CCF was, then, a movement *and* a party; unlike other
movements such as Moral Rearmament or the many nuclear
disarmament groups, it entered the political system and became
a part of it in order to effect the changes it advocated. A movement may have political goals, such as those of the disarmament
movements, but it does not necessarily engage in politics to
achieve its ends. Unlike Social Credit, the CCF retained many of
the characteristics of a movement throughout the twenty-eight
years of its history.

Where movement and party combine, as in the CCF, the aims
of one frequently frustrate the aims of the other, particularly
when these aims are in direct conflict. Because the CCF was in
some respects the inheritor of the Progressive tradition, it was to
an extent anti-party. Nevertheless, it had to operate within the
existing party system in order to achieve the goals it sought as a
movement. The history of the national CCF shows that it was
more successful as a movement than as a party, and that the
degree to which it succeeded as one and failed as the other was
determined by the effect one aspect had on the other. It is equally
true, however, that the party-movement has advantages the
"pure" party does not have. The relative permanence and stability of its electorate, the dedication and selflessness of its members, and the honest consistency of its goals provide it with
certainties "pure" parties lack. The *movement* may hinder the
party; it may also keep it alive.

A movement can be said to have succeeded when the changes
or reforms it champions have been made. When its goals have
been achieved, unless it seeks a new cause, it dies. A political
party succeeds when it wins an election and its leaders form the
government. Its goal remains essentially unchanged, however, for
it must win the next election, and the next. The regularity of
elections provides the political party with a single goal that does
not change as times change, one that is constantly renewed.
Movements, on the other hand, are themselves shaped by the

7 / Smelser, *Theory of Collective Behavior*, 325–33; see also S. M.
Lipset, *Agrarian Socialism* (Berkeley 1950); C. B. Macpherson, *Demo-
cracy in Alberta* (Toronto 1953); and John A. Irving, *The Social Credit
Movement in Alberta* (Toronto 1959).

times as are their goals. Unlike parties, the conditions in which
they operate are less certain and less disciplined. Certainty and
discipline must be generated from within the movement. As
specific goals are achieved, recede, or are rendered obsolete, new
ones must be found or the movement dies. With the signing of
the nuclear arms test-ban treaty, many of the nuclear disarmament movements disappeared and others became movements for
such causes as the diplomatic recognition of the People's Re-
public of China.

The party-movement both gains and loses because of the
combination. The discipline and certainty of the party political
system, that is, elections, propaganda, Parliament, and opposition parties, affect the nature of the movement and the clarity
with which it is able to perceive its goals, while the nature of the
movement, that is, chiliasm, dedication, iconoclasm, and sec-
tarianism, affects the operation of the party. The relationship
between the two is both beneficial and corrosive.

This was so in the case of the CCF. Although the CCF was
never in power in the dominion Parliament, and never even the
official opposition, many reforms were achieved through legislative action by the party in power as a result of the active presence
of the CCF. It brought the plight of the farmer and worker to the
attention of the government through the particularly potent
method of taking seats away from the other parties and threatening, or appearing to threaten, to win power itself. During the
forties, the political and economic establishment in Canada was
galvanized by the apparent growth of radicalism represented by
the courageous and determined band of democratic socialists in
the House of Commons and in the provincial legislatures of
British Columbia, Saskatchewan, and Ontario.

But the prime objective of a political party is not to influence
other parties or the governments they form. Parties certainly do
have this functional effect, but that is not why they exist. The
success of a party cannot be measured in terms of the number of
its policies adopted by other parties or by the legislation other
parties introduce when they are in power. There is something
slightly pathetic, if not fatuous, in a party appealing for public
support at the polls on the grounds that other parties have
enacted its program. For one thing such an appeal lacks credi-
bility to the ordinary voter, and for another it offers no basis for
proposing a change of government. Editorial writers praised the
CCF while urging that it should always remain in opposition.
J. S. Woodsworth was the conscience of Parliament, a saint and
a prophet, but never prime minister.

The success of the CCF as measured by its effect on the political　　**7** life of Canada is really the success of the CCF as a movement. The extent to which the Canadian polity moved toward the welfare state in the late thirties and forties was due in large measure to the activities of the CCF, indeed, to the simple fact that it existed. What W. L. Morton has said of Woodsworth is also true of the party he led: "More than any other Canadian public man, he helped transform Canadian politics from the politics of special and sectional interests to the politics of collective concern for the welfare of the individual in a society collectively organized."[8] From 1926, when Woodsworth succeeded in getting Mackenzie King to introduce the first old age pension legislation, to the introduction of medicare in Saskatchewan in 1963, the CCF was in the forefront of agitation for improved social legislation. And there is no doubt that the pressure exerted by the CCF through the speeches of its MPs and the upsurge in popular support in the forties pushed the Liberal government further in the direction of social reform than it would otherwise have gone. The prodigal's return by Mackenzie King to some of the ideas he first expressed in that tedious opus, *Industry and Humanity*, came about through his fear of the CCF usurping the radical role which he felt belonged to him and his party.[9] In 1942 King referred slightingly to the "immature Radicalism" of the CCF, but in 1943 he saw the CCF as a "serious threat on the national scene."[10] He was sufficiently disturbed by its growing strength to decide that the Liberal party had to counter-attack by placing more emphasis on post-war policy and by "keeping in touch with the working classes and farmers."[11] The radicalism of the post-war reforms proposed was the result of the CCF "presence."[12]

Progressive measures in labour legislation, housing, ownership of "natural monopolies," and agriculture were almost always enunciated first by the CCF. No party had a more enviable record in the defence of civil liberties even though the defence meant helping bitter enemies, as when the Communist party was persecuted under section 98 of the Criminal Code. The rescinding of that section was a direct result of CCF efforts. Members of

8 / W. L. Morton, *The Kingdom of Canada* (Toronto 1963), 443.

9 / See J. Pickersgill, *The Mackenzie King Record*, I, *1939–44* (Toronto 1960), *passim*, and J. W. Pickersgill and D. F. Forster, *The Mackenzie King Record*, VII (Toronto 1968), *passim*.

10 / *Ibid.*, 382, 9; and see p. 601 where King records that his reform measures – labour code, price floors, etc. – "cut out the ground ... from under the CCF and Tories alike ... " In 1944 King expressed the need to keep Liberal principles to the fore to avoid a CCF "sweep." *Ibid.*, 94.

11 / *Ibid.*, 643.   12 / See also R. M. Dawson, *The Government of Canada*, N. Ward, ed. (Toronto 1964), 455, 465; and N. Ward, *The Public Purse* (Toronto 1962), 258.

the party took pride in the fact that, as Stanley Knowles put it, "Canadians in every walk of life are indebted, in one way or another, to the battles waged on their behalf by the CCF, whether its strength was that of but a handful, or of the larger groups it had in Parliament from time to time."[13] The strength of purpose and determination characteristic of a movement served the CCF well in Parliament; its members were among the staunchest defenders and greatest practitioners of parliamentary democracy in the House of Commons. They enjoyed a well-deserved reputation for their devotion to their duties as members and for their mastery of procedure. It was not surprising that in 1957, Stanley Knowles, the CCF whip, was asked by Prime Minister Diefenbaker to be Speaker of the House. The parliamentary success of the CCF caused some anguish among the more radical members of the party who saw its success as fundamentally counter-revolutionary. It was, nevertheless, thoroughly consistent with the evolutionary character of the party ideology and quite in keeping with the Anglo-Saxon and British Labour party traditions of the CCF.

The achievements of the CCF were not mean. By any account it was a significant and influential force on the Canadian political scene. It altered the shape of politics, it altered the shape of policy, and it maintained a defence of principle at times when principles were forgotten by other parties and other politicians. All this won the party great respect, but no elections. In that sense, the CCF *party* was a failure, the CCF *movement* a success.

It is virtually impossible, however, to disentangle the CCF movement from the CCF party. One can say that the CCF failed as a party because not enough people voted for it. Why more people did not vote for it cannot be discovered without first seeing that the CCF was a movement which, like all movements, had characteristics that attracted some people and repelled others, and further that, although CCF strategists recognized this fact, the nature of the CCF as a movement prevented them from doing anything about it. At the beginning the CCF was more a movement than a party. The electoral process was simply a means of achieving social goals. Woodsworth made this explicit in the House of Commons when, having outlined the main points of the Regina Manifesto, he said, "We start out to bring about these changes by the old and tried political method of electing a sufficient number of people to parliament so that there will be a majority in favour of the program we advocate."[14] The end the CCF sought was the establishment of a co-operative common-

13 / S. H. Knowles, *The New Party* (Toronto 1961), 30.
14 / *Hansard*, 1934, 266.

wealth in Canada; the means was the election of enough MPs supporting that goal to enact it. The emphasis was not on forming a government, it was on getting a majority to support the CCF program – which may amount to the same thing, but the point to be made is that Woodsworth's emphasis was not on power, it was on change. Looking back to the beginnings of the CCF, M. J. Coldwell, leader of the party from 1940 to 1958, remarked, "We thought of our association as a movement of the people, not a closely knit group leading a party."[15]

As a movement makes use of the party system to achieve its ends, it must adopt the techniques of the other parties and becomes more a party in the process. Woodsworth sensed this and, with others in the group, opposed the centralization of the CCF. But as the party became enmeshed in the struggle for votes with the Liberal and Conservative parties, some of the freedom of the movement was sacrificed to the discipline of the party; some of the evangelical zeal of the movement was replaced by the drive to organize constituencies for the party. As the movement became more institutionalized, there was some dilution of the ideology, but the aspect of the CCF that was "movement" did not disappear. It had a crucial effect on the CCF as "party" until the end.

Stanley Knowles wrote in 1961 that there was still a need for a "movement of the people" and that the New Party (New Democratic Party, NDP) was in fact "a still larger movement" which the CCF and Canadian Labour Congress had created.[16] The new party laid increasingly less emphasis on education and the notion of the NDP as a movement was one held only by those who had been long active in the CCF. And even they changed: at the provincial convention of the Ontario NDP in April 1966, Donald MacDonald, leader of the Ontario party, formerly leader of the Ontario CCF and national director of education for the CCF before that, was reported as saying that the reorganization of the Ontario NDP would "transform the NDP from a movement to a party: 'It's becoming a serious political organization instead of a fumbling amateur one.' "[17]

It has been suggested that the progress of the CCF from movement to party that was continued in the development of the New Democratic Party was one of the organization coming to terms with the world.[18] The implication of this analysis is that the CCF

15 / Interview with the author, Aug. 1963.
16 / Knowles, *The New Party*, 32–3.
17 / David Scott, "The NDP Prepares to Take Over," *Globe and Mail*, April 30, 1966, 7.
18 / Leo Zakuta, *A Protest Movement Becalmed* (Toronto 1964), and

was, at the outset at any rate, unrealistic or other-worldly. It did, as do all movements, become institutionalized, but its creation was a realistic approach to the exigent circumstances by those involved. The reaction of the wheat farmer to the conditions in which he lived and worked was shrewdly realistic. The analysis of the ills of Canadian society provided by the socialists in the CCF was valid and demonstrably realistic. Within the context of the CCF as a movement the zeal of Woodsworth and the belief in the effectiveness of political evangelism were realistic or worldly.

Yet, at the same time, had the CCF not taken the electoral road to the co-operative commonwealth, had it not been in a position even to appear as a threat to as pure a political animal as Mackenzie King, then the many aims of the movement that were achieved would not have been achieved. The success of the movement, such as it was, was through the instrumentality of the party; the failure of the party was largely through the crippling effects of the movement. The CCF hung suspended between the realities of its doctrine and origin on one hand, and of the Canadian party system on the other.

The distinction between norm-oriented parties and value-oriented movements, like all such typologies, suffers if pressed too hard. To some extent all parties at some time display some of the characteristics of a movement and most movements actively engaged in politics display many of the characteristics of political parties. To put it another way, there are no pure elements in social science. The goals sought by the CCF, as expressed in the phrase "co-operative commonwealth," clearly involved significant changes in widely held values in Canada; the policies it advocated on the hustings were for the most part predicated on these values, but were often quite clearly proposals for reform or normative change. They could be, as indeed they were, enacted by a party which did not seek the same ultimate goals as the CCF. For the purpose of studying the CCF, the party-movement distinction is a useful one because it casts light on the reasons for the successes and failures of the CCF and provides a useful explanation of some aspects of political behaviour in the context of the Canadian party system. It is this general distinction that is applied throughout this study. It is a distinction which helps provide answers to the questions surrounding the success – or failure – of socialism in Canada.

"The Radical Political Movement in Canada," in S. D. Clark, ed., *Urbanism and the Changing Canadian Society* (Toronto 1961).

THE RADICAL BACKGROUND

2

As all traced their particular grievances to the same cause, the capitalist system, so all saw in a socialist society the one and only remedy for those grievances.

SAMUEL BEER
British Politics in a Collective Age

The CCF has generally been seen by students of Canadian politics as an agrarian protest movement, in some ways the successor to the Progressive party, with much in common with the Social Credit party and similar movements of agrarian radicalism in the American middle west.[1] In general, this view is misleading. For, although the CCF first formed a government in Saskatchewan, won more rural than urban seats, had as its statement of principles the Regina Manifesto, and owed a great deal to the tradition of agrarian radicalism that flourished in the Canadian wheat belt, it would be foolish to ignore the vital role played in the establishment and growth of the party by labour and urban socialist elements. The distribution of its votes in national elections is a further indication of the strong urban strain in the CCF. Although the votes were infrequently translated into seats, the CCF had more supporters in the urban areas of Ontario, Manitoba, and British Columbia than it had among the wheat farmers. Professor McNaught has pointed out that "the movement of the 'Thirties sprang from urban labour, the Christian social gospel of the Protestant churches and ... the radical urban intellectuals – as well as from the soil of the wheat belt."[2]

The party's founders recognized these roots at the Calgary conference in 1932. They insisted on appending the words "farmer, labour, socialist" to the full name of the party.[3] Among its supporters the CCF was often referred to as a "farmer-labour" party,[4] but since not all farmers were socialists, and the Fabian intellectuals of the League for Social Reconstruction were neither farmers nor labour, the Calgary appendage makes more sense. Clause three of the Calgary resolution was quite explicit: "The general viewpoint and program involved in the socialization of our economic life, has already been outlined and accepted by the

1 / See, for example, S. M. Lipset, *Agrarian Socialism* (Berkeley 1950), *passim*, and F. H. Underhill, who casually states, "Progressivism was reborn in the Cooperative Commonwealth Federation," in his "Political Parties and Ideas," in G. Brown, ed., *Canada* (Berkeley 1950), 341. See also G. Carter in S. Neuman, ed., *Modern Political Parties* (Chicago 1956). John Irving, "Prairie Ideals and Realities," *Queen's Quarterly*, LXIII (Summer 1956), sees the CCF "as a development from the more radical wing of the UFA," 194.

2 / K. W. McNaught, "CCF Town and Country," *Queen's Quarterly*, LXI (Summer 1954), 213. See also his *A Prophet in Politics* (Toronto 1959), 255–6, n. 1. And see Appendix III.

3 / Minutes, "Conference Resulting in Formation of the Co-Operative Commonwealth Federation," CCF Minute Books, Aug. 1, 1932, CCF Papers, Public Archives of Canada (hereafter CCFP and PAC).

4 / See, for example, David Lewis and F. R. Scott, *Make This Your Canada* (Toronto 1943), 118–19, and M. J. Coldwell, *Left Turn Canada* (Toronto 1945), 20.

Labour, Farmer, Socialist and other groups affiliating."[5] Why these forces should have come together in the Canadian West at the time they did was the result of a combination of factors, the roots of which extend back beyond the period of the First World War. It is enough to say for the moment that given the nature of rural society, the political traditions of the prairie provinces, and the effect of the depression on the western economy, the West offered the most fertile soil for the establishment of a party like the CCF. But without the presence of the urban labour parties, it is likely that the CCF would have suffered the same fate as the Progressives.

The background of agrarian protest in Canada has been carefully and exhaustively studied elsewhere.[6] Only brief mention needs to be made here of the growth and development of the agrarian movements and labour parties in order to provide a background for the events immediate to the formation of the CCF. Simplicity would seem to require that the CCF be seen as the lineal descendant of the Progressive party. This proposition, however attractive, does not sustain close scrutiny because the Progressive party was never in any sense a socialist party, and it clearly showed its dislike of radical labour politics on several occasions. The *Grain Growers' Guide*, organ of the Progressives and usually in the van of Progressive political thought,[7] vigorously opposed the Winnipeg General Strike. During the 1921 election campaign no effort was made to solicit labour support and those elements of the Progressive platform shared by the labour parties were deliberately understated. The Progressives were radicals in that they advocated change, but the change they favoured was not socialism. They were, in Morton's apt phrase, "crypto-Liberals,"[8] particularly in the Manitoba wing of the party though less so in the Alberta movement. Agrarian politics in Alberta were more radical and more class-conscious, a result of the activities of the United Farmers of Alberta and the Non-Partisan League. The "Ginger Group" of Progressive MPs who bolted their party and made common cause with J. S. Woodsworth's Labour group in Parliament were largely Albertans.

5 / Minutes, "Conference Resulting in the Formation of the CCF," CCFP.

6 / Lipset, *Agrarian Socialism*; C. B. Macpherson, *Democracy in Alberta* (Toronto 1953); W. L. Morton, *The Progressive Party in Canada* (Toronto 1950); P. F. Sharp, *Agrarian Revolt in Western Canada* (Minneapolis 1948); John Irving, *The Social Credit Movement in Alberta* (Toronto 1959).

7 / Morton, *Progressive Party*, 117–18.

8 / *Ibid.*, 200–1.

Progressivism was more a product of the same forces that subsequently gave rise to and sustained both the CCF and Social
Credit parties than it was their progenitor. The Progressive party
was not class-oriented; it supported reform within the established
system, not fundamental change of the system itself. The fleeting
success which the Progressives enjoyed did demonstrate that such
movements could succeed, just as their failure demonstrated that
such movements would also collapse unless they were prepared
to enter the political arena as an organized, disciplined party,
competing with the others. The Progressive movement was a
product of the same feelings of economic and political isolation,
of "quasi-colonial" exploitation,[9] and of frustrated ambitions
that led to the establishment of the CCF and Social Credit parties.

Many who later played an active part in the formation of the
CCF were members of the Progressive party, since it was at that
time a logical vehicle of protest against the studied refusal of the
political establishment in the East to recognize the special problems of the rural and urban inhabitants west of the Lakehead.
M. J. Coldwell, who succeeded J. S. Woodsworth as leader of the
CCF, remained a member of the Saskatchewan Progressive party
until it was superseded by the Farmers' Political Association in
the rural areas and by the Independent Labour party in the cities
and towns. The Progressive party was equally a home for those
in all three provinces who moved into the Conservative party –
although in Manitoba most Progressives entered happily into
formal union with the Liberals in 1932.[10] In Saskatchewan the
decline in Progressive strength was matched by a parallel growth
in Conservative support. Between 1921 and 1930 the Progressive
share of the vote fell from 61 to 12 per cent and the Conservative's share rose from 16 to 38 per cent.[11]

The Progressive party was, in fact, something different in each
province. Its legacy to the CCF was a heightened awareness of
the feasibility of political action and of the importance of a distinctly radical platform to discourage the cannibalistic enthusiasms of Mackenzie King. In Alberta, Progressivism can best be
equated with American populism for the reasons advanced by
Sharp, chief of which was the predominance of American settlers
in the province, many of whom had some experience of agrarian
politics in their own country.[12] The predominance in Manitoba

9 / Macpherson, *Democracy in Alberta*, 6 ff.
10 / See M. S. Donnelly, *The Government of Manitoba* (Toronto
1963), 63–4.
11 / Election statistics are from the *Reports* of the Chief Electoral
Officer (Ottawa, Queen's Printer) and Howard Scarrow, *Canada Votes*
(New Orleans 1963).
12 / See Sharp, *Agrarian Revolt*, ch. 1.

of settlers from eastern Canada provided the basis in that province for agrarian liberalism in the Grit tradition of rural Ontario. In Saskatchewan a stronger concentration of British and
European immigrants meant a population to whom protest meant
socialism.[13] The pedigree of the CCF bears traces of all three
strains from urban as well as rural antecedents. Much of the
struggle over doctrine within the party was caused by the ming-
ling of these strains. To this day there are oldtimers in the CCF/
NDP for whom socialism is a fascinating blend of American
populism and Social Credit monetary reform. Most of these oldtimers are from Alberta.

Two of the early antecedents of the CCF deserve some comment. The Non-Partisan League and the United Farmers of Alberta represented the purely North American strain in the CCF's
pedigree. Both had something in common with British socialism,
which helped attract support from those immigrants familiar
with that body of doctrine, but American ideas were more dominant. Henry Wise Wood, leader of the UFA, for example, was
born in Missouri, and came to Canada in his forties. Like many
of his compatriots who had emigrated to Alberta, he had been a
member of the Populist party and put an emphasis on active non-
partisan citizenship that was clearly more an American than a
British concept.

The Non-Partisan League was a direct import from the United
States, fresh from its triumphant capture of the government of
North Dakota. Although it was an agrarian movement, the outright socialism of much of its platform attracted a number of
urban radicals to its ranks when it first appeared in Canada in
1916.[14] J. S. Woodsworth likened its program to that of the British Labour party, and along with Salem Bland, William Irvine,
and Fred Dixon, worked as an organizer for the League.[15]

Unlike the UFA, the League had little success. Its forthright
opposition to conscription in the 1917 election appeared to do

13 / See R. England, *The Colonization of Western Canada* (London
1936), 86, 310–11, and *Report on the Seventh Census of Canada* (1931),
"Population of Canada by Racial Origins" (Ottawa 1933).

14 / The best discussions of the League are in Sharp, *Agrarian Revolt*,
and Macpherson, *Democracy in Alberta*.

15 / Salem Bland, Methodist clergyman and professor at Wesley College in Winnipeg, a notable preacher of the Social Gospel, was dismissed
from the College in 1917 for his radical views. He remained a social
gospeller and later wrote a column for the Toronto *Star*. Fred Dixon, a
close friend of Woodsworth, ran as Social Democratic candidate in the
1910 Manitoba provincial election, was elected in 1914, and edited the
Western Labour News with Woodsworth during the Winnipeg Strike and
was arrested with him. William Irvine, at various times in his career
Labour and UFA MP, CCF MP, pamphleteer, journalist, and preacher, was,
16   in one way or another, always in the van of western radicalism.

more harm than good, despite the feeling of many farmers that it was another instance of the government's refusal to appreciate their needs. But despite its failure, the League provided considerable impetus to the reform movement: it sharpened class consciousness and put a more vigorous and radical language on the tongues of many farmers.[16] Woodsworth's brief spell as organizer provided him with contacts with the rural community that served him well fourteen years later when he filled the role of catalyst in bringing the farm and labour groups together in a single party. More specifically, the League had a profound influence on the development of the UFA, laying the foundation for its subsequent success in Alberta politics.

Although not as socialistic as the League, the UFA was both more radical and more class conscious than the Progressives. Its repudiation of the competitive system in economics and politics and its willingness to co-operate with other economic groups made it an easy companion for labour and socialists alike. The spokesmen of the UFA were not blind to the traditional antagonism between farm and labour, but they were sufficiently realistic to see the necessity of closer ties. In any case the size of the labour "group" in Alberta was too small to be a problem. As Wood put it in 1921, the year the UFA became the government of the province,

If we turn away from Labour, who are we to turn to? The salvation of the world depends upon the mobilization of a democratic strength sufficient to work social redemption and social salvation. The mobilization of this force depends upon the co-operation of democratic elements. It may be a difficult road to travel but there is no other.[17]

Characteristically, the first minister of labour in the UFA government was Vernon Smith, elected on the Labour ticket.

The UFA philosophy was similar in some respects to guild socialism. Co-operation with labour was simply a case of one economic group working with another in the effort to establish group government and thereby "fundamental democracy," in which the economic groups making up society are represented.[18] Wood believed that democracy was citizens in action organized around their economic interests. Parties had no place in this system; they not only belonged to the past but were demonstrably

16 / Macpherson, *Democracy in Alberta*, 39, n. 26; Sharp, *Agrarian Revolt*, 102–3.

17 / Reprinted in *Alberta Labour News*, Sept. 26, 1925.

18 / See Macpherson, *Democracy in Alberta*, ch. 2; Morton, "The Social Philosophy of Henry Wise Wood," *Agricultural History*, XXII (April 1948), 114–23; and W. K. Rolph, *Henry Wise Wood of Alberta* (Toronto 1950).

corrupt.[19] Farmers and workers entered politics to preserve – or
establish – their group identity and to exercise their rights as participants in the economic and political processes. Government
was the process of arriving at decisions that were in the interest
of all groups through non-partisan discussion of the issues. The
activities of the UFA helped generate a class consciousness among
the rural population and paved the way to co-operation with the
labour parties by emphasizing the common grievances and common interests of farmer and worker.

The road to co-operation was not a difficult one in Alberta.
Nor was it difficult in Saskatchewan, but in Manitoba the situation was different. There the working-class population was much
larger, less Anglo-Saxon, and generally more militant and radical.
The memory of the General Strike lingered to sour relations. Co-
operation was never fully achieved. Even in Alberta and Saskatchewan there were many workers who saw farmers as pro-
prietors and employers, and many farmers who viewed labour's
agitation for the eight-hour day as some kind of sick joke. But
when the mills of the Depression ground out destitution and
misery on the farm and in the cities alike, there was no real
difficulty in bringing the farmers' groups into close liaison with
the labour parties in the cities.

One serious obstacle, as far as the UFA was concerned, was the
persistent opposition of Wood to party activity as such. Engage-
ment in politics as an economic group was one thing; emerging
as a united political party was another again. The understandably
strong anti-party sentiment in the UFA and the persuasive advocacy of Henry Wise Wood made co-operation with labour
parties virtually impossible while Wood was in command.

Wood retired in 1931 and was succeeded by Robert Gardiner,
an MP and a member of the Ginger Group who had been working closely with Woodsworth's two-man labour party in the
House of Commons since 1924. The 1932 convention of the UFA
passed a resolution offering close co-operation with other political groups and pledged its support for the establishment of a co-
operative commonwealth which was defined as:

A community freed from the domination of irresponsible financial and
economic power, in which all social means of production and distribution, including land, are socially owned and controlled either by volun-
tarily organized groups of producers and consumers, or – in the
case of the major public services and utilities and such productive
and distributive enterprises as can be conducted most efficiently when

18   19 / William Irvine, *The Farmers in Politics* (Toronto 1920), 56–7.

owned in common – by public corporations responsible to the people's elected representatives.[20]

The definition is a socialist one, more so in fact than the Regina Manifesto turned out to be, at any rate with respect to land ownership. At the end of June 1932, the UFA executive, MPs, and the provincial Legislature endorsed the convention resolution and drafted a ten-point manifesto outlining the aims of the UFA. They reiterated the invitation to other groups, "urban and rural, whose aims are fundamentally the same as those of the UFA," to co-operate with them in order to realize these aims.[21] Specifically, they invited all such groups to attend a conference in Calgary in August to discuss action in their common cause. There is little doubt that the specific invitation was instigated by Robert Gardiner in his capacity as co-chairman of the parliamentary group which that May had decided to begin the process of bringing the radical movements together. For this reason the third conference of the Western Labor Political Parties, originally scheduled for Regina, was held in Calgary.[22]

The moment was propitious. By 1932 the Depression had stalked across the plains and the good times of the post-war period had totally disappeared. There had been crop failures before, in Alberta in the years 1917–20, and a disastrous fall in the price of wheat between 1920 and 1923, but the boom which followed 1923 had restored confidence and injected optimism into the prairie economy. The price of wheat was nevertheless exceptionally vulnerable, whereas the fixed costs of the farmers were not. The post-war slump demonstrated the interdependence of farmer and worker, for, as the farmers' incomes declined, fewer manufactured goods were purchased and unemployment resulted, most noticeably in those industries directly related to farm purchases. Both were adversely affected by the steadily rising cost of living.

The fat years that followed the 1920–3 slump brought the National Policy to full fruition. The western plains were occupied; 3,000 miles of track were added to the railways in the West; virtually all the arable land was within easy reach of the railhead. Saskatchewan and Alberta enjoyed a 20 per cent increase in population and their economies flourished, but there was little

20 / *Declaration of Ultimate Objectives* (n.p., n.d., [c. Feb. 1933]), CCFP.

21 / *The Co-operative Commonwealth Federation (Farmer, Labour, Socialist), An Outline of its Origins, Organization and Objectives ...* (Calgary, n.d. [c. 1932]), CCFP.

22 / *How the CCF Got Started* (Regina, n.d., mimeo), CCFP.

diversification, as there had been in Manitoba. The growth was almost all in agriculture and most of that in wheat farming. British Columbia experienced economic expansion as well. The opening of the Panama Canal and the general health of the overseas market for lumber and minerals contributed to a growth rate that was the highest in Canada, but dependence on overseas markets and primary production meant that its economy was vulnerable. The growth rate attracted to the province a host of unskilled labourers who accentuated the unemployment problem in Vancouver when the Depression came.

In the twelve months from January to December of 1930, the price of wheat fell by 57 per cent. By December 1932 farm prices generally had fallen 70 per cent from the levels of July 1929. The expansion during the boom had been financed extensively with borrowed capital and the farmer was quickly crushed between the upper and nether millstones of declining income and fixed costs. Drought exacerbated the situation in Saskatchewan. By 1932 two-thirds of the farm population in that province were destitute.[23] The greatest decrease in income occurred in Saskatchewan, then Alberta, Manitoba, and British Columbia, in that order. Winnipeg and Vancouver were centres of severe unemployment. Farm yields were higher in Alberta, where the drought was less severe, but higher fixed debt charges offset what advantage this brought the farmers in that province. Across the country from Port Arthur westwards, the Depression was a time of impossible debt, high unemployment, and utter destitution.

It deepened the conviction of those already committed to the radical point of view and made new recruits among those whose farms were repossessed or who were living on the dole or spoiling in a labour camp. The traditional western distrust of the established political parties was not diminished by the countless stories of privilege and influence peddling in the distribution of jobs and relief to party hacks and hangers-on.

By 1931 the militant and politically oriented Saskatchewan section of the United Farmers of Canada had begun to work closely with the Farmers' Political Association and the Saskatchewan Independent Labour party. The United Farmers had been formed in 1926 through the fusion of the Grain Growers Association and the Farmers Union. The Farmers' Political Association was formed two years earlier in the federal constituency of Last Mountain by a group of politically conscious farmers led by George Williams. Its objectives were more radical and its leaders more militant than those of the Saskatchewan Section (ss) of

23 / *Report of the Royal Commission on Dominion-Provincial Relations* (Ottawa 1954), Bk. I, 169.

the UFC, but both organizations were a product of widespread disappointment with the failure of the Progressives. Initially, the UFC(SS) was more reluctant than the Political Association to become directly involved in politics. The two groups developed separately and gradually came together in 1929 and 1930.

Political activity on the urban front in Saskatchewan intensified as economic conditions worsened. The Independent Labour party was organized by M. J. Coldwell following his success in the 1926 Regina civic elections when he topped the aldermanic poll on a labour ticket. The ILP was distinctly Fabian in outlook and drew heavily on traditional British socialist material. Mimeographed pamphlets from the National Labour College and old copies of Robert Blatchford's Clarion were circulated among the membership.[24] Sections of the party were established in Melville and Saskatoon. It was not long before contact was made with the more militant of the farmers.

In 1929 the Farmers' Political Association and the ILP nominated three candidates under the joint banner of the Farmer-Labour party. The same year, the Saskatchewan group was in touch with the Manitoba ILP. Woodsworth spoke at the July convention of the Saskatchewan ILP and John Queen and Abraham Heaps spoke at a general meeting in Regina that fall. Links with other similar groups were established by exchanging speakers and by the contacts provided through the conferences of the Western Labour Political Parties which had begun in 1929. In 1932 the Weyburn Labor Association was formed by the Rev. T. C. Douglas to provide assistance to the unemployed in Weyburn. He had written to Woodsworth about his activities and was asked to get in touch with M. J. Coldwell. The result was the formation of the Weyburn branch of the ILP.[25] By this time Coldwell was very active in politics in the province; his regular Monday evening radio broadcasts on socialism and economics had made him a well-known figure in the Regina district. At this juncture the aim of the ILP was to set up locals throughout the province and then work to amalgamate at that level with the local UFC(SS) lodge.

The Farmers' Political Association became a province-wide organization in March of 1930. The following month a joint conference with the ILP was held in Regina at which the three hundred delegates approved a joint constitution and statement of objectives. Coldwell was elected a vice-chairman of the Farmers' Political Association, linking the urban and rural movements

24 / Interview with M. J. Coldwell, July 1962.
25 / Transcript of interviews with T. C. Douglas by C. Higginbotham, 1958–60.

together. The meeting did not merge the two groups; it demonstrated their decision to pool resources in what was increasingly referred to as the common struggle.

The two groups nominated 13 candidates in the federal election of 1930 and succeeded in electing 2 of them. More impressive were the 40,000 votes cast in favour of the radical candidates. The enthusiasm was reflected in the decision of the UFC (SS) to endorse political action by farmers as such. A resolution calling for the UFC itself to engage in political action failed by only 9 votes. The following year a similar resolution passed with a good majority.

G. H. Williams, founder of the Farmers' Political Association, was elected president of the UFC(SS) in 1930, bringing the three radical political groups in Saskatchewan still closer together. At that convention the delegates adopted a thirteen-point program prepared by Williams which declared that: "the present economic crisis is due to inherent unsoundness in the capitalistic system which is based on private ownership of resources and capitalistic control of production and distribution and involves payment of rent, interest and profit."[26] In July 1932, the ILP and the UFC(SS) held their conventions in Saskatoon. At a joint meeting they decided that fusion was undesirable but that a joint program and joint action were essential. Although executive positions were shared by people in all three organizations – the Farmers' Political Association had been virtually absorbed by the UFC at this point – and the separation was in reality only nominal, years of struggle to achieve class consciousness and a sense of identity precluded any submerging of farm and labour movements into a single inclusive movement.

The two movements decided to contest the provincial elections under the old Farmer-Labour banner. M. J. Coldwell was elected president and leader of the joint venture. G. H. Williams had intended to stand for this post, but he was advised that his impromptu visit to Russia after the world wheat conference in 1930 had lowered his political stock. There were obvious limits to the radicalism of the farmers and the Regina Fabians. The two groups did, however, instruct their delegates to the UFA-sponsored Calgary conference later that month that the new party to be built should be called "The Socialist Party of Canada."[27] And the emphasis in Coldwell's provincial party was to be "fundamentally socialistic."[28] The ideological raiment of the Farmer-Labour party was provided largely by the urban socialists, while

26 / *Canadian Annual Review, 1930–31* (Toronto 1931), 258.
27 / Lipset, *Agrarian Socialism*, 104.
28 / Morton, *Progressive Party*, 280; Coldwell, *Left Turn*, 3.

the reformist energy and the "troops" were supplied by the farmers, who outnumbered the five hundred members of the Saskatchewan ILP.

The urban and rural wings of the Farmer-Labour party came together with little rancour. The labour wing was relatively young and the nature of the provincial economy ensured that there was a clear appreciation of the farmers' problems. In other provinces there was less understanding and consequently less co-operation, particularly of a formal kind, prior to the formation of the CCF. Some of the labour parties, however, had been active in politics before any of the rural movements had begun to consider political action.

For the most part the urban labour parties that participated in the formation of the CCF had a long history, one of division and, consequently, impotence. However, labour candidates did manage to win seats in Parliament. A. W. Puttee and Ralph Smith were the first and were followed by J. S. Woodsworth, William Irvine, and A. A. Heaps. It is uncertain whether more concerted action would have produced better results; what is clear is that a good deal of time and energy were expended in waging internecine war and in establishing "new" branches of the old parties to hold the true doctrine. The Winnipeg ILP was formed in 1921 when Fred Dixon, S. J. Farmer, and William Ivens, among others, left the Dominion Labour party which, in their view, was too conservative.[29] The Canadian Labour party was founded in the same year under the aegis of the Trades and Labor Congress although the TLC was not affiliated with it.

By 1921 there was a host of various labour parties in Canada, most with branches – some with headquarters – in the western cities.[30] In addition to those already mentioned, there was a Labour Representation League, a Federal Labour party, a Federated Labour party, a Workers' party, and the Socialist Party of Canada, to mention a few. In the 1917 Dominion election, the labour parties contested 25 seats; in 1921 there were 29 labour/socialist candidates – at least one in every province. That year, in which two candidates were elected, Woodsworth and Irvine, was the pinnacle of activity and the number of candidates declined from then until the CCF was formed.

The results of the effort and debate that went into left-wing politics were, from an electoral point of view, rather dismal. But the enthusiasm of the labour parties and their prodigious feats of

29 / See McNaught, *A Prophet*, 147–8.
30 / The rise and fall of the many labour parties and the Labour Representation League is catalogued in the annual reports of the Department of Labour, *Labour Organization in Canada* (Ottawa 1910–59).

publication and propagandizing through public meetings and such
left-wing newspapers as *Citizen and Country*, *The Federationist*,
Western Labour News, and *The Clarion* made them particularly
effective in popularizing the radical point of view. Within the
subculture of working-class politics in the cities and in the log-
ging and mining camps, these papers were widely read and the
current topics eagerly discussed.

Woodsworth made an abortive attempt to knit together the
disparate socialist groups in 1926. At a meeting in the Vancouver
home of Robert Skinner with Angus MacInnis, John Sidaway,
and John Price – all active in the Vancouver branch of the Canadian Labour party – the formation of a national socialist party
was discussed. Woodsworth provided Skinner with the names
of 22 people whom he considered to be key contacts. Skinner
wrote to them but the response was disappointing and served to
confirm a suspicion the five men shared that the labour and
socialist parties were "all mixed up like a dog's breakfast."[31] Yet
Woodsworth and the others recognized the inevitability of failure
if the elements of the urban left were unable to make common
cause in their opposition to capitalism.

Three years later the move toward unity began in Regina with
the first formal convention of the western labour parties. The
meeting took place as a result of the initiative of the Brandon
local of the Manitoba Independent Labour party. Invitations
were sent to all elected labour representatives and all labour and
socialist parties west of the Lakehead. The purpose of the gathering was to "correlate the activities of the several labour political
parties in Western Canada."[32] The *Manitoba Free Press* saw
more to it than that: "From the flux of individual labour groups
existent in Western Canada, a skeleton framework of a Western
Canada Labour Party was built Saturday and today at a conference of labour representatives from points from Winnipeg to
the Pacific Coast."[33] The significance of the conferences of the
western labour parties has generally been overlooked by students
of CCF origins. The conferences helped knit together the urban
left and eventually provided a point of contact for the farmers'
organizations. The possibility of forming a united party from
among the diverse protest movements became real when order
began to appear among what had previously been the most

31 / Interview with Robert Skinner, July 1966. See also the unpublished MA thesis by R. Grantham, "Some Aspects of the Socialist Movement in British Columbia, 1898–1933" (University of British Columbia
1942), Appendix 15.

32 / *Alberta Labour News*, Nov. 2, 1929.

33 / *Manitoba Free Press*, Oct. 28, 1929, Regina *Leader-Post*, Oct.
26, 1929.

chaotic element in the complex of western radicalism. M. J. Coldwell remarked some years later that the conferences of the labour parties deserve "much of the credit for the formation of the CCF."[34]

The program adopted by the first conference was not so much radical as it was practical, containing nothing of an ideological nature that would either deter other groups from affiliating or lead to dissension at the conference itself. As old practitioners of left-wing politics, the leaders of the conference knew when to leave well enough alone. The program called for pensions for the blind, relief for the unemployed, and a minimum wage standard. Like so many agrarian manifestos, it also demanded public ownership and development of natural resources. In any case, the main point of the gathering was not to put together a workers' platform – there was no shortage of them in any case – but to "unify the activities of the affiliated parties, to arrange common action, and to bring about the unification of the entire labour and socialist movement throughout Western Canada."[35]

J. S. Woodsworth was among the delegates at Regina that year, along with representatives of the branches of the Canadian Labour party in Calgary and Edmonton; the Vancouver, Edmonton, and Regina Trades and Labour councils; the Dominion Labour party of Lethbridge; and locals of the Manitoba Independent Labour party. Eight of the nineteen delegates were from Saskatchewan, six from Alberta, four from Manitoba, and one from British Columbia. M. J. Coldwell, Clarence Fines, and Fred White, all destined to play important roles in the CCF, were delegates. At Woodsworth's request each delegate reported on the state of labour political organization in his particular region. It was useful for Woodsworth to have some notion of the degree of support each party had so that he could arrange speaking tours for his colleagues in the House of Commons to best advantage and, of perhaps greater importance, through his good offices, pool the resources of the farm and labour groups where such pooling seemed feasible.

The second Western Conference of the Labor Political Parties met in Medicine Hat in September 1930. A more detailed program was adopted, one which demanded improved old age pensions, consumer co-operatives, and social control of credit and currency, in addition to the points made in the first program. Among the additions was a call for immigration restrictions limiting entry to those "who willingly come and who are finan-

34 / Interview with Coldwell, July 1962.
35 / "Minutes of the Western Conference of Labour Political Parties," 26–7, Oct. 1929, CCFP.

cially equipped to be self-supporting."[36] The tone of the resolutions was more radical: the unemployment resolution emphatically declared that "The problem of unemployment cannot be solved under the capitalistic competitive system of production." W. J. Bartlett of the Vancouver and District Trades and Labour Council and the Vancouver Independent Labour party was elected president of the conference.

The third and most significant gathering of the labour parties was held in Winnipeg in 1931. The *Manitoba Free Press* again observed that the conference was likely to result in the formation of a Canadian party "corresponding to the British Labour Party."[37] Invitations to attend had been sent to labour groups in Montreal, Hamilton, Toronto, and "other centres." Woodsworth had personally invited those members of labour parties in the East that he knew. Conference secretary W. E. Small reported that the replies received indicated that the groups in the East, while unable to send delegates, "favoured the formation of a Dominion political body."[38] A major obstacle for all delegates outside the immediate vicinity was the cost of travel. Vancouver was a vigorous centre of socialist activity but only W. J. Bartlett could attend the conference. He worked for the CPR and had a railroad pass. The conference had also invited the United Farmers of Canada (ss) and other farm groups to send delegates and a number did so. A. J. MacAuley of the United Farmers addressed the meeting. According to the *Labour Statesman* "it was as if a radical Labour man were setting forth the aims and ideals of the workers."[39]

This was the most radical of the three conferences, "resolutions galore were offered to the effect that capitalism must go and socialism be established."[40] The decision to set up a committee of five farm representatives and five labour representatives to "work out a plan for the effective education of the workers and farmers looking to the establishment of the co-operative commonwealth" was the first formal exercise in farmer-labour co-operation at other than the local level.[41] During the discussion of this proposal it was pointed out that the Independent Labour party had been working with farmers and farm groups in British Columbia as well as in Brandon, Souris, and Melville. The problems of the Depression occupied much of the time of the delegates and resolutions were passed dealing with the situation in

36 / *Ibid.*, 1930.
37 / *Ibid.*, July 6, 1931.
38 / *Ibid.*, July 17, 1931.
39 / *Ibid.*, July 31, 1931.
40 / *Ibid.*
41 / *Ibid.*, and see also *Manitoba Free Press*, July 18, 1931, and "Minutes of the Western Conference," 1931, CCFP.

relief camps and with the handling of relief funds. At the conclusion of the conference, the delegates called upon "workers
throughout the world to organize politically and industrially for
the abolition of capitalism and the establishment of a co-operative commonwealth."[42] Rejecting a suggestion that the labour
parties "get together" with the Communist party, the conference
agreed that representatives of the labour parties in the East
should again be invited to the fourth conference to be held in
Regina the following year (1932).

The location of the fourth meeting was subsequently changed
on the advice of Woodsworth in response to the UFA invitation to
hold a joint meeting in Calgary.[43] The Calgary meeting was the
culmination of the gradual intermingling of the radical farm and
labour movements in western Canada. The labour parties' conferences gave radical leaders like Coldwell and Woodsworth an
insight into the extent of radical thought and feeling in western
Canada. And latterly they provided those whose experience had
been limited to purely labour activities with contact with the
farmers' political groups and *vice versa*. The consolidation of
the forces of the socialist, labour, and farm groups had begun in
the West under the aegis of these conferences before the co-
operating groups in the House of Commons had decided to form
a Dominion-wide party based on farmer-labour co-operation.
That the MPs could see the need for action and the possibility of
unity was to some extent due to the meetings of the labour parties, for these at least demonstrated the viability of a broadly-
based political organization. They provided both a framework
for the future party as well as a solid core of members. There
were, for example, approximately four hundred members of the
Independent Labour party in Regina alone.[44]

Woodsworth and his colleagues in the House were also aware
of the feverish though disparate activity of the labour parties in
Ontario. This activity, and the evidence of the three conferences
in the West, provided what would appear to be reasonably conclusive proof of the viability of a Dominion-wide socialist party.
The Labour MPs had sent letters to all trade unions in Canada
urging political action and the general support the replies indicated led Grace Woodsworth, caucus secretary, to conclude with
some optimism that the unions were "almost ready for political
organization on a large scale."[45]

42 / "Minutes of the Western Conference," 1931. For the first time,
delegates are referred to as "comrade."
43 / Morton, *Progressive Party*, 279–81, and see below.
44 / *Alberta Labour News*, July 18, 1931.
45 / G. Woodsworth, "Trade Unions and Political Action," *Labour
Statesman*, Sept. 18, 1931.

When the urban and agrarian radicals did combine their forces under the spur of the Depression, the ease with which the combination – for it was never a union – took place was due in large measure to the presence of men who were *persona grata* with farmer and worker alike. The key figure was Woodsworth. As spokesman in the House of Commons for the radical group, he was the institutional leader. He was also the inspirational leader, a position derived from his religious background and close association with the struggles of the persecuted and the alienated in the West almost since the turn of the century. Countless people in the halls and school houses of the western provinces had heard him speak and witnessed his honesty and conviction. For some he was the dedicated evangelist of the Social Gospel, for others one of the martyrs of the Winnipeg General Strike.

The message of the Social Gospel was relevant for the urban worker as much as for the wheat farmer. Although more closely associated with labour politics, his association with the Non-Partisan League and his own travels through the prairies gave Woodsworth a clear understanding of the farmers' problems. Because he was the parliamentary leader of a mixed urban-agrarian alliance, if only in an informal sense, and because his obvious sincerity and conviction removed him from any suspicion by either side, Woodsworth became the linchpin between the urban labour groups and the farm groups, providing a central figure around whom the parties could unite.

His own political views were more radical than those of many of the farmers and less radical than those of many of the labour party figures. His "middle of the road" position made him more acceptable to both sides. He was, in a sense, above politics. He was not a politician in the way that his successor, M. J. Coldwell, was. For Woodsworth, party politics were anathema and throughout his career his vision was of a great movement, not of a great party. The CCF was to be a movement of men and women motivated by Christian ideals, volunteering their services and determined upon the reformation of society to achieve the co-operative commonwealth. It should be pointed out that these ideals were shared by Coldwell who was, nevertheless, more pragmatic. Although he was no fonder of the two-party system than Henry Wise Wood, Woodsworth had serious reservations on the subject of group government.[46] Apart from opposing cabinet dictatorship and supporting "true representation" of the constituencies, Woodsworth displayed whole-hearted support for the institutions of parliamentary democracy. Like his colleagues and those who came after him in the CCF, he had great skill in the techniques of

46 / McNaught, *A Prophet*, 168.

Parliament and was prepared to use the available machinery to
achieve the goals of his movement, as he did in 1926 to force
Mackenzie King to establish old age pensions.

Although he could on occasion demonstrate the skills of management and the thrust and determination of a political leader –
notably in the remaking of the Ontario CCF in 1934[47] – his
leadership of the co-operating groups and later the CCF was as
much a tribute to his vision and the devotion he aroused as to
his skill as a politician. As a symbolic leader he represented the
ideals of the farmer and the working man. The comparative ease
with which the federation of the farm and city parties and movements was completed was in no small way due to Woodsworth's
personality and the image it fostered in his followers.

His parliamentary ability was instrumental in separating the
"Ginger Group" from the Progressive party in 1924. Following
their election to the House of Commons in 1921 in the Progressive landslide, Woodsworth and William Irvine made a point of
meeting frequently with "certain Progressives who recognize their
responsibility to the labour section of their constituencies."[48] By
1923 Woodsworth had established his right in the Commons to
speak after Robert Forke (who had succeeded T. A. Crerar as
leader of the Progressives) as the leader of a party, even though
there were only two in his party, that is, Irvine and himself.

By 1924 Forke was experiencing some difficulty in holding the
Progressives together. During the debate on the budget that year
Woodsworth moved an amendment which was essentially the
same as one moved by Forke the year before. Woodsworth's
amendment placed the Progressives in an awkward position.
Support it and they defeated Mackenzie King's government,
which had been wooing them assiduously. If they voted against it
they were repudiating their own principles. The bulk of the Progressives followed their leader and supported the government. A
small number, known subsequently as the Ginger Group,[49] voted
with Woodsworth and Irvine. All the members of the original
Ginger Group became members of the CCF, most of them for the
remainder of their political careers: W. C. Good withdrew when
the doctrine became too much for him, and Agnes Macphail was
more in than out although she carried her own label.

47 / J. S. Woodsworth in *The Independent*, March 24, 1922, cited in
McNaught, *A Prophet*, 164.

48 / See the unpublished MA thesis (Toronto 1961) of Gerald Caplan,
"Socialism and Anti-Socialism in Ontario, 1932–45," *passim*.

49 / The group consisted of Robert Gardiner (who became leader of
the UFA in 1931), E. J. Garland, H. E. Spencer, G. G. Coote, D. M.
Kennedy, J. T. Shaw, all of the UFA; M. N. Campbell of Saskatchewan; W.
J. Ward of Manitoba; Preston Elliot, W. C. Good, and Agnes Macphail of
the United Farmers of Ontario.

After the separation of the Ginger Group from the decaying hulk of the Progressive party, the way was clear for more formal co-operation. A document was drawn up in 1930 providing for regular consultation, something which had, in fact, taken place since the break in 1924. The preamble of the document stated:

Whereas, we the Farmer and Labour groups in the House of Commons, Ottawa, in conference assembled, find that we have much in common and recognize that we are engaged in the common fight against a strongly entrenched system of special privilege, which is functioning through the party system, recognize the advisability of each Group retaining its identity in Parliament, thus enabling the groups to give voice to the distinctive viewpoint held by the electorate represented by them, and also that in working together, we may assist in the development of a cooperative system of administration.[50]

Despite the tentative tone of the preamble, the co-operation proposed was fairly close and involved the appointment of a steering committee and a secretary. Most significantly, it included a statement of intent to find a common stand on major issues and to choose a spokesman who would represent the whole group. A chairman was to be elected with power to act on behalf of the co-operating groups in the event that there was insufficient time for a conference.

From this close and formal co-operation came the parliamentary impetus for the establishment of the CCF. On May 26, 1932, the members of the group met in William Irvine's office, which served as group caucus room, and agreed to extend their parliamentary organization into the country at large. They decided to set up a federation of groups to promote co-operation between the constituent organizations in the provinces. The new organization was to be called the "Commonwealth Party."[51] Woodsworth and Robert Gardiner of the UFA were appointed co-chairmen. Agnes Macphail was to organize Ontario; Coldwell was invited to organize in Saskatchewan; the Socialist Party of Canada and the ILP were to undertake similar duties in British Columbia and Manitoba; and Gardiner was put in charge of the Alberta organization, where his position as president of the UFA had enabled him to lay the foundation for the Calgary conference.

A final fillip was given to their growing enthusiasm by the organization of the League for Social Reconstruction in January 1932. A Canadian version of the Fabian Society, the League

50 / CCFP and Henry Spencer Papers, PAC. According to W. Eggleston, "Groups and the Election," *Toronto Star*, June 6, 1930, the document was drawn up following the budget debate of that year.

51 / McNaught, *A Prophet*, 259–60; Woodsworth Papers, scrapbook, v. 1932–7, PAC; and see also *How the CCF Got Started*.

provided intellectual leadership for the CCF for the better part of its history, and at the beginning demonstrated to Woodsworth and his colleagues that there was support for their new party outside farm and labour circles.

The League for Social Reconstruction, or LSR as it was usually called – initials seem to be a characteristic of left-wing politics in Canada – was the direct result of a conversation Frank Underhill and Frank Scott had while on a hiking trip in the Berkshire hills of Massachusetts. They agreed that Canadian politics needed a third party, one which would not be readily absorbed by the Liberals as the Progressives had been. They decided to establish an organization in Canada that would be similar to the British Fabian Society or its American equivalent, the League for Industrial Democracy. This body would work out a program for the new party that would clearly distinguish it from the Liberal party.

The first meeting of the LSR was held in Toronto in January 1932. It was attended largely by Underhill's colleagues from the University of Toronto and Scott's from McGill. A link with the established left was provided by Woodsworth, who was made honorary president. The LSR described itself in its inaugural manifesto as " ... an association of men and women who are working for the establishment in Canada of a social order in which the basic principle regulating production, distribution and service will be the common good rather than private profit."[52] The task the LSR set itself was "to work for the realization of its ideal by organizing groups to study and report on particular problems and by issuing to the public in the form of pamphlets, articles, lectures, etc., the most accurate information obtainable about the nation's affairs in order to create that informed public opinion which is necessary for effective political action."[53] It did not affiliate with the party it helped create, but it became increasingly involved in the affairs of the CCF; members of the LSR were frequently officers in the CCF and often candidates for election under the party banner. For this reason, among others, it was gradually absorbed by the party and never did achieve the status of the Fabian Society.

The existence of the LSR had an undeniable effect on the CCF not merely in the initial stages of its development, when the first draft of what was to become the Regina Manifesto was prepared by a committee of the LSR, but throughout the first half of the

52 / LSR *Manifesto*, papers in the possession of Professor G. M. A. Grube. See also F. R. Scott, "A Decade of the League for Social Reconstruction," *Saturday Night*, Jan. 24, 1942.
53 / LSR *Manifesto*.

party's life when the books and pamphlets published by the LSR shaped the party's doctrines. Its influence was also exerted through the pages of the *Canadian Forum* which was, for the most part, the organ of the left in Canada and for a time the journal of the LSR.[54] The League also provided the new party with at least a patina of eastern sophistication. It was a little more difficult for the opposition to stereotype the party as readily as it had stereotyped the Progressives. In this way the LSR assisted the CCF in creating a slightly more palatable image of itself for the urban radical who had cause to suspect the purity and consistency of the socialism of many agrarian members.

The League grew fairly rapidly in the first year or two of its existence. In 1933, the Toronto branch of the LSR held a series of public lectures given by some of its leading figures, Underhill, Scott, and King Gordon. The average attendance at these meetings was 135. The Toronto branch had a membership of 145 by 1933.[55]

Support in academic circles in Montreal and Toronto with the promise of expansion was undoubtedly of value to Woodsworth, who was at this point in the process of determining what should be done with the radical farm and labour groups in the West. The knowledge would be doubly encouraging for, apart from the fact that there was a natural desire on Woodsworth's part for intellectual support, the aims of the League were entirely consistent with his own. Woodsworth was an educator and evangelist in the cause of reform. The aims of the LSR were similar. It was an organization of educators with no personal political ambitions.

By 1932 it was clear to the leaders of the co-operating groups that there was almost a national base of popular support for a new radical political movement. The election of Angus MacInnis on the ILP ticket in Vancouver South in 1930 underlined the growing strength of socialism in British Columbia, and added a vigorous spokesman to the "group" in the House of Commons. The arrival on the scene of the LSR merely added to the proof and extended the support of the party eastward into the universities and the urban middle class.

At this point there was reason for believing that a national urban-agrarian socialist movement could be established with good prospects for success. The formation of the LSR meant that the new movement would have its "brains trust." The willingness of the labour parties and farm groups to co-operate and the

54 / See the unpublished MA thesis (Toronto 1953) by Margaret Prang, "Some Opinions of Political Radicalism between Two World Wars."

55 / LSR "Minutes," 1935, Grube Papers.

apparent similarity of their aims pointed to success. The old antagonism between farm and labour appeared to have been submerged by their common plight. The farm and labour groups took advantage of the UFA invitation, and the farm, labour, and intellectual groups gathered in Calgary in 1932 to create the Co-operative Commonwealth Federation.

The Depression made the union possible but could not guarantee its success. The return of prosperity in the forties opened the old wounds of farm-labour antagonism. In Saskatchewan, where labour was a relatively minor element, the CCF succeeded. In Manitoba, where the two elements were more closely balanced and the major impetus for the movement came from the ILP in Winnipeg and Brandon, union between the two was never fully achieved and the CCF had only limited success. The United Farmers of Manitoba never did affiliate, although they did give the CCF access to their lodges and district organizations for the purpose of spreading propaganda. In Alberta the UFA found no difficulty in co-operating with labour; indeed in some respects the Dominion Labour party, as one member put it, was merely "the city side of the UFA."[56] But the defeat of the UFA government in the 1935 election, which the CCF naturally did not contest, put the Social Credit party into office. In Ontario and eastern Canada generally, the CCF never did find an agrarian base. It remained an urban labour movement, "finding its greatest strength in those districts where old country Britishers predominate."[57] British Columbia was similar to Ontario, for there the party remained a socialist labour movement with insignificant rural support. The CCF was, in the East and far West, an urban labour party but, paradoxically, with relatively little support from organized labour until it was almost too late.

The existence of all the groups examined above spelled success for the CCF's organization, although there was really no fundamental compatibility in the doctrines the various groups espoused. There were, on the one hand, the doctrinaire socialists from British Columbia who viewed the farmers with suspicion and distrust, seeing them for what they really were – frustrated *petit bourgeois*.[58] The members of the Dominion Labour party, the Canadian Labour party, and the Independent Labour party in Alberta and Saskatchewan were either Fabians or trade unionists, schooled in the socialism of Bellamy and Blatchford

56 / Transcript of an interview with Fred White in the possession of Professor Paul Fox. White was a member of the Dominion Labour party in Alberta.

57 / *Ibid.*

58 / See Dorothy Steeves, *The Compassionate Rebel* (Vancouver 1960), ch. 7.

and the Social Gospel. Along with their compatriots in Winnipeg they were familiar with the literature of democratic socialism and for the most part clear on their doctrine. The members of the LSR were socialist intellectuals who saw the new party as the vehicle for an ideology, and to this they lent their energies. The farm groups were seeking reform. For the most part they were led by men who were acquainted with socialism and had, in many instances, urban backgrounds. The farmers who supported them were less familiar with the doctrines of democratic socialism. Their interest was in reform, not social revolution. Thus William Irvine and Henry Spencer could, as "socialists," frequently advocate what was essentially Social Credit monetary reform.[59]

What brought the groups together was a shared belief in the need for a co-operative commonwealth, though this meant different things to the different groups; and a common recognition of the inadequacy of the existing system to provide even the necessities of life. The urban socialists made the protest coherent and gave it specific content. They provided, in men like Woodsworth, Coldwell, MacInnis, and Irvine, the cement to bind the groups together. But the fundamental differences that existed could not be eradicated, and for this reason the party started its career as a federation of rural and urban protest movements. The federal structure was to be one of the stumbling blocks in the development of the party, yet it was necessary if the party was to get off the ground.

The ideological disagreement that existed between the various elements could not have been easily reconciled within the framework of a single party. The federal structure meant that each constituent group could retain to a large degree its original doctrine under the broad umbrella of the Regina Manifesto. As well, and perhaps most important, all the elements which formed the new organization were, to some extent, the result of sectional and occupational discontent. They represented those regions and occupations which were on the economic periphery and largely in the control of the vested interests in the East. The anti-centralism and individualism of the prairies that had typified the Progressive groups had not disappeared and was reasserted in the Depression. It would hardly have been consistent with a protest that was to some extent the result of an inability to establish a local identity and status to create as a vehicle for this protest a party which required members and groups to submerge the identity they had succeeded in building for themselves in that

59 / See *Hansard*, 1935, 446 ff. In an interview with the author Frank Underhill described Irvine's address at Toronto's Hygeia Hall in 1932 as "pure social credit."

larger whole. There was, in addition, the anti-party bias of the agrarian radical.

Membership in a radical political movement is usually the result of a moral and an intellectual conviction about the fundamental iniquity of some aspect of the existing social and economic system. It is also, for some, the result of a need to establish an identity in an alien society. In societies that are clearly class-structured, the need for identity is less pressing because membership in a class is in itself an identity. In so-called classless or open societies the need is more pressing, particularly so when the economic and social systems leave the individual free of social ties and place him in a state of competition with actual and supposed equals.[60] Lacking the reference points of a clearly defined class structure, involved in a competitive struggle which he feels – and usually rightly – he is losing, the individual searches for some locus of his existence and for some satisfactory explanation of his apparent failure.

Only those with a fanatical devotion to the existing system or incredible psychological stamina could undertake to explain, in terms of their own shortcomings, their failure to get a job, raise a crop, or get fair prices for their produce. For the underpaid, unemployed, or hailed-out, there had to be another reason for failure, for they had done all that they could. Beaten by the system, the soil, or the climate, they were themselves blameless; the fault lay elsewhere. Once the fault was found and remedied, they could receive the just returns for their labour.

Alienated by a system in which the cards were stacked against them, the farmers and urban workers found in the protest movements an identity and an explanation. They were united with others who shared the disabilities of poverty and political impotence. In a purportedly classless society, they created a kind of class. This class was provided with a doctrine by the protest movements that explained the causes of the common affliction, allocated responsibility for the condition, and offered a cure that did not do too much violence to the prevailing value system – particularly those aspects related to the ownership of real property; to this day the "family farm" is a sacred prairie concept. Capitalism was the cause, but capitalists were the enemy. The co-operative commonwealth was the cure, for it promised a society in which labour received its due reward and the institu-

60 / See W. Kornhauser, *The Politics of Mass Society* (London 1960), ch. 4; Wendell King, *Social Movements in the United States* (New York 1956), ch. 1; and Erich Fromm, *The Fear of Freedom* (London 1942), ch. 4, esp. 114–16. Ostrogorski commented on the isolation of the individual in America in 1902. See M. Ostrogorski, *Democracy and the Organization of Political Parties*, S. M. Lipset, ed. (New York 1964), II, 307–9. John

tions of liberal democracy operated as they were supposed to operate, free from the perversions of the old party system.

The intellectuals in the LSR and the Marxians in British Columbia saw more in the situation and favoured root-and-branch reform, but even they, for the most part, accepted the framework of liberal democracy and parliamentary institutions. As a result it was a moderate socialism with a wide variety of interpretation that triumphed in the CCF. In the light of the history of the several strands that made up the CCF fabric, it is in no way surprising that consistency of view where the party doctrine was concerned was not easily found. Farmers and workers responded to the doctrines of the movements that federated in 1932 as the CCF because they made sense of a chaotic situation. In Alberta three years later, farmers responded to a different doctrine for essentially the same reasons. Social Credit proposed to repair and modify the free enterprise system to make it work as it should; the CCF groups proposed to substitute a better system. Both agreed that the members of the social and economic establishment were the villains in the piece and both offered the farmer what he wanted: the opportunity for an honest man to make an honest dollar.

The men who met in Calgary in 1932 in the winter of their discontent were not revolutionaries in the ordinary sense. They did not want to overturn the system entirely; they wanted to reform it along the lines dictated by the social gospel and the doctrines of Fabian socialism. To achieve their goals they had decided to become a political party, competing with the "old-line parties" only as a painful necessity. From the beginning they showed a determination to resist the forces that would destroy the individual groups they had built up by submerging them in a larger party. Their eyes were firmly fixed on the establishment of the co-operative commonwealth because they had learned that the existing system could guarantee them nothing. When it is dark, the light on the distant shore always appears nearer than it is.

Porter points out that "it is indisputable that some form of group affiliation lying between the extremes of the mass and the individual is a prerequisite for mutual health." *The Vertical Mosaic* (Toronto 1964), 73.

3

3

THE REGINA MANIFESTO

Socialism is not a science, a sociology in miniature –
it is a cry of pain, sometimes of anger, uttered by
men who feel most keenly our collective malaise.

EMIL DURKHEIM
Socialism and St. Simon

Those men and women who came together in 1932 and 1933 to create the Co-operative Commonwealth Federation believed that the solution to the *malaise* afflicting Canada was socialism. The Regina Manifesto was the articulation of their *weltanschauung*; it formed the core of the ideology of the CCF. There were many departures from the letter of the document, but its spirit informed the ideals and attitudes of the CCF activists during the party's life.

It is almost a truism that ideological parties do not succeed in Canadian politics, and the CCF is usually the example cited as proof. Ideological parties, the argument goes, are by their nature exclusive: only those who accept the ideology can, or will, become supporters. Their popular appeal is therefore limited. Brokerage parties, on the other hand, appeal to a much broader spectrum of the populace since they seek the lowest common denominator. But this may be a false distinction because it is possible to argue that all parties are ideological, the so-called brokerage parties being merely those whose ideology is more consistent with the outlook of the majority of the populace and therefore appearing less distinctive and specific. In such cases, the ideology need not be spelled out in any specific document or manifesto. The so-called ideological parties do not fail because they are ideological, but rather because their particular ideology is, in this context, dysfunctional to the prevailing values. As a movement the ideological party is not, clearly, like the "brokerage" parties, which are functional in the context of the prevailing value system.

The party which sets itself up in opposition to the prevailing system of values is obviously more distinctive and clearly requires a statement of the belief that underlies its opposition. Running, as it were, against the current, it needs a marker to measure its progress, to rally its adherents, and to safeguard its faith. Its ideology stated in a manifesto is such a marker. As a movement seeking to change values or attitudes, such a party attracts to its cause a wide range of dissidents. There may be little consistency of view among them. But to wage war successfully in the political arena, there must be some general unity of belief and purpose. A documented ideology provides the basis for unity. It imposes a discipline of belief and hence of outlook on what would otherwise be a fissiparous gathering of the discontented. The Progressive party failed partly for this reason; there was neither certainty nor unity of belief beyond the general discontent.

Once the dogma has been laid down and the goals prescribed, the party-movement advances its specific policies predicated on the achievement of the goals. The distance of the goals from actual achievement may vary – indeed it usually does – but un- **39** less the policies advocated are in clear conflict with the stated goals, the party-movement remains consistent with its ideology. The prime difficulty a movement faces when it engages in political activity and becomes a party, that is, seeks to win elections, is that it must widen its support. It must expand its membership and its electorate. This necessarily affects its policies and may affect its goals, if only causing them to recede. The nature of ideology itself means, as well, that there will be differing interpretations of means and ends within the party-movement itself. The CCF was no exception.

Judging by the Regina Manifesto alone, it would seem that the federation of movements and parties that emerged from the conferences at Calgary and Regina in 1932 and 1933 was unmistakably socialist. But an examination of the speeches of members of the CCF, of the literature and election programs published by the party, casts some doubt on this judgment. The Manifesto did remain the core of the party's doctrine until it was superseded by the Winnipeg Declaration in 1956 – for many in the CCF it remained the core even after 1956 – but it was overlaid with an accretion of revised statements of socialism made largely by the leading figures in the party. When the official revision came in 1956 it was really little more than a formal recognition of what had taken place some years earlier.

From the beginning there was no unanimity about what the new federation stood for. Socialism is susceptible of a wide variety of interpretation. At both Calgary and Regina there were some who rejected even the word itself with some vehemence. Laconically, David Lewis and Frank Scott point out that "there was great division of opinion among the delegates."[1] If there was any consistency of view, it was among the urban socialists from the prairie cities and the intellectuals in the LSR. Their socialism was British Fabian socialism, particularly so in the case of the intellectuals, most of whom had been educated in Britain. The group around M. J. Coldwell from Saskatchewan had read Blatchford's *Merrie England* and old copies of his *Clarion* were circulated along with mimeographed material from the National Labour College in Britain. According to Coldwell, the Saskatchewan ILP doctrine was "very much a British Socialism."[2] On the one hand, the notion of fellowship, the value of co-operation, and the importance of the family as a social prototype, all central to the ideology of British socialism, were consistent themes in the socialism of these urban delegates. On the other hand, the

1 / David Lewis and F. R. Scott, *Make This* YOUR *Canada* (Toronto 1943), 119.
2 / Interview with M. J. Coldwell, 1963.

doctrine of the Socialist Party of Canada in British Columbia
owed more to Marx than Blatchford, and the members at Regina
and Calgary were at pains to demonstrate the difference.

The rural delegates, however, are perhaps best classified as
liberal reformers in the populist tradition. Certainly the delegates
to Regina from the United Farmers of Ontario were not socialists.
They, and many of their colleagues from Manitoba and some
from Alberta and Saskatchewan, were liberal. Scott wrote that
the farmers never indulged in the Marxist phraseology of the
socialist labour delegates and were frankly baffled by it; they
"vigorously supported principles of constitutionalism, and compensation for owners of nationalized industries."[3] They were
more interested in monetary reform and economic tinkering than
in any fundamental shift in values; their sympathies probably
lay more with Major Douglas than with Marx or Blatchford.[4]
But like the urban socialists in the labour parties and the MPs,
they recognized that without some form of co-operative enterprise no reform could be achieved. All agreed that capitalism
was the cause of their discontent.

When the fourth conference of the Labour Political Parties
met in Calgary on June 30, 1932, it was in anticipation of the
subsequent joint meeting with the farmers' groups, the United
Farmers of Alberta and the United Farmers of Saskatchewan
(SS). There were some delegates from the LSR there, although
who they were is not known – they were seated at the meeting
with voice but not vote. Also in attendance was A. R. Mosher of
the Canadian Brotherhood of Railway Employees of the militant
All-Canadian Congress of Labour. The joint meeting took place
August 1, on which day the plans for united action were discussed and ratified and the CCF founded. There was time left
over for the provisional national council of the new organization
to hold its first meeting.

The resolution setting out the purpose of the new federation
of groups and parties was moved by M. J. Coldwell on behalf of
the "Labour Political Parties." It had been drafted by Coldwell,
Robert Gardiner, and G. Latham of the Canadian Labour Party,
Edmonton. The object of the new organization was to promote
co-operation between the member organizations and "correlate"
their political activities. The organizations in the federation were
to be those whose purpose was, "The establishment in Canada

3 / F. R. Scott, "The CCF Convention," *Canadian Forum*, XIII (1933),
447.
4 / This was particularly true of the UFA delegates, who had some
familiarity with Douglas Social Credit as their 1933 *Declaration of
Ultimate Objectives* indicates; and see also *Hansard*, 1934, 268–89.

of a co-operative commonwealth, in which the basic principle regulating production, distribution, and exchange, will be the supplying of human needs instead of the making of profits."[5] The name of the new body was the Co-operative Commonwealth Federation (Farmer-Labour-Socialist). The appendage was included on the insistence of the delegates from British Columbia who wanted it known that not all the affiliates could claim the title "socialist." Woodsworth was unanimously elected president and Norman Priestley of the UFA, secretary. The provisional national council consisted of George Williams (UFC), John Queen, MLA (ILP), A. R. Mosher (CBRE), Mrs. George Latham (Canadian Labour party), Angus MacInnis, MP (ILP), William Irvine, MP (UFA) and Louise Lucas (UFC).

The resolutions committee presented the meeting with a fourteen-point program which the group undertook to enact "if elected." It was prefaced with a clear statement of the federation's endorsement of radical solutions:

That believing the present economic crisis is due to inherent unsoundness of the capitalist system, which is based on private ownership of resources, and capitalist control of production, distribution and exchange which involves the payment of rent, interest and profit, that we should organize Nationally to change the system.

We [sic] further declare that we recognize that social ownership and co-operative production for use is the only sound economic system.[6]

The fourteen points included both the specific and the general. After some discussion the plan was revised and passed as an eight-point platform for the CCF.[7] The revision eliminated some of the specific proposals such as the development of Churchill, Manitoba, as a free port, and some of the woollier plans such as one which called for the "removal of the burden of debt which hangs over society."

The eight points were radical enough, calling for the socialization of banking, credit, and the "financial system" and for the social ownership of utilities and natural resources. The platform also spoke of the need to maintain existing welfare legislation "during the transition to the socialist state." Despite this, Frank Underhill suggested to Frank Scott that if the new group was not prepared to go any further than the eight points proposed, it would suffer the same fate as the Progressives.[8]

5 / Minutes, "Conference Resulting in Formation of the Co-operative Commonwealth Federation," CCF Minute Book, CCFP.
6 / *Ibid.*
7 / See Appendix I.
8 / Interview with F. R. Scott, 1962. In the light of this interview it is interesting to speculate on the extent to which Underhill's determination

The original fourteen points were a combination of the proposals presented by the various founding groups at their individual conventions prior to the Calgary meeting. The United Farmers of Manitoba had resolved in January 1932 that "the present economic crisis is due to inherent unsoundness in the capitalist system ... "[9] The manifesto of the Manitoba ILP called for the establishment of a co-operative commonwealth based on production for use rather than profit and advocated socialization of banking, industry, and finance.[10] It was consistent with the declared intentions of the UFA, the LSR (although without the elegance of style), and of the UFC (SS) and the Saskatchewan ILP.

The Calgary program was succinct and couched in language that was neither revolutionary nor foreign to the experience of the people to whom it was primarily addressed. It lacked the ringing prose of the Regina Manifesto but, as Frank Scott said much later, it would have been a much more effective political instrument for the new party than the Manifesto ever was.[11] But as far as the new federation's ideology was concerned, as far as its plan for the ultimate society went, the delegates "oozed idealism to the detriment of practical expediencies."[12]

During the winter of 1932–3, the federation directed its attention toward the preparation of a manifesto for presentation to the convention at Regina. At its meeting of January 24, 1933, the provisional national council agreed to establish a committee to draft a manifesto based on the eight-point Calgary program.[13] The council instructed the committee to ask the research committee of the LSR in Toronto to help prepare the manifesto. The Regina Manifesto was largely the product of this committee, particularly of its chairman, Frank Underhill.

In June 1933 Underhill prepared a draft manifesto at his summer home in Muskoka. He took the draft to Toronto where it was discussed and revised by the members of the LSR research committee in Toronto at that time. Among those who participated in the discussions were Harry Cassidy and Escott Reid. The final version was rewritten entirely by Underhill to provide some uniformity of style[14] and was then forwarded to the provisional national council, which met on July 16, 1933.

to be "radical" resulted in the radicalism of the Regina Manifesto, of which he wrote the major part.

9 / *Canadian Forum*, XII (1932), 124.

10 / *An Outline*, appendix and p. 8.

11 / F. R. Scott, "Canada's New Political Party," unpubl. ms. 1942, Scott Papers.

12 / A. Key, "Creating a National Federation," *Canadian Forum*, XII (1932), 451.

13 / Minutes of the Provisional National Council, Jan. 24, 1933, CCFP.

14 / F. H. Underhill to F. R. Scott, Jan. 26, 1951, Scott Papers.

At the same time that the CCF manifesto was being considered, the leading figures in the LSR were meeting to discuss the preparation of a book, published in 1935 as *Social Planning for Canada*. In April 1933, Underhill, Frank Scott, King Gordon, Elmore Philpott, Escott Reid, Edgar McInnis, A. F. W. Plumptre, G. G. Coote, J. S. Woodsworth, Eugene Forsey, E. J. Garland, Graham Spry, and J. F. Parkinson met to discuss the book and, undoubtedly, talked about the CCF manifesto as well. The Regina Manifesto was clearly the product of the League, both directly and indirectly.

When the provisional national council met on July 16 in Regina, it had before it the document prepared by the LSR committee and Frank Underhill. Three days were spent discussing the Manifesto, paragraph by paragraph.[15] The draft as revised by the council was then presented to the convention and was read through in its entirety by Norman Priestley, with no little homiletic intonation. At the conclusion, with the ringing phrases of the final sentence, "No CCF government will rest content until it has eradicated capitalism and put into operation the full programme of socialized planning which will lead to the establishment in Canada of the Co-operative Commonwealth," the convention rose as one and cheered.[16] The manifesto was then debated, section by section. The changes that were made by the council and the convention were, in general, toward a more moderate position. It is difficult to document these changes precisely since there is no copy of the original draft extant.

Attempts were made through the debate to cleave to a more doctrinaire socialist position. These came most frequently from the British Columbia delegates. The principle of compensation for socialized industry was opposed by those delegates, forcing the deletion of a paragraph of the section on social ownership and the substitution of a compromise drafted by Scott, King Gordon, and Eugene Forsey during the luncheon adjournment.[17] But the Manifesto, as it finally emerged from the convention, still bore the mark of the Fabian intellectuals in the LSR. Although new paragraphs were drafted and a new section on social justice inserted, the major draftsmen in most instances were the LSR delegates. The document left room for a relatively wide interpretation and avoided antagonizing overmuch either the right or the left. It was typical that the provisional national council opposed an amendment that would have committed the party to

15 / Minutes of the Provisional National Council, July 16–20, 1933, CCF Minute Book, CCFP.

16 / Interview with F. R. Scott, 1962. Coldwell later described this sentence as "a millstone around the party's neck." Interview, 1963.

17 / Interview with F. R. Scott, 1962.

socializing "the means of production and distribution" instead of "the principal means of production and distribution,"[18] and also that the convention should defeat an amendment to delete the sentence "We do not believe in violent change."[19]

In his address to the convention, Woodsworth, as president of the new federation, outlined his hope for the development of a distinctively Canadian socialism:

Perhaps it is because I am a Canadian of several generations, and have inherited the individualism common to all born on the American continent; yet with political and social ideals profoundly influenced by British traditions and so-called Christian idealism; further with a rather wide and intimate knowledge of the various sections of the Canadian people – in any case, I am convinced that we may develop in Canada a distinctive type of Socialism. I refuse to follow slavishly the British model or the American model or the Russian model. We in Canada will solve our problems along our own lines.[20]

The CCF did not quite succeed in this task. Britain, and later Sweden, served as models throughout the party's history.

The socialism in the Regina Manifesto is a mixture of Christian, Fabian, and Marxian socialism, shot through with progressive reformism. There was in the CCF, if not explicitly in the Manifesto, a strong underlying belief that man is both a rational and social creature, capable of creating a perfect society by abolishing the corrupt social order.

The preamble of the Regina Manifesto avoids the standard Marxist phraseology in favour of the language of a more moderate and Christian reformism in its moral condemnation of the capitalist system and its insistence that "the supplying of human needs and not the making of profits" ought to be the principle regulating production, distribution, and exchange. At the same time the institution of the co-operative commonwealth would mean a "much richer individual life for every citizen." The CCF sought a new social order to replace the existing one which crushed the essential human values beneath the iron-heeled necessities of capitalism. These necessities involved the fluctuation between "feverish periods of prosperity in which the main benefits go to speculators and profiteers, and ... catastrophic depression, in which the common man's normal state of insecurity and hardship is accentuated."[21] It was a system which was, as the

18 / Minutes of the Provisional National Council, July 17, 1933.
19 / "Minutes of the First Annual Convention of the C.C.F.," July 19–21, 1933, CCF Minute Book, CCFP.
20 / Report of the First National Convention (1933) CCFP.
21 / Unless otherwise noted, this and subsequent quotations are from the Regina Manifesto.

Manifesto put it, "marked by glaring inequalities of wealth and
opportunity, by chaotic waste and instability; and ... poverty and
insecurity." Within the framework of a liberal democratic society
such a system was inefficient and immoral. In the language of
the Manifesto the capitalist economy had produced a situation
intolerable in a democracy, for it meant that "Power had become
more and more concentrated into [*sic*] the hands of a small
irresponsible minority of financiers and industrialists and to their
predatory interests the majority are habitually sacrificed." According to the Manifesto, the aim of the CCF was to remedy the
defects by overpowering capitalism. But even within that document it was stated that only the "principal means" of production
and distribution were to be owned, controlled, and operated by
the people.

The analysis of the party system in the Regina Manifesto owes
as much to Marx as to Henry Wise Wood, for parties are seen as
"the instruments of capitalist interests ... bound to carry on government in accordance with the dictates of the big business interests who finance them." But far from wanting to overthrow the
system in its entirety, the CCF wanted simply to "put an end to
the capitalist domination of our political life." The desire to reform through constitutional means a system gone wrong is distinctly Fabian.

Although the CCF saw the division between the "haves" and
"have-nots" as a division between classes and spoke in the Manifesto of the "exploitation and domination of one class by another," the analysis of the class struggle ended there. Class consciousness was not, apart from that expressed by the Socialist
party affiliates from British Columbia, an awareness of a fundamental antagonism that would lead inevitably to conflict; it was
more a recognition that many people were being deprived of the
benefits of a liberal democratic society. It was a social consciousness imbued with the egalitarianism and individualism of liberal
thought.

The Manifesto, read carefully, could satisfy most shades of
opinion on the left in western Canada with the exception of the
communists. It proposed revolutionary change by non-revolutionary means in order to provide a society in which Christian
principles prevailed – or, more accurately, Protestant principles
prevailed – within the framework of parliamentary democracy.
Its failing was the failing of all compromise solutions: whereas
it had something in it for everybody, it satisfied no one completely other than the members of the LSR who, as one member
reported in a letter to a friend, "scored a brilliant success at the

convention" and "succeeded in having their views accepted pretty generally with respect to the programs."[22]

The liberal reformism of the Manifesto upset the delegates from British Columbia, while the Ontario and, to some extent, Alberta farm delegates were less than happy with what they saw as distinctly revolutionary overtones. The CCF was to the Canadian left what the Liberal party was for so long to the centre: a concatenation of philosophies, some mutually inconsistent. It failed, as the Liberal party did not, because the CCF insisted on spelling out its beliefs while the Liberal party, from 1896, lived largely on assumptions in the absence of any clear statement such as the Regina Manifesto. The Liberal assumes his position is consistent with that of the party and in the absence of any clear body of doctrine, who is to gainsay this assumption?

The Manifesto disturbed the Ontario and Alberta farmers with such phrases as "the functionless owner class" and the "parasitic interest receiving class." W. C. Good of the UFO was concerned about the socialism in the program,[23] as were G. G. Coote and Alfred Speakman of the UFA, both of whom had participated in the development of the party as members of the co-operating groups in the House of Commons. Coote felt that the "socialist element was very much over-represented at the Regina conference and ... on the body that drew up the Manifesto ... "[24] He felt that for this reason it would be difficult for the new organization to hold the support of many of the farmers since he did not think it possible to "harmonize [the] extreme left wing views of the socialist-labour element with the farmer elements."[25] He informed Good that he was telling the farmers in his constituency that socialization of credit was all that was needed and that the government could control industry "with regard to hours of work, rates of wages, and prices of products, without having to socialize ownership of all industries."[26] Alfred Speakman wrote to Good: "I cannot feel that the majority of our Alberta farmers, either in or out of our UFA [sic] are prepared to support the more radical attitudes by certain of our affiliated friends."[27] Speakman also pointed out in the same letter that he had "stated at every

22 / H. Cassidy to K. W. Taylor, July 1933, Grube Papers.
23 / W. C. Good to Alfred Speakman, July 31, 1933, and Good to Stanley McConnell, Sept. 29, 1933, W. C. Good Papers, PAC.
24 / G. G. Coote to Good, Oct. 24, 1933, Good Papers. E. E. Winch, doughty left winger in the British Columbia section, thought the reverse; in his view the effete easterners were the conservatives in the movement. Winch to J. King, June 9, 1935, CCFP.
25 / Coote to Good, Oct. 24, 1933, Good Papers.
26 / Ibid.
27 / Alfred Speakman to Good, Nov. 1, 1933, Good Papers.

meeting that the C.C.F. has not joined the Socialist Party, nor has become a Wholly Socialistic body [*sic*]."[28]

As a program it was not specific and therefore not completely satisfactory. As a statement of attitude it was more satisfactory since it did express the anger and frustration of the intellectual, the farmer, and the labour groups. But even then the Manifesto tended to be less than adequate. Its elaborate idealism made it essentially unworkable as an electioneering document. Some aspects made it a distinct liability in this respect. As Good pointed out, it was "too elaborate and complicated," and the final paragraph "highly misleading and injurious to the cause the C.C.F. ostensibly espouses."[29] The farmer could accept the demands for some social ownership – notably the agricultural implements industry – as well as monetary reform and the regulation of marketing. He was not, however, as ready to accept the demands for sweeping social change. The moral criticism in the Manifesto he could accept; the detailed centralist panacea baffled him. It was a long way from the eight-point Calgary program.

The letters between Good, Speakman, and Coote also indicate a lack of sympathy for the political ends of the CCF. The frequent references to "a CCF government" disturbed them because they felt that political action should be but one of many agencies for reform.[30] They were clearly not prepared to admit they had established a political party, nor were they willing to allow that the amalgamation of federated movements was to be as broad and sweeping in its approach as the Manifesto indicated. In short the disparity of viewpoint between the farmers and the draftsmen of the Manifesto, between the farmers and the urban radicals from the cities in the East and West, was clear from the outset. The intellectuals had set a pace that placed the CCF some distance ahead of the political aims of many farmers in the West and in Ontario, so much so that the UFO withdrew from the CCF in 1934, the UFA in 1939.

The Manifesto was not a people's document in that it proposed to give to the people what the "magnates" and "vested interests" had taken from them. It proposed a managed economy to be directed by panels of professors, engineers, and other experts. The desire to provide experts to run the country was on the face of it inconsistent with the individualist ethic of agrarian radicalism, but was not inconsistent with the recognition by the farmers of their own inability to cope with the situation and, more obviously, of the influence which the Wheat Pools and the

28 / *Loc. cit.*
29 / Good to Stanley McConnell, Sept. 29, 1933, Good Papers, PAC.
30 / Good to Speakman, July 31, 1933, Good Papers.

Co-operative movement had. From this point of view the Manifesto bore a resemblance to the proposals of Major C. H.
Douglas.

There would be, to start with, a national planning commission: "a small body of economists, engineers and statisticians
assisted by an appropriate technical staff." There would be
"Managing Boards of the Socialized Industries" and "Investment
Boards" and, remarkably, a kind of "crime and punishment"
commission composed of "psychiatrists, psychologists, socially
minded jurists and social workers" who would "deal with all
matters pertaining to crime and punishment and the general
administration of law."[31] This was a far cry from the rural simplicity of the agrarian myth. It was evidence of the utopian character of the movement and the influence of the LSR, which was
founded on the rationalist premise of liberal democracy:[32] all
things are possible with intelligence, expertise, and the democratic
method.

The revolutionary tenor of parts of the Manifesto made it an
easy target for the enemies of the movement; they remained
political bulls'-eyes during the life of the CCF.[33] As a movement
which at the same time sought, if only obliquely at the start, to
influence the electorate, the CCF was hampered by the Manifesto
because it set the tone of the party without providing, apart from
section 14, any specific and immediate remedies for the ills of
society. The task of modification, softening, and amplification
began almost as soon as the convention adjourned, but the strident tone of many sections of the Manifesto offered encouragement to radical sentiment and offset the efforts of the moderates.
Thus the editors of the *C.C.F. Research Review*, a publication
of the CCF Research Bureau in Regina,[34] were able to publish
the "CCF Immediate Program" of 1934 and follow it with an
editorial condemning gradualism and stating: "we will not hesi-
tate to tramp on gradualists' necks with the iron heel of ruthless-
ness."[35]

Having started from what was, in the context of party politics,
a rather doctrinaire position, the party had to move to the right
to attract wider support. This need became evident when the
party did not succeed as rapidly as had been expected by the

31 / Regina Manifesto.
32 / LSR Manifesto; see also *Social Planning for Canada* (Toronto
1935), ed. Eugene Forsey, J. F. Parkinson, F. R. Scott, Graham Spry,
Frank Underhill, J. King Gordon, Leonard Marsh, ch. 1, 21.
33 / Ch. 6 below.
34 / The Bureau was set up after the Calgary conference by a group
of young men who had been working in the ILP with Coldwell. Jack King
was editor of the *Review*.
35 / *C.C.F. Research Review*, I (Aug. 1934).

enthusiasts. The Winnipeg Convention in 1934 had as its major
piece of business the drafting of an Immediate Program dealing
with finance, agriculture, labour, social services, and peace. It
was more moderate, calling for the socialization of the banking
and financial machinery of the country, the prevention of farm
mortgage foreclosures, the reduction of farm debt, crop insurance, and the full panoply of pump-priming programs popular
at that time.[36]

The CCF was dedicated to the propagation of a faith even more
than it was to the winning of political power, although each defeat at the polls caused alarm because it was seen as both a
measurement of the success of the evangelism and as evidence
of the party's distance from the real exercise of power. It was
true of the CCF as it was of the Fabian Society that, "It [sought]
to achieve [its] ends by the general dissemination of knowledge
as to the relation between the individual and society in its economic, ethical and political aspects."[37]

A profound and abiding belief in the essential rationality of
man dominated the CCF and reinforced the conviction of both
leaders and followers that the people of Canada could be educated
to accept and understand socialism. A mimeographed instruction
sheet dealing with electoral organization stated that "The C.C.F.
is primarily a great educational crusade." And there can be no
doubt about Woodsworth's views:

My experience in politics has shown me that at election time one has
a splendid chance for carrying on educational propaganda. I believe
that at this stage of the development this should be one of the main
reasons for entering candidates. We must get away from the old idea
of winning at any cost and by any method, and steadily build up a
convinced and educated constituency.[38]

Following the failure of the party to win more than two seats in
Saskatchewan in the federal election of 1935 (a defeat for the
CCF which had a "drastic effect" on the leaders of the Saskatchewan party, who "had been counting too heavily on the rational
persuasiveness of their cause"),[39] there was no reassessment and
change in policy; there was instead an increased determination

36 / Report of the Second National Convention (1934), CCFP.
37 / Max Beer, *History of British Socialism* (London 1929), ch. 2, 286.
38 / J. S. Woodsworth to A. B. Macdonald, March 14, 1935, CCFP.
It was a view shared by E. E. Winch, provincial secretary of the Socialist
Party of Canada (British Columbia), who felt that the primary task of
the CCF was not electing candidates, it was "the making of socialists."
Winch to Jack King, June 9, 1935, CCFP.

39 / Lipset, *Agrarian Socialism*, 109.

to press forward in the same manner as before. G. H. Williams,
at this time provincial leader in Saskatchewan, wrote:

The lesson of the election of the c.c.f. must be that if there is to be any future for the c.c.f. movement in Canada that future can only be as an intelligent socialist organization. Such an organization to be successful must form Study Groups and put over Radio Broadcasts [*sic*] not just at election time but continuously from week to week and from year to year.[40]

M. J. Coldwell wrote to Grant MacNeil on the same topic, urging a meeting to lay plans for a new educational campaign aimed at establishing "a group of c.c.f. supporters studying the economic and social situation in every community in Canada."[41]

This emphasis on education was not simply a stage in the early phase of the development of the ccf. The report of the Education and Information Division of 1948 stressed the need for more research and publication since, as the report put it, "we are failing as a movement to provide enough educational opportunities to develop socialists among newcomers."[42] This was more than simply a reflection of the Fabian influence through the LSR. Among other equally important factors was the tradition of education and self-betterment that was so much a part of agrarian movements like the Grange, the Patrons of Industry, and the various grain growers' associations. Nor can one overlook the fact that the leading figures were either teachers, such as M. J. Coldwell and Clarence Fines; or clergymen, such as Woodsworth, Irvine, Ivens, Coote, King Gordon; or journalists, such as Roper, Pritchard, and E. A. Partridge, to name only a few.

Woodsworth was very much the pedagogue. M. J. Coldwell, himself a school principal, described Woodsworth as "an ideal teacher" and as "essentially an idealist; he didn't believe in organization, he believed that when the time was right the people would flock to an idea rather than a party."[43] Woodsworth on tour was a teacher, complete with charts and pointer, lecturing his audiences in remote country school-houses.[44] He was not an orator like William Irvine; he preferred to convince rather than convert. It was largely through his example and the fact that the leading figures in the ccf were either clergymen, teachers, or academics that education played such an important part in the

40 / G. H. Williams to W. D. Summers, Oct. 22, 1935, sas.
41 / M. J. Coldwell to C. G. MacNeil, Oct. 18, 1935, ccfp.
42 / National Council Minutes, April 1945, ccfp.
43 / Interview with M. J. Coldwell, 1962.
44 / Interview with F. H. Underhill, 1962.

CCF approach to politics, an approach clearly more consistent with a movement than with a party.

These were men who saw their task as educating a rational public to the needs of a crippled society; who tended to see the CCF as a movement designed to teach the truth about capitalist economics and bourgeois society. The ironic fact was that the tradition of self-betterment in the agrarian movements upon which they capitalized and to which they contributed was fully consistent with the *petit bourgeois* individualism that formed the core of progressivism, the basis for the Social Credit success in Alberta and which was, at bottom, anti-socialist.

It was a characteristic of the CCF that, like most democratic socialist movements, it assumed that the people could be taught. Indeed they *had* to learn because, unlike contemporary Conservatism and Liberalism, the socialism of the CCF demanded an intellectual commitment, one strong enough to offset the social stigma attached to open support of a socialist cause. Support for the Liberal and Conservative parties was inherited and habitual, requiring no commitment to speak of. The Liberal and Conservative parties are, in Robert Fulford's wise observation, like the Unitarian Church: they require no acceptance of dogma, only attendance.[45] It would be wrong to argue that people belonged to and supported the CCF for purely intellectual reasons. There is a wide range of explanation for membership in a protest movement or deviant political party. What is true is that the CCF required considerable intellectual commitment from its members and, therefore, had to devote time and attention to education.

A socialist movement, since it is challenging the validity of the existing social order, must educate. This places it at an immediate disadvantage. The CCF did, however, have one advantage in that its educational efforts were facilitated by the necessity and social importance of group activity in the rural communities of western Canada. The obvious problems of communication meant that public meetings and group discussions played a large part in organizational activity. The radio discussion groups held by M. J. Coldwell prior to the formation of the CCF and the weekly "Citizens Forum" he held in Regina were all part of this group activity. The opportunity to instruct and the desire to learn were both present. The missionary zeal of the socialist gave him an advantage over the non-socialist politician in that he was prepared to travel anywhere at any time to talk to any group. His zeal enhanced his availability; his conviction meant that he seldom turned down a request for a meeting. At a period when information and education were anxiously sought this was a

45 / Robert Fulford, *Maclean's*, July 6, 1963, 53.

distinct asset.[46] Having been formed from the federation of urban and agrarian groups which had in many cases this common point of origin, it was not unnatural that the CCF should continue in this direction and seek to expand such activity to all parts of Canada, overlooking the fact that such groups and such zeal for knowledge were more typical of the rural West than anywhere else, and even in the West, of only certain kinds of people.

But this was also a reasonable course for the party to take, based as it was on the nineteenth-century liberal view of the perfectibility of man through rational argument and persuasion. As Lipset put it, "They [the CCF] believed that socialism was the correct solution to the social and economic problems of the day and that, if it were honestly presented to the people, it would be accepted."[47] Rejecting the Marxist view of the impersonal forces that moved societies, the CCF produced more publications in both variety and volume than any other Canadian party. It was the only party that organized correspondence courses, provided lengthy and detailed reading lists, provided study guides for important socialist books, established study groups, and ran summer schools. It was the only party in Canada to have, at one time, six party newspapers in simultaneous publication under separate editorial boards in six provinces. In addition it became the only party with a press service, the Co-operative Press Association, set up to provide copy for these newspapers.[48] In one correspondence course it was stated that "the C.C.F. must be, in essence, a vast adult education movement."[49] In 1938 a "Winter School" was held in Regina at which ten topics were discussed including "Socialist Theory," "Socialism in Practice," and "Duties of Poll Captains," although the emphasis was on program and philosophy.[50] In short, there was never a time during the history of the CCF that a vast amount of time and money was not devoted to education, although there was less emphasis on this aspect in the 1950s.

The pedagogical strain was augmented by the utopian evangelism and the chiliasm of the leading figures in the movement. Woodsworth's support of socialism was based on religious and

46 / M. J. Coldwell has a fund of tales of hair-raising adventures in the early period when no effort was spared to carry the party "gospel" to the farthest corners of the land in any weather. Lipset makes much of the importance of group activity – and rightly so.

47 / Lipset, *Agrarian Socialism*, 109.

48 / See the Reports of the Education and Information Director in the National Council and National Convention Minutes, CCFP.

49 / *Correspondence Course II*, "Educational Techniques," Lesson I, CCFP.

50 / E. J. Garland, "Organizer's Report," Dec. 1938, CCFP.

moral grounds as, to a lesser extent, was the socialism of the whole movement throughout its history.[51] It was a modified utopian socialism, the sort that one finds in the writings of Edward Bellamy, whose "Parable of the Water Tank" was a popular piece of CCF literature, and whose *Looking Backward* was recommended as required reading as late as 1953, in a pamphlet published by the Provincial Education Committee of the British Columbia-Yukon section of the CCF.[52] What gave this variety of socialism its impact was the moral indignation at poverty and inequality and the evangelical promise of a better world. Edward Bellamy was the American messiah of this outlook. Like Bellamy, the members of the CCF came to see their philosophy as a panacea for the ills of society – moral, political, and economic.

Because of this, the socialism of the CCF inspired service and sacrifice; it was a faith worth crusading for since it offered everything that was good and opposed all that was bad. It was more Christian than the socialism of the British Labour party which, understandably, after the collapse of the second Labour administration placed more emphasis on the class struggle and the ultimate establishment of a classless society. It was more Fabian than the Fabian Society for, certainly as far as J. S. Woodsworth was concerned and to a lesser degree M. J. Coldwell, education was more important than political power. The CCF was less socialistic than either the Labour party or Fabian Society, and less so than its American counterpart under the leadership of Eugene Debs and Norman Thomas. There was little of Marx in the Regina Manifesto. Frank Underhill, its chief architect, admitted that he had never read Marx.[53] The CCF doctrine laid more emphasis than the more doctrinaire Marxist parties upon the protection of the farmer's land from foreclosure, and made much of promises of more property for all. In this respect the CCF gave proof of its agrarian ancestry, particularly that of the Progressive strain, but more the Progressivism of the United States than that of the western Canadian provinces.

Having, as it were, a doctrine with no flaws – one consistent with Christian societies, liberal democracy, bourgeois ideals, and the North American myth of prosperity for all – the CCF as a movement exacted from its leaders and supporters a degree of service to its cause hitherto unknown in Canadian political his-

51 / McNaught, *A Prophet*, 13, 96, and *passim*. See also M. J. Coldwell, *Am I My Brother's Keeper* (Ottawa [c. 1948]), and W. Irvine, *Can a Christian Vote for Capitalism* (Ottawa 1935).
52 / *Socialism*, no. 4 of a series: *Understanding the C.C.F.* (Vancouver 1953), publ. by Education Committee of B.C.-Yukon CCF.
53 / F. H. Underhill, tape recording, "The Angry Thirties," Seminar at Carleton University, 1963.

tory. The creed was one which lent itself to evangelism and its adherents lost no opportunity to proselytize. Woodsworth drove himself relentlessly until his health forced him from the field. In 1935 he gave more than 200 speeches outside of Parliament. In the first six months of 1936 he made over 50.[54] David Lewis, national secretary from 1936 until 1950, did the work of three men for a pittance. His starting salary in 1938 was $1,800 per year.

The CCF doctrine was one which elicited total commitment to the movement. And party officials expected total commitment. Membership involved time and responsibilities which the party felt should be placed foremost in the minds of the members: "I would say most emphatically that when a member of the C.C.F. becomes too busy with other activities to accept the responsibilities which go with membership in this movement, he is too busy."[55] Members travelling to conventions would seek from the various provincial offices names and addresses of people in cities en route who would be interested in arranging public meetings for them as they passed through on their way.[56] The activities involved in the day-to-day affairs of the movement required a faith and a dedication to the cause that of itself necessarily restricted membership to those willing to make such sacrifices.

The leaders and members had to be fired by great conviction to continue as they did with little money, little support, frequent failure, and constant attack from opposition parties, chambers of commerce, most newspapers, some clergy – indeed, at one time or another, from virtually every vocal association or organ in Canadian society. There is little doubt that for many in the movement it was the party's relative failure that kept it going. For them it was the battle and not the winning of it that provided the impetus. The congenital rebel, the crypto-anarchist – and there were several such in the CCF – is less concerned with the ultimate achievement of success than with the struggle. For some members of the CCF the success of the party lay in its providing a forum for the discontented and the crank, whose delight in life was to champion the lost cause or rail against established order.

This attitude toward the party was not the attitude of the majority; it was, however, one which on occasion produced the best oratory and the worst publicity. But for party officials and leaders the doctrine was practical and workable. As the first postwar correspondence course put it: "Socialism is not so much a

54 / "Chairman's Address" to the 1936 National Convention, typescript ms, CCFP.

55 / Elmer Roper, "A Call to Action," address to the annual convention of the Alberta CCF, Dec. 5, 1952.

56 / E. E. Winch to N. Priestley, June 10, 1934, CCFP.

theory to be studied 'off in an ivory tower' as a way of life that
must be put into practice." These people believed that socialism
would triumph in time, given effort and education. In a letter to
Angus MacInnis, David Lewis summed up this view: "My point
is the very deep conviction that if we could only find a way of
getting our message graphically to the people, we would obtain
support to an extent we don't even dare dream of."[57] A party
worker in Nanaimo wrote:

> The purpose of our organization is not to elect C.C.F. politicians to
> office but to place the management of their own business in the hands
> of a people aware of the necessity for and bent upon the achievement
> of a planned and socialized economy. A vast responsibility rests upon
> this C.C.F. to which a bewildered people is turning. We must systematically teach them how to work out their own salvation.[58]

Both statements demonstrate not simply the firm belief in education but, of course, the assumption of the educability of the
people: the belief in the ultimate triumph of rational man.

The essential ingredient of successful evangelism is a firm belief in the rightness of the cause. This was present in the CCF. The
workers were missionaries who gave their time and money freely
to the movement. Woodsworth recognized the fact in his address
to the 1936 convention when he said:

> I think of stenographers and office workers who, receiving only a car
> ticket and a lunch, make it possible to keep our offices open. I think of
> the hundreds who will never win office or even experience the exhilaration; with scant recognition these men and women patiently, almost
> doggedly carry on [sic] the most unobtrusive ways – distributing bills,
> painting signs, driving cars, making lunches, talking to their neighbours. It is they who are making more converts than all the rest of us
> put together. Making converts – yes, after all that is our job – leading
> people to seek a new way of living, the cooperative way, through
> which alone a true brotherhood may be established.[59]

The same view was expressed by David Lewis a year later:

> Yet there were times when one's moral indignation was even stronger
> than it is normally. The thought of how much more beautiful life
> could be, of how much loveliness there really is if only people had a
> chance to observe and appreciate it, often made me feel that the convention in Winnipeg could not be and must not be allowed to become
> just another meeting. If it were only possible to communicate to the

57 / D. Lewis to A. MacInnis, Jan. 25, 1945, CCFP.
58 / A report of the 1935 federal campaign in Nanaimo riding signed
by M. E. James, candidate's agent, CCFP.
59 / J. S. Woodsworth, Address to the 1936 Convention, CCFP.

people in our movement the urgency and the tremendous adventure
in createdness [*sic*] which are the essence of our movement, then
Canada would quickly become ours and that means the peoples [*sic*].[60]

And it was a natural concomitant of this position that the party
activists would see their movement as being of great value and
importance in Canadian political life. In 1939, E. J. Garland,
national organizer, said: "If there is an election this movement
will be needed more than ever. It is the only bulwark we have
protecting civil liberties, against any attempt on the part of local
authorities to exercise oppression."[61] There was an automatic
assumption that, in this case, "local authorities" would oppress in
the absence of the CCF.

It was the belief in the rightness and necessity of the CCF cause
that enabled party workers to continue when party fortunes,
both fiscal and political, were in decline. It provided, as one
party supporter put it, "a kind of backstop in our minds, a sort of
mental reinsurance, which we are not required to express publicly, that politics is an uncertain game, and public favour sometimes whimsical, but the C.C.F. carries on against that inevitable
day when the public will recognize that they need us."[62] However, there were those in the party who based their faith less on
hope and more on dogma: "... no matter what our setback or how
static we may appear to be, we have one consolation – we know
economic determinism is on our side and that eventually we must
forge ahead."[63]

It would be an exaggeration to state that the CCF was concerned only with its own clear-sighted image of the future to the
exclusion of new ideas or to the ignoring of changing circumstances. Under M. J. Coldwell, who was less the apostle and
more the politician than J. S. Woodsworth, party doctrine did
evolve and change. But even so, the righteous, utopian, and
holier-than-thou attitude, which is in many respects the hallmark
of a socialist movement, never completely disappeared. And it
was necessary that it should never disappear. It was only on
Woodsworth's retirement that any significant change began to
occur for, "No 'politician' in the ordinary sense of that word,
utterly devoid of skilled oratory or demagogic appeal but inspired by a deep social vision and a burning faith in the common
man, he gave the new movement a quality of leadership which at

60 / Lewis to MacInnis, Aug. 20, 1937, CCFP.
61 / Minutes of a meeting of federal MPs, Sept. 13, 1939, CCFP.
62 / Eric Havelock, "The Party and the Public" report of the Electoral
Committee to the annual Ontario provincial convention, 1945, Grube
Papers.
63 / H. Winch to F. R. Scott, n.d. (*c.* 1935–8), Scott Papers.

once lifted it above mere party politics."[64] In 1944 Frank Underhill, who was critical of the CCF for its failure as a party some
fifteen years later, said in an address:

The C.C.F. is still what Mr. Woodsworth left it, a movement devoted
to social and economic change in the interests of the great mass of the
plain common people. Let us resolve to keep it a movement and to
save it from sinking into being merely a party intent on collecting
votes.[65]

Even though the attitudes and direction provided by the party
leadership during and after the Second World War were away
from the movement concept and directed more toward the successful operation of a political party, the CCF remained to its
members and leaders as much a movement as a party because of
the central myth or ideology. As long as there were socialist goals
unachieved, as long as the co-operative commonwealth remained
an ideal to work toward, there was a need for the CCF and abundant evidence to support the rightness of its cause.

The CCF remained a movement because its members were
concerned with the "ought" of politics and saw political parties
as mere practitioners of the "is." The distrust of the prairie farmer for the "old line parties" was a result of his transference of
the failure of these parties to improve his economic condition
into a statement of their ethical bankruptcy.

The importance of the "ought" in the socialism of the CCF
was demonstrated by Woodsworth in his address to the fifth
national convention when he said: "In our efforts to win elections
we must not yield to the temptations of expediency. Let us stick to
our principles, win or lose,"[66] and more specifically in 1955 by
Frank Scott: "A democratic socialist party is held together by a
group of ideals, which are essentially moral concepts. All policies
applied from time to time are attempts to realize these ideals in
a given country at a given time."[67]

The CCF espoused moral ends upon which its leaders were
determined to act. Unlike the other parties in Canada, the CCF
faced the dilemma posed by Lord Acton and described by Daniel
Bell as "the irreconcilable tension between ethics and politics,"
a tension arising from the question "are politics an attempt to

64 / F. R. Scott, "Canada's New Political Party," unpubl. ms, Sept.
1942, Scott Papers.
65 / F. H. Underhill, "J. S. Woodsworth," address given at the in-
auguration of the Ontario Woodsworth Memorial Foundation, Oct. 7,
1944; reprinted in *In Search of Canadian Liberalism* (Toronto 1960).
66 / Report of the Fifth National Convention, 1938.
67 / F. R. Scott, notes for an address to the Quebec provincial convention, Aug. 1955, Scott Papers.

realize ideals, or an endeavour to get advantages, within the The Regina Manifestolimits of ethics?"[68] The CCF answer to this question was given by Woodsworth in 1935: "we are fighting for a principle and ... we should fight for this principle even if we should go down to defeat."[69] This view is consistent with the goals of a movement but not with the goals of a political party, if these are seen to be the achievement and maintenance of political power. The goals of the party are immediate and the neglect or sacrifice of principle has always been accepted by political parties in order that power should be won or held. For the pure movement it is change and not necessarily power that is desired; hence principle may always be kept pure.

As a political movement – one which sought political power in order to achieve the reforms it advocated – the CCF faced a dilemma that was, to some extent, the result of its devotion to two ends or two ethics: the ethic of responsibility and the ethic of conscience or ultimate ends.[70] The CCF as a movement was enthusiastically dedicated to the achievement of an ideal, yet it was at the same time prepared to work within the system – abide by the "rules of the game" – and accept the responsibility of office or of official opposition when it had to. The strain between these two aspects generated tension within the party and hostility towards those who seemed to be either ignoring the party's role in the Canadian party system or subverting principle in order to win office or the support of some segment of Canadian society, for example, the trade unions.

It has been argued that the distinguishing feature of modern society is the separation of ethics and politics.[71] Although this "either-or" analysis is too sweeping, it does suggest a root of much tension within the CCF. Some of its members steadfastly refused to accept any accommodation with the Canadian political system, their anti-party bias having either a Marxist or a populist origin. Others accepted the political system and were prepared to modify the party's doctrine when changing conditions made alteration not only sensible politically, but theoretically necessary. The CCF sought office with noble intent and grand design. The internal contradiction made its career difficult, but the party's

68 / Daniel Bell, "Marxian Socialism in the United States," in D. D. Egbert & Stow Persons, *Socialism and American Life*, I (Princeton 1952), 217. See also G. Himmelfarb, "The American Revolution in the theory of Lord Acton," *Journal of Modern History* (Dec. 1949), 312, cited in Bell.

69 / J. S. Woodsworth to John Mitchell, May 14, 1935, Woodsworth Papers, PAC.

70 / See Gerth and Mills, eds., *From Max Weber* (New York 1958), 121.

71 / Bell in Egbert and Persons, 218.

leaders pursued this goal with remarkable determination and, by and large, equally remarkable consistency. Only in the latter years of the party's existence did electoral considerations appear to brook large in the presentation of platforms. This did not mean that aspects of the party program were conveniently forgotten or deliberately obscured, it meant only that the program became reduced to simpler homiletics. The central myth was retained, but referred to less frequently, and only at ritual gatherings.

The increasing attention that was paid to electoral activity, the increasing emphasis on organization, and the lessened emphasis on education marked the decline of the movement aspect of the CCF and the predominance of the party aspect. This development reached its zenith in the formation and subsequent political activity of the New Democratic Party, in which electoral organization achieved the status of a high art. The doctrine was neither forgotten nor betrayed in its development; the shift was one of emphasis. And it is, as well, one which resulted from the growing recognition of the ineffectiveness of education from the side lines; the election of one good socialist achieved more than ten pamphlets.

To return to the Weber-Bell dichotomy, it can be seen that the shift from movement-party to party-movement necessarily involves a risk that principles may suffer in the drive to power. Leaders learn to exercise greater care in making statements, avoiding those which, however accurate, may disaffect possible supporters and hence are better left unsaid. Political leaders in Canada are no strangers to the process of selective disquisition and the leaders of the CCF and its successor, the NDP, learned the art. The dichotomy is not clear-cut; the areas between the ethic of responsibility and of ultimate ends and between the party and the movement are grey and indistinct. What is certain is that the CCF grew less utopian, more pragmatic, and more oriented toward the "game" as it grew older.

When these changes took place is difficult if not impossible to determine with precision, for, as Lipset points out in reference to the Saskatchewan CCF, "the ideology was in a state of continuous adjustment."[72] It is possible to dip into the records of speeches by all leading figures in the CCF at any given point and find vigorous statements of both the doctrinaire and the more pragmatic positions. This apparent inconsistency is not so much the result of ideological ignorance as of the pressures upon a party-movement in twentieth-century Canada. Unlike their

72 / Lipset, *Agrarian Socialism*, 151. The ambivalence can be seen in the following excerpt from a letter to Harold Winch from David Lewis, April 4, 1944, "there is a great deal to the concept of socialist competition although I hate to use the word ... ," CCFP.

American socialist counterparts, the leading figures in the CCF
were involved in the political game and in many instances had
been before the CCF itself was formed. It was inevitable that there
should be ambivalence. And if any distinction can be found, it
is between speeches made between elections and on the hustings
and statements directed toward the public and party members.
But since most CCF utterances were public, the point of the
distinction was usually lost.

It is not even possible to say that the ideals of the party remained unshaken although of all aspects of the party ideology
the ideals – or the utopian goal – remained the least altered. In
1944 M. J. Coldwell, speaking in Washington, D.C., outlined
the goals of the CCF:

Our aim, then, is to replace the present capitalist system with its injustice and inhumanity, by a social order from which exploitation of
one group by another will be eliminated and in which economic planning for abundance will supersede unregulated private enterprise. The
social order we desire is not one where individuality will be crushed
by regimentation, but will make possible a greater opportunity for
individual initiative, more leisure and a richer life for our citizens.[73]

In 1950 the national executive drafted the following resolution
for submission to the national convention:

Democratic socialism is based on the philosophy of human dignity
and equality. Its moral purpose is to abolish exploitation of man by
man, to eliminate competitive greed, and to remove injustice and
unnecessary human suffering. Its economic aim is to replace capitalist
chaos by social planning and monopoly power by social ownership.[74]

David Lewis, in an interview with Professor Paul Fox, pointed
out that the ultimate program of the CCF was "a complete reconstruction of society wherein the means of production and
distribution etcetera were publicly owned." He went on to say:

what will always distinguish our kind of party is that we do not believe
that profit is the be-all and end-all of life. On the contrary, we believe
that the profit idea is immoral rather than a moral one [sic], and that
people are capable of being motivated by things other than profit in
society, and that society ought to appeal to these other sources of mo-
tivation rather than to their self seeking search for private gain.[75]

Yet in 1934 Woodsworth argued in the House of Commons that
"the C.C.F. has never thought of socializing all industries. The

73 / U.S. *Congressional Record*, appendix, 1944, XC, part 8, 353.
74 / Minutes of the National Council, May 1950, CCFP.
75 / Transcript in the possession of Professor Paul Fox of an interview with David Lewis in 1962.

charge is without foundation."[76] In 1936 T. C. Douglas said
"Only where a monopoly exists do we say that there should be
government ownership."[77] In the same speech Douglas drew a
distinction between the kinds of goods in society and indicated
the concern of the CCF with one kind: "I mentioned that there
were two kinds of goods, and that the public goods are the only
ones we propose to take over. Public goods are goods which any
person may have ..."[78] This was a distinction that was maintained
for the obvious reason that much of the impetus behind the movement on the prairies had been the result of the farmer's determination to be master of his own economic destiny, that is, owner
of his own land. Speaking to the national convention in Toronto
in 1942, Coldwell provided this enunciation of the party's goals:

We seek to raise the general level of society and liberate that individual initiative that capitalist regimentation denies. We desire greater
opportunities for education, greater opportunities for worthwhile service with adequate rewards for jobs well done. We want to see more
personal property for more people, but we want to see no public
property privately owned or used to exploit the community in the
interest of monopolistic corporations or anti-social individuals.[79]

There is nothing in this statement at all inconsistent with that
petit bourgeois individualism attributed by Professor Macpherson
to the supporters of the UFA and Social Credit.[80] Though apparently inconsistent, socialism and *petit bourgeois* individualism,
in the context of agrarian radicalism in Canada, seem to be inter-
changeable terms. The CCF program as spelled out in speeches
and leaflets, like Bellamy's *Looking Backward* already alluded
to above, "stimulated the appetites of its readers for material
things, but it held them out as a bait, as a reward that could be
secured only after a thorough-going application of the village
ideals of equality and neighborliness."[81] G. H. Williams, leader
of the party in Saskatchewan, wrote in a pamphlet published in
January 1939: "Socialism not only recognizes the right of the
possession and enjoyment of personal property, but wants to
make it possible for people to enjoy a great deal more of it."[82]
In a radio address in 1947, Coldwell drew the standard distinction between private and public property, the former being "a

76 / *Hansard*, 1934, 268.
77 / *Hansard*, 1936, 476.
78 / *Ibid.*
79 / Address by the national chairman to the 1942 National Convention (mimeo.), CCFP.
80 / Macpherson, *Democracy in Alberta*, 225 ff.
81 / Daniel Aaron, *Men of Good Hope* (New York 1951), 94.
82 / G. H. Williams, *Social Democracy in Canada* (Regina 1939), 52.

home, the land we till, furniture, clothing, a car, so forth" and the latter "the kind of property we cannot use personally but which can be used to exploit the whole community."[83] The policy of the CCF as he outlined it in this address was to operate the productive machinery in the interest of the people "rather than for profits" and thus produce "more private property ... for the use of individual Canadians."[84] One pamphlet published in Saskatchewan put it rather succinctly: "The C.C.F. aim is to raise all wages and give everyone more goods and more private property."[85]

The same ambivalence can be seen with respect to the question of profit which, as stated above, David Lewis saw as immoral yet which Frank Scott saw as "a valuable incentive when kept in its proper place."[86] The Saskatchewan section felt it necessary to delete from its own manifesto the phrase "not for profit" which in the Regina Manifesto was part of the slogan "Production for Use and not for Profit."[87]

If any clear position emerges, apart from the consistent desire to change society, it is the unshaken opposition of the CCF to monopolies. Any statement of CCF policy makes this clear; one will suffice here.

These [economic] problems mainly arise from the monopolistic control of the machinery of production and of distribution. Farmers no longer own their own land; a glance at mortgage statistics will give ample proof of such a statement. Workers in industry are completely divorced from the control of the tools they must use in order to earn their daily bread. Both groups are being reduced steadily to a position of propertyless dependence upon giant corporations who own and control every means of life.[88]

It is also clear that seen in perspective there was a gradual development of a less militant attitude toward business *per se* and that the CCF was, at the same time, becoming more a party and less a movement. Indicative of this development was the variation between the views expressed in a confidential memorandum circulated to the members of the party's national council

83 / M. J. Coldwell, script for radio address, "The Nation's Business" series, July 30, 1947 (mimeo.), CCFP.

84 / *Ibid*.

85 / CCF pamphlet, n.d., CCFP.

86 / F. R. Scott, "The C.C.F., The League ... ", 26.

87 / "Saskatchewan farmers and small businessmen, when they read the words 'not for profit,' immediately concluded they could not earn their own living, an erroneous impression the Saskatchewan members of the C.C.F. wanted to correct." *Winnipeg Tribune*, July 28, 1937.

88 / M. J. Coldwell, Address to the 1938 National Convention (mimeo.), CCFP.

in March 1946, largely prepared by Scott who was national
chairman at the time, and notes prepared by him for an address
to the Quebec convention in 1955. The 1946 memorandum
states:

The socialist principles of the c.c.f. do not vary. Our objective is
always the same – the creation of the Co-operative Commonwealth,
combining economic and political democracy, and placing human
needs and human values first. Every experience that Canada has
undergone during the war has strengthened our conviction that a
socialist commonwealth is not only a magnificent ideal but an absolute
necessity if civilization is to survive.[89]

The notes state:

Nationalization of industry, in so far as we are concerned with it, is
a policy, not an ideal. Three socialist ideals – equality of opportunity
Wealth is made by all, all have the right to share in it. Freedom –
political and economic – Econ. freedom [sic] means right for business
to determine its own policies, within rules laid down by the state and
collective agreements, but not the right to combine and monopolise,
and equality and brotherhood for all races on this earth.[90]

There was as well, a diminution of the chiliasm of the movement. The early history of the CCF bears out the validity of Bell's
statement that:

Every socialist, every convert to political messianism, is in the beginning something of a chiliast. In the newly found enthusiasm, in the
identification with an oppressed group, hope flares that the final conflict will not be too far ahead. But the revolution is not always immediately in sight, and the question of how to discipline this chiliastic
zeal and hold it in readiness has been the basic problem of socialist
strategy.[91]

It was felt in the CCF that the Depression would result in the defeat of capitalism and then that the post-war period would bring
depression and CCF success. The flexibility of capitalism and the
gradual infusion of ameliorative liberalism into the policies of
the Liberal party prevented this occurrence. The resulting continued prosperity went some way toward quenching the fires that
had earlier burned in the breasts of some of the leading militants
in the CCF. They saw, with bitter satisfaction, some of their
policies adopted by the Liberal party.

89 / "The c.c.f. and Postwar Canada" (confidential memorandum),
March 1946, CCFP.
90 / F. R. Scott, "Notes for an address," Scott Papers.
91 / Bell in Egbert and Persons, 219.

The CCF did not aim its blows against the individuals in the system *per se*; it did, consistent with Mannheim's description of the chiliast and chiliastic movements, attack the evil principle "active in them."[92] It was not opposed to the men in business; it attacked the institutions of capitalism which placed men in the position that made them into oppressors of their fellows. This was made clear in Woodsworth's address to the Nova Scotia convention in 1939 when he said that he had no quarrel "with the individuals in the great corporations which at present controlled and dominated transportation, finance, industry and also the political field." His quarrel was "with the set-up which permitted them to have such power."[93] At the same time there are many examples which show that this distinction was not always maintained. In a radio broadcast in November 1947, Coldwell argued that "profiteering is rampant. Never before have unscrupulous businessmen wrung such big profits out of the Canadian people."[94] Many similar examples can be found in the minutes of council meetings, in pamphlets and manuals. It is true, however, that whenever this point was raised it was clear that the CCF was opposed to the system that corrupts and not the corrupted as such.

In the discussion that follows it will become clear that this aspect of the CCF which reflected its roots in the farmers' movements, its Fabian and Christian socialist heritage – that which made it a movement – began to fade. The main watershed was the Winnipeg Declaration of 1956, which marked the formal recognition of what had become increasingly evident since the end of the Second World War. Time and experience made politicians of many of the ideologues, but the ideologue was never far from the surface.

Throughout its history, the CCF was in the forefront of the defence of civil liberties in Canada with a determination and honesty that showed no regard for the niceties of party politics. It made no difference that Tim Buck was leader of a party that was a menace to the CCF; his arrest and imprisonment were vigorously opposed by the CCF.[95] It was at the same time the champion of parliamentary democracy and constitutionalism.[96] The socialism that emerged as it became more involved in the political game was, more and more, a kind of remedial liberalism. Lewis could write in 1943 that "only a socialist organization of

92 / Mannheim, *Ideology and Utopia* (New York 1936), 217.
93 / *Star*, Halifax, May 30, 1939.
94 / Script for radio broadcast, Nov. 29, 1947, CCFP.
95 / *Hansard*, 1932–3, 2096 ff.
96 / See Lewis and Scott, *Make This* YOUR *Canada*, chs. 5, 10, 11, *passim*.

society, democratically controlled and directed, with complete
and ever expanding freedom of speech, organization and religion
can establish equal opportunity for all and eliminate injustice,
depression and war."[97] And Coldwell, speaking in 1938, could
demonstrate the attitude that came to supersede that expressed
by Lewis: "I am more anxious to preserve and promote institutions and ideals which will, when the time comes, enable us to
achieve progressively ultimate aims, than I am in simply propagating ultimate ideals."[98] Both demonstrate the evolutionary
attitude that was to be clearly expressed in the Winnipeg Declaration; both demonstrate the clear acceptance of essentially liberal
ideals which, the argument proceeded, could only be achieved
through socialization. Although it could be said that this serves
merely to underline the inherent contradiction in the party philosophy so expressed, it serves equally well to demonstrate the
development of the non-revolutionary nature of the CCF doctrine
in that its concern was not the complete re-shaping of society,
but the more just and adequate utilization of the machinery that
existed. The more this attitude came to prevail, the closer the
CCF moved to 1956 and away from the spirit of 1933. As already
indicated this strain was evident at the convention which adopted
the Regina Manifesto. What is clear is the ambivalence and, indeed, the doctrinal confusion and contradiction that existed.

Doctrinal confusion and contradiction tend to be the lot of
most democratic socialist parties because democracy mitigates
against any great consistency of doctrine. In the case of the CCF
the presence in one movement of a wide range of political attitudes served to compound the problem. It was difficult for the
leaders of the party to operate effectively because their public
statements were not only subject to close scrutiny by the doctrinaire members of the party, but were also examined by an
opposition press which delighted in discovering lapses from
principle in party statements – as any brief survey of editorial
comment on the 1956 Declaration will show.

A common view of CCF policy was that it had never been
tested by the fires of office and that if the party spokesmen were
at all close to power they would soon trim their sails.[99] Such
critics missed the point, since the central ideology of the CCF was

97 / Memorandum of notes on points raised in William Irvine's letter
of Oct. 16, 1943, typescript, in D. Lewis to M. J. Coldwell, Nov. 15,
1943, CCFP.

98 / M. J. Coldwell, ms for an address to the University Club, Ottawa,
Feb. 2, 1938, CCFP.

99 / Or that "with nothing to lose and everything to gain, they can
afford to advocate new ideas." J. R. Mallory, "The Structure of Canadian
Politics," in Thorburn, *Party Politics in Canada* (Toronto 1963), 25.

not practical in their sense. It was a belief in a goal, like Christianity, and not, therefore, to be modified by the forces of political expediency or scrapped because it had not been achieved. What changed, as the CCF became more a party and less a movement, was the acceptance of the goal as further distant and less readily achieved than had been believed at Regina in 1933. The urgency of the times convinced the delegates at Regina that results could be achieved quickly – because they saw that they had to be achieved quickly. By 1956 it had become clear that change, because less urgent, could be achieved gradually; and that the goal of the movement – essentially unchanged – was more distant and would be better approached by the successful activities of the party.

In the years which followed the founding of the CCF, the immediacy which was so evident at Calgary and Regina waned, increased again in the early forties, and faded once again. After Regina the groups which federated to form the CCF were submerged as events and necessity welded them into a single movement and a single party. Although the CCF never matched the strength of the Progressives in the House of Commons, it avoided the error that helped dissolve that experiment. The leaders of the CCF gradually centralized control and helped shape the movement into a party.

MOVEMENT INTO PARTY, 1933-40

To build the socialist society we must first win; to
win we must build the socialist movement; to do
that we must work and give and study tirelessly.

DAVID LEWIS

In the early period of the CCF's existence, almost all those associated with the new federation of farm, labour, and socialist groups were motivated by the vision of a co-operative commonwealth in Canada. What united the movement was the zeal and determination of its adherents and a loose consistency of view. There was a wide difference in specific matters, and, as already mentioned, a difference of scope. But for each, as T. C. Douglas has said in countless speeches, paraphrasing the Labour party hymn, there was a desire to build "a new Jerusalem in this green and pleasant land."

As the CCF grew, as it became more a political party with national ambitions, its centre of control – if not of gravity – moved eastward. From the beginning there were forces pulling in this direction. As a national political organization the CCF naturally had its headquarters in Ottawa – in 1935 a permanent office was established there. The leading figures in the national CCF were mostly MPs and consequently spent a large part of their time in that city. The Saskatchewan and British Columbia sections were parties apart because although an effort was made by the national CCF to provide closer contact with the West than had been the case with the "old line" parties, it was nonetheless true that those in power in the CCF were often unable to understand or were out of sympathy with the western sections.

The movement east began with the Regina convention and the drafting of the Regina Manifesto. It then continued virtually unabated and was given impetus by Woodsworth's illness, which placed more authority in the hands of the national secretary. The development of closer relations with organized labour, the presence in the East of the party's intellectual leadership in the League for Social Reconstruction, the fact of the war – which solidified the eastern leadership – the nature of Canadian politics, and the inescapable facts of geography and transportation all exerted an irresistible pull eastward.

Represented by Eugene Forsey, Frank Scott, King Gordon, and J. F. Parkinson, the LSR was a major influence at Regina and in party councils afterward.[1] Its members – who were almost all in their late twenties or early thirties – provided the sophisticated and consistent analysis of society that was lacking in the farmers' programs. In addition they had the important status of eastern intellectuals whose counsel was needed. It was not that the far-

1 / F. H. Underhill, "Report of L.S.R. Activities," Oct. 3, 1933, Grube Papers. Of the key figures in the LSR, Underhill, Spry, King Gordon, Forsey, and Scott had studied at Oxford; Parkinson at the London School of Economics; and Marsh at London University.

mers were unable to see the whole picture; they were, however, more concerned with rapid cures than with analysis, and wanted less a change and more a repair job carried out under the aegis of their new party. The difference in approach was evident enough at the time. It was felt necessary to minimize the part played by the intellectuals in the early development of the party, largely, no doubt, to assuage the anti-intellectualism of the farm element. In the LSR book, *Social Planning for Canada*, this need is obvious: "It is worth emphasizing that it was the farmers and workers themselves, not some group of 'academic theorists' from outside, who created the new movement, gave it its name ... and its first programme, of which later programmes are simply detailed expansions."[2]

The revised and abridged version, *Democracy Needs Socialism*, states that "it is worth noting that the so-called intellectuals had no hand in the original formation of the C.C.F., but only came in later."[3] The minutes of the 1932 Calgary convention show that the members of the LSR were granted voice without vote at that convention.[4] This was probably in response to criticism that the party was an academic's dream, divorced from reality; it was also an attempt to avoid any indication that the new party was anything but the creature of those who formed it, the farmers and workers – although in the early stage the division was, in fact, farmers and intellectuals, since the labour parties had more intellectuals in them than workers.

The urban intellectuals became more and more involved in shaping the doctrine of the party. Having provided the Manifesto, they went on to provide the working documents in *Social Planning for Canada*, and the condensed version, *Democracy Needs Socialism*. In the foreword to *Social Planning for Canada*, J. S. Woodsworth wrote, with unconscious understatement, "on the whole the book is undoubtedly in line with the Regina Manifesto. It should be of great service in the formulation of the future policies of the C.C.F."[5] The books and their authors[6] played an important part in determining the policies and direction of the CCF. Woodsworth wrote in the foreword that "Every C.C.F. member ought to be able to give a reason for the faith that is in him." The books, pamphlets, and advice provided by the LSR made such reasons available. *Social Planning for Canada*, an indignant and at times devastating attack on Canadian capitalism, provided

2 / LSR, *Social Planning for Canada* (Toronto 1935), 472.
3 / LSR, *Democracy Needs Socialism* (Toronto 1935), 49.
4 / CCF Minute Books, Calgary Conference, 1932, CCFP.
5 / LSR, *Social Planning*, vi.
6 / Eugene Forsey, J. King Gordon, Leonard Marsh, Frank Underhill, J. F. Parkinson, F. R. Scott, Graham Spry.

a sustained academic critique that was a far cry from the more superficial criticisms of the farmers' organizations.

As the party's centre of control moved to the East, the CCF came more and more under the influence of the intellectuals who had formulated the critique. The farmers in the heyday of the Progressive Movement had feared that their MPs would be seduced by the wiles of the eastern magnates and had proposed the recall as a political chastity belt. In the case of the CCF, the members and elected officials of the party were seduced by the eastern intellectuals. The national CCF became less and less the semi-agrarian party it was at its foundation. It was more a party with support in the West but with urban and intellectual leadership from the East.

The LSR was centred in Toronto and Montreal, although there were chapters in other centres, notably Winnipeg and Vancouver. The leading figures in the league were either from the University of Toronto or McGill University. And it was through these individuals, particularly Frank Scott and Frank Underhill, that the LSR exerted its influence. The 1935 election address of the CCF was largely Underhill's work.[7] In 1936, Scott wrote several of the national council resolutions for the Fourth National Convention and was providing advice and information on the CCF provincial program to Harold Winch for the British Columbia CCF.[8] In 1937 the national council asked the LSR to draft a provincial program "covering those subjects common to every province."[9] Indeed the demise of the league was largely the result of its members becoming too absorbed in their work with the CCF to devote time to the activities of the LSR.

During the sessions of the House of Commons, close liaison between the LSR and CCF MPs was maintained,[10] partly through joint conferences. In 1936 the CCF and LSR met to hear reports on the party's progress and discuss drafts of the proposed party policy prepared by Underhill. In the same year a conference was held to discuss legislative proposals for presentation in the session.[11] At the latter conference it was decided to leave the Manifesto untouched while drafting a new Immediate Program. At the conference in May 1936, resolutions from the party branches for the national convention were discussed, the Immediate Program which the 1936 convention approved being largely the work of this joint group. Officially the LSR had no status in the party

7 / J. S. Woodsworth to M. J. Coldwell, July 31, 1935, CCFP.
8 / F. R. Scott to Harold Winch, June 5, 1936, CCFP.
9 / National Council Minutes, Jan. 30, 1937, CCFP.
10 / Reports of LSR secretaries, 1933–5, Grube Papers.
11 / Minutes of the CCF–LSR conferences, March 28, May 24–5, 1936, CCFP.

structure, yet it was more influential in shaping policy than constituency resolutions or the convention itself in the period 1932–40.

The LSR was in every sense the CCF "brains trust."[12] The minutes of the CCF national executive for this period indicate that although Underhill, Forsey, King Gordon, and Scott were not members of the executive, they were frequently in attendance and actively participated in the deliberations of that body.

The intimate connection between the CCF and the league meant that the formal political and economic thought of the movement was provided very largely by the leading figures in the LSR through their contact with the CCF leadership and in the two books and various pamphlets published by the league. They provided the analysis of the social and economic system to which members of the CCF turned again and again. Despite the prominence of this single source, the ambivalence that one would naturally expect, in a movement of diverse origins such as the CCF, remained. On some points the critique of the LSR reinforced the attitudes prevalent in the farmers' movements; on others the aims were contradictory. The contradictions were not evident during the first decade or so of the party's life, when the Depression obscured the fact that the farmers were really capitalists *manqué* or, as Macpherson has pointed out, *petit bourgeois*.[13] In the forties the CCF came to concentrate its attacks on monopoly capitalism rather than on capitalism as such out of deference to the farmers and the small businessmen, whose support was needed to win elections.

In the beginning, all members could sit comfortably beside this statement with its Marxist flavour:

The great condemnation of our system is that it makes an interest in "things" the major interest to the almost complete exclusion of an interest in values. The basis of privilege is wealth, the creed of privilege is a belief in the making of money, the measure of human achievement is a monetary yardstick. The philosophy of acquisition renders impotent the finer impulses. So are members of the privileged group known rather for a vulgar display of houses and lands, of yachts and automobiles, than for their contribution to the cultural life of our age.[14]

Buttressed by the report of the Stevens Royal Commission on Price Spreads, the LSR argued that capitalism was the cause of

12 / See G. V. Ferguson, "The C.C.F. at Regina" and "The C.C.F. Brains Trust," *Winnipeg Free Press,* July 24 & 25, 1933.
13 / C. B. Macpherson, *Democracy in Alberta,* 148, 230, and *passim.*
14 / LSR, *Social Planning,* 37.

vulgar hedonism. This view was in harmony with a dominant
theme in the philosophy of the agrarian movements, the theme
that stressed the simplicity and purity of rural life and its freedom
from the seductive and soul-destroying ostentation of urban living. The *CCF Research Review*, published in Regina, attacked
popsicles, processed cheese, and packaged breakfast cereal as
examples of the corruption, dishonesty, and impurity of capitalist
society.[15]

But this was a point of view that was rather awkward for a
political party to espouse when it had to canvass the public for
support. A movement may crusade to convert the infidel but it
can hardly expect to do so by going among the godless and
soliciting their votes in order to elect a government pledged to
eradicate their way of life. As a political party, the CCF could not
attack homes, cars, yachts, and the level of public taste while
soliciting votes. And, philosophical declarations aside, this kind
of campaign was inconsistent with the aspirations of the farmers
and workers who wanted nothing more than a share of bourgeois
affluence. The tension produced made it difficult for the CCF to
avoid providing ammunition for its enemies through its apparent
willingness to equalize down and to elevate public taste by legislative fiat. It may have been good philosophy to attack vulgarity
and ostentation, but it was bad politics. Good revolutionary stuff
during a depression, it might be argued, but only if the attack is
coupled with a promise that a CCF government would bring these
good things for everybody. And the CCF did subsequently make
such promises.

The intellectuals in the LSR could be more objective in their
opposition to capitalism than the agrarian radicals. They opposed
it because of the social and economic inequality it caused, because it perverted democracy, caused maldistribution of income,
produced an execrable level of culture and, finally, because it was
inconsistent with Christian fundamentals.[16] In short, because it
perverted the liberal democratic ideal. Only socialism could make
democracy work; politics would then be freed from the unwhole-
some influence of monopoly capital and government would reflect
the best interests of the whole nation. Only in such a society
could the full and free development of the individual be assured.

Unlike the intellectuals in the LSR, the farmer was personally
involved. As a producer he was badly treated by the system both
economically and socially; economically because his income was
inadequate and bore no relationship to his labour or its product,

15 / *C.C.F. Research Review*, II (March 1935), 15–16; and see R.
Hofstadter, *The Age of Reform* (New York 1955), ch. 1.
16 / LSR, *Social Planning*, ch. 1.

and because he was exploited by large corporations against
which he was powerless; socially because he was alienated from
society physically and culturally – which is why he created his
own society on the prairie with its own manners and mores.[17]
The individualism which brought him to farming became meaningless in a corporate industrial society. During the inter-war
period he was frustrated economically and socially.[18]

Socialism was a personal weapon for the farmer, one that could
make the economy work for him by providing a countervailing
power against big business. He firmly believed that through it the
government would line up on his side instead of staying on the
other. Social ownership was an acceptable means of providing
access to power and property for those who had neither ownership nor influence under capitalism. Co-operation was a social
necessity on the plains and an economic virtue among independent producers who were dependent upon markets beyond their
influence or control; it was an attractive substitute for competition. The concern of the farmer was, naturally enough, with the
lot of the farmer. Improve that and the problem was well solved.
The intellectuals were more concerned with the broader picture
of which the farmers' problems were only one aspect. Their focus
was broad; the farmers', narrow.

During the Depression, the two analyses reinforced each other.
At the point in time when the capitalist system is in a depression
while in a period of transition to an urban industrial society, the
concern of the intellectual socialist with society is consistent with
the concern of the farmer for his wealth and status because the
economic sensitivity of the farmer's position makes him one of
the dispossessed. Once this point is passed the two positions
diverge. The socialist's attention remains focussed on the underprivileged, who are the urban workers. The farmer's position
improves with good times and he achieves his goals, independence, and proprietorship.

In the thirties, the farmer's fight was against a progress in
which he had no part and which seemed to be depriving him of
his rightful share of the world's goods. He was in the classical
petit bourgeois position, neither bourgeois nor proletarian, and
increasingly conscious of the disparity and anomaly of his position. Although he was able to join with labour parties making
common cause against a common enemy, there does not seem to
be any evidence that he really understood the problems of the

17 / Lipset, *Agrarian Socialism*, chs. 1, 2; and see the now notorious
article by H. F. Gadsby, "The Sons of the Soil," *Saturday Night*, June 1,
1918, 4, ridiculing the farmers' delegation to Ottawa.

18 / See Irving; Macpherson, *Democracy*; Lipset, *Agrarian Socialism*;
Hofstadter, *The Age of Reform*, esp. p. 8.

industrial worker. Even in hard times the farmer is master of
the productive process in a way the worker is not. He is aware
of the significance of his part as a producer in the final product
while the industrial worker is only aware of the insignificance of
his role in the production of the finished goods. In this respect
the frustrations of the urban worker are fundamentally different
from those of the farmer. Both could agree with the analysis of
the LSR when capitalism had broken down. But when prosperity
returned, it made more of a difference to the situation of the
farmer than it did to that of the urban worker.

The CCF was an indigenous prairie party for the farmers; one
set up to oppose the "old line" parties of the East and their
backers, "the vested interests." The CCF provided a vehicle for
the active involvement denied the farmers by the old parties, an
involvement they lacked in the economic and social spheres as
well.[19] It was a manifestation of the hinterland standing up to
the metropolis in a struggle for the preservation of its independence and was, in that sense, a conservative force.[20] For the intellectuals in the LSR, the failure of the party system and of liberal
democracy was a product of capitalism. To cure the ill, more was
required than a dose of agrarian isolationism because more was
involved than the stability of the family farm.

In the long run it was urban socialism rather than agrarian
isolationism that was the more lasting and influential force in the
CCF, a fact recognized in the founding of the New Democratic
Party in 1961 at which the presence of representatives of farm
organizations had more historical than political significance. The
LSR was more influential in the CCF than any of the affiliated
farmers' groups. After 1935, when a permanent national office
was established in Ottawa, all the writing and thinking in the
national party was done by people whose contact with the western
grain farmer was superficial and intermittent. David Lewis, national secretary from 1936 to 1950 – and in a real sense the
centre of the party – was not a product of agrarian unrest. He
was an urban socialist in the European tradition.

The political necessity of keeping close touch with agrarian
questions was never overlooked, for the obvious reason that the
party won seats in the farm belt and generally had more rural
members in the parliamentary caucus than urban. But the leading
figures of the party: Woodsworth, Coldwell, Lewis, Scott, Mac-
Innis, and Knowles, were urban socialists who believed strongly
that the party had to move closer to labour. Indeed, during the
crucial formative period after the 1935 election, only three of

19 / Lipset, *Agrarian Socialism*, 218–19.
20 / *Ibid.*, 226.

the party's MPs were from rural ridings; the other five were all from urban constituencies. None of the eight were farmers.[21]

It is not surprising that the socialism of the LSR and the leaders of the CCF was more pertinent and durable in the context of an urban industrial society, for it was greatly influenced by the political thought of the Fabian Society and the British Labour party. Nor is it surprising that it prevailed in view of the greater voting strength of the CCF in the more urban provinces of British Columbia and Ontario. Woodsworth was nothing if not a labour man. His interest in farm problems was partly a result of his concern with the plight of the farmer in the thirties and partly the result of his recognition of the support for socialist reform that could be achieved in the agrarian West. In his pamphlet *Labour in Parliament*, no mention is made of farmers or their problems at all. Lewis said in an interview that the farmer "never was in the core of the CCF – he was always a person prepared to accept us, you know, in the way in which a voter who doesn't commit himself to his party – who goes from one party to another."[22] It would be an exaggeration to say that the CCF was a labour party from the beginning; it was an urban socialist party at the top and consequently more inclined in the direction of labour.

There had been contact with organized labour through the labour parties in western Canada, and J. S. Woodsworth was no stranger to the union movement. A. R. Mosher, of the Canadian Brotherhood of Railway Employees, attended the founding convention in Calgary and was appointed to the provisional executive. He subsequently resigned the office largely as a result of the consternation his association with the party caused in the Gompers-oriented international trade union movement.[23] His position was awkward in any case because there was no provision in the CCF constitution for the affiliation of a national trade union. The nature of the CCF as a federation of local and provincial bodies offered some justification for this restriction, but it was as much the result of hostility on the part of rural delegates toward labour unions as anything else. If the party's doctrine reflected the influence of the eastern radicals, its structure reflected that of the rural delegates.

21 / M. J. Coldwell (Rosetown-Biggar), T. C. Douglas (Weyburn), and Agnes MacPhail (Grey Bruce), held the rural seats. The others were: J. S. Taylor (Nanaimo), Angus MacInnis (Vancouver South), C. G. MacNeil (Vancouver North), A. A. Heaps (Winnipeg North), J. S. Woodsworth (Winnipeg North Centre). Taylor subsequently left the party.
22 / Interview with David Lewis, 1962, Fox transcript.
23 / E. J. Garland to Lewis, June 27, 1936, CCFP.

The hostility was not all on one side. The Gompers tradition of eschewing political alignment was strong in Canadian trade unions. It was an article of faith with the TLC right up to the merger with the Canadian Congress of Labour in 1956. The TLC was so opposed to any kind of political favouritism or alignment that it made no effort to bar Communists from its ranks. One of the objectives of the Communists in the TLC was the prevention of any move toward closer association with the CCF. The failure of the CCF to establish close relations with the labour movement in Ontario in the thirties can be attributed in no small degree to the activities of Communists not only in the TLC but in other local unions and labour councils as well.

The All-Canadian Congress of Labour was equally unwilling to endorse the CCF at the start because the CCF was not socialist enough. When the ACCL was established in 1927 one of its primary purposes, according to the *Canadian Unionist*, "was declared to be 'to assist the workers, through education, to realize the necessity of working-class political action.' "[24] Through its journal, the Congress was critical of the CCF for its lack of revolutionary aims: "one is constrained to marvel at the confidence of those who undertake the regeneration of society by act of Parliament,"[25] and for its support of the farmers:

The concessions made to the farmers have been ill required and might well be withdrawn. What is needed is an undiluted labour policy defined with such clarity as to leave no room for self deception or mental reservation by those who subscribe to it. The substance of a true Labour program at this time would seem to be the acquisition of the basic industries by the nation and the direct provision therefrom and sustenance for the people.[26]

After the first failure of the party to attract strong labour support, little was done until the party headquarters moved to Ottawa and Lewis became national secretary. In 1936 he wrote to a number of unions inviting them to send fraternal delegates to the Fourth National Convention of the party. Not much enthusiasm for this was shown by the unions and even less by some members of the CCF national executive.[27] Despite this lack of enthusiasm, a resolution drafted by Lewis was passed by the convention calling upon members of the CCF

To associate themselves actively with the organization of their trade, industry or profession. The purpose of the C.C.F. is to release industry

24 / *Canadian Unionist*, v (Oct. 1931), 79.
25 / *Ibid.*, vi (Aug. 1933), 79.
26 / *Ibid.*, vii (March 1934), 164.
27 / E. J. Garland to Lewis, June 27, 1936, CCFP.

from the control and domination of private ownership and consequently to put an end to the exploitation of the wealth producers. To
assist in this great work we appeal to the trade unionists to associate
themselves in active membership of the c.c.f.[28]

Lewis proposed this resolution since, as he put it, "I have become
more and more convinced about the need for a Trade Union base
for the party even though there are undoubtedly many disadvantages in a Trade Union political set up."[29] A similar resolution
calling for every effort to be made by the national council to
"facilitate the affiliation of economic groups, such as Co-operatives, farm organizations and trade unions" was passed at the
national convention in Winnipeg in 1937.[30] At the same convention a resolution was passed which greeted "with enthusiasm the
great strides in Trade Union organization ... and supports entirely
the expressed determination of the workers to organize in Trade
Unions of their own choice." In his report to the convention,
Lewis urged political action for the unions and described the CCF
as "the political party of the workers," and as "the party representing trade unions politically."

The increasing emphasis on association with labour was the
result of both the eastern bias of the party's national leadership
and its growing awareness of the party's need for an industrial
base. In 1937 the national council had asked John Mitchell,
Ontario CCF president, and Angus MacInnis, MP and trade
unionist from Vancouver, to investigate what help the CCF could
give "to trade union organization generally and particularly to
the organization work being prepared by the c.i.o. in Canada."[31]
The CCF had not grown significantly in the industrial communities in Ontario and in 1937 there was a general feeling of malaise

28 / Report of the Fourth National Convention (1936). There was at
this point no procedure for national affiliation, a further deterrent to
CBRE affiliation. See ch. 6 below.

29 / Lewis to Scott, July 12, 1937, Scott Papers. In 1942 Lewis wrote
"I would like to say, without qualification or reservation, that I am convinced that until such time as the Trade Union Movement in Canada
becomes the base of the c.c.f., our political movement will not be the
controlling force which it must be to aspire to power. We have always,
therefore, worked toward the end that the Trade Union Movement should
become part of the political movement." Lewis to Monroe Sweetland,
April 28, 1942, CCFP.

30 / Report of the Fifth National Convention (1938). Apart from
those farm groups which affiliated to form the CCF in 1932, the party had
no success in attracting other farmers' organizations such as the United
Farmers of Manitoba and the National Farmers' Union. The UFO withdrew in 1934. See G. Caplan, "The Failure of Socialism in Ontario,"
Canadian Historical Review, XLIV (June 1963), 94–6. At no time did
any co-operative societies affiliate.

31 / National Council Minutes, Feb. 3, 1937, CCFP.

in the party. J. King Gordon, in a letter to F. R. Scott, referred to the "obvious symptoms of decline" which he had observed while attending the 1937 convention.[32] He pointed out that he and Lewis had been resisted by the convention in their attempt to promote closer co-operation with local labour parties, affiliation of trade unions, and "greater toleration of the communists." Lewis had written to Scott earlier in a similar vein, complaining that there was "a complete lack of personnel and resources" and a need for the party to become more involved in "the daily struggles," which would, he argued, "attract many eager men and women who are really ready for a Social Democratic Party but have so far failed to be inspired by the CCF – and I don't blame them."[33] A letter from Harold Winch to Scott expressed similar views and feelings.[34] In short, the party leaders felt that after four years of life and one federal election the state of the party was poor. As Lewis wrote to Angus MacInnis, "The situation is terribly bad. The Movement is at a low ebb. Whatever there is of it is fairly united but rather ineffective."[35]

The solution to the decline was seen to be closer co-operation with the trade union movement and, if possible, affiliation of local unions to the CCF. This, in the view of Herbert Orliffe, provincial secretary in Ontario, was the only way to keep the party alive.[36] The Ontario section took a lead in these matters and called a conference on CCF-trade union co-operation in February 1938. The conference produced no concrete results other than a continuing committee in the Toronto area to study the matter and "try and work out a plan by which trade unions or part of the membership of a trade union could be organized as a C.C.F. club."[37] The labour participants indicated that few unions were ready to affiliate with the CCF for various reasons, one of which was that, paradoxically, the CCF was too closely associated with the ACCL.[38] The conference recommended that

32 / J. King Gordon to Scott, Aug. 1, 1937, Scott Papers.
33 / Lewis to Scott, July 16, 1937, Scott Papers.
34 / H. Winch to Scott, July 30, 1937, Scott Papers.
35 / Lewis to Angus MacInnis, Aug. 23, 1937, CCFP.
36 / H. Orliffe to Woodsworth, Jan. 31, 1936, CCFP.
37 / "Trade Union Cooperation," CCFP. Present at the meeting were J. S. Woodsworth, David Lewis, and Angus MacInnis from the CCF national council; H. Orliffe, John Mitchell, E. B. Jolliffe, and Bert Leavens of the Ontario CCF provincial council; John Bruce and J. W. Buckley of the Toronto and District Trades and Labour Council; Charles Millard and "Alb." Sheelty of the Oshawa UAWA and H. E. Langer of the ILGWU represented trade unions.
38 / The All-Canadian Congress of Labour was formed in 1927 by the uniting into a single congress of the CFL, the CBRE, the OBU, and IBEW, and ten smaller unions. H. A. Logan, *Trade Unions in Canada* (Toronto 1948). See also Forsey, "The Movement Toward Labour Unity in Canada," *CJEPS*, XXIV (Feb. 1958), 70–1. A more detailed discussion of

the CCF's national council clarify the relation of the party to trade unions generally and to international unions specifically. In 1938 some approaches were made to union leaders in the United States with respect to the closer co-operation of the CCF with the international unions, but they were fruitless.[39]

The CCF, while anxious to attract trade union support, was not anxious to become involved in the convoluted internecine struggles that were at this point racking the labour movement in Canada. In view of the troubles, the national executive decided in 1939 that it would not solicit further support from the trade union movement until the situation was more stable, although the party agreed to step up its efforts to co-operate with organized labour in expanding union membership.[40] In April that year, the CCF sent a leaflet which was titled "Strengthen the Trade Unions" and which began "Dear Comrade," to every local labour council in the country. The parliamentary caucus maintained close liaison with leading figures in the labour movement throughout the period.[41]

A. R. Mosher, who was president of the All-Canadian Congress of Labour and later of the Canadian Congress of Labour when it was formed in 1940, remained an active supporter of the CCF and in close touch with the national executive. The United Steelworkers of America led by Charles Millard – previously of the United Auto Workers – was unequivocally a CCF union. In 1940 its entire head-office staff was active in the CCF. The president of the United Packinghouse Workers in Canada, Fred Dowling, was also a CCF supporter, but it was from the Steelworkers that most support came at this point. Myrtle Armstrong, a member of the Steelworkers head-office staff in 1940, has written that:

To claim that trade union staffs of the new industrial unions at this time (1939–40) were hired solely on the basis of their political affiliations would not be an exaggeration. After 1943, with the establishment of a permanent organization, the office personnel and trade union organizers began to rise from the membership of the local trade unions. However, in a less open and direct way, their political attitudes were scrutinized prior to their appointment and they were encouraged to participate and become members of the C.C.F.[42]

---

the question of the CCF and national and international unions can be found in H. Orliffe to J. S. Woodsworth, Jan. 31, 1938; and J. S. Woodsworth to H. Orliffe, Feb. 1938; CCFP.

39 / Scott to Lewis, June 14, 1938, Scott Papers.
40 / National executive minutes, Feb. 15, 1939, CCFP.
41 / Caucus minutes, *passim*, 1938, 1939, 1940, CCFP.
42 / See the unpubl. MA thesis (Toronto 1959) by Myrtle Armstrong, "The Development of Trade Union Political Activity in the CCF," 41.

Silby Barrett of the United Mineworkers of America, who was in 1938 director of the Steelworkers in Canada on UMWA salary,[43] was also an active CCF supporter.

Through the activities of Lewis, the CCF and organized labour moved closer together. Lewis, who provided shape and direction for the party from 1938 through to the founding of the New Democratic Party, was no agrarian radical. He saw the party as a labour party rather than a farmer's party. His socialism was learned in the working-class district of Montreal, in the activities of the clothing workers' unions, the Jewish *Verbund*, and from the British Labour party. Lewis's contacts were not with the farmers; they were with the unionists and intellectuals at McGill and, to a lesser extent, Toronto. His was not the reformist socialism of the prairie radical, it was the hard, determined, and organizational socialism of the trade unionist, the class-conscious anti-capitalist.[44] Consequently Lewis had much more drive and was less prepared to accept half a loaf than were others in the party. This is not to deny the zeal and idealism which motivated the man; it is, rather, to point out the foundation for that zeal and the will to action that drove him. Unquestionably, without Lewis the party would not have maintained and developed its contact with labour. Indeed it is not an exaggeration to say that without Lewis the party might have subsided into nothingness altogether during the dark days after 1945, if not before.

In August of 1938, District 26 of the United Mineworkers of America affiliated *en bloc* with the CCF. In addition to the money which the UMW contributed to the national office from the one cent per capita levy in the nineteen locals of the unions, it contributed funds for election purposes.[45] In 1942 the UMW District 26 bought the Glace Bay *Gazette* and operated it as a pro-CCF newspaper. The editor and manager were chosen after consultation with Lewis.[46] The UMW affiliation meant, among other things,

43 / Logan, *Trade Unions in Canada*, 252–3.

44 / In the interview with Paul Fox in 1961, David Lewis described the socialism of the Young People's Socialist League to which he belonged as "the normal non-communist brand of social democracy, the Karl Kautsky type of socialism; the Eugene V. Debs American type of socialism, anti-communist because the communists had broken away." This is in contrast to the socialism of Coldwell whose roots, like those of the members of the LSR, were in British Christian and Fabian socialism.

45 / In 1940–2 the UMW affiliation provided $1,844.00 or almost half the total receipts from fees and dues. Report of the Seventh National Convention (1942). In 1944, it provided $2,000.00 for the election fund. CCF Record Book, CCFP.

46 / A. A. McKay to Lewis, July 3, 1942, CCFP. This came at a time when, in Ontario particularly, trade union support was essential for the party was in a sad state. British Columbia MLA Harold Winch toured Ontario and reported that there was "a general feeling of defeatism

that affiliation was feasible. This injected new hope into the party at a time when, as indicated above, there was some concern over its apparent failure to make the expected inroads into the strength of the "old line" parties. The members of the national executive worked closely with the UMW in the Maritimes following the affiliation, offering advice and assistance on such matters as the staffing of conciliation boards.

In September 1940 the All-Canadian Congress of Labour and the Canadian CIO Committee united to form the Canadian Congress of Labour. A. R. Mosher was president of the new Congress, Pat Conroy of the UMW was vice-president, and Silby Barrett and Charles Millard were on the executive committee. All were sympathetic toward closer CCF-trade union relations. At the 1941 CCL convention, attempts were made to affiliate the Congress with the CCF but with little success.[47] In 1942 the CCL in convention resolved that the Congress support "only those candidates who had demonstrated their friendliness toward labour and promise to continue such a policy if elected."[48] While the resolution itself is meaningless within a parliamentary system of government and a disciplined party sysem, it shows the determination of the leaders of the CCL to prepare the Congress affiliates for open support of the CCF.

The success of the CCF in Ontario in 1943[49] increased the enthusiasm in the trade union movement for closer ties and at the 1943 convention of the CCL, Eamon Park of the Steelworkers, with CCL executive approval,[50] presented a resolution calling for endorsation of the CCF as the political arm of labour.[51] The most vigorous opposition to the resolution was led by the Communists. This placed the delegates of unions wedded to the Gompers tradition in a difficult position. If they opposed the resolution they would be supporting the Communists; if they supported it they would be departing from their principle. In the end the resolution passed but it was felt by many to be too radical and was generally misunderstood as committing the Congress to support the CCF.

throughout the movement in Ontario." Report to the national office on the Ontario CCF, n.d., CCFP.

47 / *Proceedings*, CCL convention, 1941.

48 / *Ibid.*, 1942.

49 / The party won thirty-four seats and 31.1 per cent of the vote. Eighteen of the successful candidates were trade unionists. See ch. 7 below.

50 / Armstrong, "Development of Trade Union Activity," 43.

51 / *Proceedings*, CCL convention, 1943: "Whereas in the opinion of this Congress, the policy and programme of the CCF more adequately expresses the views of organized Labour than any other party;

"Be it therefore resolved that this convention of the C.C.L. endorse the C.C.F. as the political arm of Labour in Canada, and recommend to all affiliated and chartered unions that they affiliate with the C.C.F."

Many delegates refused to advise their locals to support the CCF, feeling the resolution went too far.[52]

The reasons for the lack of support for the endorsation of the CCF are not difficult to find. The tone of working-class militance that one could observe in the pages of the *Canadian Unionist* in the thirties had largely disappeared, partly as a result, no doubt, of the withdrawal of the leftist One Big Union from the ACCL in 1936, and partly as a result of the prosperity which the economic activity of the war had produced. Equally effective in dampening the move to support the CCF was the active opposition of the Communists in many of the key unions such as the United Auto Workers, the United Electrical, Radio and Machine Workers, the Mine, Mill and Smelter Workers, and the International Woodworkers.[53] This meant that the resolution had no immediate effect apart from cheering the CCF national executive. Despite nine years of active CCL support, the UMW still accounted for half of the affiliated trade union membership in the party.[54]

One result of the resolution was the formation of the CCL Political Action Committee. Its president was Charles Millard and it was accurately characterized by its own vice-president as being under the domination of the CCF.[55] At its meeting in August 1944, the PAC drew up a program of immediate and long-range aims of the unions affiliated to the Congress. It was published as a pamphlet with the 1943 resolution in a prominent position, although the program itself made no mention of the CCF. The publication drew such a storm of protest that it was withdrawn.[56] At the convention of the CCL in October 1944, A. R. Mosher clarified the position of the Congress and its affiliated unions and the CCF. He said that while the CCL endorsed the party it was not affiliated with the CCF and that "no Congress union whether chartered or affiliated, is under any compulsion to become affiliated with the CCF, so far as the Congress is concerned."[57] The Congress, while not disavowing the 1943 resolution, retreated some distance from it. The PAC program was submitted to the various parties, but only the CCF endorsed it unequivocally.[58]

The trade union movement was not moving toward the CCF

52 / Armstrong, "Development of Trade Union Activity," 45 ff.; and see Logan, *Trade Unions in Canada*, 554 and the *Proceedings* of the Fourth and Fifth CCL Conventions, 1943 and 1944.
53 / See Logan, *Trade Unions in Canada*, 556–60 and ch. 8.
54 / Report of the Twelfth National Convention (1952).
55 / Logan, *Trade Unions in Canada*, 558.
56 / Armstrong, "Development of Trade Union Activity," 45.
57 / *Proceedings*, Fifth CCL Convention, 1944.
58 / Logan, *Trade Unions in Canada*, 560.

freely and of its own accord. There was close consultation and
contact at all times during this period between leading figures in
the CCF and the CCL. Fred Dowling, director of the Packinghouse
Workers in Canada, was chairman of the Toronto CCF Trade
Union Committee in 1941, a committee which that year set for
itself projects which included establishing contact with all local
unions "by personal visit to offer the services of the CCF members
of parliament at Ottawa."[59] The Toronto CCF Trade Union Committee held a conference July 25, 1942, attended by sixty-nine
locals of thirty-four national and international unions. The discussions at the conference were concerned with "the conditions
of organized labour, the numerous Orders-in-Council and their
effect on trade union work, and the relations [sic] of the trade
unions to political action and the CCF."[60] The resolutions passed
by the conference affirmed that "labour will be doing itself a
great service and hastening the realization of its aims by entering
into affiliation for political action with the CCF at the earliest
possible moment." It called upon unions to contribute funds to
the CCF. The CCF convention later endorsed these resolutions
with only one unidentified dissenting voice.

As the trade union leaders maintained close contact with the
affairs of the CCF, so the CCF kept in touch with the affairs of the
unions. In 1940 members of the CCF caucus met with Tom
Moore, TLC president, and Mosher of the CCL to discuss the
rights of labour under the defence regulations.[61] Lewis was a
confidant of many senior figures in organized labour. He attended
the 1941 convention of the CCL and his record of his activities
there warrants quotation at length.

My presence in Hamilton last week proved very useful from our point
of view and undoubtedly helped towards organizing our forces so as
to defeat the determined attempt of the Communists to capture the
Congress. The people elected to office were Mosher, President, A. A.
MacAuslane of your own city, Vice-president, and Pat Conroy of
District 18 of the U.M.W. Calgary, Secretary-treasurer ... The switch
in the officers was made through mutual understanding between the
members of the executive in which I took an intimate part ... As far as
we are concerned we have more solid support in the Congress now
than ever before. MacAuslane ... is a member of the B.C. CCF and
Conroy is extremely sympathetic. My own position with these people
is unshakeable. They called me in on every one of even their most
intimate discussions and always treated me as if both I personally and

59 / Dowling to D. Lewis, March 16, 1941, CCFP; and see also Dowling's report in Report of the Seventh National Convention (1942).
60 / Report of the Seventh National Convention.
61 / Caucus Minutes, Nov. 20, 1940, CCFP.

our movement were a full fledged part of the show ... My expenses to Hamilton were paid by them and it was certainly a most useful week for us.[62]

Throughout the labour strife in Hamilton in 1941, C. H. Millard kept the CCF national office fully informed of the progress of the affairs of the Steelworkers of Canada at the Stelco plant and forwarded to Lewis copies of his correspondence with Norman McLarty, Minister of Labour in the King government.

The Trade Union Committee under Dowling had continued its activities and by spring 1943 had managed to secure the affiliation of 2 unions, 30 locals, and the endorsation of one union and 4 locals, including the 4,000 member Steelworkers' local at Algoma Steel in Sault Ste. Marie. The committee had set up a "Continuations Committee" of 31 trade unionists to win "the endorsations and affiliation of unions to the C.C.F."[63] It had, in addition, secured the services of Clarence Gillis, CCF MP for Cape Breton South, as director of the Continuations Committee's work.

Following the 1943 resolution of the CCL convention – which Lewis attended in order to keep the CCF supporters "supplied with ammunition"[64] – there were meetings between Lewis, Coldwell, and Gillis, the only active trade-unionist MP in the party caucus, with Mosher and Conroy to work out the details of implementing the Congress resolution.[65] The contact Lewis had with the Congress at the executive level was reciprocal in that Conroy and Dowd, executive secretary of the CCL, attended meetings of the CCF national executive.[66] In 1944, the CCL was invited to send a representative to the regular meetings of the CCF parliamentary caucus.[67] If the party files are any guide, no similarly concerted attempt was made at this time to woo any farm organizations such as the National Farmers Union. Active contact with farmers' organizations was left largely to the provincial parties.

Starting in 1943, regular CCF–trade union conferences were held in Ontario and, as the report of the third conference held in 1944 indicated, there were "approximately 35,000 unionists affiliating [sic] and endorsing the C.C.F." – this involved 47 locals. The affiliated locals and unions contributed two cents per capita per month of which half went to the provincial party and

62 / Lewis to Angus MacInnis, Sept. 16, 1941, CCFP.
63 / Report of the CCF Trade Union Committee for 1942, Grube Papers.
64 / Lewis to MacInnis, Sept. 21, 1943, CCFP.
65 / Lewis to MacInnis, Oct. 1, 1943, CCFP.
66 / National Executive Minutes, Jan. 29–30, 1944, CCFP.
67 / Caucus Minutes, June 23, 1944, CCFP.

half to the national party. By April 1945 these figures had fallen
to 16 locals and 12,500 affiliated members.[68] How serious the
decline was is difficult to assess since the figures for the Ontario
conference in 1944 possibly included endorsation that did not
necessarily involve affiliation. As events following the war were
to prove, the CCF–trade union connection was not entirely satisfactory.

To what extent the disappointing results of the CCL endorsation of the CCF were due to the efforts of the Communists in the
unions is difficult to determine. It is equally difficult to assess the
effect of the strong non-partisan tradition that was nurtured in
the TLC and undoubtedly had its effect on the members of the
CCL affiliated unions. Lipset has pointed out that "Labour leaders,
like the farmers, were primarily interested in the party as a
means of advancing their own economic objectives,"[69] and it is
possible that the CCL endorsation was a ploy in the game of
applying pressure on the Liberal government. Another factor,
which Myrtle Armstrong discusses, was the continuing dependence of Canadian trade unions upon legislation, raised, as they
were, in a "legislative cradle."[70] There was, consequently, no
lasting militant tradition as in the case of British trade unionism.
Indeed the reverse was true: the dependence on the government
buttressed the value of the Gompers tradition as much as the
parliamentary system of government tended to undermine it.
Whatever the reason, by the war's end the activities of the PAC
had not borne the fruit expected by the CCF members inside and
outside the trade union movement.

The period 1938–45 was one of steady urbanization for the
party and the stabilization of its control in eastern Canada. It
was still referred to by its members as a movement but it was
seen less a farmers' movement by its leaders – if any of them had
ever seen it as such – than distinctly as a workers' socialist movement. Even the most casual survey of the correspondence files
for this period indicates that the leaders, notably the national
secretary, saw the party as serving the interests of the workers.
References to the party as a farmers' movement are almost non-
existent and confined to public pronouncements. Party propaganda continued to stress the problems of the farmer but gradually the emphasis shifted to the problems of an industrialized
society, as would be expected during a war which heightened the
pace of industrialization. The war also provided the farmers with

68 / Report of the Third Annual CCF-Trade Union Conference, Grube
papers.
69 / Lipset, *Agrarian Socialism*, 145.
70 / Armstrong, "Development of Trade Union Activity," 50.

what they were looking for, more government control of marketing, and prosperity. The CCF was a sufficiently dynamic movement and had established itself firmly enough in the prairie soil
that it did not die under such conditions. The pragmatic Saskatchewan section flourished, as the results of the 1944 election
demonstrated.

The national CCF continued to fight for the co-operative commonwealth, but during and after the war it was within the context
of an urban industrial society. The stress was no longer on a fair
deal for the farmer; it was, as the slogan of the 1940s put it,
"Humanity First." Inhumane practices are not associated with
the family farm; they are clearly an aspect of urban industrial
society. It is indicative of the urban strain in the CCF policy and
in the Manifesto that the party could slide easily from its semi-
agrarian role to the urban one it adopted. It was this move which
brought the CCF closer to the trade unions which, in their turn,
aided the move and accelerated it. The CCF had never had the
full endorsation of the major farm organizations and they were,
in any event, less wealthy and, relatively speaking, less powerful
than the unions.

The close association with the unions and the urbanization of
the party meant that it became less a movement and more a party.
The business of practical politics became more important and
the party leaders came gradually to adopt trade union practices
for the operation of the conventions. The transition from movement to mass party – in the sense of the techniques and machinery
if not in numbers of members – was also gradual. And this transition sat well with the strong reformist bent in the party. The
program became somewhat less socialist and more unionist.

After 1939 more time was spent on direct propaganda and
organization. In 1940 the Ontario CCF was organized on a constituency basis and E. B. Jolliffe hired as an organizer with a
salary unofficially subsidized by the United Steelworkers.[71] The
same protestations of purity continued to be made, however, to
the effect that only a socialist victory was sought and that there
would be no sacrifice of principle for "the CCF was concerned
with the political process only in so far as political success enhanced the goals of socialism."[72]

Of necessity the party became less a socialist movement and
more a socialist labour party as it came to work more closely
with unions, few of whose members were socialists and whose
aims were not socialistic. The old socialist zeal remained and
found expression often enough in speeches and propaganda. To

71 / Armstrong, "Development of Trade Union Activity," 58.
72 / Ibid., 59.

it were added the hard bargaining and careful political arrangements so necessary in establishing a party.

The change can be seen in the campaign literature published
by the party in the period from 1935 to 1945 when the emphasis
changed from that of a "populist" attack on the "fifty big-shots"
with all the vigour and moral fervour of agrarian radicalism, to
the carefully phrased proposals for bringing security, abundance
and full employment, and all the other good things consistent
with urban middle-class values.

In the 1935 federal election, a series of pamphlets was published which ran the gamut of all the populist bogeys. One was
headed "Bank Robbers Get Billions but the BIG-SHOT BANKER IS
A BIGGER CRIMINAL THAN THE GUNMAN because the banker's
greed hurts all the people all the time." The similarity with the
Social Credit slogans[73] does not end there, for the pamphlet con-
tinues to urge that there be created a "People's Bank [that]
would issue money corresponding to the creative power of the
Canadian people." The pamphlet was printed in Toronto. In the
same series, Mackenzie King was charged with being the office
boy to the fifty big shots, the Liberal party was accused of launch-
ing the Depression, proposing wage cuts, expressing sympathy
with the millionaires, and generally with perpetrating all kinds of
larceny on the Canadian people. Only one section of one pamphlet in the series was devoted specifically to "the workers,"
while the farmers had an entire pamphlet devoted to their problems. No mention was made of trade unions in any of the
pamphlets.

The peroration of the series is worth quoting in full:

SMASH THE BIG SHOT MONOPOLY
You can end this drift downwards to a coolie civilization! You can
foil men like C. L. Burton who want to exile your children to a Cana-
dian Siberia.
You can save youth from a lifetime in the slave camps.
You can smash the Big Shot Monopoly.
Elect a C.C.F. government to restore to the people their stolen property.
To release Canada's vast wealth for you and your children.
To end poverty exploitation and profiteering.
To establish freedom, security, wealth, and health for you, the long
forgotten citizen!
Disregard the Big Shots' newspapers and their lies, the C.C.F. can
reconstruct Canada for you!
Smash the Big Shots' slave camps and sweat shops! Smash their
Liberal and Tory office Boys! Vote C.C.F.

73 / See Irving, *Social Credit Movement*, 233 ff., and Macpherson,
88 *Democracy*, 202–3.

A Vote for King is a vote for the Rich.
A Tory Vote is a Lost Vote.
A Vote for the c.c.f. is a Vote for Yourself.

The "Immediate Program" of 1934, upon which the CCF election campaign was based, made no reference to trade unions or trade union organization.

The party's federal platform, published in 1938 and entitled *Towards the Dawn*, dealt more extensively with labour, stating that it was the intention of the CCF to "guarantee labour its legal right to organize and bargain collectively," but in the three pages of elucidation of this and other points dealing with labour, no mention is made of trade unions, not even in the description of the role of labour in the co-operative commonwealth. It is significant, however, that more space is devoted to labour than to either farming or co-operatives, although the document indicates that at this stage the party was more anxious to offer encouragement to the formation of co-operatives than it was aware of the problems and needs of trade unions *per se*.

By 1938 the trade unions and the CCF were actively in contact. In that year, Woodsworth introduced for the second time since 1937 a bill providing for the amendment of the Criminal Code to protect the right of workers to organize and to prevent employers from interfering with the process.[74] The CCF national office sent a copy of the bill to every union local and trades council in the country. The bill attracted widespread support in the trade union movement and was referred to by the TLC as "the Woodsworth bill."[75] In the same year at the national convention, the secretary could report that "the Council is happy to record a steady growth of friendly and effective co-operation between the c.c.f. and the trade union movement."[76]

In 1939 the national office published a pamphlet entitled "Strengthen the Trade Unions." In it the party aligned itself squarely with the unions, stating that "a strong trade union movement is indispensable not only to the welfare of the workers themselves but also to maintain and extend our Canadian democracy." The leaflet included a brief history of CCF activity in the House of Commons in defence of the rights of trade unions covering the three years of 1937, 1938, and 1939.

It would be incorrect to argue that the CCF suddenly became

74 / Woodsworth introduced the bill again in 1939. *Hansard*, 1939, 16. He had the satisfaction of seeing Ernest Lapoint, Minister of Justice, incorporate it in an amendment to the Criminal Code in April of that year. *Hansard*, 1939, 2657.

75 / Logan, *Trade Unions in Canada*, 417.

76 / Report of the Fifth National Convention (1938).

pro-union in the 1937–40 period. The party was, after all, originally called the "C.C.F. (Farmer, Labour, Socialist)." At the time the party was formed, however, "labour" meant the several labour parties and did not refer specifically to organized labour as such. With the decline of the labour parties and the movement away from purely agrarian problems in the CCF, the pro-union emphasis became more marked. A survey of the speeches made by CCF MPs in the House of Commons in the period from 1933 to 1940 indicates a sharp increase in the attention paid to the problems of organized labour. The same is true of the reports of the national conventions. The secretary's report to the Fifth National Convention in 1938 included specific mention of trade unions, but only a passing reference to farmers. On balance the convention spent more time discussing matters that affected labour than it spent on agricultural matters, despite the fact that the convention was held in Edmonton, facilitating a heavier attendance of rural delegates. The report of the Sixth National Convention underlines the same general trend.

The 1939 national office publication, *A Handbook for CCF Organizers and Workers*,[77] includes this statement in the section "The CCF and Economic Groups: Farmers": "the CCF was from the very start a farmer as well as a labour party." The main emphasis of the section is on farmers as a valued adjunct to a labour party: "One of the main weapons of the vested interests in their fight against labour has been to set the farmer against the industrial worker," and "It is the job of the CCF organizer to point out to the farmer his community of interest with the industrial worker," and "The standard of living of the farmer ... is directly dependent on the standard of living of the worker." The following section, which deals with trade unions, makes no mention of farmers at all. The booklet also includes an appendix discussing the CCF work on behalf of organized labour but no appendix on the CCF efforts on behalf of farmers.

The 1940 campaign fought by the CCF was somewhat less vehement than that fought in 1935, although, as one would expect, there were unmistakable traces of the old ardour. But this was more evident in the cartoons than in the policy. The main concern was with the war, and hence little mention was made of the problems of trade unions or the needs of the farmers. The war itself produced a major upheaval in the party because not only was the party's national president, Woodsworth, a declared pacifist, but the Regina Manifesto left no doubt as to where the CCF stood in these matters: "We stand resolutely against all participation in imperialist wars." F. R. Scott, the leading intel-

77 / CCF national office, n.d. (*c.* 1939), CCFP.

lectual in the party and a member of the national council, had written an article in the January 1939 issue of *Foreign Affairs* advocating Canadian neutrality in the advent of hostilities involving Great Britain. The Fifth National Convention of the party in July 1938 heard Grant MacNeil move the national council resolution on foreign policy which stated:

If collective action should fail and war break out, the C.C.F. believes that our decision as to participation must be based on the determination to keep Canada out of any war whose purpose is really the defence of imperialist interests; recognizing that in future, as in the past, an attempt will be made to dress up imperialist wars in a guise acceptable to the general public.[78]

An amendment moved by a delegate from British Columbia calling for non-participation in *any* war excepting "a case in which Canada may be actually invaded by an enemy"[79] was defeated with only six votes supporting it. A second amendment from British Columbia calling for a national referendum on participation in the war was defeated by a similar vote. The Third National Convention, held in Toronto in 1936, had passed a resolution calling for the reorganization of the League of Nations, failing which Canada would stay out of future wars.[80]

Although it is obvious that there was a degree of ambivalence in the party policy over the interpretation of the kind of war that existed, it was fairly clear, at the national level at least, that the party was not officially committed to support Britain in any way.[81] The resolution of the 1936 national convention was clear enough but there was a strong sentiment in the party, notably in Saskatchewan, to the contrary.

In February 1937, G. H. Williams, leader of the Saskatchewan CCF and leader of the opposition in the Saskatchewan legislature, refused to appear on the same platform as J. King Gordon because Gordon was going to discuss pacifism and neutrality and, Williams felt, this subject was not a settled policy of the CCF. Williams was rebuked by the national executive for his action.[82] In the letter administering the rebuke David Lewis pointed out that the policy of the 1936 convention was clear and was hardly

78 / Report of the Fifth National Convention (1938).
79 / *Ibid.*
80 / Report of the Third National Convention (1936).
81 / See McNaught, *A Prophet*, ch. 20; and *Hansard*, 1157 ff., 1937, and 3214 ff., 1938.
82 / Lewis to G. H. Williams, March 9, 1937, CCFP. At the 1937 convention Williams moved an amendment to the resolution to include the word "imperialist." The amendment passed and the resolution read: "Canada should remain neutral in case of *imperialist* wars." (italics added)

pacifist. In his reply, Williams indicated that the popular view of the party position was that it was pacifist, particularly in the light of a speech by M. J. Coldwell in which he counselled conscientious objection.[83] Williams made it clear that there was little similar sentiment in Saskatchewan. Later the same year he wrote to Woodsworth on behalf of the Saskatchewan Provincial Council asking him to refrain from discussing neutrality on a projected tour of the province.[84] Woodsworth promptly cancelled the tour.[85]

At its meeting of January 14–15 in 1939, the national executive took the position that Canada must have the right to decide whether to enter a war or not, and that the CCF would only support that degree of defence necessary for local purposes. It also expressed the refusal of the party to support the Chamberlain foreign policy.[86] During the discussion Woodsworth opposed armaments of any kind on the ground that Canada would be safer without them, relying instead on international social justice. The executive decided that the CCF would go on record as opposing those items of the defence estimates that were not necessary for territorial or local defence. Throughout this period Woodsworth maintained a position which, if not realistic, was at least consistent. In a letter written in March 1939, he expressed the view that there was no danger to Canada of "anything more than sporadic attacks" going on to point out that "we should be morally in a far stronger position if we frankly repudiated the whole idea of safety through military strength."[87]

During the month of August the party was in ferment. Despite the views of Williams, a strong pacifist and neutralist element was developing in sections of the Saskatchewan party; the British Columbia CCF wanted the party to declare the war an imperialist war and state that Canada should, for that reason, have nothing to do with it. Correspondence during this period indicated that Coldwell, Angus MacInnis, and Lewis struggled to keep the party from breaking up by urging members to await the decision of the special national council meeting which was held September 6 in Woodsworth's office in the House of Commons.

Woodsworth opened the meeting by expressing his unequivocal opposition to the war.[88] Williams of Saskatchewan took

83 / Williams to Lewis, April 5, 1937, CCFP.
84 / Williams to Woodsworth, June 11, 1937; Letter endorsed by T. C. Douglas, MP, CCFP.
85 / Woodsworth to Williams, June 14, 1937, CCFP.
86 / National Executive Minutes, Jan. 14–15, 1939, CCFP.
87 / Woodsworth to Earl Orchard, March 27, 1939, CCFP.
88 / National Council Minutes, September 1939, CCFP. McNaught,
92   *A Prophet*, 300 ff., provides the best discussion of these events.

the opposite view. Stanley Knowles, speaking for the Manitoba Provincial Council, supported the Woodsworth position as did F. R. Scott, Dorothy Steeves, British Columbia MLA, Frank Underhill, and Chester Ronning. Entry was supported by Angus MacInnis, David Lewis, A. A. Heaps, and H. Gargrave. Despite Woodsworth's wish that the council vote on the straight issue of for or against the war, it finally formulated a policy that was a decided change from that of the 1938 convention. Of the 22 members of the council present on the morning of September 7, 13 accepted the draft statement of the CCF position on the war and 9 opposed it. Subsequently Knowles and Williams withdrew their opposition and the final vote stood at fifteen for and seven against.[89]

The council statement was sent to all council members and provincial offices and was subsequently included in a "white paper" on the CCF position on the war which was prepared by the national executive as instructed by the council. The council position included support for economic assistance to Britain, the preservation of civil liberties in Canada, reasonable provision for home defence, and unqualified opposition to an expeditionary force. The "white paper" elaborated the policy and reiterated the party's conviction that "the root causes of war lie deep in the nature of our present society."[90] The paper also pointed out that the "essence of this statement [the Council statement] is the sharp line drawn between economic assistance and military intervention overseas."

The "white paper" was originally to have included reprints of the speeches made by Woodsworth, Coldwell, and MacNeil in the House of Commons. Woodsworth had opposed the "white paper," preferring the speeches to be published and circulated alone, arguing that the censor might seize the pamphlet but would not touch the speeches.[91] The executive had decided to include the speeches with the pamphlet. When the pamphlet was finally published it did not contain the speeches and Woodsworth expressed some concern and annoyance, to which Lewis replied that he had taken the decision not to include them after consultation with MacInnis, MacNeil, Coldwell, Scott, and Garland, on the grounds that they would only confuse the issue.[92] The party leadership was clearly in the hands of Lewis in this, as in other

89 / National Council Minutes, Sept. 6, 7, 8, 1939, CCFP.
90 / "Canada and the War: The C.C.F. Position" (Ottawa 1939), 4, CCFP.
91 / Woodsworth to Lewis, undated memorandum, CCFP; and see below n. 121.
92 / Lewis to Woodsworth, Oct. 2, 1939, CCFP.

matters, and while he maintained contact with the other leading
members, he was setting both the direction and the pace.

The council policy was not accepted throughout the party.
The Ontario youth section rejected it, while the Saskatchewan
party led by G. H. Williams, who thought the official position
too lukewarm, refused to distribute the pamphlet, indicating that
members who wanted it could write to Ottawa for copies. Jolliffe
was concerned about a split in the party in Ontario and felt that
it was essential that the people be told that the CCF was opposed
to all but economic participation.[93] The Ontario provincial secretary wrote that the provincial executive endorsed the council
statement by a vote of five to four "after a lengthy and acrimonious debate."[94] The Nova Scotia provincial council wanted
the CCF position amended to include conscription and overseas
service.[95] There was little support in British Columbia for the
council position and, according to Grant MacNeil, some bitterness toward Angus MacInnis and Coldwell.[96] MacInnis himself
was aware of the situation but maintained his position, pointing
out in a letter to George Williams that he felt the "white paper"
was an "attempt at apologizing for the Council's statement."[97]
Williams was specific in his criticism of the policy and voiced the
prairie antagonism to the intellectuals:

The thing that boils me up about the "Intelligentsia" group in the
East is their continuous attempt to foist upon the c.c.f. an Isolationist
policy and to explain the decision of the National Council from the
Isolationist point of view, entirely overlooking the fact that the policy
was agreed to by some because it was considered neither wise nor
necessary to send an expeditionary force at the time. I say without any
fear of being proven wrong that those who take that point of view will
be backed by three quarters of the members of the c.c.f. as against
the position of the isolationist.[98]

Coldwell attempted to prevent those who supported the council
position from acting rashly. He wrote to MacInnis: "this is the
time when we must keep cool, and stand by the c.c.f. ship in

93 / E. B. Jolliffe to Lewis, Sept. 11, 1939, CCFP.
94 / H. Gargrave to Lewis, Sept. 18, 1939, CCFP. The CCYM felt that
Lewis and MacInnis had "railroaded" the decision through. MacInnis
to Lewis, Feb. 7, 1940, CCFP.
95 / Borgford to Lewis, Oct. 17, 1939, CCFP.
96 / C. G. MacNeil to Lewis, Sept. 18, 1939, CCFP. MacInnis' constituency considered dropping him. The provincial council of the British
Columbia CCF passed a resolution which accepted the national council
statement as an "opinion." MacInnis to Lewis, Feb. 7, 1940, CCFP.
97 / MacInnis to Williams, Oct. 4, 1939, Saskatchewan Archives,
Saskatoon. Hereafter referred to as SAS.
98 / Williams to MacInnis, Feb. 7, 1940, SAS.

spite of irritation we may sometimes feel at the narrow viewpoint
expressed by some of our good friends."[99] Nevertheless MacInnis
resigned from the national council because of the "lack of support given me by the other representatives from British Columbia
on the National Council in regard to our war statements."[100]

Clearly at this point the conflict that emerged was not only one
of right versus left but of leaders versus membership. Throughout the crisis the direction of the party was provided largely by
MacInnis, Coldwell, MacNeil, and Lewis, who managed to bring
the party as close to an endorsation of the war effort as could be
achieved over the opposition of Woodsworth, the *de facto* and
spiritual leader of the movement, and many of their intellectual
colleagues. In the case of MacInnis, his views were similar to
those of Williams – and of T. C. Douglas, who would have gone
overseas with the South Saskatchewan Regiment had he not been
medically disqualified. In the case of Lewis, there is little doubt
that his decision was based more on a realistic assessment of the
politics of the situation which, he felt, required him to modify his
own philosophical position. In his speech before the national
council he said:

If I thought socialism could be advanced by a complete isolation from
the war, I would support it. But I think such a policy would lose the
possibility of the c.c.f. getting any position in the minds of the people
of Canada by which we could be of service to them.[101]

For Woodsworth and his supporters, the CCF was primarily a
movement and within the operating framework of a movement
clear consistency of principle was possible. For Lewis the movement was also a party and a devotion to pacifist principle or to
socialist principle such that the war would be defined as imperialist and therefore be insupportable, was simply not consistent with the role of the CCF as a party within the Canadian party
system.

The tragic ambivalence that mitigated against the success of
the CCF was never more clearly seen than at this time. The party
was badly divided over the question of participation in the war,
but, as the council wisely saw, this was not the question since
Canada was going to participate and there was nothing the CCF
could do to change that fact. The decision reached on this premise
was that participation should be economic only. Yet even this
was a mistaken decision, the result of the internal contradiction
inherent in the party-movement. Lewis supported limited par-

99 / Coldwell to MacInnis, Oct. 18, 1939, CCFP.
100 / MacInnis to Lewis, April 18, 1939, CCFP.
101 / National Council Minutes, Sept. 1939, CCFP.

ticipation because he was a politician; he opposed anything more than economic assistance because he was a dedicated socialist. Yet it was a position which clearly could not be maintained and indeed was not maintained.

The war also emphasized the fairly prevalent attitude in the CCF that the party was the underdog and bound to be persecuted. In the early stages of the war this amounted almost to group paranoia. This attitude was partly the product of the constant criticism the CCF had received from the press and opposition groups, most of which depicted the CCF as un-Canadian.[102] It was also partly the product of the composition of the CCF. Active members were, for the most part, outsiders socially as well as politically and they had learned to accept the persecution which their attacks on the Canadian establishment occasioned.[103] This was particularly true in the urban segments of the party. Unlike the wheat farmers who supported the party, the urban CCF members were not vigorous protagonists of the North American dream.[104] They were strenuous critics of the society around them and of the attitudes of their middle-class neighbours. They had come to expect criticism and the shared experience of vilification undoubtedly contributed to the cohesion of the party.

The discussions in the national council that September of 1939 displayed a remarkable pessimism. Lewis pointed out that civil liberties would be encroached upon and that meetings would be banned. He opened his comments with the statement "assuming that we will be able to carry on during the war as a legal movement ... "[105] The tone of his remarks leaves little doubt that he was thinking in terms of the CCF going underground. Stanley Knowles shared this pessimism as did Eugene Forsey, who stated it explicitly at the same meeting. Angus MacInnis and M. J. Coldwell seemed to be the only members sufficiently detached to recognize the reality of the situation. MacInnis pointed out that "There is one sure way of being put out of business and that is to take an hostile [sic] attitude to everything the government suggests."[106] Coldwell urged that the council study the means of conveying the policy to the members and the public. Lewis feared the banning of CCF newspapers and suggested amalgamating them. Herbert Gargrave, provincial secretary in British Columbia, opposed the move because it would invite sabotage. The general tenor of the discussion, particularly from the more

102 / This criticism and the anti-CCF propaganda reached its height in 1944–6.
103 / See John Porter, *The Vertical Mosaic* (Toronto 1965), 342–3.
104 / *Ibid.*, 270, 311–12.
105 / National Council Minutes, Sept. 1939, CCFP.
106 / *Ibid.*

radical socialists, was one of deep pessimism about the future of the movement during the war.

One possible explanation for the pessimistic attitude could be that the leaders of the CCF had, by virtue of their vehemence in attacking the government and capitalists, lost some objectivity. The general disregard of the Liberal government for civil liberties, plus the accusation of "fascist tendencies" which the CCF had made often enough, may have clouded some of the CCF leaders' vision.

Despite the party's active support of the parliamentary system there was evident at this gathering a feeling that the war offered the enemies of the CCF and socialism an opportunity for destroying the movement. Alternatively it may have been simply that Lewis, Knowles, and Forsey thought that the CCF opposition to the war would necessitate its proscription to facilitate the war effort. Clearly those who had first-hand experience of Parliament – Coldwell and MacInnis were both MPs – were more in touch with the realities of the political situation and with the spirit of the government. It is worth noting here that Lewis, the key figure in the CCF, was never in Parliament and held no elective office outside those within the party. In all the seats he contested he was defeated.[107]

There was no need for pessimism. Although few in the party saw the war as an opportunity to advance, it would not be far short of the truth to argue that the immediate result of the war was that it helped to save the CCF. The signs of decline were unmistakable in the late thirties and leading figures in the party were aware of them. Closer relations with trade unions had been one means of injecting new blood and purpose into the movement, but as a cause it drew little active support. The CCF was not enough of a party to remain alive without a cause to champion. The movement needed to be recharged as the old cause of social and agrarian reform receded into the background with wartime prosperity. The gradual adoption by the Liberal government of many CCF reforms had taken some of the steam from the movement. The prosperity induced by the crisis in Europe was equally effective in this respect.

The war provided a new panoply of evils against which the forces of democratic socialism could be arrayed. The whole area of civil liberties and the undeniable profiteering that occurred following the lifting of the 5 per cent profit limitation, which the Liberal government had first accepted on the suggestion of T. C.

107 / David Lewis contested the Cartier by-election in Aug. 1943, Hamilton West in the 1945 general election, and Wentworth in the 1949 general election.

Douglas, provided targets for the CCF attack. The rallying cry of
"Conscription of Wealth and not Manpower" was a potent one
in the movement.

In addition, the war had an unquestionably unsettling effect
on Canadian society. People were uprooted, the normal course
of their lives altered or obliterated, and their concern for the
future heightened. This made society more receptive to the utopian context of the CCF program. It provided the same reality
and degree of necessity to the program that the conditions on the
prairies had provided in the twenties and early thirties. People
were more receptive to CCF doctrines. The Gallup Polls for the
period demonstrate the rise in popular support for the party
during the war. From the 1940 federal general election in which
the CCF received 8 per cent of the popular vote, the party's support, as judged by the poll, rose to 10 per cent in January 1942,
21 per cent in September of the same year, 23 per cent in
February of 1943, and reached a high of 29 per cent in September
1943. Support remained at 20 per cent or higher until the election
in June of 1945, when it fell to 15 per cent.[108] This could not be
entirely due to changes in the CCF platform, for while there was
some moderation of the zeal, it was offset by the continuance of
the same doctrinaire denunciations of the system. In short, there
was little real change in the CCF program as presented to the
general public.

The war was also valuable as a morale booster for the CCF in
that it made the party's insistence on planning meaningful. Wars
are fought not as a long-term enterprise but as a form of human
activity that looks forward to a specific conclusion. It was recognized by political leaders in the First and Second World Wars
that public morale and support for the war effort is enhanced if
the war aims are clearly spelled out, however spurious they may
in fact be. The CCF was the only political party in Canada that
had the future as its stock in trade. Here was an opportunity to
campaign for the planning of the future when everyone was concerned about the future and at a time when society was in a state
of some chaos. The war offered the CCF a renewed lease on its
cause and on its existence as a political movement.

But in the long run the war made the task of the CCF more
difficult for, among other things, it led to a significant redistribu-
tion of income and a mobilization of manpower that robbed the
party of some of the basis of discontent on which it depended.

108 / Results of Canadian Institute of Public Opinion Surveys, *Public
Opinion Quarterly* (Winter 1946–7), 633. The results of these surveys
may, of course, be inaccurate and the strength of the CCF at its height
somewhat less than they indicate. See also ch. 7 below.

And, despite the profiteering, the war did usher in a more Key-
nesian approach to the national economy than had been evident
before 1939. It helped to change capitalism. At the war's end
there was a natural reaction against state controls that did little
to help the CCF, which argued for more controls. Admittedly the
controls the CCF sought were not those the average individual
disliked during the war, such as rationing, but the average individual does not make fine distinctions. Advocacy of controls
was to give the CCF a negative image in post-war Canada.

From its beginnings in Calgary and Regina the national CCF
had moved eastward, leaving behind its rural antecedents and
taking on the trappings of an urban socialist movement which,
through interlocking leadership, began in the late nineteen-
thirties to establish closer relations with the trade union movement. The withdrawal of the UFO in 1934 and later of the UFA
underlined this development. The intellectuals in the LSR and
union leaders such as A. R. Mosher and Fred Dowling found
ready supporters in Lewis, the party secretary, and Coldwell,
the party leader.

The party was moving in the direction that the *Canadian
Unionist*, the militant organ of the ACCL, had wanted:

In due time, as experience is gained, it is reasonable to expect that the
c.c.f. will either adopt a working-class philosophy itself or make way
for a political Labour party which shows a better comprehension of
the alignment of forces within capitalism and of the issue at stake.[109]

The cementing of the ties with labour continued throughout the
war and the organization and structure of the party became more
closely knit and centralized. The changes that occurred in the
ideology of the party were related to the development of closer
ties with labour and a greater awareness of the importance of the
rules of the political game in Canada. Under the parliamentary
leadership of Coldwell, the less radical strain in the party was
enhanced, while Lewis, at the centre of the party's structure,
exercised a moderate left-wing influence and held tight reins over
the party's organizational and propaganda activities.

Going into the war, the CCF was in the doldrums. The war
revitalized the party; more money and effort were directed toward expanding membership and support for it. The awareness
of the leaders that there was a real possibility of success spurred
them on. Lewis wrote to Angus MacInnis in January 1941,
pointing out that there was "a rising tide but no vessel." He outlined his estimate of the needs:

I have a feeling that a six months' Blitzkrieg on Canada would shake

109 / *Canadian Unionist*, VII (Aug. 1933), 37.

the country. To do this we need to take about two dozen men and women off their present jobs, pay them the salary they make and let them loose on the country. We need radio, literature, posters and sign-boards. We need organized work in accordance with a specialized programme among farmers, industrial workers, middle class people, women and youth. My point is the very deep conviction that if we could only find a way of getting our message graphically to the people, we would obtain support to an extent which we don't even dare dream of.[110]

The pessimism among the leaders about the fate of the CCF in wartime was, as suggested earlier, unwarranted. At that time the CCF saw itself as a greater threat to the establishment in Canada than the establishment did. With the increase in the popularity of the CCF in the 1940s, opposition stiffened and a strong offshore wind arose to counter the rising tide. The optimism generated by the increase in support was frustrated by the failure of the party to capitalize on its greatly enhanced strength. The irony of the post-war period was that the support of organized labour came too late, for the worker was now enjoying the fruits of affluence and was not attracted to the CCF. But as the party's hopes dimmed, the CCF movement stayed alive, buoyed up by its belief in the rightness and ultimate success of its cause. It was this buoyant core that kept the party alive after 1951, when, like the Progressives before it, it should have disappeared.

110 / Lewis to MacInnis, Jan. 22, 1941, CCFP.

5

5

SUCCESS AND FAILURE: 1940-60

... the C.C.F. in its progress toward political power
must continue to be a movement as well as a party.

EDITORIAL
Canadian Forum, 1945

When the CCF met in convention at Winnipeg in October 1940, Canada had been at war for over a year. The party had fought the election of 1940 and had emerged virtually unchanged in strength. Party members were more conditioned to accepting the war, as was indicated in the policy enunciated by the national council in September 1939, which had about it an air of obsolescence. Canadian troops were serving overseas – among them G. H. Williams, leader of the Saskatchewan CCF, one of many CCF members who had enlisted. Canada was participating in the war on an economic front through the provision of various kinds of war material and through the Commonwealth Air Training Plan. There had been no suppression of the CCF or of its press and although the censorship imposed by the government was admittedly unnecessary and overdone, it had worked no noticeable hardship on the party. At the convention there was general satisfaction with events within the CCF; there was almost a pause while it took its bearings in a situation that was changing with increasing rapidity.

The CCF fought the 1940 campaign on a combination of its declared war aims as formulated by the council and the executive in 1939 and of the statement issued by the national convention in 1938. Its call for equality of sacrifice in the war effort was perhaps too altruistic or not sufficiently belligerent because it fared no better than it did in 1935. Party leaders were not discouraged, however, for despite 23 fewer candidates in the field, the popular vote increased in every province except Ontario, where only 24 CCF candidates were nominated compared with 50 in 1935.

The CCF position on the war effort was at variance with that of the trade union movement and with the attitude of most Canadians. Angus MacInnis pointed out that the CCF could make a sound and positive case for all-out economic aid to the allies who, at that point, did not seem to need troops.[1] However valid such an argument might be, it did not alter the impression of the public that the CCF was opposed to the war. Statements made by Woodsworth and Grant MacNeil in the House of Commons and, notably, by Colin Cameron and Dorothy Steeves in the British Columbia legislature, gave credence to the impression. In fact most CCF members probably were against the war, one way or another. The council had tried to put a good face on the political necessity of supporting the war effort, however hesitantly, but there was little it could do to avoid the rancour which followed the decision. MacInnis's suggestion of a campaign urging full

1 / A. MacInnis to D. Lewis, Sept. 22, 1939, and Nov. 8, 1939, CCFP.

economic support might have offset the effect of the party's attitude toward the war but the election came too quickly for much
to be done. On the hustings it seemed that Woodsworth and
Coldwell were more concerned about profiteering and post-war
planning than about patriotism.[2] The CCF campaign was inconsistent with the public mood in March 1940.

Lewis could insist, as he did to Inge Borgford, Nova Scotia
party secretary, and to the Ontario CCYM, that:

the National Council has not laid down any regulation requiring from
any section of the CCF, as a condition of continued affiliation, acceptance of the policy. You are therefore at liberty to express, and act
on, the view which you hold without it in any way affecting your status
in the movement. The only, but important qualification to this is that
whenever a member or section of the CCF expresses a view different
from or opposed to the National Council official policy they should
make it clear that it is their view they are expressing and not the CCF
position.[3]

From the public point of view this distinction was non-existent
and a section of the CCF or a prominent member of the CCF in
opposition to all or any aspect of the war effort meant, of course,
that the CCF as a whole was opposed. Although the trade union
movement was strongly in favour of the war, there was no evidence of any cooling of what ardour there was for the CCF. The
UMW continued to send its per capita dues to the national office
without protest, and relations with the individual unionists remained cordial.

In his report to the Sixth National Convention, Lewis indicated
the gradual change that was taking place in the attitude of the
party toward the war. Whereas socialism had been considered by
many in the movement as being antithetical to war, in the short
space of a year it had become essential to a successful war effort:
"the faith and policies of democratic socialism are indispensable
not only to win greater justice in time of peace but also to win
military victory in a war fought for democracy."[4] Britain's
courageous stand was, Lewis pointed out, largely due to "the
power of the British Labour Movement which is playing so vital
a role in the government and defence of that country." In this
latter respect it is interesting to note that one of the strongest
influences in shaping the attitude of many prominent figures in
the CCF toward the war was the attitude of the British Labour

2 / See *Winnipeg Free Press*, March 1–26, 1940, *passim*, for reports
of the campaign.
3 / D. Lewis to I. Borgford, Nov. 16, 1939, CCFP.
104   4 / Report of the Sixth National Convention (1940).

party. In the debates during the council meeting of 1939 and throughout the issues of *News Comment* during the war, there were constant references to the policies of the Labour party. A regular feature of the paper was the use of quotes from Bevin, Attlee, and Morrison as "fillers."

That the party in convention was generally unwilling to depart from the direction being provided by the national council and the parliamentary group was demonstrated by the fact that the council's report, which outlined party policy for the coming year, was accepted with relatively little debate. What debate there was concerned deletion of the reference in the report to the CCF's opposition to an expeditionary force. In defending this section, Lewis urged the convention to accept the report and specifically the recommendation that "the policy as applied and developed by the CCF parliamentary group should be continued in substance."[5] The council was upheld. An attempt by the British Columbia delegates to have policy between conventions changed only with the consent of provincial councils and executives was defeated on the recommendation of the resolutions committee.

The main policy resolutions which the convention dealt with came from the national council. They concerned agriculture, civil liberties, control of industry and financial institutions, peace aims, post-war reconstruction, the Rowell-Sirois Report, and labour. There were no significant departures from the policies laid down at the convention in 1938 and elaborated during the 1940 election campaign. One measure of the party's renewing zeal was the decision to institute a national newspaper or magazine. This appeared in March 1941 as *News Comment*, a mimeographed bulletin of some ten pages published twice monthly. A second measure was the decision of the national office, despite the loss in 1940 of E. J. Garland as national organizer,[6] to embark on a more extensive organization campaign in those provinces where the CCF showed signs of promise yet unrealized. These were Alberta, Manitoba, New Brunswick, Nova Scotia, Ontario, and Quebec. The total receipts from these provinces in 1939–40, exclusive of UMW affiliation fees, were less than the total received from Saskatchewan alone. In the year ending June 30, 1940, the party had spent $2,942 in organizers' expenses in these provinces.[7] In the year previous less than half of this had been spent, most of it in Ontario.

When the CCF met in Toronto in 1942 to celebrate its tenth

5 / *Ibid.*
6 / E. J. Garland accepted an appointment as secretary to the Canadian high commissioner to Ireland.
7 / Report of Sixth National Convention (1940).

anniversary, the rising tide of support could be felt. The party
had moved noticeably away from doctrinaire opposition to the
war toward extension of the war effort to include an expeditionary force. It was not as adamant as it had been about the ownership and control of the war industries, although this remained a
favourite target for socialist barbs. Determined and vigorous
socialist criticism of the war continued to come with undimin-
ished fervour from British Columbia, but the national party,
under the parliamentary leadership of M. J. Coldwell was, by
and large, more concerned with the successful prosecution of
the war.

The rising optimism was warranted. In the 1941 provincial
election in British Columbia, the party won a plurality of votes.
In February 1942 an unknown CCF candidate, Joe Noseworthy,
defeated Arthur Meighen, the national leader of the Conservative
party, in a by-election in the Ontario riding of York South. In
February 1941 Grant MacNeil was appointed full-time national
organizer and started his work in Ontario, spending most of that
year there.

The Seventh National Convention was notable for the changes
in policy which were introduced and accepted, indicating the
determination of the party's national leadership to bring it closer
to the views of the trade unions on the support of the war effort
and other policy questions. During this period the national newsletter, *News Comment*, devoted roughly twice as much space to
matters of interest to labour and the trade unions as to agriculture and farm problems.[8]

The changing attitude toward the war effort can be seen in the
party's conscription policy. The CCF urged its supporters and the
nation at large to support the conscription plebiscite, although in
a radio address on the subject Coldwell added that "we have not
changed our opinion ... that conscription of manpower is not the
most vital issue at this time."[9] Support for the plebiscite and its
implications was not unqualified within the ranks of the CCF.
According to George Grube there were many people in Ontario
who feared that the CCF group in the House would support conscription for overseas service. If they did so, he argued, it would
be "a mortal blow to the party in Ontario."[10]

In the convention itself the party adopted a policy statement
prepared by the national council entitled "For Victory and Reconstruction." In essence the program was a slightly modified

8 / In Vol. II, Nos. 1–12 (Jan.–June 1942), 13 items on agriculture, 5
on co-operatives in Canada, 80 on labour.

9 / M. J. Coldwell, *Go to the Polls, an address on the Issues of the
Plebiscite* (Ottawa 1942), 3.

10 / George Grube to M. J. Coldwell, June 26, 1942, Grube Papers.

version of the 1940 program, "A New Order Shall Arise." The 1940 program demanded that "all munitions and war industries should be mobilized and nationalized under the Mobilization Act immediately"; whereas in "For Victory and Reconstruction" this became "Public ownership, or, where this is not feasible in wartime, at least complete government control of all war industries."

In his address to the convention, Coldwell answered critics of the CCF and reiterated the party's attitude toward private property, an attitude which he certainly had espoused from the beginning, although it is doubtful it was shared by everyone in the movement.

There are those who say that the C.C.F., like the Labour Parties of Great Britain, New Zealand, Australia and other countries with similar political parties, desires to bring all to a dead level, to do away with private property, and to kill individual initiative. On the contrary, we want to build up, not to tear down.

We seek to raise the general level of society and liberate that individual initiative that capitalist regimentation denies. We desire greater opportunities for education, greater opportunities for worthwhile service with adequate rewards for jobs well done. We want to see more personal property for more people, but we want to see no public property privately-owned or used to exploit the community in the interests of monopolistic corporation or anti-social individuals.[11]

And the slogan he advanced for the CCF was "Total mobilization for total war."

The exegesis of one man's speech, even though he may be the national president and leader of a party, does not necessarily provide an accurate picture of the views of all or even a majority within the party. But when coupled with the policy statement that came from the 1942 convention, it provides some indication of the direction party policy was taking. The fact that the policy statement devoted so much space to a program for post-war Canada would seem to indicate that there was rather less concern, in the national council at least, with the war and the war effort in relation to CCF policy than with the party's position after the war. This in itself indicates an acceptance of the existing situation and an optimism with respect to the future. The party had forsaken many of the targets selected in September of 1939 as being either out of range or not valid targets after all, and was directing its attention to peacetime pursuits.

This shift of attention – at a time when the war had not yet turned in favour of the allied cause – was a necessary reaction of the party leaders to changing circumstances. It was also a shift

11 / Report of the Tenth National Convention (1948).

of considerable tactical importance because it identified the CCF with peacetime solutions; it aligned the party with what would seem to be the common frame of mind during war: that of looking ahead to reconstruction and stability. In the case of the CCF there is no evidence that this was a deliberate decision. It was probably a response dictated by the nature of the situation: Canada was at war and the range of policy options was narrowed by that fact.

A political movement with a diverse membership and a democratic structure is more likely to arrive at positions in harmony with popular feeling than autocratically-controlled political parties which rely more upon the decisions of a small group of leaders. This would seem to be particularly so in times of great national crisis such as war or depression, when there is a wider consensus than in normal times. The democratic party-movement is more effective as a political antenna, being closer and more responsive to popular feeling than autocratic parties. The CCF was at this juncture riding a groundswell of public opinion. The optimism created by this groundswell provided the conditions for gradual changes in policy and for a less hostile and less militant approach in the party propaganda. Within the circle of leaders at this point, it must be remembered, there were a number of prominent trade unionists whose contact with the union members made them valuable channels of popular feeling at the time.

In the report of the 1942 convention there is evidence of the buoyancy within the party. Although receipts were down from the previous convention and the party operated with a deficit, the treasurer, A. M. Nicholson, presented a budget that called for an expenditure of $17,000 in 1942–3, twice the normal annual expenditure.[12] The additional money was to be used to expand the staff of the national office, to set up a research and publicity department, and to enable the appointment of a French-speaking organizer for Quebec. The funds were to be raised by the provincial sections; each was assigned a quota. In the case of Alberta and Manitoba the quotas were unrealistic, for both provinces had been heavily subsidized by the national office. Despite these weak spots, the CCF was convinced in 1942 that it could move ahead. The party members were prepared to bend to the task once more, this time buoyed up by the growing awareness that the CCF was more popular than it had ever been before.

The re-orientation of emphasis in the party program toward

12 / The financial statement presented to the Seventh National Convention (1942) treated the two-year period, July 1, 1940–June 30, 1942, as one; earlier statements were year by year. On June 30, 1940, the preceding year's receipts were $2,273.94. For the two-year period ending June 30, 1942 they were $4,408.04 or approximately $2,204.02 per year.

the post-war period was abetted by the publication in Britain of
the Beveridge Report. The CCF became the North American
advocate of the welfare state. Speaking about the party program
in October 1942, Frank Scott enunciated what amounted to
welfare socialism:

The CCF program contains ... three very basic and simple ideas. The
first is that the primary duty of the state is to secure the welfare, both
cultural and material, of the people who form the great majority of
the population. The second is that this welfare must be provided now,
in very tangible forms, such as health, education, good homes, etc. ...
The third is that this welfare will be attained only if the state develops
the national resources of the country under a general economic plan,
free from the dictates of private interests, so that the material foundation for a just society can be securely laid.[13]

It was the Beveridge Report in slightly more radical dress, but
basically Beveridge. The eradication of capitalism through public
ownership was no longer the major aim.

The remarkable success of the provincial CCF at the polls in
Ontario in 1943 appeared to be the justification of all that had
gone before. Since the national party was based in Ontario, this
success was extremely important for it represented the success
of the provincial wing that most closely resembled the national
CCF in ideology and outlook. And although the 1944 victory in
Saskatchewan was greeted with considerable enthusiasm, it was
the success of an element more remote from the national leadership. There had been little close contact or real communication
between the Saskatchewan party and the national headquarters.[14]
The Saskatchewan party operated on its own as it had always
done, changing CCF policy to suit what it saw as the Saskatchewan conditions. It was in no way dependent upon the national
office, although financially the national office was very much
dependent on Saskatchewan.

When E. B. Jolliffe led the Ontario CCF to within inches of
forming the government of the largest and wealthiest province,
optimism ran high. As the front page of *News Comment* for
January 15, 1944, stated, quoting *Maclean's Magazine*, "There
is no gainsaying the fact that the CCF has gripped the imagination
and harnessed the hopes of a large number of people."[15] There
was good reason for the optimism even before the victory in

13 / "The C.C.F. Program Today," typewritten ms for address, Oct.
1942, Scott papers.
14 / A survey of the index for *News Comment* shows references to
Ontario and British Columbia outnumber those to Saskatchewan and
the other prairie province roughly 2:1.
15 / *News Comment*, IV (Jan. 15, 1944), 1.

Ontario, for the Gallup Poll indicated a dramatic increase in
CCF popularity. The poll showed that CCF support had trebled
since 1940.[16] According to the report of the Ontario secretary
to the provincial convention in April 1943, membership had
quadrupled during the previous year and twenty-five trade union
locals had affiliated.[17] In *News Comment*, the victory in Ontario
was attributed to organization. "Now is the time to organize for
the federal elections," the article concluded.[18] The sweeping
success in Ontario was followed by two federal by-election vic-
tories when William Bryce and Joseph Burton won seats in the
Selkirk and Humboldt constituencies respectively. The effect of
the Ontario success reverberated through the party and the nation. Followed as it was by the Canadian Congress of Labour
endorsation of the CCF as the political arm of labour, it was a
significant factor in increasing affiliations and membership.

It was with a real sense of their party's destiny in both federal
and provincial affairs that senior members of the provincial sections and the national officers gathered in Regina in December
1943 for a conference on provincial policy. The purpose of the
confidential conference, which had no official policy-making
function, was to enable the provincial sections to outline for discussion and comment their policies for the various areas of provincial government. The assumption was that in several of the
provinces such policies might soon be enacted by newly elected
CCF governments. The programs that were presented are not
relevant here other than as indications of soaring confidence in
the party. What is significant is the discussion of socialism contained in the address to the conference given by Frank Scott, who
was national chairman at the time.

Scott made no reference to the social ownership of any specific
enterprises although he stressed the nature of the CCF as a socialist party: "Our socialism is scientific. We think it out in terms of
Canada – the country in which it is to be applied, and to whose
basic social and economic facts it must adapt itself. We have a
more scientific socialism than any other party in Canada, bar
none."[19] At the same time he provided the provincial leaders
with general directions toward the implementation of the welfare
state:

The C.C.F. is not just a humanitarian party, promising welfare and
security to all; it is primarily concerned with the control and planning

16 / See *Public Opinion Quarterly*, x (Winter 1946–7), 633.
17 / Report of the Eleventh Annual Ontario Provincial Convention
(1943).
18 / *News Comment*, III (Aug. 15, 1943), 2.
19 / *Report* of the Regional Conference on Provincial Policy, Dec. 29–
Jan. 2, 1943–4, CCFP.

of the productive resources of the country so that a secure economic base can be laid on which to build the social services. With greater production and secure employment there will be available the wealth which can support the costs of education, health, leisure, etc. Without the economic base, all promises of welfare are futile.[20]

Despite the fact that the provincial parties were, in three provinces at any rate, closer to power than the federal party, Scott underlined the premise of the Regina Manifesto that socialism could come only if the party was successful at the federal level: "The Regina Manifesto was basically sound. We must carry back to all parts of the movement the fundamental fact that unless we elect a C.C.F. government federally, the people of Canada will not have economic security, no matter how strong our provincial movements may be."[21]

Optimism was undiluted at the 1944 convention. Income for the year ending June 30, 1944 exceeded $28,000, an increase of more than 300 per cent over the same period in 1942 and up $11,000 from 1943. Ten thousand dollars had been spent during the year on a special dominion-wide publicity campaign, $6,000 on literature, and almost $17,000 on salaries, including subsidies to provincial organizers.[22] As the national secretary indicated in his report, there was ample reason for optimism. Since the 1942 convention the CCF had won three federal by-elections and three provincial by-elections – two in British Columbia and one in Manitoba – had become the government in Saskatchewan, doubled its vote in Alberta, become the official opposition in Ontario, increased its poll in the Maritimes, and elected a member to the Quebec legislature. It was phenomenal progress. The CCF was represented in seven of the nine provincial legislatures and held a total of 109 provincial seats.

Organizational growth was parallel. Total membership in the party had been less than 30,000 in 1942; in 1944 it approached 100,000.[23] There were more than 2,000 local CCF organizations – clubs, constituency associations, and study groups. The party was publishing six English-language papers provincially and one French-language paper, as well as *News Comment*.[24] David Lewis estimated that "during the winter months, at least fifty CCF broadcasts are heard each week across Canada."[25] He sum-

20 / *Ibid.*
21 / *Ibid.*
22 / The discrepancy in these figures is due to the fact that the publicity campaign was a separate account supported by provincial contributions.
23 / Report of the Eighth National Convention (1944).
24 / The total "Paid up" circulation of all papers combined was "just over 90,000"; there would be some duplication of subscribers.
25 / Report of the Eighth National Convention (1944).

marized the situation: "in short, the CCF is no longer a struggling little movement striving for recognition. On the contrary, it is now a powerful and growing political force."

Significantly, the report stressed the organizational work done and pending and the need for greater efforts. The national council and executive had devoted the greater part of their time to dealing with these matters. In his address to the delegates, the national secretary made an appeal that tacitly recognized the dual nature of the CCF at this time. In the penultimate paragraph he urged greater effort to carry the CCF message into every hamlet, warned of the impending capitalist attack as the party grew in strength, and said, "we can meet this challenge successfully only as wc are willing to make ever greater sacrifices for the cause which, in our view, is the hope of Canada and the world." He began the peroration by saying: "Our task for the *immediate future, as a political party*, is to prepare for the coming federal election."[26]

The distinction implicit in his statement was that the CCF *qua* movement must press forward with greater sacrifice toward the millennium, while the CCF *qua* political party must prepare for the next election. There were, in short, two tasks – two roles to be played by members of the party. The second role, that of organizers and party politicians, sat ill with many of the members. Myrtle Armstrong has pointed out in her study of the CCF and trade unions that the members of the movement objected to the creation of the position of leader in the Ontario party in 1942 because they saw this move as an erosion of the societal nature of the CCF and as evidence of the determination of trade unionists to make it into an organization that primarily sought political power.[27]

The expansion in the support of the CCF, its victory in Saskatchewan, its proximity to power in British Columbia and Ontario, and its increased membership meant that it was no longer possible to deal with the party as a small movement; procedures had to be changed. As party membership increased, attendance at conventions increased, and it was no longer possible for everyone to speak, nor for each speaker to have unlimited time. At the 1940 convention speakers were allotted five minutes each; at the 1942 convention, at which there were 106 delegates compared with 56 in 1940, the time limit was reduced to three

26 / *Ibid.* Italics added. The convention defeated a resolution which stated: "Whereas members of the c.c.f. are firmly convinced that their organization is something more than just another political party ... be it resolved that the words 'A People's Movement' be used on letterheads, pamphlets, etc."

27 / Armstrong, "Development of Trade Union Activity," 59 ff.

minutes; at the 1944 convention there were 208 delegates.
Clearly the CCF could not continue to operate as it had in the past, yet some of the leading figures in the party, such as William Irvine and Harold Winch, found it difficult to accustom themselves to the demands and restrictions that, of necessity, fall upon a party but that are uncommon in a movement. A simple change in a rule, such as the time limit for speakers, made for perfectly practical reasons, gave the leaders more influence by restricting the participation of the veterans in the ranks, and made the proceedings seem less democratic.

To some extent this restriction on speakers at conventions was mitigated by the fact that the newcomers were unaccustomed to debate. This enabled the old hands to enjoy a slight advantage, but that often served to annoy the newcomers who were, for the most part, less committed to the movement and consequently slightly discomfited by the lucubrations of the fiery few. The new members were more prepared to accept leadership from the top and were made uneasy by the extent of participation demanded by the older members. The CCF had increased in size, but it had not become a mass movement. Rather it had become a larger party, for those who helped swell the membership rolls and who voted for it in the forties were not throwing themselves into a movement. The ease with which many later left it underlines this point. In 1945 the party nominated 205 candidates; in 1957 it could muster only 161.

It was not the movement that succeeded in 1943–45; it was the party that attracted support and members. The dramatic increase in support for the CCF is perhaps best seen as the product of abnormal times. With the approach of normality, the effort of the traditional parties to recoup their losses by moving leftward, and the massive anti-CCF campaign, all acting to produce a return to traditional patterns of political behaviour, sustained support of the CCF was unlikely. By 1949, all that was left was a residual increase, the legacy of successful educational activity among the recruits provided by the war.

The struggle between those who would shape the CCF more in the image of a political party and those who opposed such apostasy was most evident at the 1944 national convention in Montreal. The crucial debate was on the election manifesto drafted by the national council. The war was nearing its end, and with the good news from Saskatchewan ringing in their ears, the party leaders were poised for the final leap to power.

The section which became the focus for much of the debate was that dealing with the place of small business in the "cooperative commonwealth." The evolution of this section prior to the convention is significant. A draft dated November 4 (the convention opened November 29) made the following proposal:

Smaller concerns whose owners carry on the functions of managers and receive from their operations incomes no larger than are required for a comfortable standard of living, will be left in private hands until, if found necessary, they can be absorbed into the national plan. As this takes place, opportunities will be afforded for the present owners to continue their function as managers.[28]

The draft presented to the convention had been substantially revised by the council:

The Socialization of large-scale enterprise, however, does not mean taking over every private business. Where private business shows no signs of becoming a monopoly, and operates efficiently under decent working conditions, and fulfils its obligations to the community, it will be given every opportunity to function, to provide a fair rate of return and to make its contribution to the nation's welfare.[29]

The final version approved by the convention did not differ substantially from the above, apart from the substitution of "and does not operate to the detriment of the Canadian people" for "and fulfils its obligations to the community"; and the final word being changed to "wealth."[30]

In his defence of the council proposal, David Lewis argued that it was included for the purpose of assuring small businessmen that a CCF government would not deprive them of their businesses.[31] Colin Cameron, British Columbia MLA, replied that the CCF "need hardly be concerned with the feelings of small businessmen if we are to carry out an extensive socialization program."[32] For the national secretary, the problem was one of avoiding the alienation of possible support for the party; for Cameron, it was a question of doing what the movement had set out to do in the first place, that is, eradicate capitalism.

These tensions only compounded confusion, for there is no doubt that Lewis fundamentally agreed with what Cameron thought at this juncture. Lewis, however, was more frequently in touch with the more pragmatic and conventional views of the trade unionists; he was also very much aware of the need to sustain the party's advance in electoral support. This required a less militant, less socialistic approach, in order that inroads might be made in the ranks of the middle-class voters. Lewis's opinion

28 / Documents, 1944 Convention file, CCFP.
29 / *Ibid.*
30 / Report of the Eighth National Convention (1944).
31 / *Edmonton Journal*, Dec. 1, 1944.
32 / *Ibid.*

prevailed, and in the issue of *News Comment* covering this part of the program, the following statement appeared: "The C.C.F. does not propose to socialize business just for the fun of it, *or for some doctrinaire reason*. It proposes to socialize only when that step is necessary for *severely practical* reasons, to achieve the great social ends it has in view."[33]

In 1944, as in the past, the CCF was opposed to monopolies. It was not openly opposed to competition, despite the fact that it had opposed competition in the past and would again in the future – but not in policy declarations or election manifestos. The CCF in the forties stood for "more things for more people": "The C.C.F. will not only protect farmers and workers in the ownership of homes and other personal property; it will make possible far more ownership of homes and other personal property by the mass of the people than there has ever been since pioneer days."[34] Business was accepted; big business – monopolies – was not.

A rationale for this position was provided earlier by Lewis in a letter to Angus MacInnis dealing with an editorial in the British Columbia CCF paper the *Federationist*. The editorial pointed out that the economic problems Canada faced were not those of distribution but of ownership. Lewis supported this position: "It is an elementary fact to socialists that upon the ownership and control of the economy depends the problem of distribution as well as that of production."[35] But he quarrelled with the publication of the editorial because it did not take into consideration the people who would be reading it. His analysis of the position of the party in this letter is significant and must be quoted at length:

I think the *Federationist* is probably the best CCF paper in the country but its usefulness is definitely marred and frequently destroyed by a reckless pedantry which ignores consequences and, therefore, ignores the purpose of our work and our purpose, surely, is not the search for truth as bourgeois theoreticians erroneously describe their work, but to mobilize the workers for action on the basis of the truths of scientific socialism. If this is so then, obviously again, what we say and do must be measured by the effect which it will have on our purpose of mobilizing the people for action. If what we say and do will blunt or harm our purpose in the particular circumstances in which we work, then, we are saying and doing a false thing even if, in the abstract, it is true. The difference between the honest democratic socialist and a dishonest political demagogue whether of the Right or of the Left lies

33 / *News Comment*, v (Feb. 15, 1945), 5. Italics added.
34 / *Ibid.*
35 / D. Lewis to A. MacInnis, Oct. 1, 1940, CCFP.

only in that the former will not do or say anything false simply because it may serve his purpose best.[36]

It was the desperation of a politician in a movement that caused him to write: "When, in Heaven's name, are we going to learn that working-class politics and the struggle for power are not a Sunday-school class where the purity of godliness and the infallibility of the Bible must be held up without fear of consequences."[37]

The second conference on provincial policy, held in Winnipeg December 29–January 1, 1944–5, continued the trend of general moderation. In the discussion of socialization it was decided that the best approach to the problem was by taking over shares, "for it is least disturbing to the established enterprise."[38] It was felt as well that with this method a province need only take over a majority of the stock to control the firm in question. The concern of the CCF with what must be done when a CCF government is formed was the product of the electoral successes and membership increase already mentioned, and the belief that the end of the war would bring a depression in its wake which would result in the CCF being called upon to assume the responsibility of government. This view was expressed by several speakers at the conference and frequently in correspondence originating from the national office. In a letter to the Nova Scotia provincial secretary at the beginning of the war, Lewis spoke of the "difficulties and suffering" that were "bound to come at the end of the war."[39] It was the task of the CCF to be ready.

Professor Zakuta has seen the move away from pure socialism as the product of the party's approach to success.[40] Yet both the moderate and the radical view were present from the time of the party's foundation. Both elements were mixed in varying proportions in all the CCF leaders. Success did move the party closer to the reformist element and away from the socialist element. The conflict was partly rationalized by the assertion that "the best way of advancing the socialist cause [is] first to get elected."[41] It may be more accurate and more just to the CCF leaders to see the changes in policy as an honest attempt to make the unchanging principles of the party better understood and more acceptable. What was seen by the radicals as a flight from prin-

36 / *Ibid.*
37 / *Ibid.*
38 / Minutes of the 1944–5 Conference on Provincial Policy, CCFP. No brief was presented by the Quebec section. Only British Columbia, Saskatchewan, Ontario, and Nova Scotia actively participated.
39 / D. Lewis to I. Borgford, Nov. 16, 1939, CCFP.
40 / L. Zakuta, *A Protest Movement Becalmed* (Toronto 1964), 60–2.
41 / *Ibid.*, 61.

ciple was perhaps a shift in presentation for good political and pedagogical reasons.

In the first place, what was said by the moderate element in the CCF in the late forties was not very different from what Woodsworth and Coldwell had been saying in the thirties. What differed was that the language of moderation was spoken more frequently after the war. In the second place there is no evidence that there had been any softening of the *moral* condemnation of the capitalist system; the Winnipeg Declaration of 1956 offers proof of this. Both elements in the party were agreed on the fundamental nature of sin; they differed in their attitudes toward the evangelical process. It is difficult, if not impossible, to find one explanation for the changes; there were many. As will be discussed in the following pages, no one approach was followed consistently.

The optimism of the party came to an abrupt end with its crushing defeat in the Ontario provincial election of 1945. The CCF vote fell by only 4,000 votes but these were so distributed that 26 seats were lost. This is not the place to analyze in any detail the Ontario defeat and the fall of that provincial organization.[42] The defeat has been described as the result of the last-minute "Gestapo Speech" by CCF leader, E. B. Joliffe, in which he accused the Drew government of using secret agents to ferret out information about politicians and parties; as the failure of the CCF to recognize the potency of the anti-socialist campaign being waged by B. A. Trestrail and Gladstone Murray; and as the product of over-confidence in the inevitability of CCF victory.[43]

The Ontario disaster was only slightly mitigated by the subsequent federal election. In Ontario the CCF dropped 130,000 of the votes it had won in the provincial contest a week earlier, although the party won 28 seats; but, apart from one in Nova Scotia, all were west of the Lakehead, in Manitoba, Saskatchewan, and British Columbia.

Those critics who directed their attention to the question of policy were generally agreed that in both elections the party had been too vague and too general. In place of slogans, it was argued, there should have been more specifics, more answers to

42 / See Caplan, "The Failure of Canadian Socialism," *Canadian Historical Review*, XLIV (June 1963); and Caplan, thesis.

43 / See G. Grube, "The Lebel Report and Civil Liberties," *Canadian Forum*, XXV (Nov. 1945) and (Dec. 1945). See also D. P. O'Hearn, "What Happened to the C.C.F. in Ontario," *Saturday Night*, 61 (Jan. 8, 1946); F. A. Brewin, "What the C.C.F. Needs," *Canadian Forum*, XXVI (Feb. 1946); and "The Meaning of the Elections," *Canadian Forum*, XXV (July 1945).

obvious questions about the degree and kind of socialism the CCF
would introduce as a government.[44] Others in the party thought
that the close alliance with organized labour, which was particularly strong in Ontario, was detrimental. It was thought that
the trade unions wanted power and that they ran the Ontario
provincial campaign with this in mind – not entirely a foolish
approach, but one which incensed socialist militants. The prominence of Jolliffe as leader in the campaign literature, the reliance on slogans – a "five star program" – and the fact that the
pamphlets distributed in the last weeks of the election were
drafted in their entirety by the Political Action Committee of
the Steelworkers' union were seen by the militants as reason
enough for the retribution meted out. At the 1945 Ontario provincial convention a resolution to expel Jolliffe and Lewis, because
"the campaign tactics of the 1945 election had been decided by
Mr. Jolliffe with the advice of Mr. Lewis and the democratic
processes within the CCF had been ignored,"[45] was defeated.

There was some validity to the criticism. In the Ontario provincial election the CCF campaign had been based on the "five
stars" which were: "Job Security, Home Security, Health Security, Farm Security, A United People." There were fewer of
the "no-holds-barred" attacks on capitalism and the establishment that had characterized earlier campaigns – apart from
Jolliffe's final speech. In the Dominion election the criticism of
monopoly and business was even more moderate; although in
many ridings, and in some of the national pamphlets, the danger
of post-war depression was conjured up with pictures of haggard
old men hunched over soup bowls or of workers crowding on to
freight cars – the captions were "What capitalism does to Canadians" and "This must not happen again." At the same time,
however, other pamphlets offered voters electric refrigerators,
radios, houses, and cars as the fruits of social ownership under a
CCF government. The campaign slogans were "Security with
Victory" and "Jobs for All." The theme was reform rather than
revolution. It was a campaign in which the CCF tried to match
the promises of the other parties – in other words, play the game
more by their rules. The difficulty was, of course, that the voter
had more experience of the Liberals producing than he had of
the CCF. It was clear that outside Saskatchewan few Canadians
were prepared to admit that only the CCF could provide jobs,

44 / "The Meaning of the Elections" (unsigned article); G. O. Rothney, "Quebec Saves our King," *Canadian Forum*, xxv (July 1945); R. E.
K. Pemberton, "The C.C.F. Should Get Wise to Itself," *Canadian Forum*,
xxv (Oct. 1945), and a letter from Joe Noseworthy in *Canadian Forum*,
xxvi (March 1946).

45 / Armstrong, "Development of Trade Union Activity," 61 ff.

prosperity, and security, particularly when it attacked the institutions that were identified in the public mind with those very things. And, as discussed below, the CCF was not prepared for the propaganda onslaught from its opponents that its successes provoked.

Defeat produced decline. Those who had supported the CCF after the 1943 success in Ontario drifted away. Membership in the party dropped, particularly in Ontario, although there was no immediate decline in income from the provinces as would have been expected. Twenty-two thousand dollars had been received from the provinces in the year ending June 30, 1945, and the amount rose to $31,000 the following year.[46] There was no immediately obvious reasons for members to feel that the CCF was a declining force in Canadian politics. Financially it had never been healthier. The results of the provincial elections in Alberta, British Columbia, and Nova Scotia had all shown an increase in the popular support, if not in actual seats won.

There were, however, signs of decay not reflected in the financial statements. In a confidential report prepared by the national chairman and national secretary and submitted to the national council in March 1946, it was pointed out that quota payments from the provinces had "almost entirely broken down" and that "precisely when domestic and international issues cry out for leadership from the CCF, we are ill-equipped to give it and not very effective even on those elementary issues on which our party had already had an important influence in the past."[47] In his address to the council, national chairman Frank Scott noted that the party was dormant: "It is as though we had lost faith in ourselves; zeal is lacking, because inside each CCF member there is an element of doubt about his function and role at the present moment."[48] The solution Scott proposed was a rethinking of the CCF position while continuing to advocate its programme, for "analysis proves it is right." He concluded by pointing out that CCF policy was "desperately needed ... in Canada," and that the party had to find ways to make people see that fact.[49]

Scott reiterated this theme in his address to the Ninth National Convention, returning to the appeal of the movement rather than the needs of the party, although the drive for power had not abated. In his address he said, "We exist in order that this [the domination of Canada by monopoly and private profit] shall be changed, and that human values shall prevail over materialistic

46 / Report of the Ninth National Convention (1946).

47 / "The C.C.F. and Postwar Canada," confidential report of national secretary to the national council, March 1946, CCFP.

48 / "Notes for Council Address," n.d., Scott Papers.

49 / *Ibid.*

interests."[50] He set as the goal the election of the first CCF government in Ottawa. The national president, M. J. Coldwell, re-
stated the truths of the Regina Manifesto in his address. Putting
election slogans and propaganda behind him, he declared: "In
a society in which private gain is the main motive of production,
selfishness and greed are encouraged. As socialists we desire to
raise the level of social behaviour by substituting the motive of
social well-being for selfish gain."[51] It was a speech filled with
zeal and moral fervour. He closed by calling for "effort, education and fidelity by all sections of our Movement [sic]." It was
unlike his 1944 convention address, which was a factual recita-
tion of party achievements and political goals.

The convention was a needed pause to drink once again at the
well-spring of chiliastic socialism in an effort to heal the wounds
of battles fought and lost, and to unite a party which had become
fragmented by the demands of electioneering. In a time of weakness, there was strength in the movement. The reassertion of
socialist principles was not an indication that there would be any
change in direction or attitude in the national leadership of
the party. The association with trade unions continued and increased, if not in support at the polls, at least in the co-operation
and participation in party affairs by union officials, and by party
officials in union affairs. But it was clear that appeals for renewed
effort could only be couched in the language of the movement.

Despite the efforts of the Canadian Congress of Labour Political Action Committee, which had called for all workers to support the CCF, rank and file trade union support did not grow. It
was nonetheless clear to the leaders of the party that success lay
in closer ties with the trade unions. Clearly there was to be no
support, or relatively little, from rural Manitoba or Alberta. In
the former, the two safe CCF seats were in working-class Winnipeg. What support the party had in Ontario was in the urban
ridings, and Ontario was the key to national success. By 1946
there were trade union committees in British Columbia, Saskatchewan, Manitoba, and Ontario, in addition to a national
trade union committee chaired by Angus MacInnis.

The approach taken by these committees is exemplified by the
activities of the Ontario committee, which sought to establish
"industrial units" in each bargaining unit or plant where there

50 / Report of the Ninth National Convention (1946). The same
attitude was expressed in the confidential report to the national council
cited above. "Every experience Canada has undergone during the war
has strengthened our conviction that a socialist commonwealth is not
only a magnificent ideal but an absolute necessity if civilization is to
survive."

51 / *Ibid.*

was a trade union, with the objective of securing the affiliation of that union to the CCF. In addition, it hoped to establish CCF political committees in affiliated unions and provide liaison with provincial and local CCF units, "to keep them informed and activized in regard to the industrial situation."[52] The chief obstacle faced by the committees was the apathy of rank and file trade unionists. This apathy was abetted in many unions by the local leaders, who were opposed to political action; often they were aided by the communist Labour Progressive party. The LPP argued that under a socialist economy there would be no place for trade unions, hence support for the CCF was support for the abolition of trade unions – a curious argument but one which had some success.[53]

The CCF continued to press home the point that it represented organized labour. At a national council meeting in January 1947, a resolution was passed that "The CCF in parliament and throughout the country is determined to achieve the program which organized labour needs, and invites unions throughout Canada to rally round a campaign to this end."[54] By April of 1948 four people were working full time in Ontario under the aegis of the Ontario CCF Trade Union Committee promoting the party among the unions.[55]

The lengths to which the party was prepared to go in courting the favour of the unions was demonstrated in 1947. The CCF was acting as host for a conference of Commonwealth Labour parties and had invited Norman Thomas, the American Socialist party leader, to attend. Thomas had accepted the invitation when Lewis had to withdraw it, explaining that Canadian union leaders had objected because of the official non-partisan policy of their American head offices. The presence of the leader of the Socialist party would be an embarrassment to their American brethren.[56]

In 1950 the development of closer ties with labour resulted in the re-activation of the joint CCF-CCL committee, which had been created in 1947 to co-ordinate the political activities of the two

52 / Report of the Ontario CCF Trade Union Committee to the Ontario provincial council, Jan. 12, 1946, Grube Papers.

53 / Report of Ontario CCF Trade Union Committee to provincial executive, March 20, 1945, Grube Papers. See also A. MacInnis to D. Lewis, Oct. 27, 1948, in which MacInnis describes the Communist influence at the TLC convention as "very strong," pointing out that "the amazing thing is to find the Liberal and Conservative members of the Executive and of the unions working with them." CCFP.

54 / National Council Minutes, Jan. 1947, CCFP.

55 / *Ibid.*, April 1948.

56 / D. Lewis to N. Thomas, Aug. 18, 1947, CCFP. The same problem arose when the NDP was formed. Some international unions found affiliation awkward because of headquarters "Gompersism." Others had no difficulty.

organizations but had been singularly inactive. Charles Millard, Pat Conroy, George Burt, and Murray Cotterill were the CCL members; Angus MacInnis, David Lewis, Andrew Brewin, and Stanley Knowles represented the CCF.[57] The new committee flourished briefly but achieved little. The close connection did, however, commit the CCL and its affiliates to assist the CCF. Financial help in the form of lump sums from CCL affiliates became a regular source of party funds from this point. In 1950 the national secretary reported that the party's financial difficulties had been partly relieved "through the generosity of some Congress [CCL] unions."[58]

Affiliation dues did not provide much money for the party since few union locals affiliated. In 1952 such dues amounted to slightly more than $1,000; in 1954 to less than $2,000. At no time did the CCF receive more than $6,000 in this way. Lump sum contributions, on the other hand, were substantial and regular. In 1953 the United Auto Workers and United Steelworkers unions contributed $30,000 to the organization fund. The Auto Workers provided $12,000 annually after 1954.[59]

Among some members of the CCF, the influx of trade unionists and the degree of control by leading trade unionists was viewed with alarm. Myrtle Armstrong has written that many of these party members refused to take a positive part in party activities and instead devoted their energy to "negative, destructive criticism."[60] The nature of the CCF had changed. More time and attention were devoted to organization and winning votes than to discussion of the many aspects of socialism and the development of more telling social criticism.

The effects of this change and of continued electoral failure soon began to be felt. At the Tenth National Convention, there appeared the first signs of the self-justification of the CCF as a perennial third choice. Both the national secretary and the national chairman pointed with some pride to the fact that the Liberal party had seen fit to adopt CCF policies.[61] The democratic nature of the CCF was held up as a shining example to other parties: "We cannot emphasize too often or too much the basic character of the CCF, the way it is built as a grass-roots people's movement, and the method whereby its inner democracy is safe-

57 / National Executive Minutes, Feb. 25, 1950, CCFP.
58 / Ibid.
59 / See National Council Minutes, Jan. 1953, and the financial statements in the reports of the national conventions for 1952–60 inclusive, CCFP.
60 / Armstrong, "Development of Trade Union Activity," 88.
61 / Report of Tenth National Convention (1948).

guarded and enriched."[62] Increased emphasis was placed on the CCF's intrinsic worth. That there was little immediate hope of the party coming to power was seen as unimportant. What mattered was that the CCF was a shining example of democracy in structure, honesty in finance, and morality in policy. The possibility of building a strong labour party depended upon the leaders holding the CCF together while closer ties with the trade unions were established. Reiteration of the virtues of the CCF helped to unite the party and make it attractive to the unions – a useful function in the presence of a divided labour movement. Despite its failure to win national elections, CCF members saw it as a worth-while organization, and, win or lose, better than the other parties which themselves recognized this worth by adopting CCF policies. This was an adequate *raison d'etre*, and a justification wholly consistent with the CCF as a movement.

The major policy statement of the Tenth National Convention indicated the further rationalization of the party's policy. The need to share social ownership between the federal and provincial governments was recognized and stress was laid on the principle of co-operative ownership. Having indicated at the outset the CCF's awareness of the strains of the Canadian federal system, the policy statement approached socialization from a more moderate point of view than had been the case in the election of 1945: "It cannot be too often emphasized that the CCF regards socialization of industry as a means to an end, and not an end in itself."[63] Social ownership would be restricted to chartered banks, transportation, basic steel production, the farm implement industry, meat packing and fertilizer production, fuel and power. Gone was the blanket condemnation of "big business" and of ruthless monopolies. In its place appeared the following:

In order to achieve effective production and distribution in both the public and private sectors of the economy, *a C.C.F. government will help and encourage private business* to fulfill its legitimate functions.

Experience has shown that where public business flourishes private business thrives also. The private trader or industrialist freed from the domination of industrial and financial monopolies will have a better chance to exercise his enterprise and initiative, to earn a fair rate of return and to make his contribution to the nation's wealth.[64]

This was the CCF "First Term Program." It was a long way from Regina, and demonstrated the decision of the party's national

62 / *Ibid.*
63 / *Ibid.*
64 / *Ibid.* Italics added.

leadership to place the CCF in a position where it would antago-
nize neither the trade unionists nor the middle-class voter – if
such a distinction has any validity in North American society. If
the gospel of the Regina Manifesto had little appeal for the
middle-class – or *petit bourgeois* – Canadian, then it had little
appeal for the trade unionist who was middle class as much as
the farmer, at least in ambition if not otherwise. From another
point of view this was a recognition by the moderate socialist of
the facts of economic life at mid-century. The nostrums of the
thirties were no longer strictly applicable in a society that was
increasingly affluent and in which there seemed to be less social
and economic injustice.

The change was not taken without grumbling and argument.
At the 1948 convention, an eleventh-hour decision by the national council to make a change in the draft program by substituting control of banking for outright ownership was fought to a
standstill by the rank and file and defeated. The handling of the
matter by the executive was clumsy; had the change been made
earlier there would not have been the same opposition. As it
happened the delegates received the original draft plus the
changed version in the form of a mimeographed addendum. Such
evidence of authoritarian whim was all that was needed.[65]

The new direction in policy did not come from the membership of the party; it came from the leaders in the East. Resolutions presented to the convention from the constituencies indicate
that the active membership was determined to maintain the
socialism of the CCF against all comers. The fact that the Regina
Manifesto was being treated merely as a talisman to ward off the
spirits of capitalism, while the policy of the party tended further
and further away from the socialism of the Manifesto, was not
lost upon the members. But it was difficult for them to do much
about it within the framework of convention procedure as it had
developed. They could not fight the leaders effectively for they
could not find replacements as able – or willing – to serve as the
incumbents. The three-minute limit on convention speeches, the
oratorical skills of a David Lewis, the mastery of policy detail by
the officers, the presence of trade union support on the floor of
the convention – all combined to make effective opposition difficult and rarely successful. The procedure for handling resolutions
from the constituencies and provincial sections was itself detrimental to effective control by the membership.

Despite the efforts of the party leaders, however, the CCF did
not recapture the position it held at the war's end. Although the
1953 election did produce an additional 10 seats in the House

of Commons, only 2 of these were east of the Lakehead – one in Ontario and one in Nova Scotia, although the Ontario vote constituted one-third of the total CCF vote. The party's share of the popular vote continued to fall both as a percentage of the total vote and in terms of actual votes received, despite the increase in population. By 1953 the party had almost two hundred thousand fewer votes and only 11 per cent of the popular vote as compared with 15 per cent in 1945. This dropped to 9 per cent in the 1958 election. The same story was told by the figures produced by the Gallup Poll. In 1953 the polls showed that only 11 per cent of those of voting age would vote CCF and of these over half were in British Columbia and the prairie provinces.[66] The party was running a deficit of over $1,000 per month and membership was falling: figures for 1950, in comparison with 1949, showed a general loss of almost half the membership. A national expansion drive, launched in 1949 following the general election, fell far short of its objectives although there were full-time organizers in all but two of the provinces.

It could not be said that there was any lack of research or education during this period. From 1945 to 1950 the party mounted its most extensive and intensive educational campaign. The national office had both a director of research and a director of education – although the two positions were later combined. In the year ending June 30, 1948, literature sales from the national office were over $5,000, compared with $1,000 the previous year.[67] In addition a national bulletin for members, *Across Canada*, was introduced in 1947. It was basically a "house organ" providing news of party activities while *News Comment*, as a research journal, provided "ammunition." Material published included a 112-page booklet, *Who Owns Canada*, published by Woodsworth House Publishers, which "revealed the concentration of economic power in Canada,"[68] as well as countless propaganda leaflets. This was in addition to the material published and distributed by the provincial sections of the party. There was no shortage of propaganda, nor indeed of study outlines for such books as *Planning for Freedom*,[69] Coldwell's *Left Turn Canada*, and Lewis and Scott's *Make This YOUR Canada*. The output of material was remarkable.[70]

66 / *News Release*, Canadian Institute of Public Opinion (CIPO), 1953.
67 / Report of the Tenth National Convention (1948).
68 / *Across Canada*, VI (Nov. 1947).
69 / Sixteen lectures given by CCF notables in 1944 and published (mimeo.) by the Ontario CCF, CCFP.
70 / The 1945 CCF Literature List included 35 leaflets and books. In 1947 five three-month correspondence courses dealing with "Group Activities," "Educational Techniques," "History of Canadian Trade Unions," "Agriculture," and "Socialism" were offered to party members.

It became increasingly evident that the Regina Manifesto was
both out-of-date and a liability for a political party in the mid-
twentieth century. The need for a restatement of the party's aims
and purposes was first proposed at the Eleventh National Convention in 1950. The process whereby the party's basic statement
of ideology was changed was a lengthy one, involving six years,
three national conventions, and a plethora of documents,
minutes, drafts, and memoranda. It was started in earnest by
Frank Scott, national chairman.

Addressing the 1950 convention, Scott laid the foundation for
a rethinking of the Regina Manifesto by stating, "We do not
oppose the making of profit in all its forms; on the contrary, the
profit motive, under proper control, is now and will be for a long
time a most valuable stimulus to production."[71] He pointed out
that the times had changed and that nationalization was no longer
invariably necessary nor an article of socialist faith. Coldwell
called for a re-definition of the party's philosophy and program
"in the light of new developments which have occurred in the
past decade."[72]

There was some concern that the decision to revise the basic
principles of the party had been taken by the officers without any
real attempt to determine the feeling of the membership. A correspondent in the *Canadian Forum* was critical of this aspect of
the convention, and referred to the decision to revise the Manifesto as evidence of "the same inclination of the leaders to pre-
determine policy."[73] He argued further that the policy was being
largely "made in Britain."

There is no doubt that the shifts in Labour party policy which
were taking place at this time had some effect on the decision of
the CCF leaders to rewrite the Regina Manifesto. It would be un-
fair to argue, however, that the decision was sudden or that the
change had not already begun. The move was a formal recognition of the changes taking place in socialist parties throughout
the western world, as an article in *News Comment* had pointed
out.[74]

A committee of the national council made a draft restatement
of principles[75] which was circulated to clubs and constituency
associations for comments and suggestions. With the suggested

71 / Report of the Eleventh National Convention (1950). For a more
detailed discussion of the formation of the Winnipeg Declaration, see
ch. 6.
72 / *Ibid.*
73 / "The C.C.F. Convention," *Canadian Forum*, xxx (Sept. 1950), 124.
74 / *News Comment*, x (Aug.–Sept. 1950), 1–2.
75 / The committee consisted of T. C. Douglas, Hazen Argue, Andrew
Brewin, Clarie Gillis, Lorne Ingle, François LaRoche, David Lewis,
Grace MacInnis, Joe Noseworthy, and Frank Scott.

changes from the various sections of the party in hand, the statement was re-drafted and published in October 1951, not as a
final statement but as a basis for discussion and for presentation
to the convention in 1952. It was published in *Comment*, the
successor to *News Comment*, along with an article on the Socialist International and the Declaration of the International
adopted at Frankfurt in July 1951.[76] The revised version was not
acceptable to the provincial parties and was not formally presented to the convention.[77]

From 1952 to 1956 no suitable drafts had been prepared until,
in some desperation, the national executive, acting on instructions
from the national council, appointed David Lewis, Lorne Ingle,
Omer Chartrand, and Morden Lazarus to prepare a draft statement of principles for the July convention.[78] This draft was presented to the 1956 convention and became the Winnipeg Declaration of Principles. In the intervening period of 1952–6 party
fortunes had continued to worsen. There was no reason for with-
holding any change in policy. Total membership was falling[79]
and the party had become almost totally dependent upon financing from Saskatchewan and the trade unions.

There were countless recipes for success at the time. In the
pages of the *Canadian Forum* a series of articles under the general
title of "What's Left?" debated the problem. One writer insisted
that the need was for a "renewal of moral fervor" and a campaign
of "muck-raking and debunking."[80] Carlyle King, president of
the Saskatchewan CCF, was more specific:

The trouble is that socialist parties have gone a-whoring after the
Bitch Goddess. They have wanted Success, Victory, Power; forgetting
that the main business of socialist parties is not to form governments
but to change minds. When people begin to concentrate on success at
the polls, they become careful and cautious; and when they become
careful and cautious, the virtue goes out of them.[81]

The CCF had always seen education as one of its major tasks, and

76 / *Comment*, 1 (Nov. 1951); and see National Council Minutes,
Oct. 1951, CCFP.
77 / Report of the Twelfth National Convention (1952).
78 / David Lewis resigned as national secretary in 1950 and was
replaced by Lorne Ingle. In 1950 Lewis was elected vice-chairman and
in 1954 he became national chairman. Omer Chartrand was Quebec
provincial secretary and Morden Lazarus was the Co-operative Press
Association correspondent. The CPA was the news service for the CCF
papers – it had a few non-party subscribers as well.
79 / L. Ingle to F. Welton, Nov. 1954, CCFP; and see Appendix B.
80 / L. Harrington, "What's Left," *Canadian Forum*, XXXI (March
1952), 270.
81 / Carlyle King, "What's Left," *Canadian Forum*, XXXII (April
1952), 3.

the work of education had been carried on with immense energy
during the post-war period. But it was education for those already
committed and had little effect on the party's electoral strength.
From the beginning, the CCF had seen one of its aims as the
winning of political power. The Regina Manifesto was specific
on this point: "The CCF aims at political power in order to put
an end to this capitalist domination of our political life." But
since 1945 the party had been slowly bleeding to death at the
polls.

When the national council met in January 1956 to discuss the
new manifesto, those who had been in the movement from the
start reviewed the decline of the party and suggested ways of
turning the tide. For some, like Herbert Herridge and William
Irvine, the solution was more socialism. As Irvine put it, there
was nothing that could replace the Manifesto; "we were born in
the manger of poverty and the old capitalists are still the same."[82]
For others, like Lewis, Scott, MacInnis, and Coldwell, there had
to be a more pragmatic appeal, one related to daily issues. "We
should be empirical rather than dogmatic," Coldwell argued. The
party's appeal should not be based "on the premise of depression
coming." The division between the "party" men and the "movement" men was clear. Scott argued, "the best program [is] no
substitute for organization," while Lewis insisted that, "com-
placency with the rightness of the cause is not enough." For
Colin Cameron, on the other hand, capitalism had not changed;
the CCF needed to "speak hard truths boldly." For Herridge the
solution lay in providing "a small core of socialist students to
keep us away from expediency." Despite the division it is also
clear that there was a common dedication to a cause for almost
without exception every speaker stressed the need to emphasize
the "moral and ethical appeal" of democratic socialism. Scott
could argue that "psychology [is] more important than economic
theory," and still insist that what was needed was "more talk on
morals of our society, its materialism, corruption through advertising, starving of education." And Lewis, arguing in support
of a restatement of the party principles said, "restating does not
destroy principle or weaken moral indignation."[83]

The Winnipeg Declaration lacked the fire of the Regina Manifesto and was accepted only after long, and at times bitter, debate.[84] The members resented the change in policy despite their
earlier acceptance of the need for change. The leaders of the CCF

82 / F. R. Scott's Notes on the national council meeting of Jan. 13–15,
1956, Scott Papers.
83 / *Ibid.*
84 / See the *Winnipeg Free Press*, Aug. 2, 3, 4, 1956, for reports of
the convention.

were attempting, in good faith, to provide the party with a central body of doctrine that had none of the revolutionary overtones of the Regina Manifesto and which would, they earnestly hoped, be more acceptable to the public and place their party in a more favourable light.

It was a much shorter document than the Regina Manifesto. It opened with a similar statement of aim: "the establishment in Canada by democratic means of a co-operative commonwealth in which the supplying of human needs and the enrichment of human life shall be the primary purpose of our society."[85] And it included the same note of moral determination in a section headed "Capitalism Basically Immoral" which stated that "a society motivated for private gain and special privilege is basically immoral." But as far as the radicals in the CCF were concerned, it petered out, offering in the peroration a gentle statement which any party in a democracy would accept: "The CCF will not rest content until every person in this land and in all other lands is able to enjoy equality and freedom, a sense of human dignity, and an opportunity to live a rich and meaningful life as a citizen of a free and peaceful world."[86] It was a far cry from the ringing declaration of the original manifesto.

The inclusion of the phrase "and in all other lands" and of two sections dealing with peace and support of the UN is significant because it demonstrates the increasing attention to external affairs that typified the discussions at post-war conventions of the CCF. As the party faced a society in which more and more of the reforms it supported and fought for were implemented, there seemed to be less for it to say about conditions in Canada. The national target for attack was diminishing with the gradual establishment of the welfare state under Liberal aegis. The moral fervour of the movement was increasingly directed toward international affairs. This was partly the result of the general widening of horizons which the revolution in communications had produced, and of the increased awareness of international affairs which resulted from the war, the atomic bomb, and the UN. It is interesting to note that more resolutions dealing with international affairs were submitted to national conventions after the war than before. The contentious issues at conventions became such questions as German rearmament, the Korean War, and, for all conventions after 1949, Canadian membership in NATO.

If the party had failed to become the government, it had nevertheless accomplished much. The indirect success of the CCF was recognized in the first paragraph of the Winnipeg Declaration:

85 / *Winnipeg Declaration of Principles.*
86 / *Ibid.*

"The Regina Manifesto, proclaimed by the founders of the movement in 1933, has had a profound influence on Canada's social system. Many of the improvements it recommended have been wrung out of unwilling governments by the growing strength of our movement and the growing political maturity of the Canadian people." It was possibly as a result of the improvements made by the "unwilling governments" that the CCF had to spell out in the Declaration that the CCF in power would "provide appropriate opportunities for private business." The explicit change in party principles was made as a public declaration that much of what had been said about the CCF as an agency of total government control was false. The statement of moral aims and of the success of the CCF even without power was made to indicate to the members of the movement that the CCF was still worthwhile.

Some effort was made by leading figures in the CCF to argue that the Declaration did not constitute any major revision of party doctrine. Andrew Brewin wrote in the *CCF News*, "the Winnipeg Declaration is, like its predecessor, the Regina Manifesto, a thoroughly liberal document."[87] And T. C. Douglas in a province-wide radio broadcast cited speeches by Woodsworth and himself in the House of Commons in 1934 and 1936 to demonstrate that "the CCF have [*sic*] never believed that all economic functions should be owned by the State."[88] The dilution of the policy of social ownership was not a flight from socialism, in his view it was a simple recognition of the realities of the political and economic situation. If total nationalization could have been achieved without at the same time causing economic dislocation as a result of the withdrawal of foreign investment capital, then it is likely that there would have been less insistence on changing the Manifesto. Only the tools of change had been modified.

The members of the CCF remained committed and dedicated socialists. The high moral condemnation of profit-making, of the social, political, and economic inequities which they saw in Canada, was still within them. Their idealism had not disappeared. The Winnipeg Declaration was not a manifestation of the departure of CCF members from socialism as much as it was a manifestation of their leaders' anxiety to win elections, of their recognition of the fact that the CCF was not, as a party, attracting enough votes. And it had to do this to achieve socialism.

87 / F. A. Brewin, "Not 'Liberal' but Liberal," *CCF News* (Nov. 1956), cited in Zakuta, *A Protest Movement Becalmed*, 97.
88 / "The Winnipeg Declaration II: The Structure of a Co-operative Commonwealth," Provincial Affairs series, broadcast Oct. 24, 1956, mimeo., CCFP.

There was another reason, the pending unification of the two major labour congresses in Canada, the Canadian Congress of Labour and the Trades and Labour Congress. In 1949 the CCL convention had passed a resolution favouring unification and in 1950 there had been considerable progress toward unity.[89] In 1956 the merger took place. No specific mention was made at the merger convention of the earlier CCL decision endorsing the CCF as the political arm of labour. There was little doubt, however, that the sympathies of the new Canadian Labour Congress lay with the CCF. The resolution on political education and action passed at the founding convention of the new congress stated that:

The Political Education Committee be authorized to initiate discussions with free trade unions not affiliated with the Congress, with the principal farm organizations in Canada, with the co-operative movement, and with the Co-operative Commonwealth Federation or other political parties pledged to support the legislative program of the Canadian Labour Congress, excluding communist and fascist dominated parties, and to explore and develop co-ordination of action in the legislative and political field.[90]

The Political Action Committee was made up largely of pro-CCF unionists, while the Political Education Committee was chaired by Howard Conquergood, a member of the CCF. The Winnipeg Declaration made the party more attractive to a national labour body that included the old TLC, an opponent of the CCF for so long. In this instance it was again political necessity that compelled the change in party policy.

The change seemed to make little difference to the electorate. Indeed, one observer of the 1957 election has noted: "The CCF approach to Canadian problems, while far from being Marxist, was nevertheless clearly rooted in the socialist tradition. The party's aim was not only to replace the government, but to transform much of Canadian society."[91] In 1957 the campaign slogan was "Share Canada's Wealth," and the emphasis was on welfare policy. It made little difference to the voters and while the party did win more seats than in the previous election its share of the popular vote fell slightly. What was most significant was that the party's vote in Saskatchewan fell by 8 per cent and the Saskatoon seat was lost to a Conservative. The general election of 1958 was

89 / E. Forsey, "The Movement Towards Labour Unity," 73.
90 / Proceedings of the First Canadian Labour Congress Convention, April 1956.
91 / John Meisel, *The Canadian General Election of 1957* (Toronto 1962), 220.

a disaster. The CCF share of the popular vote fell by only one percentage point but the party lost seventeen seats, including those of M. J. Coldwell and Stanley Knowles. Fourteen of these seats were in Alberta and Saskatchewan. It was clear to the leaders of the party, as it had been for some time, that a simple restatement of principles was not enough to rescue the cause of democratic socialism in Canada.[92]

The decision to establish much closer ties with organized labour had been made following the merger of the two congresses. At the CCF national council meeting in October 1957, the matter of broadening the base of the party was discussed and there was general agreement that a new kind of political alignment was needed.[93] It was pointed out that at the next convention of the CLC, a stand would be taken on political action and the members of the CCF in the congress wanted to know in what direction they should move. One member said that Claude Jodoin, CLC president, did not believe the Congress should take political action itself but that it should have a parallel organization for political action in the manner that the British Labour party and the Trades Union Congress co-operated. Colin Cameron believed there was a need for a new political alignment but felt it could only arise "when we get class consciousness into labour." It was his view that Canadian labour "does not believe the dice are loaded against them."[94] There was, however, general agreement that the movement for a newer and broader base for the CCF should get under way.

In February 1958 the executive council of the CLC decided to prepare a resolution for presentation to the Congress convention which would instruct the executive council "to establish a consultative committee with the CCF for the purpose of developing an effective political instrument patterned along the lines of the British Labour Party."[95] At the convention in April a resolution was passed which stated the need for a "broadly-based people's political movement which embraces the CCF, the Labour Movement, farm organizations, professional people and other liberally-

92 / See Frank Scott, "Notes on the January 1956 national council meeting," Scott Papers; and Arnold Webster to Lorne Ingle, Dec. 29, 1955, CCFP. Broadening the base of the CCF was discussed in November 1956, at a meeting of Lewis, Coldwell, Knowles, and some members of the CLC executive at Claude Jodoin's home in Ottawa. The matter was further explored at a second such meeting in Jan. 1957. David Lewis to Carl Hamilton, Nov. 12, 1957, CCFP.

93 / Frank Scott, "Notes on the National Council Meeting of October 19, 1957," Scott Papers; and national council minutes, Oct. 1957.

94 / *Ibid.*

95 / "Canadian Labour Congress Executive Council Meetings," *Canadian Labour*, III (April 1958), 29. See also the unpubl. MA thesis (Toronto 1962), "The Formation of the N.D.P.," by Fred Schindeler.

minded persons."[96] The executive council was instructed to give immediate attention to building such a party.

The massive CCF defeat that took place between the CLC executive council meeting and the CLC convention undoubtedly gave some urgency to the deliberations. The movement toward the establishment of the new party was also hastened by the election of Stanley Knowles and Bill Dodge to vice-presidencies on the Congress executive. Dodge was an active member of the CCF in Montreal.

The national council of the CCF welcomed the invitation of the CLC and appointed David Lewis, Hazen Argue, Stanley Knowles, Andrew Brewin, Carl Hamilton, T. C. Douglas, Harold Winch and F. R. Scott to meet with representatives of the Congress to pursue the matter.[97] The "CLC-CCF Political Committee," as it came to be called, held its first meeting on June 25, 1958. It was later expanded and became the "National Committee for the New Party." At the national convention in July 1958, the CCF welcomed the Congress invitation, endorsed the council decision, and stated that any new party "must continue to be dedicated to the principles of democratic social planning and to the widest forms of social security and individual liberty."[98]

The process of establishing the new party continued in the period between 1958 and 1960 through seminars, intra-party education campaigns, and the establishment in some provinces of "New Party Clubs" to attract the "other liberally minded persons" who had not previously supported the CCF. At the party's convention in 1960, the establishment of the New Party was endorsed unanimously. It had, in effect, been endorsed when the 1958 convention agreed to enter into discussions with the CLC. Indeed it was almost a foregone conclusion when the merged labour organizations indicated their willingness to back such a development. If the CCF grew naturally from the grass roots, the party which succeeded it was grown artificially, from the top down, in the way the Liberal and Conservative parties came into being.

It was the culmination of some twenty-five years of effort on the part of David Lewis, above all, to make the CCF into a Canadian version of the British Labour party. The CCF started off as a federation of farm, labour, and socialist groups but became, at the national level, an organization directed entirely by individuals whose orientation was urban and socialist and whose model was

96 / Proceedings of the Second Annual Convention of the Canadian Labour Congress, April 1958.
97 / National Council Minutes, May 1958, CCFP.
98 / Report of the Fifteenth National Convention (1958).

the British Labour party. Despite the obvious geographic advantages, the contact of the CCF with the American socialist movement had been minimal.

The CCF seldom invited American socialist party dignitaries to address conventions, whereas tours were arranged for visiting British socialists and conventions were addressed by such people as Clement Attlee, Richard Crossman, and Jenny Lee. Appropriately enough, Hugh Gaitskell, leader of the Labour party, was the guest speaker at the founding convention of the New Democratic party. The political orientation of the CCL had been toward Britain. The pages of the *Canadian Unionist* from the first issue contained countless articles by Raymond Postgate, George Lansbury, Ernest Bevin, and other Labour party luminaries. The CCF news-letter, *News Comment*, carried as a regular feature excerpts from speeches and statements of British Labour party figures. There is no question that the CCF leaders saw the party as a Canadian version of the British Labour party in the same way that the LSR was to be a Canadian Fabian society. Great spiritual and doctrinal sustenance was drawn from Britain by all sections of the movement, but particularly by the national movement and by Lewis, who was a close acquaintance of many of the figures in the British Labour party.

The formation of the New Democratic Party was, in this sense, the fulfilment of the aims of Lewis and Scott and Coldwell. Their socialism remained, as a moral faith, unchanged. They, like their socialist counterparts in Britain, were prepared to modify the explicit doctrine and to allow a closer relationship with labour to evolve and to provide, it was hoped, a program acceptable to the public, as well as votes and money.

But it remains a fact of politics that the program does not change the popular image of the party, nor does it change the individuals who stand on it. It may have been the Winnipeg Declaration that formed the basis of the party platform in 1957 and 1958, but it was the old CCF that stood on the platform and provided the same arguments, the same criticisms of the system and its faults that had been heard from 1933 onward. It was not enough to point out that small businesses – indeed any business that was not a monopoly – would not be nationalized. The question should never have come up for the implication was clear that the CCF did intend to "take over," and blandishments of security rang falsely on the ears of those who feared any kind of government takeover.

Throughout the history of the CCF, the policy and, to some extent, the ideology of the party changed because the leaders

came to feel more and more the need to attract a larger number of the electorate. Admittedly the policy was largely shaped by the times and by experience both in Canada and in Great Britain. But basically it was felt that those aspects of the party programme which alienated support – such as the policy of socialization of business – had to be dropped or explained away. The leaders of the CCF recognized that without a broader base of support than that which they had, they could never become the government. There was, therefore, an effort to win middle-class support.[99] And this meant appealing to middle-class sentiment.

It was not too difficult for the CCF leaders to do this. Coldwell, Scott, and Lewis were at home in the bourgeois milieu, and while this does not imply any weakening of the socialist resolve, it does indicate an ability to see things the way the middle classes in Canada saw them and therefore to disparage the wilder statements and less practical, although doctrinally more acceptable, schemes of the Winches and Camerons. As leaders they had a dual responsibility: to the party and to the movement. They had to keep the movement alive and inspired while struggling to build a successful party. The two roles were at times complementary and at times contradictory.

The irony in the history of the development of the CCF ideology from Regina to 1961 is found in the fact that it really did not make any difference to the party's success or failure. Indeed it might be argued, as those on the left of the party argue still, that had the party maintained its staunch socialism and not diluted the CCF "clause four," the party might have been more successful. As it was, it became more liberal and less socialist. It remained a movement in that the zeal was there, the idealism remained, and the moral antipathy to capitalism and profit-making was present in the Winnipeg Declaration and in the speeches of all the members; but as a party it looked to the objective observer increasingly like the other middle-of-the-road parties. And, it would be argued, the CCF could never compete with the Liberal party on the Liberal party's terms. Only if it stayed as a radical left-wing party could it succeed.

On the other hand it seems more accurate to say that it made little difference what the CCF said, how its pamphlets looked, or what program emerged from its conventions. There is no evidence that the popularity of the CCF in 1943 and 1944 was due to what it was saying in 1942 any more than its rapid fall from public favour in 1945 resulted from its program. No party ever tried harder than the CCF did in those two years and in the years

99 / See for example the report of the national organizer to the 1952 national convention in which he said he felt the PAC had been driving away *middle-class* votes.

which followed the war, to say the right things to the electorate. Its leaders did so, it must be pointed out, in a way as consistent with their aims as possible. But they tried everything. In 1953 and 1957 they used comic papers to outline the story of the CCF program for welfare and prosperity for everyone, and to depict the Liberals as purveyors of poverty for the many. The fact remains that when they gained or lost popularity it was largely in spite of themselves.

The image of the CCF was hardly affected latterly by its program or its manifestos. The party image was formed in the Depression and very largely retained throughout its history. The CCF tried to solidify its ties with labour but it did not become a labour party, initially because of the division in the Canadian labour movement. When it did move into union in 1960 the union was incomplete; labour support was only partial and the popular image of organized labour was not much more advantageous to the party. Its attempt to build a broad base was constantly hampered by the militants within it, whose activities fostered the popular view of the CCF as a haven for revolutionaries and, after the war, for Communists and fellow travellers.[100] These same people resented and resisted the encroachment of organized labour on their preserve for this reduced their range of action, limited their ability to sway the party, and introduced the unwelcome machinery of bureaucracy.[101]

In another sense it could be said that in changing its policy the CCF was merely re-thinking the means whereby the socialist end or ethic could be achieved.[102] There is some truth in this argument. But in re-thinking the policy the party leaders were re-thinking it within the framework of a party rather than of a movement. The means they sought to achieve the socialist ends of co-operation, fellowship, and equality were, as it turned out, means which were consistent with the developing status quo – with the mixed economy. The CCF party could not attack competition as immoral while defending the mixed economy; it could not appeal for middle-class support while condemning middle-class values. The party leaders struggled to build a party which did not repudiate the ideology of the movement. The resulting tension explains such phenomena as the unbridled vehemence of

100 / See for example the articles signed "M. F. B." in the *Winnipeg Free Press* for Aug. 19, 20, 21, 1948; in which the left-wing members of the CCF (Dorothy Steeves, Harold Winch, Colin Cameron, etc.) are referred to *ad nauseam* as "travellers" and "fellow travellers." A cartoon in the same paper (Aug. 19) describes Tim Buck, the Communist leader, as being "Well to the rear [of the CCF 'parade'] but catching up."
101 / Armstrong, "Development, Trade Union Activity," 90 ff.
102 / F. H. Underhill, *In Search of Canadian Liberalism*, 223–6.

the election campaign of 1957 in which the CCF depicted business as causing misery and hardship to "John and Jane Public" who, the comic strip showed, lived in a shack with twins but no washer or other conveniences – such as chairs.

As the CCF re-thought its program to take into consideration the post-Keynesian revolution and the advent of the mixed economy, it ran the risk of losing its *raison d'être* as a party, for it appeared that the Liberals could do almost as much in the field of welfare and were probably better equipped to manage a mixed economy. The movement, however, maintained its *raison d'être* by pointing to the fact that poverty, inequality, injustice, and greed still existed in Canada. There was no evidence that the mixed economy was any closer to the situation where "the principle regulating production, distribution and exchange will be the supplying of human needs and not the making of profits." Hence the more doctrinaire could ask "why abandon the Regina Manifesto?" The Winnipeg Declaration did imply a change of ends in that private profit and corporate power were not to disappear as much as they were to be subordinate to social planning. The exegesis of the two documents serves a useful purpose because both have the internal inconsistencies that reflect the ambilvalence or schizophrenia of socialism in Canada.

The development of the CCF program and ideology demonstrates the struggle within the movement to establish the party and the belief of the party leaders that the CCF's failure was somehow due to a failure to make the socialist message register. To overcome this deficiency they tried to accentuate those aspects of CCF policy that promised more property for more people. They reshaped and changed their policy to make it more consistent with contemporary socialist thought and with the middle-class attitudes and values that predominated in the Canadian electorate. It was an attempt to make the message more meaningful while avoiding any dilution of the ultimate ends of socialism. They found they could dispense with social ownership and at the same time retain their moral convictions about the inherently evil nature of capitalism. Their liberalism kept them from being communists while their socialism prevented them from becoming liberals.

6

ORGANIZATION AND STRUCTURE

No matter what the form of government the
universal fact is the rule of the many by the few.

GAETANO MOSCA
The Ruling Class

The ruling elite of a political party, regardless of its make-up, does not have absolute control. It cannot act with indifference toward the multitude of factors that are operative within the context of its particular political universe. All parties are not the same, however. In some the leaders have more authority, in others they have less. The variables which affect the leaders and determine the nature of their control are diverse and include the personality of the individual or individuals holding positions of leadership, the nature of the party's ideology, the extent and attitude of its membership, and the constitution of the party. The extent to which control varies from party to party is largely a matter of degree: no party leader is absolute; no party rank and file has complete authority. And the extent of control varies within a single party from time to time as the party faces the exigencies of political warfare.

Mosca's statement is a truism unless anarchy can be described as a form of government. It was a truism ignored by the Progressives, who refused to accept the limitations implied by party structure and disintegrated as a result. The paraphernalia of direct democracy so dear to the hearts of agrarian reformers merely substituted one ruling group for another. The use of the recall meant that the local constituency committee or local party leaders took the place of the party caucus – the few were still making decisions for the many. The "old line" Liberal and Conservative parties are ruled by an elite and make no provision for real membership control of policy, allowing participation only in the selection of a new leader.[1] But in neither case is leadership exercised in isolation. The leaders must anticipate the reaction to their decisions of their immediate colleagues, the provincial sections of the party, and the rank and file. This consciousness of the pressures exerted by the party structure in its formal and informal aspects produces a kind of lop-sided democracy. The successful leaders in this context are those who are able not only to sense the pressures but to predict them for any given act or policy. The members of the party may not always get what they want, but the leader seldom has his own way either. If a party is not a mass membership party and places a low value on political activism, the leaders' constituency is a narrow one indeed and more freedom of action results. But the outer limits remain and the leaders' consciousness of these determines the success of their stewardship.

The CCF has been described as a party with a democratic structure that enabled the members to make policy and select

1 / See Porter, *The Vertical Mosaic*, 373–85 and ch. 13.

their leaders.[2] The official view the CCF had of itself corresponded
with this picture and much time and effort were devoted to ex-
pounding the theme of membership democracy. It is true that
the constitution and ethos of the party reflected a belief in the
rightness and efficacy of the democratic process. When the party
had little to offer the electorate in the way of seats in Parliament,
it always had this belief to set it above the other parties.

The interesting thing about the CCF in this respect is not the
degree to which its structure was more democratic than other
parties', but that the structure made possible a degree of leadership control and manipulation which, given the nature of party
factions, would not have been possible in any other kind of structure. Under any other kind of structure the party would have
simply blown apart; the techniques of democracy and the firm
direction of the leaders kept it together. It is also true that the
democratic constitution, providing regular opportunities for some
members to attack the leadership and for others to raise the
banners of Marxist socialism to public view, weakened the party
and threatened on more than one occasion to reduce it to little
more than a national forum of dissent. The nature of the CCF as
a political movement with a mass membership base and a well-
developed and articulated structure provided both opportunities
and the necessity for control by the leaders that was, in some
respects, inconsistent with the democratic theme of the constitution. The CCF provided an example of the operation of Michels'
Iron Law of Oligarchy.[3]

On the assumption that the prime function of a political party
as organization is to win elections – the other functions such as
finding candidates and developing platforms are generated by
the prime function – then it follows that its structure will reflect
and further this end. If one were constructing a party, one would
design its organization in such a way as to make it an effective
electoral machine. In most democratic states the make-up of the
political parties tends to be fairly uniform; a party will resemble
its competitors because party competition tends to produce the
optimum machinery.

Variations in party organization stem from functions performed by the party that are not generated by the prime function.
Its structure will reflect purposes that are additional to that of
winning elections and may not even be connected with it. The
CCF started as a federation of movements and party-movements

2 / Dawson, *Government of Canada* (Toronto 1957), 514–16; and
Corry, *Democratic Government* (Toronto 1951), 262.
3 / Robert Michels, *Political Parties* (New York 1959).

and came to see itself as a single movement. Because it was a Organization and Structure
movement with agrarian anti-party and non-partisan antecedents,
its founders took pains to eschew features of the "old line" parties
they abhorred and deliberately set out to construct a unique instrument which shared only one recognizable feature with its
competitors – an ambition for government – but even that was
tempered with a passion for a cause that enabled members and
leaders alike to view politics as a kind of Pilgrim's Progress.

The constitution of the CCF was not an instrument to be used
in forging a political party; it was more a declaration of faith in
the procedures of democracy.[4] It was designed to ensure that the
new party would be free from the disabilities of the old ones.
Part of the constitution's purpose was the demonstration of effective internal democracy in the face of the autocratic and elitist
Liberal and Conservative parties. Democracy in the CCF was an
end in itself; its own justification.

The democratic structure of the CCF was retained without ever
being seriously questioned or reformed, not because it was shown
that it enabled the party to achieve power, but because it reflected
the faith of the members and was a demonstration of democracy
at work that satisfied them. It was as well a splendid advertise-
ment of the party's *bona fides* as the true party of democracy. It
was never seen as an impediment, largely because it was seldom
seen as a means but always as an end in itself. Socialism and
democracy were inseparable in society and in the party.

The CCF did not originate as a centrally directed and controlled
political party but as a confederation whose object, according to
the second article of the constitution, was "to co-ordinate the
activities of the member organizations in order to promote
through political action and other appropriate means, the establishment in Canada of a Co-operative Commonwealth ... "[5] The
third article of the 1933 Constitution defined the membership in
the federation as follows: "Membership in the Federation shall
consist of approved provincial organizations which accept the
Co-operative Commonwealth Federation Programme." More
specifically the approved organizations were those which founded
the CCF and therefore endorsed the 1932 eight-point program
and the 1933 Manifesto. The *Alberta Labour News* was quite
explicit on this point:

the CCF is not an amalgamation of the groups which compose it. It

4 / The fact that it was designed at the time of the party's formation
sets it apart from the constitutions of the Liberal and Conservative parties,
which produced theirs as an *ex post facto* rationale for their structure.
5 / CCF Constitution, 1933.

is a federation of those groups for the single purpose of achieving the major objective of them all which is to establish by constitutional methods a Socialist order of society.

The purpose of the federation is the co-operation of affiliated groups throughout Canada to gain political power to consumate the social and economic objectives of the affiliated groups.[6]

There was no individual membership in the CCF as such at this time, only membership in those groups that were affiliated with the CCF. For Woodsworth the idea of federation was important. He wrote in October 1933, "we must preserve the fundamental principle that each affiliated organization has the right to preserve its own identity."[7] He went on in the same letter to emphasise the determination of the UFA and the Manitoba ILP not to be submerged. The initial structure of the party, as it was drafted, was in fact a confederation. The national party was to be nothing more than the sum of its constituent parts – the co-ordinating agency. As will be discussed below, before the party was more than two years old, the fact did not conform to the letter. The CCF became more centralized and more "federal."

Woodsworth's comments make it clear that the CCF could only have been established on a basis that preserved the identity of the constituent groups. For this reason individuals could not join the CCF as such; they had to join one of the affiliated bodies or establish a club and apply to the provincial section for affiliation. This restriction of entry to provincial sections, however, also effectively prevented any national body from affiliating. Had the 1933 constitution permitted national affiliations it is likely that the Canadian Brotherhood of Railway Employees would have joined, thereby producing far-reaching effects on subsequent CCF-trade union relations.[8]

The confederated structure of the party was also indicative of the anxiety of the founding groups to avoid establishing a party that would have a centralized organization of the kind they associated with the Liberal and Conservative parties. By preserving the indigenous nature of the movement and, they thought, preventing the accretion of power at the centre, the CCF constitution would provide the kind of constituent democracy that Canadian politics had lacked. The letter of the law was the logical outcome of a party formed by members who had learned their theory in the context of the group government ideas of Henry Wise Wood and the notions of co-operative fellowship of British socialism

6 / *Alberta Labour News*, Aug. 6, 13, 1932.
7 / J. S. Woodsworth to Arthur Mould, Oct. 2, 1933, CCFP.
8 / See McNaught, *A Prophet*, 261.

and the Social Gospel. In addition, the hostility of the founding members to established order dictated this kind of approach. And, finally, the great diversity of viewpoint and objective among the founding groups made some kind of federal structure inevitable. Lewis and Scott underline this factor in their chapter on the formation of the CCF:

There was unavoidable suspicion and strangeness. There were provincial parties which had achieved some political success and were determined to retain their identity. There were differences of social philosophy, ranging all the way from pure reformism to doctrinaire socialism. Every group brought its particular approach.[9]

There were thirteen affiliated groups across the country, each attached to the particular provincial section and through it to the national party. Some, such as the Ontario Labour Conference, were themselves a federation of still smaller groups – in this case of various labour parties. The prairie provinces were well covered by the existing parties or coalitions of parties and organizations such as the Saskatchewan Farmer-Labour party, but in British Columbia, Ontario, and Quebec, clubs had to be set up to accommodate those who did not belong to any established party or organization. As Woodsworth pointed out, "The CCF Clubs were organized simply as a third group which, together with Farmer and Labour, would constitute the federation ... "[10] Originating as a convenience, the clubs were to remain a thorn in the flesh of the party throughout its history for, as could be expected, they developed an identity of their own and tended to attract as members those who were either more middle class or more doctrinaire than members in other affiliated groups. In Ontario, many became cells of ideologues who more often than not split the party with their doctrinal quarrels.[11]

As the constituent parties at the provincial level – the ILP and Saskatchewan Farmer-Labour party, for example – faded away; their place was taken by CCF constituency associations. Despite the fact that the disappearance of these founding groups removed the need for the clubs, they, for the most part, remained. By 1943, there were three classes of members in the CCF, all with the same rights as far as the organs of the national body were concerned: club members, members-at-large attached to constituency associations, and members of affiliated trade unions. One distinction that was made, with the example of the British Labour party in mind, was that affiliated trade unions did not have a

9 / *Make This* YOUR *Canada*, 119.
10 / J. S. Woodsworth to John Mitchell, March 31, 1933, CCFP.
11 / See Zakuta, *A Protest Movement Becalmed*, 46–7.

block vote and were entitled to fewer convention delegates per total membership than either clubs or constituency associations.[12]

Although the purpose of the national body was to co-ordinate the activities of the groups at the base, it soon developed an identity and purpose of its own, quite distinct from the activities of the various provincial groups, whose main concern was provincial politics. In Woodsworth's view, the national CCF was the creation of the federation process and while its members belonged through the provincial bodies, it was quite properly a distinct entity.[13] The federal nature of the CCF meant that the party developed as the Liberal and Conservative parties had developed. The provincial sections quickly became provincial parties with a life and purpose of their own within the province and the national party followed suit. The national CCF did not co-ordinate the activities of the provincial parties; it went about the business of a national party in much the same way as the national Liberal and Conservative parties. What co-ordination and intervention in provincial affairs there was occurred during the early years when the proliferation of elements at the base in the provinces necessitated direction from the national body. In 1934 dissension in the Ontario section necessitated swift and decisive national intervention and the complete reorganization of the provincial party to a design approved by the national officers. The incident is noteworthy because it illustrates the authority the national party had and one major instance of its use. After 1935 there was little interference or direction of provincial parties by the national party – except when provincial activities interfered with the activities of the Ottawa-based CCF.

The CCF had from the very beginning decided to have nothing to do with the Communist party or any of its front organizations such as the Canadian Labor Defense League.[14] There were, however, many people in the CCF clubs and the various labour parties who were sympathetic either to the Communist party or, what amounted to the same thing, to the cause of labour unity.[15] The United Farmers of Ontario, on the other hand, were nervous of even Fabian socialists and were only conditionally affiliated to the CCF. The indictment under section 98 of the Criminal Code of A. E. Smith, secretary of the Labor Defence League, split the Ontario CCF on the question of how much support should be given to the protests over this action. A number of CCF members

12 / See CCF Constitution, 1942, article 3; D. Lewis to King Gordon, March 10, 1943, CCFP. No more than ten delegates per affiliated union were permitted.
13 / J. S. Woodsworth to N. F. Priestley, May 25, 1934, CCFP.
14 / "Official Statement," July 22, 1933, CCFP.
15 / See ch. 9 below.

joined Smith in a public protest. The Ontario Provincial Council passed a resolution forbidding participation in such protest meetings by CCF members. The following night Smith attacked the CCF from the stage of Massey Hall in Toronto, several CCF members being on the platform with him. A member of the Ontario Labour Conference denounced the provincial council ruling in an address to a club. The Ontario Association of CCF Clubs met and called upon the national council to expel the Labour Conference. The national council ruled that there would have to be a provincial council meeting, which there was and which ended in deadlock. The UFO then withdrew from the CCF, as did Elmore Philpott, a key figure in Ontario and president of the Association of CCF Clubs. Woodsworth suspended the Ontario CCF's provincial constitution and, with the help of Graham Spry and Angus MacInnis, proceeded to reorganize the CCF in Ontario, although he had no formal authority to do so.[16]

The reorganization abolished the Labour Conference and the Association of Clubs; labour parties and clubs were to affiliate with the Ontario CCF on an individual basis.[17] These gradually gave way to constituency associations and a few clubs. The Ontario section became a centrally controlled body as the provincial executive assumed functions previously held by the intermediate bodies and became the sole channel of communication between associations and clubs.

The 1934 national convention found the CCF with 59 branches of the Socialist Party of Canada in British Columbia, as well as 154 clubs; 11,000 locals of the UFA, Canadian Labour party, and Economic Reconstruction Clubs in Alberta; a Farmer Labour party in Saskatchewan; locals of the ILP, Social Reconstruction Clubs, and a farmer section in Manitoba; a few clubs in the Maritimes and Quebec, and some 1,600 members in Ontario.[18] By 1937 only Manitoba and Alberta had a federal structure; elsewhere the provincial organization was unitary, based on the constituency association and clubs.[19]

As this development strengthened the provincial councils and executives, the consolidation of the provincial parties enhanced the independence and authority of the national party. It was not an agency of the provincial parties; it was a separate party, ad-

16 / See the "circulars" to the CCF Clubs from D. M. LeBourdais, Feb. 27, and March 12, 1934, CCFP. See also the correspondence between Graham Spry and Frank Scott of March 8, 12, 20, 1934, Scott Papers; and McNaught, *A Prophet*, 266.

17 / See the correspondence from J. S. Woodsworth to N. F. Priestley, Feb. 26, March 6, 13, 19; April 16, 23; May 25, 1934, CCFP.

18 / Report of Second National Convention (1934); and see Zakuta, *A Protest Movement Becalmed*, 44.

19 / Report of the Fourth National Convention (1937).

mittedly sharing personnel but separate and with superogatory
powers which it could exercise if necessary. The constitution of
the party provided that the national convention was the supreme
governing body. The national council was to direct the party's
affairs between conventions,[20] which were annual until 1938 and
then biennial. The council was to keep provincial councils informed and consult with them before making major policy decisions.[21] This proviso in practice was only a means of keeping
the provincial sections in touch with executive activity, for the
council seldom met more than twice a year, was too large to be
effective if all delegates attended, and, more often than not, was
somewhat less than representative since not all delegates could
find the time or the money necessary to cover expenses of a
weekend in Ottawa.[22]

The council was chosen initially by the national convention
and was composed of three members from each province chosen
by that province's delegation at the convention, plus the members
of the national executive, giving a total of 39 members.[23] This
procedure was later changed to provide for the election of council delegates by the respective provincial conventions.[24] Until
1937, the council elected the party officers from among its numbers with the exception of the national chairman, who was elected by the convention.

From the beginning, the party officers considered themselves
charged with the responsibility of initiating party policy. The
preparation of the Regina Manifesto by a committee of the LSR
was the result of decisions taken by what was essentially an
executive committee set up by the Calgary convention in 1932.
Resolutions before conventions that dealt with major national,
international and, occasionally, provincial crises came almost
without exception from the council, which had them supplied
ready-made by the national executive.[25]

The executive was the real centre of power in the party. It
consisted of the national president, the national chairman, two
vice-chairmen, the treasurer, the secretary, and six additional
members. The dominant influence of this body was a natural de-

20 / CCF Constitution, 1933, articles 7, 8.
21 / Report of the Fifth National Convention (1938); see also amendments made at the 1942 and 1946 national conventions.
22 / Report of the Seventh National Convention (1940). As Lewis
pointed out, the cost of bringing delegates to Ottawa prevented more
frequent meetings of the national council.
23 / CCF Constitution, 1933, article 6.
24 / Report of Third National Convention (1936).
25 / For example, the resolutions dealing with the draft election
manifesto of 1937, the Manitoba coalition in 1940, and the 1942 policy
statement "For Victory and Reconstruction."

velopment. It was charged with the administration of the CCF between meetings of the council, its decisions being subject to council ratification. Its meetings were frequent, and even more frequent were the meetings of the officers of the party, the president, chairman, vice-chairmen, treasurer, and secretary.[26] Since a quorum was six the officers often constituted the national executive among themselves.[27] The executive met in Ottawa at the national headquarters and was, therefore, in constant contact with the centre of national politics and with the national party staff.

Woodsworth had opposed the development of a central party office in Ottawa and the appointment of full-time party officials. He was concerned about the cost and felt that more valuable work could be done on the hustings: "Then again there is the whole question of centralization. I recognize a good deal can be done at Ottawa, but at this stage of development it seems to me most of our energy put into a central office is apt to draw from the various localities where money and energy are much needed."[28] Coldwell, national chairman at this time, was insistent. Earlier, in 1935, he had written to Woodsworth complaining of the lack of co-operation that he, as national secretary, had been getting from the constituent bodies. He wrote: "I feel very strongly that we have to unify our national efforts. I have been national secretary for nearly a year and responses to our communications have been very disappointing."[29] The following year Coldwell wrote to E. J. Garland, the newly appointed national organizer,[30] pointing out the need for better organization:

At the present time the movement consists of a number of independent and quite largely inactive provincial organizations. The lack of direction from the national point of view is, I believe, largely responsible for the chaotic condition of the CCF picture throughout Canada. This is not the fault of any person or persons either in the national

26 / See the reports of the national secretary in the national convention reports: for example in 1942 the council met 3 times, the executive 6 times; in 1940 the council 3, the executive 17; in 1950 the council 6 and the executive 15. No record of the meetings was kept.

27 / CCF Constitution, 1946, article 8.

28 / J. S. Woodsworth to M. J. Coldwell, Sept. 9, 1938, CCFP. In an interview with the author, Frank Scott pointed out that Woodsworth wanted to establish a crusading movement and felt that a salaried official would destroy the idea of voluntary assistance, and that if that happened all would be lost.

29 / M. J. Coldwell to J. S. Woodsworth, Oct. 18, 1935, CCFP. See also the letter from M. J. Coldwell to G. H. Williams, in which he refers to the "lack of cohesion in the national movement," Oct. 26, 1936, CCFP.

30 / Garland performed prodigious feats as organizer; in 1937 he held 282 meetings at an average cost, including travel, of $2.80 per meeting. Report of Fifth National Convention (1938).

organization or in the provincial councils. It is due wholly, in my
opinion, to the fact that we have never had either a national office or a
national organizing official ...[31]

Coldwell's view was supported by Frank Underhill, who wrote in
the *Canadian Forum* that the lack of a "strong, well-organized
central office"[32] was a major weakness in the CCF. In September
1938, when Lewis was anxious to become national secretary on
a full-time basis, Coldwell replied to Woodsworth's letter, indicating that the need for central control was urgent:

You fear that our movement may become too centralized. I am not
afraid of that. Indeed, we are in the same position as the Dominion
itself with loosely associated units duplicating and multiplying activities that ought to be national in scope ... Unless the movement shows
that it really is in earnest, I personally, do not choose to remain as its
national chairman for I do not agree at all with the present lack of
policy in regard to National Office matters.[33]

Coldwell was successful and Lewis assumed full-time responsibilities in rather spartan office space donated by the law firm with
which he had articled.

The process of national centralization was recognized at the
1938 national convention when the original confederational structure was abandoned in favour of one similar to the federal organization of Canada: a national CCF with provincial sections,
joined in a federal structure.[34] The party constitution was amended at the national convention in 1940 to give the national council more authority in the provincial sphere where provincial
activities affected other provinces or the national party. At the
same convention it was decided that any conflicts between the
national and provincial bodies would be resolved in favour of the
national body.[35] In 1943 provincial offices were instructed to
send the national office copies of their executive and council
minutes and of "every piece of literature ... as soon as it is published."[36] By 1944 the process had progressed to the point where
it was possible for the national secretary to feel that he could
advise the leader of the Saskatchewan party as to who should be
hired or fired in the establishment of the first CCF government
in that province.[37]

31 / M. J. Coldwell to E. J. Garland, Dec. 11, 1936, CCFP.
32 / "The CCF Takes Stock," XVI (Aug. 1936), 10.
33 / M. J. Coldwell to J. S. Woodsworth, Sept. 12, 1938, CCFP.
34 / Report of Fifth National Convention (1938).
35 / Report of Sixth National Convention (1940); and see also D.
Lewis to E. Roper, Nov. 23, 1940, CCFP.
36 / National Council Minutes, Jan. 30–1, 1943, CCFP.
37 / D. Lewis to T. C. Douglas, June 21, 1944, CCFP, and see n. 95
below.

A significant step was taken in 1946 when the national membership fee was introduced. Financing previously had been by provincial quota, a haphazard method at best.[38] With a single national membership the financial dependence of the national party on the provincial sections was removed. The national office thus had a ready check on the state of membership in every province and could allocate its resources more effectively. The self-sufficiency of the centre which this situation produced created a sense of unity under a single directing body.

Several decisions taken by the 1950 national convention helped centralize party control. The national executive had undertaken to chastise and correct provincial party newspapers for editorials considered to be inconsistent with the party's policy or with what the executive considered the party's interests.[39] This move was ratified by the national convention in 1950:

Therefore be it resolved that the convention requests provincial councils and executives to take all necessary measures to ensure that editorial policy in CCF provincial papers express national and provincial policy, and
Be it further resolved that this convention instructs the national executive to draw to the attention of provincial bodies any failures by provincial papers to observe this policy.[40]

The same convention passed an amendment to the constitution which gave the national council the power to take disciplinary action "where the interests of the National Movement are involved" and where the provincial section in question has "failed to take appropriate action."[41] In both cases the resolutions originated with the national executive through the national council. In 1952 the Council agreed that election programs should be drafted by the national executive rather than prepared far enough in advance for convention aproval, but too far for campaign strategy.[42] The inter-provincial conferences which were held every two years from 1943 to 1952, although designed to provide contact between provincial sections as such and between sections and the national office, had the effect of co-ordinating policy under central direction and subjecting the provincial officials to the direct influence of the national officials. The presence at these conferences of David Lewis and Frank Scott, for ex-

38 / Report of the Ninth National Convention (1946); Frank Scott said in an interview with the author that this was one of the most significant developments in the party's history.
39 / National Executive Minutes, April 20, 1947, CCFP.
40 / Report of the Eleventh National Convention (1950).
41 / *Ibid.*
42 / National Council Minutes, March 1–2, 1952, CCFP.

ample, served to demonstrate the pre-eminence of the national
movement.

The CCF was constantly concerned with organization, partly
for the obvious reason that the national party had to establish its
network throughout the country. E. J. Garland was the first full-
time organizer in the field. He was assisted by CCF MPs when
they were free to travel, since it was party policy that MPs were
full-time servants of the movement, contributing a percentage of
their income annually and virtually all of their free time for
meetings and speeches.[43] William Irvine became organizer following Garland's departure; he was succeeded by Grant MacNeil
and later by Donald MacDonald. The provincial sections em-
ployed their own organizers, but the senior men in the field were
those from Ottawa.

As the CCF came more and more to assume the role of a political party under the leadership of Lewis and Coldwell, there was
greater stress on unity. Unity was provided by the factors already
mentioned and also by other less concrete factors such as frequent tours by the party leader and party secretary, the national
membership bulletin *Across Canada*, and the research journal
News Comment. The nature of the party was such that discussion
was important and therefore the most able and intelligent members, those with expertise in discussion, assumed and retained
positions of prominence. Equally important was the fact that the
party was a mass membership party – in nature if not in actual
numbers – and one which assumed a high level of membership
activity in all phases of party life. As Michels has pointed out,
this inevitably produces heightened power at the centre.[44] In such
a party those prepared to become active automatically establish
themselves as leading figures by virtue of their willingness to
assume party responsibilities.

A major portion of party activity was directed toward getting
and keeping members:

But to the CCF, membership is the basis of the entire organization ...
we organize our CCF members into local committees, units, clubs,
study groups, discussion groups, in every community, and from every
occupation. And these groups are organized, not only, nor even
mainly, for work at elections. They are organized as living instruments
of democracy. Through them CCF members learn collectively about
the economics and social problems of our country and of the world;

43 / Transcript of interview, Chris Higginbotham with T. C. Douglas,
Sept. 1958, 138; copy in possession of the author.
44 / Michels, *Political Parties*, 32.

they learn how to work together for a common purpose, how to govern themselves, and how to defend their rights together.[45]

This activity was thoroughly in keeping with the nature of the CCF *qua* movement – and consistent with this kind of party in Duverger's typology[46] – and, as discussed by Lipset in his study of the CCF in Saskatchewan, was the basis of the party's success in that province.

The mass membership base posed problems from a structural viewpoint. It meant that the party devoted a great deal of time and money to finding things for the members to do and on membership education. Dependent as it was upon membership contributions of money and time, at least until the fifties when trade union contributions increased, members had to be found and kept. It was not difficult to sustain this kind of organization in Saskatchewan, but elsewhere there was not the same social basis for it. It assumed a high level of political orientation and interest on the part of a large portion of the Canadian population, and yet the only evidence for the assumption was the interest shown in the West during the twenties and thirties. Only those people who were prepared to involve themselves wholeheartedly in politics became active CCF members and these people were not, as a rule, typical of the Canadian electorate except in Saskatchewan. The Saskatchewan conventions have been described as "a representative gathering of the province" and those in Manitoba and Ontario – and one could add British Columbia – as more "like meetings of special interest groups, sprinkled with malcontents and radicals ... "[47]

When it appeared that the CCF was going to win power, people attached themselves to it and swelled its ranks, but when the bubble burst, they rapidly disappeared. Zakuta underlines this factor, pointing out that for many people, the prospect of victory produces adhesion to the party, but when this prospect evaporates, they depart.[48] Equally damaging to a party that relied upon membership for its life was the fact that, in urban society particularly, and in post-war agrarian society in general, there was more to do and consequently less willingness to become involved in politics, especially when there were relatively few elections.

45 / Script for broadcast, "The Nation's Business," David Lewis, Oct. 8, 1947, CFFP.

46 / Duverger, *Political Parties: Their Organization and Activity in the Modern State*, 23–7.

47 / F. C. Engelmann, "The Cooperative Commonwealth Federation of Canada; A Study of Membership Participation in Policy Making." Unpubl. PHD thesis (Yale 1954), 79.

48 / Zakuta, *A Protest Movement Becalmed*, 82 ff.

In Canada, unlike the United States, when one election was over
the next seemed a long way off. Victory was always a receding
factor. Even the tried and true became tired. As Lewis pointed
out in 1948, "The real problem is that large sections of our
movement are no longer working as hard as they did, mainly
because they have worked very hard for so many years that they
have become a little tired."[49] In post-war Canada, political clubs
or constituency associations were not significant social nuclei but
the CCF was built on the assumption that they were. The nature
of the party demanded the kind of commitment that required the
basic units to be viable social groups. Fred Zaplitny, MP for
Dauphin, summed up the problem in a letter to Lewis in 1946:

> The turnover in membership in our party is terrific. We get people to
> join, but we don't seem to be able to keep them joined. We have to
> admit that the apathey [sic] and inertia in our ranks has been particu-
> larly bad in the past two years. Part of our recession can be written off
> as election weariness, part of it, perhaps as the effect of the Trestrails,
> but we must face the fact that the dynamic which put us into the
> Major League three years ago appears to have petered out.[50]

In his report to the national council in April 1948, Lewis concluded that the party had made little progress since 1945. It was,
he felt, largely the result of member apathy.[51]

Heightened activity by the central office and an increase in the
number of "professionals" seemed to make little difference. As
the party became more centralized and its members less active,
the size of the bureaucracy increased. A librarian, a research
director, and an education and information secretary were added
during the period 1944–50. The additions made little impact on
the party's electoral fortunes because their activities were directed
toward serving existing members and the parliamentary caucus.
In any case, an increase in the number of members did not necessarily produce an increase in votes and what kept the clubs and
constituencies busy did not necessarily add to the number of
members or CCF voters.

It was a dilemma because the party was financed for the most
part by membership dues; consequently the number of members
had to be maintained or increased. To hold members, it was
believed that the party had to provide them with educational material and general party literature to extend their knowledge of
socialism and keep them involved in the cause. Membership

49 / D. Lewis to Ralph Bell, Feb. 21, 1948, CCFP.
50 / F. Zaplitny to D. Lewis, Dec. 24, 1946, CCFP.
51 / National Council Minutes, April 20, 1948, CCFP.

could not be casual. Yet the effort and expense directed toward
servicing the membership diverted resources that would have
been better spent fighting elections or hiring organizers between
elections. The CCF depended upon its membership base to stay
alive but the nature of membership, involving as it did a commitment to the movement, effectively prevented its growth. The
movement aspect provided a body of dedicated members who
would work unstintingly for the party on the hustings; it also
precluded people from offering the kind of casual membership
typical of the other parties. The problem was solved when the
trade unions became more closely associated with the party –
they provided large sums of money on request and asked little in
the way of literature in return.

By the forties, even the dedicated party members found less
relevance in the kind of activity associated with the party during
the Depression. There were frequent appeals to members to participate in the "daily struggle," but the leadership realized that
such appeals had little effect. So too the role of the party membership in policy-making declined. The party officers accepted
this as inevitable; members could hardly be expected to play a
significant role in policy-making unless they devoted considerable
time and effort to national affairs. Recognition of this fact was
indicated at the meeting of the CCF Interprovincial Conference
in 1944: "the rank and file simply cannot be doing their ordinary
full time job and still expect to keep up on everything that is
being done in parliament or the legislature, much less be con-
sulted on every step by the elected MLA's."[52] By implication, the
same rank and file could not be expected to generate policy for
the party at provincial or national conventions. Their role was
tacitly accepted as one of ratification of executive action. Resolutions submitted to conventions by constituency associations
were often ill-conceived and hastily drafted. Increasingly they
were the work of the zealots, malcontents, or radicals in the party
who were prepared to devote the time to constituency activities
that invariably earns them office in the constituency mainly because they are always there and willing. Outside Saskatchewan
policy-making in the party at the national and provincial levels
was confined to the party officers and the militants.[53] The spirit
of the movement embodied in the structure tended at times to
work against the party.

Nevertheless, it remained an article of faith that party policy

52 / CCF Interprovincial Conference Minutes, Dec. 28, Jan. 3, 1944–5,
CCFP.
53 / Engelmann thesis, 67. See n. 47.

was made at the national conventions. The basic principle was, as Engelmann has described it, "membership participation in policy making." It was a cardinal principle in party dogma:

It is my profound conviction that a political party which is in itself undemocratic – whether its policy is formulated by the large corporations as in the Liberal and Conservative Parties, or is controlled by a small clique at the top as in the Communist Party – can never build a really democratic society. In the one case we have political rights without economic justice, and in the other ostensible economic justice, certainly without political rights. Real democracy is a balanced combination of both these rights; either without the other is a negation of democracy. This is, I believe, a fundamental principle of the c.c.f. We apply this principle by safeguarding jealously the democratic processes inside our own movement.[54]

In the book for which Coldwell wrote the above, Lewis and Scott underlined this argument by pointing out that the CCF "builds its programme on a profound faith in the capacity for creative achievement by the people."[55] The same theme was reiterated in party pamphlets and election literature and was used as one of the major points in appealing to people to join the CCF.

In the original constitution representation at the party's national conventions was on the basis of the number of federal constituencies in the particular province. This was amended in 1940 to provide for the election of delegates by the constituency associations and to guarantee representation to provinces where the CCF was weak.[56] In 1946 this provision was amended to provide maximum and minimum representation on the basis of federal constituencies. Representation was also provided for affiliated organizations such as trade unions. The changes in the basis of representation at the conventions reflected the expansion of membership at the time. Such expansion indicated the success of the party in attracting more people to its ranks; it also restricted participation in the policy-making process at conventions. The time limit for speakers at the conventions mentioned above was one result.[57] Another was the increased influence of the leaders, whose experience made them more than a match for the new members.

Participation meant that party members were involved in the process of preparing resolutions in the constituency associations for presentation at the national conventions. Resolutions came

54 / M. J. Coldwell, "Introduction," Lewis and Scott, *Make This Your Canada,* vi–vii.
55 / Lewis and Scott, *Make This Your Canada,* 144.
56 / CCF *Constitution,* 1940, article 8.
57 / Report of the Fourth National Convention (1937).

from three sources primarily: the clubs and constituencies, provincial executives and councils, and the national executive and council. The national executive and council had the greatest record of success with their resolutions before conventions. Although party membership fluctuated, the number of resolutions submitted by constituencies and clubs increased steadily. In 1948, 54 of a total of 105 resolutions came from this source; in 1952 there were 69 such resolutions of a total of 107, and in 1956, 40 out of a total of 65 resolutions.[58] After 1944 all resolutions were processed by a resolutions committee appointed by the national executive prior to the convention.[59] The committee combined redundant resolutions, redrafted and rejected resolutions, and submitted its decisions to the convention for ratification. The services of the committee were essential, but resented by the rank and file who recognized it as a further limit on their participation in policy-making and as evidence of the growing dominance of the party "brass" in CCF affairs.

Even in the resolutions committee – which was carefully chosen as a rule to reflect regional and doctrinal variation in the party – there was a good deal more membership participation and control in the CCF than in the other political parties in Canada, although not quite as much as party propaganda made out.[60] The crucial policy decisions were those taken by the national executive or council or based on resolutions from those two bodies. It should be kept in mind that the people who sat on the executive and council were elected by the party membership. And if major policy decisions did not emanate directly from clubs and constituencies, resolutions from these sources provided party leaders with valuable insight into the feelings and attitudes of the party members and with useful guidelines for party direction. Decisions taken by the officers were naturally conditioned by their anticipation of convention reaction, which alone was an important restraint.

It would be difficult to defend the proposition that CCF members actually made and shaped party policy; this was the function of the party leaders. But it would be equally difficult to deny the vital role played by the membership in the process, if only by their mere presence and the leaders' consciousness of the democratic structure. The party leaders could not make policy decisions and public pronouncements with quite the same sense of

58 / Resolution books were published prior to each convention. In this regard it is interesting to note that the number of resolutions tended to increase as party fortunes declined. In 1944, 96 were submitted, in 1958, 200, CCFP.

59 / Report of the Eighth National Convention (1944).

60 / See R. M. Dawson, *Government of Canada*, 577–86.

impunity and power as could the leaders of an elitist or caucus party. Equally restrictive in this sense was the framework of the party ideology. It provided a guide for the leaders and a yardstick by which the members could measure official deviation.

The advantages of this kind of structure were both theoretical and practical. Theoretically, the CCF offered a demonstration of the relative viability of democratic party structure in a competitive electoral situation. Practically, the role of the member provided a proprietorial interest in the party and reinforced his commitment to the cause. It was satisfying to party members and leaders alike to acknowledge their innovation in a field where democracy of any kind was a curiosity. There may have been some propaganda advantages as well.

The disadvantages were those normally associated with the operation of democracy. The CCF was an anomaly on the political landscape. It amused and satisfied opposition press and parties to witness internecine squabbles being worked out in public on the floor of party conventions. They were quick to take advantage of the situation by publishing widely statements made by the more radical CCF'ers. The CCF leaders could not seize electoral advantage as readily as could the other parties if it involved any deviation from party policy or party principle. Honesty is not intrinsically disadvantageous, but in combat situations it is more advantageous as a tactic than as a principle. For the CCF, waging electoral war against Mackenzie King Liberals, it proved to be a liability on a number of occasions.

In the final analysis, despite the reciprocity between members and leaders in the CCF, the leaders did dominate. The party was ruled by a benevolent oligarchy that exerted more influence than the structure of the party implied. The nature of the CCF as a movement made this inevitable because in a movement the focus on the leader or leaders is greater than in a simple party. This naturally increases the responsibility of the leaders, but it also increases their power and influence. They stand for more than just the party; they stand for the ideals and the spirit of the movement as well.

From 1933 to 1961, the CCF had only two leaders. In the same period the Liberal party had three and the Conservative party five. There are a number of factors that explain this difference, the most obvious being the analysis of the tendency toward oligarchy advanced by Michels. Of equal importance is the fact that continuity in leadership was essential to enable the CCF to establish itself as a unified political movement. As discussed earlier, the ability of Woodsworth to represent the farmer, labour, and socialist groups was a key factor in pulling the CCF together

156

at the start and through the early years of the movement. He was, in many respects, the one essential ingredient that brought into a single movement the groups that made up the radical wing in Canadian politics in the thirties. His role was that of the charismatic leader.

A great deal has been written about the concept of charismatic leadership.[61] There seems little doubt that in the CCF Woodsworth was a charismatic leader, that is, one who has the special gifts Weber referred to when he elaborated the concept.[62] As Weber points out, the authority of such a leader is based on the devotion of the group members "to the specific and exceptional sanctity, heroism, or exemplary character of an individual person, and of the normative patterns or order revealed or ordained by him. ... "[63]

At the memorial service for Woodsworth in Vancouver, William Irvine said of him:

It was his supersensitiveness to the touch of another's pain which made his soul a flaming passion of protest against injustice and drove his frail body into prodigious dynamic action.

He not only had courage of a physical kind, the courage to face a hostile crowd, to become a longshoreman, to go to prison. But he had that courage expressed in lines which he himself quoted: the courage "to go on forever and fail, and go on again," the courage which enabled him to rest "with the half of a broken hope for a pillow at night."[64]

Bruce Hutchison wrote in the *Vancouver Sun*:

He was the most Christ-like man ever seen in Parliament, and his white beard, his flaming eye, his anger at injustice, his gentleness with everyone, and his deep booming voice of moral protest made him appear like a prophet out of the Old Testament ... He was the saint in our politics. Our politics and all men who knew him, gained a certain purity from his presence and lost a vehement flame in his passing.[65]

To his biographer, Kenneth McNaught, he was a prophet in politics.

61 / For example, K. J. Ratnam, "Charisma and Political Leadership," *Political Studies*, XII (1964); C. J. Friedrich, "Political Leadership and the Problem of Charismatic Power," *Journal of Politics*, XXIII (1961); J. J. Marcus, "Transcendence and Charisma," *Western Political Quarterly*, XIV (1961); and see A. Gouldner, ed., *Studies in Leadership* (New York 1950), *passim*; and Heberle, ch. 7.

62 / From *Max Weber*, H. H. Gerth and C. W. Mills, eds. (New York 1958), 245–50.

63 / Max Weber, *The Theory of Social and Economic Organization*, trans. H. Henderson and T. Parsons (New York 1947), 328.

64 / Grace MacInnis, *J. S. Woodsworth, A Man to Remember* (Toronto 1953), 319–20.

65 / *Ibid.*, 320.

Throughout his career, from his resignation from the church and his imprisonment during the Winnipeg General Strike, to his break with many of his followers over Canadian participation in the war, Woodsworth demonstrated a single-mindedness and devotion to principle that was consistent with the doctrines of the Social Gospel and the fundamentals of Christianity. Both before he entered the House of Commons and afterward, he gave the impression of a saint having descended into the market-place to put things right. For prairie farmers and the immigrant workers of North Winnipeg, he was one who practised what he preached, who advocated a society based on the principles of the Sermon on the Mount.

In that Woodsworth stood clearly for the ideals that economic and social conditions mocked, he assumed a place of predominance in the eyes of those anxiously seeking substitutes for a bleak existence. Leadership is to a great extent relative to the situation. It flourishes in a problem situation, the kind of role played by the leader being determined by the goals of the particular group in that situation. To lead the group, the individual must have prestige "and this he acquires by symbolizing the ideals of all members of the group."[66] Woodsworth exemplified the kind of life and the kind of society the farmers and members of the lower and dispossessed middle classes sought in the twenties and thirties. Powerless in themselves, they saw in Woodsworth the mobilization of ideals which seemed to promise solutions to their problems.

Woodsworth's reputation through his activities in the church, in the Non-Partisan League, in the Winnipeg Strike, and as a member of the House of Commons, established him as a man in harmony with the needs and anxieties of the farmer and the labouring groups. It has been said that "readiness for devotion to the leader is especially high when feelings of emptiness or discontent with drab trifles of daily living, or states of despair are prevalent."[67] Woodsworth's leadership was accepted and became a vital factor in the creation of the CCF because the time was ripe.

Woodsworth's life represented the triumph over adversity that was consistent with established Christian beliefs. His presence reassured the radicals that their activities were sanctified by the "saint in politics": their doubts were assuaged by Woodsworth's Protestant nobility. Woodsworth's daughter, the wife of Angus MacInnis, wrote in her biography of her father that "more than

66 / C. A. Gibb, "The Principles and Traits of Leadership," *Journal of Abstract and Social Psychology*, XLII (1947), 272.

67 / D. W. Abse and L. Jessner, "The Psychodynamic Aspects of Leadership," S. R. Graubard and G. Halton, eds., *Excellence and Leadership in a Democracy* (New York 1962), 77.

any other single individual of his day, J. S. Woodsworth represented leadership for the new moral force that was beginning to
shape itself within the Canadian community."[68] His "goodness,"
recognized by friend and foe alike, made it easier for his followers
to accept the stigma of being socialists in a capitalist society.

Woodsworth was a western leader: he had little following in
Ontario, and none to the east of that province. The existence of
a common problem and the presence of a stern Protestant morality shared in adversity gave the plains the right to introduce the
CCF. The psychology of the plains that emerges in the novels of
Sinclair Ross[69] is one which provides fertile soil for the kind of
leadership Woodsworth provided, based as it is on bourgeois
morality with its "crabbed Protestant view of sensuality and
emotion, emphasising strong patriarchal authority, a thriftness of
feeling as well as money, a harsh sense of duty and compulsive
restraint, order and methodicalness, enforced by a religious impulse which glorified work and an economic impulse for the
rational pursuit of money."[70] The plight of the prairie farmer, his
toil unrewarded, denied his just deserts, and the strong strain of
Protestant fundamentalism and the popularity of the Social Gospel[71] – which preached the rights of the poor against the rich and
damned the monopolies – combined to provide the background
against which the popularity of Woodsworth stands out.

He was not a stirring orator; being rather a humourless pedagogue with a mission, "a moral crusader."[72] His trademarks were
his striking physical appearance and a pointer and a roll of charts
which he used to explain the inequities and iniquities of the
capitalist system. Like William Aberhart in Alberta, Woodsworth was teaching about the wrongs of the existing system and
offering a solution. In Aberhart's case it was a call to return to
the fundamentals of the Bible and the system; in Woodsworth's
case it was a call to abandon the system and move to one more
consistent with the Christian ethic.

McNaught sees him as a natural "protestant," zealous reformer, puritan, and leader.[73] T. C. Douglas recalls him as a
complex disciplinarian:

Biographers tend to stress his gentleness and he was a very gentle man

68 / MacInnis, *J. S. Woodsworth*, 321.
69 / See, for example, *As For Me and My House* (Toronto 1957), or
the short story, "Cornet at Midnight," in Carlyle King, ed., *Saskatchewan
Harvest* (Toronto 1955).
70 / Daniel Bell, "Notes on Authoritarian and Democratic Leadership," in A. Gouldner, ed., *Studies in Leadership* (New York 1950), 405.
71 / See McNaught, *A Prophet*, chs. 1 and 4.
72 / Interviews with Frank Underhill and Frank Scott, July 1962.
73 / McNaught, *A Prophet*, 316.

but also a very firm man. He had all the complexity of the Methodist minister. Strict with his family, I don't mean by that tyrannical, but certainly strict, strict with himself, quite a disciplinarian, hard on himself as a matter of fact, but nevertheless very kindly.[74]

Grace MacInnis writes:

We children always felt that our father was different. Other children called their father "Daddy" and looked on him much as one of themselves, only older. We called ours "Father," and there was a shade of awe mixed with our affection for him. At home or a thousand miles away, he was the keystone of the family arch, the centre round whom we grouped our living. His dominant personality made it so. Furthermore, he was buttressed by Mother, who felt that this was the natural order of things.

Mother loved us children deeply, but we knew that Father came first, and we felt that that was only right.[75]

It might be stretching the evidence beyond the breaking point to argue that Woodsworth was an authoritarian leader although it does seem clear that this characterization would be more true of Woodsworth than Coldwell. On balance it would appear that Woodsworth fits Bell's description of the authoritarian character: "An authoritarian character does not lack courage or even initiative. But his actions are rooted in basic feelings of powerlessness that have to be overcome. Strength is won by leaning on a superior power or a call or a sense of duty."[76] It seems to be more than coincidence that the passages cited above and the biographical studies of Woodsworth lead to tentative conclusions that he fitted the pattern of authoritarian and charismatic leaders; that his life, with certain clear exceptions, fitted the pattern outlined by Gouldner: "Living largely by booty, and the gifts of followers, hostile to routine, to formal organization and, typically, to the obligations of family life, charismatic leadership is ephemeral in the extreme."[77]

Woodsworth did survive largely on the gifts of followers and what he received as an MP. Contemporaries report that he was unhappy in routine work – his career is itself ample evidence of this – and that he was opposed to formal organization, so much so that Frank Scott argues that Woodsworth clearly hindered the effective organization of the CCF as a political party with a central office.[78] When the establishment of a national office in

74 / Douglas-Higginbotham interview, 1962, 212.
75 / MacInnis, *J. S. Woodsworth*, 1.
76 / Bell in Gouldner, 406.
77 / A. Gouldner, "Types of Leaders, Bureaucrats and Agitators," in Gouldner, *Studies in Leadership*, 62–3.
78 / Interview with Frank Scott, July 1962.

Ottawa and the appointment of David Lewis as full-time national secretary was being discussed, Woodsworth indicated to Coldwell his general dislike of the project.[79] It may have been that in Ontario and Quebec the Woodsworth charisma and insistence on local activity instead of on central organization and machine building was inadequate. This was certainly the judgment of Scott, who wrote Lewis in the spring of 1934:

It is clear now that there will be no mass movement for some time. Bennett's progressive conservatism, with his central bank, agricultural marketing boards and Stevens inquiry, has revived the popular illusion of salvation through capitalist planning. The C.C.F. leaders are of the wrong type for the present situation, so we shall have to build slowly and painfully from these small beginnings that we have.[80]

In the West it was a different matter. There Woodsworth the social evangelist, the leader of a great moral crusade in the countryside and in Parliament, was in the prairie radical tradition. He stood for triumph over adversity. If leadership is always relative to the situation and if Gouldner's analysis of leadership has any validity, then west of the Lakehead Woodsworth was a person who emitted "group patterning stimuli."[81] He was a combination of the "patriarchal sovereign" and "Hero" in the typology devised by Fritz Redl: one who first of all integrates the members of a group,

because they incorporate the super-ego or conscience of the central person into their own. Wanting his approval, they adopt his standards of right and wrong. They thereby come to hold similar values and are able to orient themselves to each other,

and then secondly, who

integrates the group by encouraging the manifestation of socially approved action. The Hero's initiatory act is courageous, enabling other individuals to cast off their anxieties, and permitting them to take a stand in favour of approved values.[82]

During his life and after, Woodsworth was the embodiment of the CCF. His picture was part of the furniture of every CCF office and the party halls and offices were invariably named after him. His wife, when she was able, was present as a revered guest on the platform of the national conventions after his death. In the

79 / J. S. Woodsworth to M. J. Coldwell, Sept. 9, 1938, CCFP.
80 / Frank Scott to David Lewis, April 6, 1934, Scott Papers.
81 / A. Gouldner, "Introduction," in Gouldner, *Studies in Leadership*, 20; see also Gibb, "Principles and Traits of Leadership," 270–3.
82 / Fritz Redl, "Group Emotion and Leadership," *Psychiatry* (1942), cited in Gouldner, *Studies in Leadership*, 42.

presence of Woodsworth Houses, Woodsworth Halls, Woodsworth Clubs, Woodsworth Foundations, it is not an exaggeration
to suggest that the canonization of a leader, remarkable though
this one was, is consistent with the analysis of the charismatic
leader.[83]

It was Woodsworth who provided the focus and the direction
for the several protest movements in the West. The party that
developed was built on the foundation his presence had caused to
be laid. He was, by his nature and the nature of his position, unable to give his whole-hearted support to the development of a
centrally directed political party. The CCF that grew after 1937
was largely the work of M. J. Coldwell, David Lewis, Frank
Scott, and Angus MacInnis. After 1937 Woodsworth was only
titular leader of the party. The change in the structure of the
national executive that was made at the 1937 convention was a
recognition of Woodsworth's failing strength. In fact it merely
ratified a change that had taken place earlier, as Lewis noted in a
letter to Frank McKenzie:

By the Winnipeg Convention of 1937, many of us on the Executive
saw that it was impossible for Mr. Woodsworth to perform the functions of National Political Leader, as well as the functions of administrative head of the party. However, it was felt that we did not want to
deprive Mr. Woodsworth of the title of President and we therefore
created the new position of National Chairman, to perform the
function of administrative head.[84]

In the spring of 1938 Woodsworth suffered a stroke which impaired his sight. By then his role as leader in any active sense
was confined to Parliament, but he did remain the party's spiritual
leader.

The leadership of Lewis and Coldwell was to last until Coldwell's defeat in the 1957 election. Lewis continued as administrative and ideological leader of the party until the formation of
the New Democratic Party. The fact that the CCF held together
in 1939 despite the severe strain imposed upon it by the decision
to support the war effort is testimony both to the fact that it had
outgrown its need for Woodsworth as the central figure and that

83 / See Michels, *Political Parties*, "The masses experience a profound
need to prostrate themselves, not simply before great ideals, but also
before the individuals who in their eyes incorporate such ideals," 67.

84 / David Lewis to Frank McKenzie, April 30, 1950, CCFP. See also
M. J. Coldwell to David Lewis, Sept. 6, 1938, CCFP: "J. S. has had a
holiday and now he wants to be kept busy. Club lectures would suit him
but I am not sure of the wisdom of sending the *President* around
addressing little study groups and distributing literature. Still we must
keep him contented." Emphasis in the original. And see Lipset, *Agrarian
Socialism*, 152, and McNaught, *A Prophet*, 267.

it was more than a political movement. The structure of the party built by Lewis and Coldwell provided the permanence which the early movement lacked.

With Coldwell in the House of Commons to provide the parliamentary direction and the image of sound, intelligent, and progressive leadership, Lewis, by dint of prodigious energy, remarkable intelligence, and extraordinary persuasive oratory, was able to shape party structure and policy with remarkable freedom. It is difficult to exaggerate Coldwell's role in building the party at this stage; it is hardly possible to exaggerate that played by Lewis. There were others involved in the leadership of the party through the national executive; they were part of an informal caucus that was formed in 1933, grew with the party, and remained in the central position in the party throughout its life and into the life of the NDP. Partly because he was full-time and the others were not, partly because of the abilities already referred to, Lewis dominated this socialist elite, as he did the whole party.

Because the CCF was less a disorganized movement and more an organized party by 1939, Coldwell's position was clearly dissimilar to that of Woodsworth in the early period. Unlike Woodsworth, Coldwell had come through the administrative apparatus of the party, first as national secretary and then as national chairman. Much less the crusading social gospeler than his predecessor, Coldwell tended to be more a moderator than a leader. He had political sense and, save on matters of principle, was ready to strike a compromise. On matters of principle he was more a social reformer than a revolutionary. His experience was managerial, as a school principal, president and secretary-treasurer of the Canadian Teachers Federation, Regina alderman, and member of the hospital and library boards in that city.

Lewis was both more a doctrinaire socialist than Coldwell and more a politician in that he had a shrewd understanding of the realities of power and an awareness of where possible support for the CCF lay. He had, in addition, some skill in "man management." It was largely through his efforts that organized labour came to support the CCF as extensively as it did. From the beginning of 1938, when he became full-time national secretary, until July 1950, when he left that post to practise law, he was the centre of party affairs. After his retirement from the post of secretary, his election to the national executive enabled him to continue to exert more influence on party affairs than any other person in the party. The most cursory survey of the national office's files demonstrates the remarkable grasp Lewis had on the party's affairs. Unlike his counterparts in the other national parties, he was in the tradition of the European party secretary.

He was not a particularly charismatic leader; he was a manager, if not a boss. He was the leading member of an oligarchy, the senior figure in the party elite, an elite based on the skills democracy demands and on the ability to shape and use doctrine – which is so essential in a socialist movement.

There is nothing sinister about the fact of one man's control of a party when it is considered in the light of that man's abilities and the party's inability to afford more than one senior, full-time, political official. At various times there were other officials in the national office – research directors, education directors, and librarians – but their jobs were specific and they were, in the final analysis, Lewis's subordinates. The limited size of the national office staff is not unusual in Canadian politics, although it is unusual for a party which had an elaborate structure and which relied heavily upon membership participation and discussion for its decisions. The lack of a larger office staff perhaps enhanced Lewis's position in that it enabled him to apply his talents to every aspect of the party's life.

Since the national council met infrequently and was, at best, a cumbersome body, and since the national executive did not meet much more than once a month, the burden of administration fell on the officers, all of whom, with the exception of Lewis, had other full-time occupations.[85] It is a fact of voluntary organizations that where the officers are only part-time, the main burden of administration falls to the full-time secretary, who not only handles the routine matters of administration but fulfils a decision-making role as well. This may only be a matter of making up the agenda for the executive meetings, although this in itself is a significant task. It usually is much more extensive. The power which is delegated to the secretary tacitly or explicitly by the executive, will be exercised with greater or less freedom depending upon the confidence the executive has in the secretary and upon the degree of similarity and familiarity of views that exists between the elected officers and the full-time officer. In his study of the institutionalization of the CCF, Leo Zakuta points out that "whatever the specific methods of the established leadership, its real power lay much more in its own deeper consensus and close personal relations than in any of its deliberate arrangements."[86] When the incumbent has the talents of a David Lewis the domination is complete. Frederick Engelmann has argued, with more

85 / In 1943 the five "Table Officers" were given power to "deal with administration and similar matters between meetings of the National Executive ... " National Executive Minutes, June 5, 6, 1943, CCFP.

86 / Zakuta, *A Protest Movement Becalmed*, 30.

charity than accuracy, that "It is true that a great number of motions in meetings of the Executive were made or initiated by Lewis during his secretaryship; but there is no evidence that he used this initiative, which stemmed from full-time occupation with CCF problems, to dominate that body."[87]

The role of ideologue-in-chief was shared by Lewis with Frank Scott, who played a major role in shaping the party ideology, partly through direct activity, as a member of the executive, and in the writing of *Make This Your Canada* in collaboration with Lewis; and partly through indirect action in the influence he had through his close relationship with Lewis.[88] During the period 1942–3 when the book was being written, Scott was frequently in Ottawa in his capacity as national chairman and a co-author.

During his long tenure of office in the party as secretary from 1936 to 1950, and later executive member, Lewis formulated much party policy. He established the CCF attitude toward W. D. Herridge's New Democracy, drafted with Scott a statement dealing with the Spanish Civil War, prepared memoranda for the parliamentary caucus and attended most caucus meetings, advised Coldwell, gave advice on provincial issues to provincial secretaries, and provided a constant stream of propaganda in the form of editorials, press releases, and party leaflets.[89] His output in the period prior to the appointment of a full-time research director was prodigious. He was on every major committee, either *ex officio* or by virtue of his indispensability as the key man in the party. As full-time party functionary, orator, and debater, he was invariably influential. Caucus minutes demonstrate the extent to which his advice was sought on matters of policy and on the socialist position, particularly in foreign affairs.

It is clear from the correspondence in the party files that Lewis had considerable freedom in making party policy at short notice. He wrote to Coldwell in 1945 about a royal commission being set up to investigate the activities of the right-wing propaganda organization, the Public Informational Association, stating that he was expressing the CCF view in a speech that evening and issuing a press release. Coldwell replied a week later expressing

87 / Engelmann thesis, 120. See n. 47.
88 / Scott Papers, *passim*.
89 / David Lewis to M. J. Coldwell, Sept. 25, 1937, CCFP. Lewis either wrote or edited and revised most statements and literature issued from the national office. See D. Lewis to H. Gargrave, Dec. 17, 1938, CCFP; D. Lewis to CCF caucus, Jan. 8, 1940; and see caucus minutes *passim*, CCFP; and D. Lewis to M. J. Coldwell, July 5, 1945, CCFP, suggesting resolutions to be presented in the House. In February 1939, he was asked to attend all caucus meetings, "in an advisory capacity," Caucus Minutes, Feb. 23, 1959.

agreement, although the idea had not been discussed by the executive or the parliamentary caucus.[90] Lewis spoke frequently at public meetings and on the air; he often shared broadcasts with Coldwell on such series as "The Nation's Business," and did many by himself. These speeches were mimeographed, distributed to party offices, and incorporated into CCF policy. There is no evidence to indicate that he ever sought clearance with either Coldwell or the national chairman for any of these addresses. In his capacity as *de facto* editor of the party membership newsletter, *Across Canada* (1947–50), and the magazine *News Comment*, he had, in effect, full control over all the organs of communication within the party, and outside it. His address at Dalhousie University in 1946, "The Principle of Socialism Today," became a major part of the party's ideological equipment.

The extent to which Lewis dominated the party and shaped it in his image is difficult to measure. He directed the leadership and advised the party's provincial premier in Saskatchewan with an aplomb and, perhaps unwittingly, a degree of condescension that was remarkable.[91] Clearly one man can have great effect on the shape and history of one party, particularly in the circumstances surrounding the CCF. The view Lewis had of the leadership function was quite clear and involved a high degree of direction from the centre:

I know your own personal reluctance and the reluctance I think of all of us to interfere in any way with the democratic process on which the C.C.F. is built. I am myself convinced, however, that it is in no sense an interference with that process for the leadership of the party to express its opinion and its wishes clearly and emphatically, and to do its utmost to persuade the local organization of the correctness of that opinion. It is clearly unreasonable to expect a local organization in a constituency to see the problem from the point of view of the national movement.[92]

Within this context, Lewis did dominate the party and was largely responsible for the shape it took from 1938 to 1961, since it is admitted by all associated with the party that his influence was not markedly diminished after he left the post of national secre-

90 / D. Lewis to M. J. Coldwell, July 5, 1945; M. J. Coldwell to D. Lewis, July 11, 1945, CCFP. In 1944 Lewis complained to Coldwell that the caucus was acting as though it was the party executive. Lewis-Coldwell, July 3, 1944, CCFP.

91 / See, for example, Lewis to Douglas, June 21, 1944; Sept. 6, 1944; June 25, 1945; Jan. 26, 1945; and Lewis to Coldwell, July 3, 1944, CCFP; in which advice and criticism are offered on such matters as cabinet personnel, senior administrative appointments, and relations with organized labour.

92 / Lewis to G. Grube, April 18, 1944, Grube Papers.

tary. His influence was also felt in the Ontario section in a direct way after 1947 when he was elected to the Ontario provincial executive.[93]

In many respects Lewis was the party leader, although he was unable to win a seat in Parliament. It is possible that had he won a seat before the end of the forties, he would have replaced Coldwell. He demonstrated all the qualities of leadership, including "catonian strength of conviction" and self-sufficiency almost to the extent of arrogant pride.[94] It is not surprising then, that the CCF was in many respects run by an oligarchy. "Who says organization, says oligarchy," wrote Michels.[95] And the CCF, a party with a mass base and democratic institutions, was an organization and an oligarchy. If the personnel at the top in party executive positions is examined, this becomes fairly clear. Michels pointed out:

At the outset, leaders arise SPONTANEOUSLY; their functions are ACCESSORY and GRATUITOUS. Soon, however, they become PROFESSIONAL leaders, and in this second stage of development they are STABLE and IRREMOVABLE.[96]

From 1933 to 1961 the CCF had only 2 leaders and 1 parliamentary leader (Hazen Argue, from 1958 to 1961). In the same period it had 5 national secretaries, one in office from 1936 to 1950, another for less than a year. The 5 major offices in the party executive were filled by eleven people in the period 1933–61. Of a possible 80 different persons in office, on the basis of a complete change every convention, 11 persons occupied 80 posts over a twenty-eight year period. M. J. Coldwell, David Lewis, Frank Scott, Angus MacInnis, Stanley Knowles, and Thérèse Casgrain, among them held office for over 15 years. Lewis, Scott, and Coldwell held office for the longest periods, Lewis and Coldwell, of course, never being off the executive. Scott was on the national council from 1937 to 1940, national chairman from 1942 to 1950 and on the executive from 1950 to 1952 and the council from 1954 to 1960. From 1937 to 1960, 118 council positions were filled by 46 people, of whom 10 held positions for 10 years each. Grace MacInnis was on the council for 15 years, Stanley Knowles for 12, and Frank Scott for 11. It was not unusual for someone, as in the case of George Grube, to serve on the national executive for 12 years.

From a survey of the length of time as either an executive

93 / Ontario Provincial Convention Report, 1947; see also Lewis to A. Brewin, Oct. 29, 1947, CCFP.
94 / Michels, *Political Parties*, 64–72; interviews with party officials.
95 / *Ibid.*, 401.
96 / *Ibid.*, emphasis in the original.

member or one of the officers of the party, it emerges that the
ruling elite in the CCF consisted of no more than 12 people:
Woodsworth, Coldwell, Lewis, Scott, Grace and Angus Mac-
Innis, Knowles, Andrew Brewin, George Grube, Lorne Ingle,
Carl Hamilton, and Thérèse Casgrain. Length of service is no
sure indication of influence and certainly some of those listed
were of less influence than others. It is certain that of all those
who served on the national executive of the CCF, those in office
for the longest period had the greatest opportunity to influence
and shape the party. It is also reasonable to assume that their
contact with one another over a period of time would establish
a rapport and solidarity that would amount to the establishment
of an oligarchy in spite of themselves and the party members.

The reasons for the predominance of these individuals are not
difficult to find, and when found, are consistent with those outlined by Michels.[97] These include oratorical skills – of great importance in a party which placed such emphasis on discussion –
control of the organs of publication and communication in the
party, and superior knowledge of party affairs and party personalities. Of equal importance is the fact that as the party grew
in size, those known as either "names" or as personalities in the
party stood the best chance of re-election. This alone is enough
to ensure continuity in office. In the latter years of the party,
when trade union techniques came to the fore, the use of "slates"
of officers virtually guaranteed the election of the ruling group.

Dominance by the party leaders was inevitable because the
CCF retained some of the characteristics of a movement and required personalities for focus, provided first by Woodsworth, the
prophet, and then to a lesser extent by Coldwell, the astute parliamentarian, typical of the party's one great national success –
its parliamentary ability and reputation. These two figures gave
the movement its character and image for most of its members.
In parties where the leader symbolizes the goals or ideology of
the group, his position is solidified by these goals. Support for
him is a reaffirmation of faith; opposition to the leader may constitute apostasy or treachery. Ideological parties with a democratic structure, such as the CCF, are prone to oligarchy because
internal opposition tends to lack legitimacy, democracy notwithstanding.

Because the CCF party was national in scope and federal in
structure, and because it had to contest national elections with
a single platform and a national organization, centralized control
was essential. The electoral activity of a party is of great importance and is dominated by its permanent professional staff.

97 / *Ibid.*, part 1, *passim.*

In CCF practice, this meant David Lewis, at least until 1950. The character of the party that the members and the electorate saw through posters, leaflets, and speeches on radio and, later, television, was delineated by the central office staff under the direction of the national executive. This delineation provided a base for continuity, the power it generated for those in leadership positions being further enhanced by the secrecy necessary for many aspects of campaign planning.

The fact that the national office was the centre for research and publication and was in the national capital also enhanced the power of the leaders: they were, so to speak, at the centre of affairs. In a party which published much and debated more, those who did research, edited, published, who spoke knowledgeably from experience, and provided the nourishment necessary for the party, had positions that were virtually unassailable. The leaders were never seriously challenged by incipient revolt or "take-over bids" within the party from its inception to its transformation in 1961.

It would appear that there was less dominance of the provincial movements by their executives and leaders largely as a result of the proximity of leaders to members and the greater familiarity of members with party affairs at the provincial level. It does seem clear, however, that this was not the case at the national level. The fact that only those close to or resident in Ottawa could attend the frequent meetings of the officers or the national executive meant that the affairs of the CCF were of necessity left in the hands of a small group on a more or less permanent basis.[98]

The influence of this small group cannot be exaggerated. In addition to the tasks performed by the leadership group mentioned above, the minutes of the national executive indicate that these same people were almost invariably appointed to the committees that were struck to draft executive resolutions for council meetings and conventions, and to the committees that prepared party statements on specific issues such as the war, German rearmament, conscription, and the like. The committee that prepared the election manifesto for the party in 1938 was composed of Woodsworth, Coldwell, Scott, and Lewis.[99] The committee

98 / A survey of national executive minutes shows the most frequent attenders to be Lewis, Coldwell, Scott, A. MacInnis, Knowles, Brewin, MacNeil, Grube, Casgrain; in roughly that order.

99 / See National Executive Minutes, March 18, 1945 (Dumbarton Oaks), CCFP; Jan. 8, 1946 (Indonesia); Dec. 20, 1947 (general foreign policy statement by Grube, Scott, Lewis, MacInnis). The committee struck to investigate closer ties with labour (the NDP development) was Lewis, Scott, Knowles, Brewin, Hamilton, Argue, Douglas, and H. Winch. National Council Minutes, Oct. 1957. See also National Council Minutes for July 1938, Sept. 1939, and Nov. 1944, CCFP.

that prepared the same thing in 1944 consisted of Lewis, Scott, Grube, Brewin, and Dorothy Steeves of British Columbia.[100] The party was never big enough, however, to fall completely under the control of a class of managers in the manner Ostrogorski feared when he examined the Birmingham Caucus.[101]

Perhaps the best example of both the fact of a ruling oligarchy and of the existence of a degree of membership control foreign to the other political parties in Canada is provided by the process which led up to the passing of the Winnipeg Declaration in 1956, which gave the CCF a new manifesto twenty-three years after the passage of the first at Regina. Of equal significance in this respect is the process which led to the foundation of the New Democratic Party, but the evidence in this instance, for obvious reasons, is not complete.

The impetus for a change in the party's statement of principles originated with the party leaders in 1950. The first recorded discussion of the idea occurred at a meeting of the parliamentary caucus, July 22, 1950.[102] At that meeting it was agreed that an "innocuous" statement was to be brought in at the national convention in order to authorize the national council to begin the work of preparing a new statement of principles. The impetus for change came from a recognition by the leaders that there was much in the Regina Manifesto that was neither accurate or relevant, and to a considerable extent from the climate of change being generated by similar discussion within the British Labour Party and the international socialist movement. In his address to the party convention, Coldwell referred to the meeting of the International Socialist Conference at Copenhagen in June 1950[103] at which the first draft of what became the Frankfurt Declaration of the Socialist International was discussed. In his speech as national chairman, Frank Scott made the same plea as Coldwell: the basic principles of the CCF should be examined and modified to bring them up to date. Characteristically, at least two constituency associations felt that a reaffirmation of the Regina Manifesto would provide the cure for the party's troubles.[104]

Both Scott and Coldwell recognized the need to couch their requests for an examination of the Manifesto in the context of changes being made by other political parties. They recognized

100 / National Council Minutes, March 1944, CCFP.
101 / M. Ostrogorski, *Democracy and the Organization of Political Parties*, S. M. Lipset, ed. (New York 1964), I.
102 / CCF Caucus Minutes, CCFP.
103 / Report of the Eleventh National Convention (1950).
104 / Resolution Book, Eleventh National Convention (1950), nos. 30, 31, CCFP.

the need for change to enable the CCF to meet the challenges of the political situation in Canada, but in this respect they were victims of the awkwardness which afflicts leaders of democratic parties. They could not depart too quickly from support of the doctrinaire CCF position for, as leaders, they had to demonstrate their *bona fides*, so to speak, to the members of the movement. And, too, they doubtless felt morally bound to uphold the faith. They could not simply inform their followers that the complexities of day-to-day politics made shifts and changes necessary, for to do so would have been to deny the rationale of the party, its structure and ideology. They felt compelled to initiate the change but equally compelled to do so gradually and cautiously, reaffirming the true faith as they went along.[105]

In a debate marked by some bitterness, particularly on the part of delegates from British Columbia – who were in good number since the convention was held in Vancouver – the party agreed to both a reaffirmation of faith in the Regina Manifesto and an examination of its principles. The national council was instructed to prepare an appendix to the Manifesto which would constitute "a statement of the application of socialist principles to Canada and the world today."[106] There was sufficient concern throughout the party about what was meant by the resolution and the amendment that the national office felt it necessary to reassure the members in the August–September issue of *News Comment* that the Regina Manifesto was not going to be rewritten or watered down. Scott's address was reprinted and the resolution was compared with the re-definition of socialist aims taking place in Europe through the International Socialist Conference and the preparation of the New Fabian Essays.[107]

The procedure adopted by the national council, on the recommendation of a national executive committee, demonstrates the degree to which the party leaders accepted the democratic process as a framework within which they exercised their leadership. It also demonstrates that within that framework the pre-eminence of the ruling oligarchy was maintained. Admittedly – given the nature of the party members, particularly those who attended conventions – the changing of the party's basic creed was an act

105 / Samuel Beer discusses similar problems facing the leaders of the British Labour party in *British Politics in a Collectivist Age* (New York 1966).

106 / Report of the Eleventh National Convention (1950). See also Vancouver *Sun*, July 29, 1950, and "The CCF Convention," *Canadian Forum*, Sept. 1950.

107 / "CCF Methods To Be Restated," *News Comment*, x (Aug.–Sept. 1950).

that required elaborate obeisance to the democratic procedures; nevertheless the party leaders did more to provide membership participation in the process than they need have done.

At its meeting in January 1951, the national executive appointed a committee of David Lewis, Lorne Ingle, Donald Macdonald, and Andrew Brewin to draft proposals for carrying out the convention resolution.[108] The national council adopted this committee's proposals and in turn appointed an *ad hoc* committee to draft the new statement of principles. The proposals were that the council invite suggestions from the party at large, such suggestions to be incorporated in a draft by the *ad hoc* committee, the draft to be submitted to the executive for approval, circulated to national council members and provincial councils for further suggestions, and then the draft and suggestions to be debated at a national council meeting. Following this meeting a second draft would be prepared by the *ad hoc* committee; this was to be circulated and discussed at the council meeting prior to the 1952 convention, a third and final draft then being prepared for submission to the convention itself. The *ad hoc* committee consisted of Lewis, Frank Scott, Brewin, T. C. Douglas, Ingle, Hazen Argue, Grace MacInnis, Joe Noseworthy, Francois Laroche, and Clarie Gillis.[109]

By June 1951 the first draft had been prepared by the committee and approved by the national executive for circulation to council members at the national and provincial levels.[110] When the national council met in October to discuss the draft and the suggestions made by the various councils, it was discovered that there were some six major policy differences ranging from the danger of world communism to the bilingual nature of Canada. The draft itself was over thirty paragraphs in length, something more than an appendix to the Regina Manifesto. Lorne Ingle and Grace MacInnis were instructed to edit the version that emerged from the council to make the language "simple and more colourful."[111] The resulting product was published October 22 and circulated to all sections of the party for discussion.

At a national executive meeting in February 1952 it was made clear that there was general unhappiness with the draft. Two provinces, British Columbia and Saskatchewan, strongly recommended that formulation of the New Statement of Principles as it was called – the notion of an appendix having been forgotten along the way – be postponed. Saskatchewan urged that the

108 / National Executive Minutes, Jan. 28, 1951, CCFP.
109 / National Council Minutes, March 1951, CCFP.
110 / National Executive Minutes, June 16, 1951.
111 / National Council Minutes, Oct. 1951, and see *Comment*, I (Nov. 1951).

whole project be abandoned and efforts directed toward preparing a federal election program. British Columbia pointed out the serious differences of opinion the draft had evoked.[112] At a meeting of the national council a month later it was decided to postpone the project and present the new statement to the 1954 national convention.[113] The national executive felt that the draft prepared for this convention by a small committee chaired by Brewin was a "well written explanation of the CCF approach to problems in the present day," but quite inadequate as a statement of principles, and should instead be published as a single pamphlet.[114] Nothing was presented to the 1954 convention.

The matter rested until it was raised again in an address by Coldwell to the national council in January of 1955.[115] Again little was done in the year following, but in 1956 the subject was raised at the January meeting of the national council. After addresses by Coldwell and Douglas and a lengthy discussion of the CCF position and the party's principles, it was decided that a new statement of principles should be drafted for presentation to the national convention in Winnipeg that following August.[116] In February the national executive appointed Lewis, Morden Lazarus, Omer Chartrand, and Ingle to prepare the draft statement of CCF principles.[117] It was presented to the national convention in 1956 and formed the basis of the Winnipeg Declaration. The final version that emerged from the convention lacked the ring and emotional tone of the draft, which included such statements as "while glittering mansions are being erected in the suburbs, dark slums continue to blot the centres of our large cities,"[118] which the convention, after six years consideration of the revision of Canadian socialism, was prepared to drop in favour of a calmer approach.

In the final analysis, the party executive drafted the bulk of the statement but not without full opportunity for the party to participate through its councils and executives and conventions. Clearly it was the rank and file – or more accurately the activists who attended the convention – who were the keepers of the faith; it was the leaders who were the innovators. E. E. Winch, who attacked the Regina Manifesto as an essentially bourgeois document in 1933, stoutly defended it in 1950.[119] This act may show

112 / National Executive Minutes, Feb. 29, 1952.
113 / National Council Minutes, March 1952.
114 / National Executive Minutes, Jan. 5, 1954.
115 / National Council Minutes, Jan. 14, 1955.
116 / National Council Minutes, Jan. 1956.
117 / National Executive Minutes, Feb. 19, 1956.
118 / National Council Minutes, July 1956.
119 / Vancouver *Sun*, July 29, 1950, and ch. 3 above.

merely the changes in Winch; it can be argued as well, however, that it shows the essential conservatism of the membership in a mass political movement. And it is perhaps as a result of such inertia that direct and positive leadership emerges.

Oligarchy seems inevitable in democratic organizations, particularly those which aspire to and achieve a mass base. It is also necessary, and particularly so in a party which is at the same time a political movement, since leadership of a direct and forceful kind gives the focus and impetus which the movement would otherwise lack. Thus the paradox of a democratic movement is the necessity for oligarchic leadership and the inevitability of a managerial elite which, conscious of the democratic structure of the party and fully in sympathy with it, must nevertheless manipulate it in order to achieve the ends of the movement.

The ruling group in the CCF, too small to be considered a bureaucracy in the broad sense, but clearly an oligarchy, led the CCF into its companionate marriage with organized labour, and thus preserved the socialist nucleus by grafting it onto a host with greater financial resources if much thinner philosophical resources. It was this that kept socialism alive in Canada, at least the brand of socialism that was the CCF. And among the men who were responsible for this final act of the CCF were those who had been there at the beginning and who were responsible in some ways for the initial act: Lewis, Scott, Douglas, and Coldwell.[120]

The political antecedents of the CCF and the socialist ideology the party adopted called for a democratic structure. Commitment, participation, and co-operation were aspects of the party ideology that made a democratic constitution inevitable. Members of the CCF were not prepared to accept the subordination of the individual implicit in the managerial structure of the old parties. Their movement was, after all, a movement of people dedicated to eradicate bossism from politics and economics; the party that was the electoral vehicle of the movement had to reflect this goal. The CCF succeeded in demonstrating the extent to which members can run their own party and, at the same time, the extent to which leaders, often in spite of themselves, lead in a manner not quite consistent with the *ideals* of democracy. For reasons elaborated in this chapter, members are seldom able to keep sufficiently abreast of affairs to make policy intelligently, but they can, as they did in the CCF, ensure that leaders are constantly aware of their responsibilities to their followers and the professed ideals of the party or party-movement.

As one element in a national polity, democratically organized

120 / National Council Minutes, Oct. 1957, May 1958, CCFP.

political parties contribute significantly to the maintenance of
democracy in that polity. The pluralist democracy requires not
only a variety of associations, but a certainty of effective influence
in the final decision-making processes. Democratic political parties are an important channel for this influence. In Canada it is
a channel that was first navigated by the CCF. The inevitability
of oligarchy under the circumstances described above is not an
inherently evil condition; like the law of gravity it is easy to live
with as long as we keep our awareness of it.

The New Democratic Party, successor to the CCF, is less
democratic than the CCF because it is much less a movement than
the CCF. It is still more democratic than its rivals, the Liberal
and Conservative parties. These latter two bodies have moved
slowly in the direction of providing more avenues for membership influence, but this development is being outpaced by the
influence of professional public relations advisers. The optimum
political machine still remains as the elitist or caucus political
party, in which speed of decision and alacrity of policy shift remain prime virtues. Winning elections is still the prime function
of the political party.

THE CCF AND THE VOTER

7

Socialism is for all of them the expression of truth,
reason, and justice, and need only be discovered
in order to conquer the world with its power.

FREIDRICH ENGELS
Die Entwicklung des Sozialismus ...

The success or failure of a political party can only be measured in terms of its success or failure at the polls. A party which does not win many elections is not a success. A party which at no time in its history gets more than 16 per cent of the popular vote is neither a success nor a major party. If it is able to see, in the platforms of other parties and the legislation of governments formed by other parties, elements of its own platform, this in no way measures its success as a party; what it sees is evidence of its success as a movement.

The CCF did not succeed as a political party. It remained a minor party and a political movement. No single explanation can be advanced to account for this failure nor is any one analysis adequate. It can be argued that the CCF failed as a party because it was an attempt to operate outside the context of Canadian politics. There is some truth in the view that it could never have replaced the Liberal party, which was firmly anchored in the centre of Canadian politics, ever ready to adopt planks for its platform that seemed likely to appeal, whatever their source. One external factor that contributed to the failure of the CCF was the shift leftward taken by the Liberal party in the forties. Equally significant are those explanations which are based on the attitudes and voting behaviour of the Canadian electorate – what little is known about them. The effect of opposition propaganda from other parties and from various organizations in the community cannot be underestimated. The structure of the CCF, its nature as a movement, and the content of its ideology, all contributed to its failure as a party although, paradoxically, they were the basis of its success and longevity as a movement. What does seem clear is that given the premise on which the CCF was formed, there was nothing its leaders or members could have done to win power. By casting off its old name and old image, if not its old leaders, the CCF may succeed as the New Democratic Party where it failed as the Canadian socialist party.

The democratic political movement which rises in opposition to the existing political and social system faces a dilemma. To achieve its ends it must have power, and it must seek that power through the existing system. It must operate within the system and engage in the very practices it came into being to oppose. Although it may work within the system purely as an expeditious approach to reform, it runs the risk of contamination. As an alternative it may attempt to function outside the system, as a pure movement, but runs the risk of ineffectiveness.[1]

1 / E. E. Schattschneider, *The Semi-Sovereign People* (New York 1960), 48–9: "In politics as in everything else it makes a great difference whose game we play. The rules of the game determine the requirements

The CCF attempted to have it both ways. It accepted and hotly defended parliamentary democracy; it was in the beginning and throughout its history opposed to the operation of the Canadian party system. It could do little about one without involving itself with the other. As a political movement it found participation in the party contest difficult and drew satisfaction from changes produced by its presence on the sidelines. As a political party it was more prepared to engage in party combat and modify its program to meet the competition, but it did so uncomfortably and to the accompaniment of criticism from members whose orientation was more movement than party. The CCF never did resolve the dilemma satisfactorily. It vacillated from one position to the other.

Even after the establishment of the NDP, the two attitudes toward participation in the electoral contest remained. On the one hand there exists the determination shown through advertising, canvassing, and constituency organization to outdo the other parties at their own game, whereas on the other there is the determination not to offer slick posters but solid socialist education – ideological sustenance for a starved electorate. In contemporary terms it is the conflict within the party of those who would opt for the "Madison Avenue" approach as against those whose sympathies lie with the approach of Woodsworth, who was more interested in educating for the millenium than in digging out votes.[2]

It was a dilemma which tended to be solved in favour of the traditional, anti-electoral politics of a socialist movement. This was due to two factors. One was the failure of the party to win any campaigns by adopting the techniques of the other parties, thus providing the die-hards with evidence that the new way – or the way of the "old line" parties – was wrong; the other was the ethic of the party which viewed easy success the same way as it viewed easy riches, as wrong and sinful. The road for the socialist was never an easy road because if it was easy, it was not socialist.[3] The elections the party won most proudly were those won through the persistent efforts of volunteers working night and day. Living in a capitalist world and for the most part living

for success. Resources sufficient for success in one game may be wholly inadequate in another. These considerations go to the heart of political strategy."

2 / At a meeting of the national council in 1935, Woodsworth "deprecated the idea that catchy demagoguery could take the place of sound understanding." National Council Minutes, Nov. 30, 1935, CCFP.

3 / T. C. Douglas was cheered by the delegates at the 1963 NDP convention in British Columbia when he declared: "There is no easy road to political office, and if there were, I wouldn't want to use it."

a capitalist life, the socialist seems somehow to require the opportunity to immolate himself in toil, to scourge himself by labour. In addition, of course, the party's belief in the validity of
the myth of public rationality meant that talk, argument, statistics, and proof were what won elections. The CCF never did
accept the ramifications of the Freudian revolution. It could not
do so, since its whole organizational basis was founded on pre-
Freudian assumptions about the nature of man. It was assumed
that people voted for the CCF because they had been won over to
the cause of socialism; this was seldom the case.

The authors of the Regina Manifesto may have been Fabians
and educated in Britain, but they seemed not to have read
Graham Wallas: "Whoever sets himself to base his political
thinking on a re-examination of the working of human nature,
must begin by trying to overcome his own tendency to exaggerate
the intellectuality of mankind."[4] The CCF believed that it could
win by rational conversion and organization. The basis of organization was the sending of the converted into the streets to
proselytize on the doorstep, to set up clubs, to chair discussion
groups, to publish pamphlets, to educate.

At the beginning Woodsworth was antagonistic toward the
notion that the party should indulge in vote-getting, as he put it,
"at any cost":

I agree with you that the main purpose of the CCF is not to get votes,
that is, to get votes at any cost. But we are out to get votes, and the
only way to do so is to constantly *recruit* fresh groups of people, many
of whom, up to the present time have been allied with one or other of
the old parties.[5]

The British Columbia wing of the party was even more dedicated
to the non-political alternative and some of its members were
concerned that the CCF had fallen into the hands of those who
would win office at the expense of socialism. Ernest Winch complained of this failing in a letter to J. G. King, editor of the
Research Review:

First, I disagree that "the primary task at this time is the electing of
candidates to the House of Commons"; that is never our primary task
which is the "making of socialists" — something very, very different.

4 / Graham Wallas, *Human Nature in Politics* (London 1920), 21.
Subsequent research has substantiated Wallas's conclusions. See, for
example, Angus Campbell, *et al., The Voter Decides* (Evanston 1954);
Robert Lane, *Political Life* (Glencoe 1959); Angus Campbell, *et al.,
The American Voter* (New York 1964); M. Benney, *et al., How People
Vote* (London 1956).
5 / J. S. Woodsworth to Arthur Mould, Oct. 2, 1933, CCFP. Emphasis
added.

Votes alone, or a majority of representatives in Parliament, will never bring socialism. Unfortunately, there is too great a tendency for the CCF to become a vote-catching political (parliamentary) party which, if persisted in, may give too well grounded a justification for the oft repeated charge that it is "the third party of capitalism."[6]

Woodsworth's view prevailed. It was the view that the party needed votes to win but that the way to get votes was first to make socialists. As determined a campaigner as anyone, Woodsworth never lost sight of the movement and drew his greatest satisfaction from the increased numbers and activities of the members: "Making converts – yes, after all that is our job – leading people to seek a new way of living, the cooperative way through which alone a true world brotherhood may be established."[7]

The early activities of the party consisted largely in carrying the message to all parts of the country and the establishment of clubs and groups to continue similar work. The operation was typical of the CCF at that stage; it was largely *ad hoc* and consisted of individual members trudging across the country speaking at small gatherings. It was the sort of activity Woodsworth knew best from his days with the Non-Partisan League and his own experience as a labour MP for Winnipeg North. It was his view that money was better spent keeping young men on the road than on building the apparatus of a central party office:

... I have just heard that Eamon Park on his return from Convention, hitch-hiked from Winnipeg to Fort Frances, and then on to Kenora, with only two or three dollars outside help he has managed to make his way and do excellent work. I would rather subsidize a few of these young men and keep them out on the road.[8]

By 1938 organizational activity became more consistently directed toward setting up centres for campaign activity, although the educational and evangelical aspect of organization was never overlooked. The change in approach is evident in the organizers' and workers' manual which the national office produced in 1939:

Inevitably the first stage of our movement was what might be called "idealistic." Speakers and workers went about explaining the philosophy underlying the movement and endeavouring to create enthusiasm for it. Almost of their own volition people got together in clubs to listen to speakers whose talks were followed by a question and

6 / E. E. Winch to J. G. King, June 9, 1935, CCFP.
7 / "Chairman's Address, 1936 National Convention, Toronto, August 3," typewritten manuscript with marginal notes in Woodsworth's hand, CCFP.
8 / J. S. Woodsworth to M. J. Coldwell, Sept. 9, 1933, CCFP.

discussion period. Sometimes the clubs discussed the National Manifesto or pamphlets dealing with socialistic philosophy. At election time clubs and club members formed the nucleus of the election machinery.

The 1937 National Convention in Winnipeg definitely marked the end of that first stage. After almost five years of general discussion and study our membership was becoming conscious of the need for more definite and systematic activities. Members became anxious to push the CCF into a position of influence and power – not in some distant future but in the years immediately ahead. The 1937 convention marked our entry into the "realistic" period.

Our objective is a permanent organization in every community to consolidate support for our program and to elect CCF representatives to all public bodies.[9]

Despite what seems to be a clear effort to establish a political organization or machine, the contents of the handbook belie the purpose set out in the preface for it continued to place great emphasis on the educational aspect of the party activity. The handbook listed the duties of the organizer with naïve simplicity and stressed his role as teacher: new contacts had to be taught the philosophy and history of the CCF in addition to the techniques of leading discussion groups, organizing study groups, and "participation in economic struggles, etc."[10] Of the thirty-three pages in the handbook, five were devoted to "Organizing for Elections"; the remainder to "Clubs and Club Activities," "The CCF and Economic Groups," and a series of appendices dealing with "The Rise of the CCF," "Hints on Running a Meeting," and "The CCF and Trade Unions."

As late as 1944 the Ontario section put out a mimeographed bulletin on organization which began, "The CCF is primarily a great educational crusade, but even crusades need organization."[11] In 1948 the national office published the *CCF Handbook*, most of which was devoted to instruction on the formation of "CCF Groups" and to suggestions for their activity. Admittedly the declared purpose of these groups was "persuading people to support the program of the CCF,"[12] but the amount of time necessary to carry out the group's activities would in themselves fully engross most people. The emphasis throughout the book is on education and group cohesion: "The feeling of 'one-ness' in our movement can be strengthened immeasurably when its members

9 / "A Handbook for CCF Organizers and Workers" (Ottawa, n.d. [c. 1939]), 1, CCFP.
10 / "Handbook," 6.
11 / "Memorandum on Organization," Ontario CCF, Aug. 4, 1944, CCFP.
12 / *CCF Handbook* (Ottawa 1948), 17.

learn to sing and play and laugh as well as to think and work together."[13]

The predominance of this attitude had a distinct effect on the kind of campaign mounted by the CCF and on the party's assessment of the reasons for failure. In his report to the national council dealing with the party's failure in the 1945 election, Lewis laid a large share of the blame on the "lack of education to meet the propaganda campaign of the opposition against us."[14] The failure of the party in 1948 to increase either its membership or popular support as measured by the Gallup Poll was felt by Lewis and Donald MacDonald, Director of Education and Information, to be the result of inadequate membership education. In his report to the council MacDonald stated:

... our movement has been marking time since the 1945 elections. We have established an overall organization but we have not succeeded in activizing our membership. If we seek to discover the reasons for this situation I am convinced that we shall find them for the most part in the state of education and informational activities, and the community programs of which they form an integral part.

The prevalent attitude among the great majority of CCF card-holders is one of vague political protest rather than the mildest socialist conviction.[15]

And in 1955 the Ontario provincial secretary, Kenneth Bryden, reiterated the same view in a letter to Lorne Ingle: "Our feeling is that our most serious weakness at the present time is that we have failed to sell the CCF to CCF'ers. That is, we have failed to bring home to enough of our people their personal responsibilities in a people's movement."[16]

It was assumed by the party executive that the success of the CCF depended almost entirely upon the activities of the membership in educating the public, teaching the truths of democratic socialism. For this purpose the party supplied its constituency associations with an endless supply of literature both for membership education and for distribution to the general public. There is a relationship between the number of members and a party's ability to campaign more effectively on a door-to-door basis; but there is no clear indication that an increased membership necessarily increased votes by a significant amount.

Some scholars have seen a relationship between the size of a

13 / *Ibid.*, 58; emphasis in the original.
14 / National Council Minutes, Sept. 1945, CCFP.
15 / *Ibid.*, April 1948.
16 / K. Bryden to Lorne Ingle, Dec. 30, 1955, CCFP.

mass party's membership and its strength at the polls. Engelmann, for example, applies the method of relating membership figures to votes suggested by Duverger.[17] His calculations for the 1949 general election indicate, as one could expect, that the highest ratio of voters to members occurred in Saskatchewan where a high level of membership and active participation prevailed. Despite the fact that the CCF increased its poll in Ontario substantially in that election, only 10 constituencies showed a membership-to-voter ratio higher than 5 per cent. What this indicates very roughly is that where the kind of activity that the organization guides and handbooks expected of members was an accepted and fairly common social phenomenon, it appears to have helped the party win votes. Where it was not, it was of little use.

But it is also possible to state that where the CCF was accepted as a major political party, that is, in Saskatchewan in 1949, membership and votes would naturally be high, regardless of the kind of activity. The leaders of the party were mistaken in assuming that the kind of party activity that was so successful in the wheat belt would be equally successful in urban communities. In 1949 there were only 58 members in the Winnipeg North constituency, yet the party succeeded in winning 12,432 votes in the general election that year.[18] A causal relationship between increased membership, heightened membership activity, and electoral success seems tenuous to say the least.

Because the CCF was a movement as well as a party and because it depended upon its members for financial support and services during election campaigns, it had to maintain and expand its membership to keep alive. But because the kind of commitment involved was one of time as well as of ideology, it tended to attract into the party individuals who, though good members from the "activist" point of view, were not, outside of the wheat belt, typical of the community at large. Only the "dedicated" joined, stayed, and worked.

If a new doctrine can only succeed if it is based on attitudes already present in a society, then in those areas of Canada where the doctrine of the CCF was not consistent with prevaling attitudes – and this meant most areas outside of the wheat belt – the individual who undertakes to propagate the doctrine must place

17 / Duverger, *Political Parties: Their Organization and Activity in the Modern State*, 94–6; F. C. Engelmann, "The Cooperative Commonwealth Federation of Canada: A Study of Membership Participation in Policy Making." Unpubl. PHD thesis (Yale 1954), 68–70.
18 / Except where otherwise noted, election figures are from H. A. Scarrow, *Canada Votes* (New Orleans 1963).

himself outside the accepted norms.[19] The rebel in such circumstances has difficulty in avoiding the charge of disloyalty since what he seeks threatens the existence of the society of which he is a member.[20] He must be prepared to espouse the cause of socialism and to accept the tasks of the party worker and the role of the non-conformist. Such qualifications restricted the intake of members to only a few in each province. Lipset has established that this was not the case in Saskatchewan, where the CCF leaders were "normal community leaders."[21] In this respect Saskatchewan was atypical because nowhere else was there the same degree of social and economic homogeneity, with the possible exception of some urban working-class areas in British Columbia. Outside the prairie bastion of the CCF, the party leaders and activists tended more to correspond to the "deviants" described by Clark: "By the very nature of their role reform leaders tended to be people devoid of 'respectable' attributes ... The influences which promoted people to break from the established institutions and to take up the cause of reform often increased opposition against them."[22] Outside of Saskatchewan and the pockets of urban support in North Winnipeg, Vancouver, and Toronto the CCF was not a socially accepted political entity in the sense that it was not in conformity to middle-class norms.

Members of the urban immigrant groups in Winnipeg, Saskatoon, or Regina were attracted to the CCF because they were social outsiders as were the agrarian leaders *vis-à-vis* the rest of the political and economic community.[23] Some were socialists before they came to Canada. Throughout the party's national membership there were those whose support was predicated on intellectual commitment pure and simple, but it is suggested that for a significant number of the party's membership an explanation of their support can be framed in terms of social deprivation, alienation, or sheer eccentricity. The active members in the clubs and constituency associations would fit the broad category of outsiders because of either weak cultural integration or anomie.[24] The CCF membership tended to be drawn from those who found

19 / See Mannheim, *Ideology and Utopia*, 207. The CCF got more votes in Ontario than in Saskatchewan, but a smaller percentage of the total vote. See Appendix II.

20 / S. D. Clark, *Movements of Political Protest in Canada, 1640–1840* (Toronto 1959), 10.

21 / Lipset, *Agrarian Socialism*, 187.

22 / S. D. Clark, *The Social Development of Canada* (Toronto 1942), 14; and see also J. Porter, *Vertical Mosaic*, 297 and 311–12.

23 / Lipset, *Agrarian Socialism*, 191–2; and see Porter, *Vertical Mosaic*, 305–7.

24 / See, for example, Margaret Mead, *Coming of Age in Samoa* (New York 1928), 202–3; and Robert Merton, *Social Theory and Social Structure* (Glencoe 1949), 127.

greater satisfaction through membership in a protest movement than they could achieve through conforming to established norms because such conformity was, for one reason or another, denied them.[25]

The propensity of the North American to join groups and involve himself in activities of a highly organized gregariousness has been noted by such observers as Ostrogorski and Tocqueville.[26] If the basic cause of this drive is, as Ostrogorski and Tocqueville observed, the isolation of the individual which is caused by the atomization that occurs in a market society, then there is a need for identity.[27] Those who are, for one reason or another, denied access to the normal means of association through clubs, established parties, or the acquisition of status in the community, may seek identity in other ways. Angus MacInnis pointed out that in British Columbia, the CCF clubs were doing "much the kind of work formerly done by fraternal societies."[28]

The study of party membership by Peter Regenstreif, while somewhat inconclusive as a result of a low response from members contacted, is useful in demonstrating the "deviant" nature of CCF membership.[29] The validity of Regenstreif's generalizations about the CCF is less open to question because the response from the CCF members was much higher than from either the Liberal or Conservative members and was from a larger sample. Twice as many CCF members as other members completed the questionnaire, and of all the returns half were from CCF members. This alone would indicate the zeal of the active CCF member. More significant, however, are the figures for religious affiliation and membership in other organizations. Twenty per cent of the CCF respondents had no religion at all compared with one per cent for the Liberal and Conservative parties and 4 per cent for the general population. Relatively few CCF members belong to service clubs and similar organizations, with the exception of co-operatives and unions where the membership is higher than in the other parties. Regenstreif's study also shows

25 / See the catalogue of causes in C. W. King, *Social Movements*, 11–25; and also H. Cantril, *The Psychology of Social Movements* (New York 1941), 48–60.

26 / Ostrogorski, *Democracy and the Organization of Political Parties*, II, 307–9; Alexis de Tocqueville, *Democracy in America*; Henry S. Commager, ed. (London 1959), 385. See also Kornhauser, *The Politics of Mass Society*, 223.

27 / See Macpherson, *Political Theory*, 1–4, 263–4; and Porter, *Vertical Mosaic*, 312–13, and ch. 2.

28 / National Council Minutes, 30 Nov., 1935, CCFP.

29 / Peter Regenstreif, "Some Aspects of National Party Support in Canada," *CJEPS*, XXIX (Feb. 1963), 59–74.

that the CCF member is more committed to his party as measured
by faithfulness at the polls, and is more active in party work.

Regenstreif's figures are substantiated by studies of CCF-NDP
activists conducted at provincial and national NDP conventions.[30]
Of 168 delegates to the British Columbia NDP convention in
1965, 108 professed no religion at all or adherence to the Unitarian church, humanism, theosophy, or Ba'hai. The remarkable
preponderance of "deviants" is due to the fact that convention
delegates are normally the most active and committed members
of the party. In addition, the British Columbia section is more
radical than most sections. Of the delegates contacted, over 97
per cent had been active members of the CCF.

What these studies indicate is simply that the active members
of the CCF were far less likely to be "ordinary" citizens involved
in the normal activities of the community. The ordinary individual who joins a club or group does so to preserve the existing
order and work within it. The activities carried out do not involve
the propagation of new ideas, the changing of social structures,
or the criticism of the existing order. Such groups might promote
parks for recreation and physical activity; they would not campaign for health foods or sun-bathing. They might work to provide money to buy projectors for the school but not for a fundamental change in teaching methods. Nor would they be likely to
advocate birth-control clinics, free medical care, or free psy-
chiatric care for delinquents. They deal within the area of activity
Galbraith has described as expressing "conventional wisdom."[31]
There is no room in middle-class urban society and in the institutions of that society for the zealot, the reformer, or the rebel.

The CCF provided a haven for the outsiders and rebels because
it was a movement as well as a party. Their presence ensured
that it remained a movement. It was a combination Woodsworth
endorsed in 1938 when he wrote that "spiritual idealism cannot
be divorced from political realism."[32] The great asset of the CCF
for many of its members was that it provided an organized and
relatively legitimate channel for social dissent. The dissent may
have had a variety of sources ranging from rationally formulated
opposition to the *status quo* to resentment and envy stemming
from social or economic inadequacy; the CCF provided a vehicle
for the energies generated by these attitudes. It offered as well a

30 / Unpublished data in the author's possession from surveys of
party activists.
31 / J. K. Galbraith, *The Affluent Society* (London 1962), ch. 2 and
passim.
32 / J. S. Woodsworth to Paul Nanten, June 21, 1938, Woodsworth
Papers.

basically simplistic solution to the ills of society and laid the blame squarely at the feet of capitalism and its practitioners.

The significance of the nature of the CCF membership, particularly of its more active members, was that, Saskatchewan farmers apart, they were not, generally speaking, the kind of people who atttracted wide support to either the CCF or the cause of democratic socialism. They were not the normal community leaders and, far from broadening the representational base of the CCF, they tended, naturally enough, to attract to the party people like themselves. This meant that the activists in the CCF would tend to proselytize among those who were likely to vote CCF in any case and who were a minority in the community.[33] It also meant that the CCF came to be represented to the rest of the community by its members and their statements and activities as reported in the press. The kind of person active in the CCF who, like Harold Winch, was given to emotional oratory of a strong revolutionary cast, came to typify the party for the average middle-class Canadian. The party image was one of social and economic deviation. Not only was the party doctrine inconsistent with the established order, but the people who espoused and promoted it were clearly the "wrong" kind of people. They were either the "activists" already described, or trade union leaders who were equally suspect. It was easier to believe the propagandists of the *status quo*. Consequently the CCF suffered throughout its career from a decidedly negative image.

Although the structure of the CCF would lead to its being described as a mass party, its nature as a party movement with a clearly articulated ideology meant that it was more exclusive than either the Liberal or Conservative parties, which did not have or need a mass base. The CCF restricted its membership automatically to those who were against the *status quo*, and further, to those who could accept the socialist critique of the *status quo* and espouse the socialist cure. It had to accept only those who were already opposed, for whatever reasons, or it had to go out and make socialists through education. And it lacked both the resources and the climate of sympathy necessary for this kind of education. Those Canadians who voted for the CCF were, in a sense, departing from the norm of electoral behaviour; that is, voting either Liberal or Conservative. Support for the CCF, in this context, constituted deviant behaviour. The image

33 / The frequency and number of "Summer Camps" and other similar activities testifies to a high level of social intercourse and homogeneity in the party. See also P. Lazarsfeld *et al., The People's Choice* (New York 1944), 146; and Berelson, *et al., Voting* (Chicago 1954), 104.

of the party was such that it attracted deviant support, such as
support that represented dissatisfaction with the *status quo*, or
which did not find the requisite satisfaction in voting for the two
major parties. This could be nothing more than an indication of
dissatisfaction with candidates or leaders, or the often cited wish
to "give the old gang a good scare." Whatever the reasons, the
CCF was a vehicle for deviant political behaviour in this context.

The image of a party is its symbolic content for the voter or
the mental stereotype he has of the party. It is the party's more
or less permanent characteristic in the mind of the voter and
arouses a particular response. The use of the term in politics and
elections, while current, originated with Graham Wallas:

But when a party has come into existence its fortunes depend upon
facts of human nature of which deliberate thought is only one. It is
primarily a name, which, like other names, calls up when it is heard
or seen an "image" that shades imperceptibly into the voluntary
realization of its meaning. As in other cases, emotional reactions can
be set up by the name and its automatic mental associations.[34]

In a sense the image of a party consists of the set of mental
associations common to given sections of the population about
that particular party. In other words, the political party does not
exist solely as a rationally apprehended entity; for a great many
people it is something more, or less, than this. As Wallas put it,
"Something is required simpler and more permanent, something
which can be loved and trusted, and which can be recognized at
successive elections as being the same thing that was loved and
trusted before; and a party is such a thing."[35] Or, in the case of
the other parties, the opposite to these feelings exists, or no feeling at all.

The point is that although not all parties are seen as either
negative or positive, some are and by some people permanently.
It requires no feat of reasoning to argue that for most company
directors a socialist party has a negative image and that they are
unlikely to support one at any time. It is true that perceptions of
party images, like the images themselves, change over time; it is
also true that they tend to persist:

The world of politics is full of novelty, yet some of its elements persist

34 / Wallas, *Human Nature in Politics*, 83–4. See also D. Butler and
R. Rose, *The British General Election of 1959* (London 1960), esp. ch.
3; M. Abrams and R. Rose, *Must Labour Lose* (London 1960), ch. 1;
M. Beck and D. J. Dooley, "Party Images in Canada," in Thorburn;
W. D. Young, "The Peterborough By-Election; The Success of a Party
Image," *Dalhousie Review*, XL (Winter 1960–1); J. Trenaman and D.
McQuail, *Television and the Political Image* (London 1961), ch. 3;
Campbell, *The American Voter*, 27–30; Berelson, *Voting*, 179.

35 / Wallas, *Human Nature in Politics*, 83.

for relatively long periods. Moreover, the features of these objects that are most widely known may heighten the sense of their unchanging character. At the simplest level, the elements of politics, like so much else in the external world, are known to the individual by name, and these symbols are of considerable cognitive importance to the electorate. What is more, a good deal else about the objects of politics may be characterized by symbols, ... whose persistence through time may give the objects an unchanging aspect despite wide changes in their "real" properties.[36]

For the political party that enters a political system from the outside in the way the CCF did, the question of image is a vital one for, regardless of its particular ideology or program, it must compete with the established parties in the system. Its image will be framed as a result of its own appearance through the activities and statements of its leading figures and through the propaganda directed against it by its opponents.

There are three major components of the party image – party policies, party leadership, and the general reputation of the party.[37] For a new political party, and particularly for one which is dedicated to the destruction of the *status quo*, its image is very often negative since its approach to the existing situation is critical and negative. This is a serious impediment to its progress because once a particular image is established it is difficult to change:

In political communication, as in all perception, we tend to see only what we are looking for. In the short run it is idle for a party to put forward claims or to describe itself in terms which are greatly at variance with the picture the elector already has of its image. One can only build on what is already there.[38]

Since the individual will in most cases vote for the party he sees as representing his own position better than another, the image he has of the parties is crucial to his voting behaviour. If a party has a negative or a bad image for a great many people, then it is unlikely to win many seats. Obviously where it wins it does not have this image; where it loses it does – unless one is to assume that voting is a much more rational process than any of the studies of voting behaviour have indicated. If parties are "reference groups,"[39] then their significance for the voter in this respect is determined by the voter's perception of them. In the case of the radical party, it offers greater satisfaction for "adjustment needs" and, unlike the major parties, does "ameliorate

36 / Campbell, *The American Voter*, 27.
37 / Abrams and Rose, *Must Labour Lose*, 12.
38 / Trenaman and McQuail, *Television and the Political Image*, 55.
39 / Lane, *Political Life* (Glencoe 1959), 299–303.

feelings of anomie or isolation"[40] because it is usually a protest movement as well. Conversely it is seen negatively by individuals who do not have these needs.

The most accurate way to discover a party's image is through opinion surveys with questions specifically designed to elicit information on this question. In the case of the CCF this was never done and, obviously, cannot now be done. The most that can be done is to indicate the likely components of the CCF image from which some idea of the image itself can be assumed although, in the absence of data from opinion studies, it cannot be treated as conclusive based as it is on a purely subjective assessment.

Using the three components of party images suggested by Abrams, it seems clear that the most important component, particularly at the time the CCF was operating as a political party and in view of its status as a minor party, was not leadership or party policy, but the general reputation of the party. The limited CCF budget and the fact that neither CCF national leader was either prime minister or leader of the opposition, meant that the party leaders did not have as wide a public recognition as Mackenzie King or George Drew. If they had any effect on the over-all image of the party because of their personalities and the respect they commanded as men and parliamentarians, it would be on the positive side. Generally speaking, CCF policy was not a major factor in the party image since its detailed proposals meant little to most of the electorate, which was quite probably unaware of them. It seems reasonable to argue that, had it been aware of what the party was proposing in specific terms, it might have looked on the CCF with less disfavour. The business elite in Canada was aware in at least a vague way of what CCF policy was, and this awareness stimulated them to mount an attack on the party. There are two aspects to the general reputation of the CCF. One is the part of its reputation that resulted from activities of the party itself, the other from the activities of those elements in the community that were opposed to the CCF. This latter aspect includes not only the other political parties but the business community and the newspapers as well.

One factor in creating the party's reputation has already been discussed in this chapter, and that is the kind of person who was a CCF member. Clearly not all members fell into the category of crank, rebel, or social deviant. For purposes of a party's image, however, the presence of this sort of person in the CCF in larger numbers than in the other parties and in a party that prided itself on the free and open discussion that enables the rebel to take the floor, meant that these individuals came to represent the CCF for

40 / *Ibid.*, 303.

many Canadians. Admittedly this was so partly because it was
what the general public wanted to believe the CCF was like; there
was a general disposition to believe the worst about socialists.
Because the CCF was a democratic movement it ran this risk and
suffered the consequences. The presence of individuals who
were Marxists, such as E. E. Winch, trade unionists such as
C. H. Millard, or intellectuals such as Frank Scott gave the party
its tone and style. They were, each in his own way, rebels and
protestants. In a society where conformity to the values of the
competitive market society was the norm, they represented a
negative force.

The nature of the CCF, its members and ideology, meant that
there was always the likelihood of internal dissension, ideological
debate, disciplinary proceedings, and expulsions. In short, behaviour like that of no other party in Canada. From the beginning, when the entire Ontario section had to be suspended,
through to the expulsion of Rod Young from the British Columbia section in 1954, the CCF appeared to be as often at war with
itself as it was with the forces of capitalism. Unlike the Liberal
and Conservative parties, whose structure was neither open nor
democratic, the CCF carried on most of its internecine quarrels
in public. What made matters worse was that in the case of most
of the expulsions the expelled members were charged with being
Communists. For those not favourably disposed toward the CCF
in any case, this was clear evidence that it was a near Communist
organization.

In 1936 the Ontario provincial council expelled three members and four CCF groups – two clubs, a youth group, and a
workers' association – for participating in a joint May Day cele-
bration with the Communist party and other groups.[41] In a
memorandum on the matter Woodsworth pointed out that "the
daily press is having a good deal to say regarding the dictatorial
methods of the CCF."[42] In the autumn of 1936 the British Columbia section split, with the leader, Rev. Robert Connell, taking
four of the sitting MLAs and setting up his own party, a moderate
reform group called the Social Constructives.[43] In the provincial
election of June 1, 1937 the Connell group took no seats but
won 8,000 votes, and cost the CCF at least one seat. G. H. Williams wrote to Woodsworth asking, "Why can't they quit fighting
in B.C.?"[44] – a question asked in the CCF with distressing fre-

41 / Ontario Provincial Council Minutes, June 1936, CCFP.
42 / J. S. Woodsworth, "The Ontario Situation," typewritten manuscript, n.d., CCFP.
43 / See Steeves, *The Compassionate Rebel*, 107–12; and A. Webster
to J. S. Woodsworth, Oct. 12, 1936, CCFP.
44 / G. H. Williams to J. S. Woodsworth, Nov. 25, 1936, CCFP.

quency. Woodsworth replied in a memorandum to the whole movement in which he indicated his concern with the effect the troubles were having on the party's public image:

Orthodoxy is all very well, the winning of a factional fight may bring considerable satisfaction to the winners, but what about the Movement as a whole, what about the thousands of men and women who have looked to our organization for freedom. Outsiders are saying – and with a considerable measure of truth – that if we cannot keep our own house in order we are not fit to run the affairs of a province or a nation.[45]

This memorandum had little apparent effect. The Manitoba CCF convention in October 1937 was marked by a strenuous debate between the Winnipeg North Centre constituency group and the Independent Labour party that led the *Winnipeg Free Press* to state in a headline: "CCF Convention at Brandon Marked by Bitter Dispute."[46]

The cumulative effect on the party of the constant stream of bad publicity was not lost on the more politically astute members of the party. Herbert Gargrave, provincial secretary in British Columbia, wrote to Lewis about the problem following the 1940 general election:

With regard to the election results, our greatest disappointment is of course the loss of Grant MacNeil. There is no doubt his stand on the war and the resolution moved in the House, together with the utterances of Mrs. Steeves and Colin Cameron in the Provincial Legislature, had a great deal to do with his defeat, and for that matter, with the general setback we received in the province.[47]

Colin Cameron did little to further the image of the party in subsequent speeches dealing with the war effort which, although in most cases they constituted valid criticism from the socialist point of view, were inconsistent with popular attitudes toward the war. In 1941 he referred to the war savings plans as "polite blackmailing schemes," despite the fact that M. J. Coldwell had declared himself "heart and soul behind the war savings campaign."[48] Lewis commented in a subsequent letter, "Too bad we have to spend so much time and energy straightening out difficulties which should never have arisen if responsible party spokes-

45 / J. S. Woodsworth, "The Need for Unity," typewritten manuscript, n.d., CCFP.
46 / *Winnipeg Free Press*, Oct. 18, 1937.
47 / H. Gargrave to D. Lewis, April 3, 1940, CCFP. See the Vancouver *Sun*, Nov. 4, 1939, and subsequent issues for the ensuing controversy.
48 / D. Lewis to H. Gargrave, Feb. 28, 1941, CCFP, and see also *Hansard*, 1941, 1077, and the Vancouver *Sun*, Feb. 28, 1941.

men would constantly keep before them the fact that whether they like it or not, they can never speak for themselves alone."[49]

It was in 1943 that the most widely reported *gaffe* of this nature was made by Harold Winch, then leader of the British Columbia CCF, in a speech to a meeting in Calgary on November 12. The report, filed by Canadian Press and carried in most associated newspapers, quoted him as saying, "when we become the government, we will institute Socialism immediately," and that the power of the police and military would be used to force obedience on those opposed to the law. He was also reported as saying that "those who defied the government's will would be treated as criminals, if capitalism says no, then we know the answer – so did Russia."[50] For those opponents who feared that the party's success in Ontario might be repeated, Winch's speech was pure gold. It provided material for anti-CCF propaganda for some years after.

The St. John *Telegraph-Journal*[51] published a "box" with statements from Hitler, Winch, and Coldwell in it, all threatening the use of force to quell law-breakers. The statements by Winch and Coldwell were unexceptional and had they been made by the Chief Constable of Orillia they would have been applauded. But in the context of the conventional view of socialism, they appeared thoroughly totalitarian. Lewis referred to Winch's "unguarded words" in a letter in which he pointed out that "they have not been harmful everywhere, but in some places very seriously so."[52] Stanley Knowles was more specific: "A few weeks ago Brandon looked to be ours with a bang, but the capital made out of H. W. was terrific, and as one (along with Tommy) who clarified and explained Harold's position, and ours, to the satisfaction of our audiences, perhaps I can be frank enough to say that the tempest over H. W. almost cost us the Brandon seat."[53] While the party was increasing its support, it suffered unnecessarily from the failure of many of its members to avoid providing the opposition with ammunition.

It was particularly important that caution be exercised in the period 1943–5 because the CCF was approaching the status of a major party on the basis of its performance at the polls in Ontario and Saskatchewan. Opposition forces were anxious to find the slightest weakness in the party's armour. Its success seemed

49 / D. Lewis to H. Gargrave, March 3, 1941, CCFP.
50 / See, for example, the Winnipeg *Tribune*, Nov. 13, 1943 and the St. John *Telegraph-Journal*, Nov. 15, 1943.
51 / St. John *Telegraph-Journal*, Nov. 15, 1943; Montreal *Gazette*, Nov. 22, 1943; and Zakuta, *A Protest Movement Becalmed*, 71, n. 1.
52 / D. Lewis to Watson Baird, Dec. 2, 1943, CCFP.
53 / S. Knowles to D. Lewis, Nov. 20, 1943, CCFP.

to fill its radical elements with new vigour, and they stated their views with greater vehemence than before. Their attitude was typified by Colin Cameron:

... I was perturbed a short time ago to see a report of an interview Mr. Coldwell gave to *Liberty*. In this report Mr. Coldwell was quoted as saying that "business men in general need not fear the CCF as the party has no desire to cause suffering but rather to eliminate it." I should have thought that business men had a great deal to fear from the CCF – that is if they value their wealth-extracting privileges and there is no reason to suppose they don't.

It seems to me a matter of little importance whether Canada's few thousand big and little chisellers fear the CCF – though I say it is rather an unhealthy sign if they don't. What is important is that Canada's millions of workers should be convinced that the CCF means business.[54]

Cameron's position was not simply the view expected from the British Columbia wing of the party; it was shared by many others, including the provincial secretary in Nova Scotia, Lloyd Shaw. Shaw wrote to Winch about a similar speech made earlier in 1943:

Personally I think you have done a real service to the movement by making no bones about the fact that the CCF is a militant revolutionary socialist party. It is becoming more and more evident that even in the East people are looking for these fundamental changes for which the CCF stands. It will hurt us more than it will help us to mince words about the matter.[55]

The national convention in Montreal in November 1944 provided the party's opponents with an opportunity to depict the CCF as a party at war with itself and one which displayed signs of totalitarianism. The chief antagonists at the convention were Winch, Cameron, and Lewis; the chief issue was how much socialization and how soon. The question arose in debate over the party election manifesto for the coming general election.

The party leaders were anxious to reassure the "small business man" that the intent of the CCF was to nationalize only monopolies. Cameron's response was "we hardly need to be concerned with the feelings of small businessmen if we are to carry out an extensive socialization program."[56] Lewis defended his purity as a socialist but advanced an argument based on simple expedience:

54 / *Edmonton Journal*, Dec. 1, 1944; *Winnipeg Free Press*, Nov. 30, 1944, etc.
55 / Lloyd Shaw to Harold Winch, Aug. 31, 1943, CCFP.
194   56 / *Windsor Star*, Dec. 1, 1944; Montreal *Gazette*, Nov. 30, 1944.

I do not take second place to them in my belief in complete socialism as the answer to our problems, but I am in favour of applying democratic measures to gain our election. I must be concerned with the reaction ... certain phrases and words have on the voters of Canada.[57]

A Vancouver *Sun* editorial sums up the reaction of most newspapers in Canada:

Down in Montreal the CCF is having trouble in figuring out the "right" story to tell voters at the next federal election. Delegates to its eighth national convention can't agree. Harold Winch and Colin Cameron think it would be preferable to tell "all" about the party and its plans for all-out socialism. Others believe this would be too scary.

Mr. Lewis protests that he is a wolf too, only he would like to pretend to be Little Red Riding Hood until it was too late for the electors to fathom his disguise.[58]

In 1945 Berry Richards and D. L. Johnson, both members of the Manitoba legislature, were suspended from the Manitoba CCF for attacking their party in the provincial legislature and for their close contact with the Labour Progressive Party. Richards was subsequently re-instated; Johnson was expelled.[59] In 1948, 6 members of the Sudbury CCF were suspended for supporting the candidacy of R. H. Carlin, a former CCF member who, having been refused CCF endorsation as a party candidate because of his support of the pro-Communist executive of the Mine, Mill and Smelter Workers' Union, ran in the provincial election as an independent. Carlin was, at the time of the election, a sitting member of the provincial legislature.[60] In April 1955 the Ontario party had to expel 14 members. It was claimed that they were Trotskyites.[61]

These are the disabilities of any ideologically-based party; debate and disagreement are inevitable. It is one of the ironies of democratic socialist parties that the unity they require as ideological parties is denied by their democratic structure, which is itself an aspect of their ideology. But the spectacle of such activity viewed by voters unaccustomed to debate and made uneasy by

57 / Montreal *Gazette*, Nov. 30, 1944.
58 / Vancouver *Sun*, Dec. 1, 1944. See also the Canadian Press dispatches on the convention, esp. Nov. 30 and Dec. 1, which most newspapers in Canada printed.
59 / S. Knowles to D. Lewis, March 10, 1945, CCFP; *Winnipeg Tribune*, March 2, 1945; *Winnipeg Free Press*, Dec. 10, 1945, and the "Richards-Johnson" file in CCFP.
60 / "Memorandum on R. H. Carlin and Other Former Members of the Sudbury Group," July 23, 1948, CCFP.
61 / Ontario CCF Convention Minutes, 1955; *Hansard,* 1955, 2893–4, 2929; and "Onward and Upward with the Revolution," *Canadian Forum*, XXXV (June 1955).

open disagreement and by the aura of revolution that surrounded
the CCF, meant that its image was unlikely to dispose the middle-
class Canadian to support it.

The CCF's reputation was not improved by its choice of words
and the style of its statements and speeches. Attacking the big
shots and capitalism within the context of prairie radicalism was
not inconsistent with winning the wheat farmer's vote. Similar
attacks in the context of urban society were less successful if only
because the worker was too close and too dependent upon his
employer to join in wholesale condemnation of his activities.
Woodsworth could declare, as he did at the Hygeia Hall in
Toronto in 1932, that "the control of the country is in the hands
of the vampires of capitalism," but it nevertheless remained true
that for many people these "vampires" were the folk heroes of
the North American culture.

There was some point in attacking the institutions of society
in the 1930s and declaring that "A Vote for King Is a Vote for
the Rich," although in some respects, even at that time, the value
of this appeal was dubious. It makes far less sense when conditions of prosperity prevail. In 1945 most Canadians did not want
to be reminded of the Depression and few were willing to think
in terms of the rhetoric of that bleak period. Yet part of the CCF
campaign in the 1945 general election was designed to remind
voters of the Depression and warn them that if they did not vote
CCF then depression would surely follow the war. The appeal of
a pamphlet headed "Sorry Brother, No Jobs Today" is nothing
if not negative. The CCF pamphlets that did not warn of impending economic disaster promised the voters welfare, rehabilitation,
and consumer goods a-plenty through democratic planning. The
first appeal was not successful for obvious reasons, the second
because specific promises did not seem plausible from a party
that had never been even on the threshold of power and also
smacked of continued wartime controls. Anti-CCF propaganda
and the Ontario defeat did little to make the voter more receptive
to the CCF national campaign.

The constant reiteration by the CCF of the need for control,
although theoretically valid, made the party look as though it
was anxious to restrict rather than free. In 1947 Frank Underhill
pointed out, " ... when socialists keep on harping about controls
as the essence of their policy, they lend plausibility to the changes
that they are really frustrated bureaucrats with an itch to manage
other people's business for them."[62] His warning had no effect.
In a nation-wide radio broadcast in 1948, Coldwell called for the

62 / F. H. Underhill, "Random Remarks on Socialism and Freedom,"
Canadian Forum, XXVII (Aug. 1947), 110.

re-imposition of wartime controls, controls which most people remembered with distaste.[63]

Lewis could call for "pioneers of today to clear a road to progress through the jungle of capitalist monopoly to remove poverty, insecurity, and slums, ignorance, prejudice and hate from our land,"[64] but such rhetoric had little appeal for many Canadians, who were unaware of these aspects of Canadian life. And this approach collided with the Victorian attitude not uncommon in Canada, that where such conditions existed they were the fault of the individuals concerned. In the competitive market society there is little support for appeals to co-operate in rescuing those who are less well off. In a race, only a fool stops or turns back to help the others catch up.

The tone and style of the CCF appeal to the people was not, given the nature of Canadian society, such that it would be accompanied by a perception that the CCF represented the individuals' interests better than either the Liberal or Conservative parties.[65] The CCF was not seen as a vehicle for upward social mobility. In the immediate post-war mood of expansion it seemed slightly anachronistic.

Appeals by the CCF were constantly directed toward the "farmers and the workers" or the "housewives, farmers, workers and pensioners," each one a low status figure for most urban Canadians. In 1948 the Ontario CCF devised several scripts for one minute radio "spots." They included the following lines:

I'm a member of ... (union). At the end of each week I get ... (sum) in take home pay. I find it pretty hard to make ends meet. Like most working girls, I'm going to vote for the CCF.

I'll tell you why working men are giving every help they can to the CCF.

I want to give you the point of view of 150,000 workers who are members of the Ontario Federation of Labour.[66]

Of 19 scripts prepared, 11 were based on unions, labour, and workers. Only those who saw themselves as "workers" and hence had some class orientation tended to identify with the people who, on the broadcasts, were going to vote CCF. The appeal to class consciousness in post-war Canada was invalid.[67] When in the 1953 and 1957 election campaigns the CCF simplified its propaganda and used a coloured comic strip, the pro-CCF charac-

63 / "The Nation's Business," Jan. 8, 1948, CCFP.
64 / Ibid., Oct. 8, 1947, CCFP.
65 / Campbell, The American Voter, 144.
66 / Scripts for broadcast, 1948, CCFP.
67 / See below, note 102, this chapter.

ters were a labourer and a farmer, both in overalls. The figure in
ordinary middle-class dress was anti-CCF. The slogan was "Share
the Wealth."

Yet the party leaders were not ignorant of the importance of
effective propaganda. How the message was presented was sub-
jected to almost as much scrutiny by the leaders as what was in
the message. In 1934 Frank Underhill, on behalf of the LSR,
prepared a memorandum on the future of the party in which he
said:

Most of us here feel that the CCF has now gone about as far as it can
go upon the wave of emotional resentment against current conditions
which has swept over Canada in the last three years. If it is to become
a permanent movement it must achieve a more effective organization
and develop new techniques of public education and propaganda.[68]

In the 1940 election campaign literature was prepared almost
exclusively by the national office. The kind of literature that was
presented was the result of a close examination of what would be
effective by the national secretary in consultation with advertising
experts. In correspondence with Herbert Gargrave and Barry
Mather of the British Columbia CCF, David Lewis outlined the
principles on which the material was based:

(a) would deal with the immediate issues of the campaign.
(b) would be written in simple language which avoided terms familiar
to grounded socialists but which are unfamiliar to the man in the
street and therefore frighten him.
(c) would be short so that the elector can read it almost at a glance.[69]

More specifically Lewis pointed out, "if I may say so I doubt
very much the wisdom of the use in election literature of such
terms as 'class conflict' and 'imperialist struggles,'" also adding
that he clearly favoured the use of such terms in general educational literature.[70] What he failed to see was that although educational literature was primarily for party members it was not
private and, of more importance, provided the material for be-
tween-election proselytization. It was the language of the educational material that was the language of the party member canvassing and speaking. Despite these principles, the 1940 literature
did not avoid the pitfalls. The issues were, as Lewis saw them:
civil liberties, opposition to profiteering, "Making the Rich do
their Part," post-war rehabilitation, and providing "A Square

68 / F. H. Underhill, "Memorandum based on discussions at L.S.R.
Conference, Feb. 11, 1934," typewritten, Woodsworth Papers.
69 / D. Lewis to H. Gargrave, Feb. 8, 1940, CCFP.
70 / D. Lewis to B. Mather, Feb. 13, 1940, CCFP.

Deal for the Producer." They were put out in leaflets that had a single bleak cartoon and three pages of prose. It was an improvement over 1935 but only in tone. It was difficult to break with the ethos of the movement which demanded honesty and detailed accuracy. The socialist saw so much that was wrong and such potential for improvement that he was unable to stop at one slogan.

A writer in the *Canadian Forum* said the CCF presented its 1940 program in too academic a manner and seemed uninterested in winning the support of the middle class. He asked, "why was so much time and so much thunder devoted to damning our profiteers and none at all to damning Hitler?"[71] Lewis replied to the article, pointing out that it was not possible for the CCF "to compete with the old parties in patriotism and imperialism" and that it was futile to try.[72] It seems clear that he did not at this point see the war as offering an opportunity for the CCF to increase its support; it was, in his view, a time to buttress the party itself:

... to try to arrive at a correct war policy on the basis of possible electoral support is not only questionable in principle but shortsighted politically. The only consideration which is admissible, other than questions relating to the nature of the war and the Canadian socialists concern with it, is the internal unity and future strength of the party.[73]

This position is symptomatic of the paranoia with which the CCF was afflicted at the outbreak of war and of the influence of European socialist attitudes in Lewis's approach to politics. The emphasis was not on winning votes but on strengthening the party – the vanguard of revolution. In this case the change had to be won, as Lewis knew, by winning elections, but he assumed that a strong party cadre could do so. In this assumption he was mistaken.

Angus MacInnis, in many ways the most realistic politician in the party's ruling circle, pleaded for a more pragmatic approach:

We must, however, go out for a program that will have a close relation to reality, that will accept conditions as they are with all the imperfections and, if you like, contradictions which meet us on every hand. Out of this mess we must point the way which will take us step by step

71 / R. E. K. Pemberton, "The CCF, the Election and the Future," *Canadian Forum* xx (April 1940), 38. See also P. Spencer, "Pardon Me Madam, How Often Do You Take A Bath? A Survey of Surveys," *Canadian Forum*, xx (May 1940); in which the author urges the CCF to develop a strategy relevant "to the readers of Popeye and the listeners of Charlie McCarthy," 276.

72 / D. Lewis, "Wanted, Brawn As Well as Brains," *Canadian Forum*, xx (June 1940), **76.**

73 / *Ibid.*, **77.**

to the new social order. We cannot do that if our program is to consist
of sneers at the amount of, or the quality of democracy which we now
have and vague rantings about how beautiful things might be if all
people were as good and wise as we are.[74]

In 1944 a committee chaired by Morden Lazarus, Ontario
provincial secretary, and a man with some experience in publicity
and advertising, studied CCF propaganda and found it to be dull,
badly laid-out, repetitious, and lacking in personal appeal. They
recommended it be made colourful, catchy, and entertaining,
and urged, "in short, DON'T PREACH!"[75] The report recommended
that the party adopt the style and clarity of the anti-CCF booklet
prepared by B. A. Trestrail, *Stand Up and Be Counted*.

The CCF campaign literature was explicit but, like the party, it
was depression-oriented. The national executive report to the
national convention in 1946 stated "it is not difficult to foresee
the disaster toward which our country is heading." In 1948 it
pointed out that "we now again have uncontrolled capitalism,
and Canadian families feel the result in a lower standard of
living"; and in 1950 the national executive resolution "Plan
Lasting Prosperity Now" stated "not as a prophet of gloom, but
as a determined fighter for prosperity, the CCF warns the Canadian people of the possibility of economic crisis."[76] The symbolic
content of CCF propaganda was decidedly negative.

By 1955 it was clear to the leaders in all sections of the party
that a new approach had to be found or the CCF would disappear.
Fred Zaplitny, MP for Dauphin, wrote to Lorne Ingle pointing
out that the main stumbling block was fear of the CCF; "people
don't know what it would do if it came to power."[77] F. von Pilis,
chairman of the National CCF Farm Committee, reported that the
farmers who did not support the CCF – and by this time farm
support in Saskatchewan was declining steadily – believed that
the CCF stood for state socialism, was dominated by organized
labour, and was anti-religious.[78] These attitudes are urban
middle-class attitudes and show the influence of the anti-CCF
propaganda campaigns.

In 1943, when the Gallup Poll showed CCF strength increasing, the most extensive and most vicious propaganda campaign
ever directed against a single political party in Canadian history
was mounted. There were two aspects to the campaign. One was
national and extensive. The second was provincial, confined

74 / A. MacInnis to D. Lewis, Jan. 17, 1941, CCFP.
75 / "Criticism of Current CCF Propaganda," Feb. 1944, mimeo., CCFP.
76 / Reports of the Ninth, Tenth, and Eleventh National Conventions
(1946, 1948, 1950).
77 / F. Zaplitny to Lorne Ingle, Dec. 29, 1955, CCFP.
78 / National Council Minutes, January 1955, CCFP.

largely to Ontario, and intensive. Both were financed by contributions from large corporations, banks, and trust companies.
The campaign funds of the Conservative party were increased
substantially by business interests in the face of the CCF
"threat."[79]

Propaganda, as many students of politics have pointed out,[80]
seldom converts; it usually reinforces attitudes already in existence. In the case of the anti-CCF propaganda, much of its effect
was due to its confirmation of existing attitudes and suspicions
and to its appeal to existing prejudices: xenophobia, anti-semitism, and anti-intellectualism. As a movement, the CCF was
dedicated to bringing about fundamental changes in the existing
social and economic order. It was attacking those institutions
which had a vested interest in the preservation of the *status quo*
and this meant not only corporate business but the communications media as well. It started with an almost insurmountable
disadvantage in that the very people it had to win to its side
accepted, for the most part, the *status quo* as the best of all
possible worlds and, in addition, formed their attitudes and had
them reinforced by what they read and heard from the leaders
of society through the media of communication which these same
leaders controlled.[81] Unable to demonstrate the validity of its
thesis and forced to challenge the prevailing values of Canadian
society, the CCF had to resort to ideological argument, argument
which was ineffective from an electoral point of view and which
by its nature placed the CCF at a further disadvantage. Lewis
was aware of this dilemma:

... I would personally like to see us think out a strategy which would
avoid our being on the defensive in an ideological argument about
socialism. There is grave danger that this is exactly what will happen
as far as our opposition is concerned, and ideological arguments place
us at a disadvantage in view of the traditional prejudices of the Canadian People.[82]

Given the nature of the CCF there was little that could be done.

The growth of CCF popularity, beginning in 1942 and culmin-
ating in the startling success of the party in the 1943 Ontario

79 / E. E. Harrill, "Money in Canadian Politics," in Thorburn, *Party
Politics*, 68.
80 / Avery Leiserson, *Parties and Politics* (New York 1958), 268; B.
Berelson, "Communications and Public Opinion," in B. Berelson and M.
Janowitz, eds., *Reader in Public Opinion & Communications* (Glencoe
1953), 458–61; P. Lazarsfeld and R. Merton, "Requisite Conditions for
Propaganda Success," in R. Christenson and R. McWilliams, eds., *Voice
of the People* (New York 1962), 340–4.
81 / See John Porter, *Vertical Mosaic*, chs. 15, 16.
82 / D. Lewis to A. Brewin, Sept. 11, 1948, CCFP.

provincial election, drew an almost immediate response from the
business establishment in Canada. The party had never enjoyed
support from the daily press, as any survey of editorial opinion
from 1933 on will immediately show. But from 1943 it was the
object of a sustained attack that showed no sign of subsiding
until after the 1949 general election. The sniping lasted through
the party's merger with labour in 1961.

The period of greatest concentration was 1943–5. The files of
the CCF contain no fewer than forty booklets attacking the party
and twice as many pamphlets of all descriptions, not to mention
the monthly news letters of the Canadian and local chambers of
commerce and the various boards of trade across the country,
which directed a great deal of attention to what was considered
a serious menace to Canadian liberties and free enterprise. During this period the standard approach was to depict the CCF as
totalitarian with a Nazi emphasis; after the war the emphasis
was on the similarity of the CCF and Soviet communism. Not
atypical was the following editorial from the Ottawa *Journal* of
April 29, 1944:

Illustrative of this sort of thing is a story going the rounds that a "little
black book" is kept at CCF headquarters in which are recorded the
names of individuals to be "looked after" when the party comes to
power. Thus: "We were also told that the CCF has men in positions to
find out who is working against the party. Spies are here and there to
check over who contributes to this movement, who donates to that
cause. The names are all carefully noted and they are marked for
special attention when the day comes. We are interested in that little
black book of the Socialists in Canada, because the National Socialists
in Germany also kept a record of those opposed the Nazis. When
Hitler came to power in the Reich there were people who were
'looked after' by Storm Troopers, just as we are informed the CCF
intends to 'look after' the persons in the little black book. Now all we
have to do is find out who will be the CCF's Himmler." Now this sort
of tale which no sane person can believe, shouldn't be circulated in
this country; certainly shouldn't be circulated without documented
proof.

The three figures who were most prominent in the anti-CCF
campaign were B. A. Trestrail, Gladstone Murray, and Jack
Boothe, cartoonist for the *Globe and Mail* and for the Trestrail
publications. Boothe's cartoons invariably depicted the CCF protagonists as either bespectacled academics in cap and gown or
vicious looking foreigners with exaggerated semitic features.
Trestrail established the Public Informational Association and
solicited retainers from businessmen across the country in order

to finance his anti-CCF activities. Although no records are available, it seems clear that he received considerable support. His major publication, a booklet entitled *Social Suicide*, condensed from his book, *Stand Up and Be Counted!*, was mailed to every postal address in Canada prior to the 1945 general election according to claims made by Trestrail in a leaflet soliciting funds. At any rate, over 27,000 people returned a contest entry form printed on the back of each leaflet.[83] Stuart Jamieson, CCF Research Director, estimated that over five million copies of the leaflet were mailed.[84]

The burden of Trestrail's argument in *Social Suicide* was that the CCF advocated "state socialism" which would retain "wartime regimentation" and would control "through a vast army of officials, the lives and habits of *everyone*."[85] The theme was advanced by selections from various CCF publications, allusions to the "failure" of socialism in Australia and New Zealand, and thinly veiled anti-intellectualism and anti-semitism: Frank Scott "was a professor in the Faculty of Law at McGill University," and "he has had no practical business experience." Lewis, whose name was printed in quotation marks, was described as "a Russian-Polish-Jew," the son of "Mowcha Losz." They were dismissed as "professional Social Students" with no practical experience.[86] Coldwell and E. B. Jolliffe, leader of the Ontario CCF, were depicted as puppets manipulated by these two sinister figures.

Following his apparent success in the 1945 campaign, Trestrail continued his activities with the distribution in 1948 of a book of anti-CCF cartoons by Jack Boothe and, in 1949, a mailing of a second pamphlet *Is Democracy Doomed?* This pamphlet was financed by General Relations Services Limited, Public and Industrial Relations Counsel. Firms wishing to support the campaign engaged General Relations Services as public relations counsel for two hundred dollars.[87] The theme was similar to *Social Suicide*, but the format, half-tabloid and pulp, indicated that the fund raising had been less successful than before.

83 / "General Outline of the 7-Point Educational Program to be conducted by *The Public Informational Association*," mimeo., "Trestrail" file, CCFP. *Social Suicide* bears neither date nor name of publisher, although it was published by McClelland and Stewart.

84 / S. Jamieson to Roy Thorne, May 28, 1945, CCFP. Trestrail financed his campaign by soliciting funds from businesses by mail and through agents. See "Trestrail" file, CCFP.

85 / B. A. Trestrail, *Social Suicide* (Toronto [c. 1945]), 12; emphasis in the original.

86 / *Ibid.*, 7–8.

87 / Form letter (mimeo) soliciting funds, "signed" by D. A. B. Murray, Winnipeg, March 2, 1949, CCFP.

Gladstone Murray retired from his position as general manager of the CBC in 1943 and established Responsible Enterprise Ltd., contributing his knowledge of public relations to the anti-CCF campaign through the reprinting of his own and others' speeches, and the publication of *Outlook*, an anti-CCF, anti-labour newsletter. He commenced his activities on the basis of a three-year plan of action and a proposed budget of $100,000 provided, it would seem, by a small group of backers whose names he appended to a letter seeking general support.[88] Gladstone Murray's Responsible Enterprise Ltd. outlasted the Trestrail operation and flourished until the autumn of 1964 when, at the urging of his "directors," Murray retired.

Public campaigns of the sort described above could, at least, be answered through letters to newspapers, speeches, and counter-propaganda. And the CCF did what it could in these ways to meet the often scurrilous charges of its more rabid opponents. There was one kind of anti-CCF campaign that was difficult to answer: the stuffing of pay envelopes with admonitions to vote for free enterprise. The extent of this kind of activity cannot be determined. On the basis of hearsay evidence it was fairly wide and is not uncommon today. In 1945 a Montreal firm enclosed a reprint of excerpts from Friedrich Hayek's *Road to Serfdom* and the following memorandum in its employees' pay envelopes: "You may vote CCF against my advice as this is your privilege. I cannot, however, accept the responsibility of maintaining employment for you and other members of our organization for any length of time under a CCF controlled government."[89] In the absence of any empirical data from opinion surveys, the effects of this kind of propaganda, and the more specific sort provided by the Trestrails and Murrays, cannot be accurately determined. It seems safe to assert, however, that its effect on the fortunes of the CCF was considerable. For those who had been in the party since before the war, it doubtless reinforced their support of the CCF; for those who joined during the wartime boom in party support, it no doubt weakened their resolve to stay and probably caused a number of defections. And there is some indication that it was a factor in the setback the Ontario party suffered in the 1945 provincial election.[90]

88 / Form letter (mimeo) signed by Gladstone Murray, Toronto, Sept. 29, 1943, CCFP. See also "Gladstone Murray as a Point of Reference," *Canadian Forum*, XXIII (March 1944). Among Murray's backers were Stephen Leacock, Arthur Meighen, J. S. Duncan (Massey-Harris), J. Y. Murdoch (Bank of Nova Scotia), and Norman Dawes (National Breweries).

89 / "Inter Office Memo" (photocopy), Lyman House, Montreal, May 29, 1945, CCFP.

90 / G. Caplan, "The Failure of Canadian Socialism: The Ontario

By 1950 the anti-CCF campaign had largely subsided, having succeeded in achieving its goal. The daily newspapers, however, did not relent. They maintained a steady opposition through their editorial columns and, not infrequently, in their regular news coverage. No Canadian political party has ever had as consistently antagonistic a press as did the CCF. It was not unusual for a newspaper to praise a particular aspect of CCF policy, and quite common for it to compliment the party for its parliamentary skills and principled behaviour, but whenever an election was in the offing, past credits were forgotten and the CCF could expect every daily newspaper in the country to oppose it. As would be expected, the level of consistent opposition was at its height during the early forties.[91] After the end of the war, newspapers were at pains to link the CCF with communism and seized upon any statement made by party members that would lend support to this thesis. Coverage of CCF conventions invariably emphasized those aspects of the intra-party debate that would bring the party into disrepute. Statements about the CCF by its opponents were given full coverage and often major headlines. Newspapers criticized the other parties frequently, but never in the same tone or terms that were reserved for the CCF. Other parties were seen as perhaps misguided; the CCF was dangerous.

In such circumstances it would have been surprising if the CCF image was anything but negative. The effect was cumulative for, anti-CCF propaganda being as widespread and vehement as it was, the moderate were dissuaded from joining or at least actively supporting the CCF. It tended as well to encourage the rebel to join. And as a result any likelihood of the party image improving diminished, if it did not disappear entirely. What is remarkable is that under such an assault the CCF managed to survive with as much intact as it did. For those in the party, the attacks offered clear evidence that the CCF was having a decided effect on the Canadian establishment. In this fact they found considerable solace.

Once a particular image of a party is established, such as that of the CCF, otherwise innocent party statements are read into a pre-existing context that distorts their true meaning. Statements which would be seen as unexceptional when made by the Liberal

Experience, 1932–1945," *Canadian Historical Review*, XLIV (June 1963), 114–16;119–20.

91 / An inspection of the files of any newspaper, particularly for the periods preceding elections, will provide numerous examples. See, for example, the *Winnipeg Free Press*, May 23, 1944; *Ottawa Journal*, Jan. 12, 1944; Sidney *Post Record*, April 5, 1948; *Winnipeg Tribune*, Jan. 26, 1945; Vancouver *Province*, June 6, 8, 1949; and see Porter, *Vertical Mosaic*, 483–4.

party would be seen as un-Canadian if made by the CCF. It is true that, for example, planning means one thing to a liberal and perhaps another to a socialist, but where meanings converge the socialist in an anti-socialist atmosphere has a poor audience.

When a socialist party speaks to what it considers to be its audience, it often uses terms and forms of address which it considers applicable.[92] It assumes that there is a class in society that is waiting to hear and act upon what the socialist party has to say. Such parties do not as a rule make a general appeal; they are by definition exclusive in this respect. They stand for and speak to the workers, the toilers, the proletariat. They must assume that others, as well as the socialists, see and make the same distinctions in society they do.

The CCF directed its appeal primarily to the workers and the farmers. In doing so it assumed that there were class differences in Canada, that the members of the classes were aware of these differences, and, most important, that they were prepared to support the party which identified itself with their class interests. The first assumption was correct and the second partially so, at least insofar as a significant number of the wheat farmers were concerned. As Macpherson has pointed out, the wheat farmers were aware of their interests as an occupational group, if not as a class in the strict sense, and were prepared to act in defence of their common interests.[93] The workers, on the other hand, lacked both this occupational awareness and class consciousness in the strict sense. Their response, it would seem, tended to be more in the nature of status consciousness rather than class consciousness, and consequently their identification was not with the party that represented the class they were in but with the party that represented the status they sought.

Alford suggests that the fact that class voting is low in Canada, lower than in the United States for example, does not imply that there are no class interests in Canada.[94] He points out that, "class cleavages do exist in Canada and are expressed in political demands and through political parties, but they do not result in sharply divergent support by social classes for the major national parties."[95] The reason for this, he argues, is that the parties are identified as regional, religious, and ethnic groupings. This iden-

92 / From 1936 to 1959 many letters in and out of the national office began "Dear Comrade" and ended "Comradely yours." Convention delegates frequently referred to "Comrade Chairman." With the infusion of trade union support a more common form of address was "Brother Chairman." See Underhill's comments on the language problem at Regina in 1933 in the Fox transcript.
93 / C. B. Macpherson, *Democracy*, 225–8.
94 / R. R. Alford, *Party and Society* (Chicago 1963), 251.
95 / *Ibid.*

tification does not quite square with the facts nor does it help to explain why, if the CCF attracted more support from the manual than from the non-manual workers, the Liberals attracted manual support even more than the CCF.[96] One possible explanation, and one consistent with the earlier discussion of the CCF image, is simply that manual workers saw the Liberal party as corresponding more closely than the CCF to their status aspirations. Only those who were working class, conscious of it and anti-middle class – and this would include trade union officials[97] – would support the CCF.

By tying itself to the "farmers and workers," the CCF effectively denied itself middle-class support and the support of a significant portion of the working class. It could count on the votes of only those whose ambitions were frustrated, whose income was low, whose job was unsatisfactory or who, as in the case of the immigrant population, were unable to establish themselves as part of Canadian society. Those who were "occupationally upwardly mobile" were not prepared to link themselves to a party that represented the status they were discarding or were anxious to discard.[98] In other words, the CCF directed its appeal to those who were most likely to vote for it anyway. For those who, in the context of the CCF ideology, should have supported the party, it stood for the very things they wanted to forget: the working class, the Depression, rancour, criticism, iconoclasm.[99]

The fact that the CCF voter was more committed, that he tended to vote more consistently for his party both provincially and nationally, election after election, than the Liberal or Conservative voter, indicates that support for the party was more deliberate and specific.[100] It required a more conscious choice

96 / *Ibid.*, and see table B-4, 354, which shows CCF support among manual occupations as 28 per cent in 1945 (its highest) compared with 43 per cent for the Liberals.

97 / See S. M. Lipset, *Political Man* (New York 1960), 243–54. The trade union leader has higher status than the rank and file member and is probably more conscious of his exclusion from the upper middle-class society for which his rank and income would qualify him were he not a "labour man." This might account for the fact that union leaders were keener supporters of the CCF than their followers, who were too far from the status goal to perceive the barriers. See Porter, *Vertical Mosaic*, ch. XI, esp. 342–4, 395.

98 / See, for example, Lipset, *Political Man*, 240.

99 / As the CCF became more closely allied and identified with organized labour, the national party's support in Saskatchewan declined from 1945 to 1949, made a slight recovery in 1953, and fell markedly to a record low in 1963 of 18 per cent of the popular vote (76,071) compared with 21 per cent (73,505) in 1935. At its height in 1945 the CCF polled 44 per cent (167,233) of the vote in Saskatchewan.

100 / Alford, *Party and Society*, 268; and see Meisel, "The June 1962 Election," 343. Meisel refers to NDP support as the result of "commitment

for one obvious reason: it meant, in most ridings, voting for the party that had little chance of either winning the seat or forming the government. Less obvious but equally important is the point that "the interrelationship of one party with all other legitimate segments of the social structure requires a minority party supporter to accept the role of social deviant."[101] As already discussed above, this is particularly so when the minority party is clearly identified as radical and has, as well, a negative image. Only those who took their politics seriously were likely to vote CCF. This is not a characteristic of the working class.[102] The groups with the highest levels of participation as voters or party members are those at the upper end of the socio-economic scale.

The likelihood was slight that the CCF would ever reach the working class and weld it into a solid political force, sufficient to be the sole support of the party and put it into office.[103] It was slight in the absence of adequate channels of communication; it was slight because most workers accepted the assumptions of the market society; and it was slight because of the strength of the pressures to conform in Canadian society. In short, the conditions which lead to leftist voting were largely absent. The media of communication represented the middle class and propagated middle-class values. As Regenstreif points out, the workers read newspapers "which are hostile to trade unions and workers' parties and which present each attempt at group conscious activity by workers in a less than favorable light."[104] The working class is constantly exposed to the dominant values of society through the media of communications. This may lead to cross-pressures that reduce the likelihood of voting. On the other hand, in a multi-party situation where one party reflects not only the dominant values but a propensity to move left, as in the case of the Liberal party, the individual may solve his dilemma and avoid the role of deviant by voting Liberal rather than CCF.

The Political Action Committees of the CCL and later of the

to a seriously held view about the nature of society and government." This, of course, was equally true of the CCF.

101 / S. M. Lipset, et al., "The Psychology of Voting," in G. Lindzey, ed., Handbook of Social Psychology (Cambridge 1954), II, 1166–7.

102 / Lipset, Political Man, 183–9.

103 / Macpherson points out that where "there is no single class large enough to be the sole support of a party," the party tends to become unprincipled. The CCF leaders believed they could win with only working-class support and assumed that they could get that support by education and the activities of the PAC. The extent to which the Winnipeg Declaration and the formation of the NDP represent a flight from principle and hence justification of Macpherson's point seems quite clear. See Macpherson, Democracy, 59–60; and ch. 5 above.

104 / Regenstreif, "Some Aspects of National Party Support in Canada," 63; and Porter, Vertical Mosaic, 457–62; 482–7.

CLC were designed to offset the union member's lack of interest in politics and, more specifically, to interest him in the CCF. They did provide a channel of communication for CCF propaganda and for leftist views generally, but it was also generally agreed that they failed to mobilize the support for the CCF that its originators had expected.[105] After ten years of PAC activity, there were only 18 union locals affiliated in Ontario with a total of 4,130 members.[106]

The fact that the CCF was a movement which demanded time and effort of its members was another factor that militated against it deriving greater support from the working class. If the availability of leisure time and the use made of leisure time determine the interest an individual takes in politics and hence in voting,[107] how much more is this a factor in determining whether or not an individual will involve himself actively in a political party which makes great demands on his time? If one of the factors in the success of the CCF in Saskatchewan was the presence of normal community leaders in the vanguard of the party, then equally important would be the involvement of normal working-class leaders to bring working-class support to the CCF. In this respect it is important to note that trade union executives are not necessarily "normal" leaders in this respect: the shop-steward or local president would correspond more closely. For this reason the fact that Fred Dowling of the Packinghouse Workers, Charles Millard of the Steelworkers, or George Burt of the Auto Workers were active supporters of the CCF would not be of great significance because they were union presidents.

These factors and the concomitant factor of high middle- and upper-class turn-out worked against the CCF. The Ontario provincial elections of 1943 and 1945 provide an interesting illustration of these factors at work. In the 1943 election when the turn-out was relatively low, 57.9 per cent, the CCF won thirty-four seats with 37 per cent of the vote (415,441). The election was followed by a massive anti-CCF propaganda campaign which extended through 1945. In that contest turn-out rose to 66.9 per cent and although the CCF lost no more than 20,000 votes, it dropped to eight seats and 22.4 per cent of the vote. Clearly the propaganda affected those most responsive to political campaigns – the non-working class, those susceptible to anti-socialist propaganda and least likely to vote CCF.

105 / See, for example, the report of Donald MacDonald, national organizer: "The PAC has been a matter of great disappointment and soul searching not only in the CCF, but more particularly among those trade unionists who have given it leadership." National Council Minutes, March 1952, CCFP.

106 / Ibid.   107 / Lipset, Political Man, 204–7.   **209**

The people to whom the CCF came increasingly to direct its appeals, the "workers," had low turn-out characteristics, less time for active politics, fewer avenues of communication to enable the establishment of a common interest in reform, a lower level of interest in politics, and, more often than not, status aspirations inconsistent with CCF support. The character of the CCF as a movement prevented it from losing its working-class image because as a movement it required strict adherence to principle and a militance that precluded broadening its appeal and base of support.

At no time in its history had the CCF succeeded in getting more than one-third of the total vote in a national election in any province other than Saskatchewan.[108] Nationally it had never been within striking distance of office. In 1945 it polled 15.6 per cent of the vote and slipped to a dismal 9.5 per cent by 1958. There was, at this point, no likelihood of the party regaining its strength without some major change in its image and appeal. The change that was made served to align the CCF with organized labour, itself an institution with a less than happy image for the middle-class Canadian.

It is instructive to look briefly at the CCF record of achievement in Quebec because in many respects the inability of the CCF to win any support there was due to the same factors, in the Quebec context, that limited the party's appeal elsewhere in Canada. If the CCF was in many ways in conflict with prevailing values in the rest of Canada, it was doubly so in Quebec. If it faced widespread and effective opposition in the rest of Canada, it faced an even more potent opponent in Quebec. And if the nature of society mitigated against its success in the rest of Canada, so too French-Canadian society lacked the characteristics that would have led to more leftist voting. While the CCF did have an intellectual cadre in English Canada, it lacked an indigenous one in Quebec. The quasi-Fabians of the LSR had to do double duty in Quebec and the rest of Canada, and although many were Montreal-based, they were unable at that time to master the complexity of the two solitudes. At no time did the CCF have more than 900 members in Quebec; most of the time it had 400 or less. Ontario by comparison seldom had fewer than 4,000.

Chief among the factors explaining the failure of the CCF to win support of any significance in Quebec was the open opposition to the party of the Roman Catholic church. The church took the view that the CCF was "socialist" in the European sense and was

therefore godless, revolutionary, and a threat to private property.
The party was officially denounced in February 1934 in a pastoral
letter issued by Mgr. Georges Gauthier, Archbishop of Montreal.
The Archbishop offered the following explanation for the condemnation:

Le principal auteur de la c.c.f. a pu déclarer que ce programme
« est fondé sur des principes franchement socialistes. » Il dit la vérité.
Tel quel, il s'appuie sur une philosophie sociale que nous ne pouvons
approuver. Les Evêques vous rappellent que les catholiques disposent
à cet égard d'une mesure de jugement. Trois erreurs, en effet, carac-
térisent le socialisme condamné par l'Eglise : la suppression ou
l'amoindrissement excessif de la propriété privée, la lutte des classes
et une conception matérialiste de l'ordre social. Mettons en regard la
doctrine de la c.c.f. et voyons, sans discussion de détail, si nous avons
raison de l'incriminer. Une erreur sur un seul de ces points suffirait à
la vicier et à la rendre inacceptable pour un catholique.[109]

The pastoral letter was followed by a more public condemnation
by Cardinal Villeneuve in speeches before the Canadian Club
and the Montreal Junior Board of Trade, in November 1938.[110]
The position of the church lent credence to the views of Maurice
Duplessis, who in public addresses linked the CCF to communism.[111] Catholic opposition was not confined to Quebec; the
church was active in opposing the CCF in other provinces as
well.[112]

Efforts were made to have the church alter its position in the
autumn of 1942, but they met with little success.[113] In October
1943, M. J. Coldwell and F. R. Scott met with Archbishop
Charbonneau of Montreal. The meeting was followed by the
plenary meeting of Canadian bishops. They issued a declaration
which purported to clear the CCF, but which did not name the
party and included the following section which was so ambiguous
as to amount to almost a reiteration of the original condemnation:

The bishops reiterate their condemnation of the doctrines of Communism, under whatever name may be used to mislead the good faith
of the people, since Communism is that form of Revolutionary Socialism which is materialistic in its philosophy, which denies the right

109 / Mgr. Georges Gauthier, *La Doctrine Sociale de l'Eglise et la
Co-operative Commonwealth Federation*, Lettre Pastorale (Montreal
1934), 9.
110 / "The CCF and Private Property" (Ottawa, n.d. [c. 1939]), CCFP.
111 / Carbon copy of telegram, D. Lewis to Premier M. Duplessis,
Oct. 26, 1937, CCFP. See also *Le Canada*, Montreal, Oct. 20, 1937.
112 / Lipset, *Agrarian Socialism*, 137–8.
113 / See the account of Murray G. Ballantyne, "The Catholic Church
and the CCF," *Canadian Catholic Historical Association Report*, 1963.

of private property, and by concentrating all economic as well as political power in the State, sets up a system of Totalitarianism destructive of liberty and degrading to the human person.[114]

It is likely that the omission of specific reference to the CCF was deliberate, since the committee established to examine the attitude of the church toward the CCF had among its members those who feared that the rise of the CCF in Quebec would hinder the development of the Bloc Populaire. They, and others, felt that the CCF posed a threat to French-Canadian *survivance*.[115] The *Canadian Register, L'Action Catholique* and *Le Devoir* published the declaration and commented that it meant that Catholics could henceforth consider themselves free to support the CCF if they chose to do so. According to Ballantyne, Cardinal Villeneuve and Archbishop McGuigan of Toronto were visited by representatives of the other parties who protested the timing of the declaration. Other Catholic newspapers took the view that the declaration did not clear the CCF but rather established principles the CCF would have to meet if it was to be cleared.[116]

The speeches of Harold Winch in 1944 and the publication in the British Columbia *CCF News*, March 9, 1944, of an attack on Cardinal Villeneuve did little to help the party overcome the stigma.[117] Despite the efforts of Ballantyne and others to have the officials of the church declare unequivocally that they were not condemning the CCF, the church refused to clarify. Ballantyne quotes a revealing portion of a letter from Archbishop McGuigan replying to his request for permission to publish an editorial in the *Canadian Register* setting the record straight. McGuigan replied, "in order to avoid division among ourselves, I think we must be a bit cautious for the present."[118] While the church did not wish to appear to support the CCF, it was clearly unwilling to remove the obvious impression that it opposed the party.

The CCF candidate in Maisonneuve-Rosemont in the 1945 federal election wrote to Lewis that "the day previous to the

114 / As cited in Ballantyne, 41. See also M. G. Ballantyne, "The Church and the CCF," *The Commonwealth*, March 3, 1944.

115 / Ballantyne, *Report*, 36.

116 / *Ibid.*, 42.

117 / A party worker in the Maritimes wrote to M. J. Coldwell complaining, "our only hope is to angle for the atheist and criminal vote, for Winch has frightened away the ordinary people who believe what they read in the papers and do not want any revolution. The CCF News cooks our goose with the Catholics and now MacInnis tries to undo whatever we may have accomplished with the Protestants." Watson Baird to M. J. Coldwell, n.d. [c. 1944], CCFP.

118 / Ballantyne, *Report*, 44.

election being Sunday, a declaration was made by the Curate of
St. François Salano, Father Arthur Champagne to his congrega-
tion that they should not vote for the CCF."[119] In 1946 the Archbishop of Regina, P. J. Mahan, urged the delegates to a convention of the Saskatchewan French-Canadian Catholic Association
to oppose the CCF government with all their might.[120]

For its part, the CCF, at least the British Columbia section,
made the task of its Catholic and French-Canadian opponents
somewhat easier. The *CCF News* marked the occasion of Cardinal Villeneuve's death with a bitter and critical article which
was reprinted in *L'Action Catholique* and required an expression
of regret from the national executive.[121] Coldwell wrote a letter
to the editor of the French language newspaper in which he
pointed out, "Je suis sûr que vous rendez compte que les
opinions émises dans le journal C.C.F. de la Colombie britannique
ne representent pas nécessairement les vues officielles de notre
parti nationale."[122] In 1955 speeches in the House of Commons
by Harold Winch, Erhart Regier, Hazen Argue, and Angus
MacInnis which dealt with various aspects of life in Quebec and
the rights of French Canadians in general were widely reported
in the Quebec press.[123] Three members of the CCF Quebec provincial council resigned as a result of the speeches and the national executive passed a resolution expressing regret for any
offence caused and dissociating the party from the views of any
party members that were contrary to party policy.[124] Coldwell
restated the CCF policy on French language rights in a national
radio broadcast February 18 at the request of the party executive.
Frank Scott wrote to Stanley Knowles and urged that no western
MPs "even say Quebec without clearance for the next two years."
In his reply Knowles referred to "the almost irreparable damage
... that has been done our cause by a few foolish and completely
unnecessary statements."[125]

The fact that the CCF favoured centralist solutions to the economic and social problems in Canada did not bring the party a
great deal of support in Quebec and merely contributed to the

119 / R. J. Dion to David Lewis, June 15, 1945, CCFP.

120 / Montreal, *La Presse*, July 10, 1946.

121 / British Columbia *CCF News*, Jan. 30, 1947; *L'Action Catholique*, March 27, 1947; National Executive Minutes, April 20, 1947.

122 / M. J. Coldwell to the editor, l'*Action Catholique*, April 3, 1947,
CCFP.

123 / *Hansard*, 1955, 120–1, 344–6, 556–7, 596–7.

124 / National Executive Minutes, Feb. 12, 1955, CCFP.

125 / F. R. Scott to S. H. Knowles, Feb. 6, 1955; and S. H. Knowles
to F. R. Scott, Feb. 8, 1955, Scott Papers.

image of the party in that province as an alien and anti-French organization.[126] André Laurendeau wrote in 1948 that:

> The CCF has always presented itself to us with an English aspect. I have known many of our young people who normally might have been its adherents ... But they found themselves in a strange climate, they were not at home ... Our socialists haven't a truly independent outlook. They are ideologically linked up with labour parties in England, Australia and New Zealand. This is a plant which doesn't acclimatize itself easily in Quebec.[127]

A further factor would be the nature of Quebec society, where traditionalist attitudes were stronger and there was accordingly a greater predilection for either the corporatism or fascism of the Arcand movement or the paternalism of the Duplessis administration. Where industrialization had broken down the patterns of traditionalism and the strength of the Catholic church, the CCF lacked a viable channel of communication. This situation was so for the reasons already mentioned, the fact that the CCF was alien and had, for French Canada, a negative image. It lacked, as well, any strong support in the Quebec trade union movement.[128]

When the Canadian and Catholic Congress of Labour did involve itself in provincial politics, it did so in order to combat Maurice Duplessis, which meant it had to support either the provincial Liberal party[129] or the Bloc Populaire. Pierre Trudeau points out that when attempts were being made to enlarge the left in Quebec with a view to defeating the Duplessis regime, the socialists refused to participate because they felt that the CCF was there to stay and could fight Duplessis alone.[130] Trudeau argues that because of its refusal to co-operate, the Union Nationale was defeated by Liberals instead of liberals. Yet in 1937 there was a meeting of socialists at Lachute, and in reporting to Lewis the results of the meeting Frank Scott wrote:

> The way CCF'ers in Quebec talk to the Quebec nationalists must be different from the way CCF'ers in Alberta talk to disappointed Social Credulites [sic]. In Quebec the immediate need is to stop corporatism

126 / P. Trudeau, "The Practice and Theory of Federalism," in M. Oliver, ed. *Social Purpose for Canada* (Toronto 1961), 375.

127 / André Laurendeau, as translated and quoted in the *Canadian Register*, June 19, 1948; and see also David Lewis, Fox transcript, "as far as the Quebecois was concerned [the CCF] was a thoroughly western, English-speaking and therefore foreign product"; and see G. O. Rothney, "Quebec Saves Our King," *Canadian Forum*, xxv (July 1945), 83.

128 / S. H. Barnes, "Ideologies and Policies of Canadian Labor Organizations," unpubl. PHD thesis (Duke 1957), 228–41.

129 / *Ibid.*, 232, interview with Marcel Prevost, 1962, Fox transcript.

130 / Trudeau, "The Practice & Theory of Federalism," 375–6.

and fascism; the only way that this may be done lies in the chance that a genuine French-liberal party may grow; therefore we in Montreal are anxious to help liberalism, not attack it.[131]

Scott's advice was soon forgotten and the CCF's policy of central control found few supporters among the French-Canadian intellectuals. Yet these were the intellectuals the CCF needed if it was to begin to establish a base in Quebec that included more than a handful of de-natured French Canadians who were, it would seem, more at home around McGill than they were in Quebec City. In 1947 Scott wrote in the *Canadian Forum* that "the CCF intends to start Canada ... along the road to economic plenty and security, by combining the best in our traditions of personal liberty and democracy with modern techniques of national planning and social ownership."[132]

There was nothing in the CCF as a political movement that was really consistent with attitudes that prevailed in Quebec. It was a foreign element, it was opposed by the Catholic church, it preached centralism, and it had in it English Canadians who frequently demonstrated great ignorance and prejudice where Quebec and French-Canadian rights were concerned. Throughout its sickly career in that province, the CCF spoke to Quebec with an English accent. It made no difference that Lewis and Scott were fluently bilingual; the CCF simply had no roots in Quebec and was unable to demonstrate effectively any reason why there should be any.

On balance there was not much the CCF could have done to gain more support from the Canadian electorate. What kept it alive was also the same factor that kept it from winning power: its nature as a political movement. It was the CCF *qua* political movement that helped give the CCF *qua* party its negative image and constantly provided the opposition parties and press with the ammunition they used with such telling effect. Because the zeal and determination of its active members kept it alive, the CCF was able to capitalize on the discontent of many during the war and raise a small but steady wave of dissatisfaction with the *status quo* for twenty-eight years. By 1953 affluence had broken the crest of the wave, the leaders of the party were twenty years older and growing weary. There was no roaring cause to bring young radicals to the ranks as the Depression had brought in the Underhills, Lewis's, Coldwells, and their ilk. The discussions at the national council meeting in January 1956, which laid more

131 / F. R. Scott to D. Lewis, July 11, 1937, Scott Papers.
132 / F. R. Scott, "Alignment of Parties," *Canadian Forum*, XXVI (March 1947), 271. See ch. 5, n. 25, above for a description of the "centralism" evident in CCF policy in the period 1944–6.

emphasis on moral and ethical criticism of the existing society than on the standard socialist critique of the economy, indicate the extent to which the party and the leaders had found themselves unable to revitalize the CCF as it then stood. They were leaders of a movement of aging zealots and a party of defeated MPs. At that point the image of the CCF was firmly fixed in the minds of the voters and there was nothing that could be done to change it.

In this context the decision to start the "new party" was a good one, although it was hampered at the outset by the fact that under the new green banner the observer could descry many of the same faces that twenty-eight years earlier had brought the CCF into being in Regina. But the memories of the electors are short and if the leaders of the CCF are old, those who remember the CCF are also old. The New Democratic Party was an attempt to start with a clean slate, if not a completely new one.

8

8

THE CCF IN PARLIAMENT

The Canadian people don't give a damn about Parliament.

FRANK UNDERHILL
"The Angry Thirties"

The CCF had its greatest success in the House of Commons. Its leaders and, for the most part, its members, were admired and respected by critics, opponents, and impartial observers. The admiration and respect were a product of the selfless devotion of the CCF members to both their cause and their duties as members. Mackenzie King said of Woodsworth that "there are few men in this Parliament for whom, in some particulars, I have greater respect than the leader of the Co-operative Commonwealth Federation. I admire him in my heart because time and again he has had the courage to say what lay on his conscience regardless of what the world might think of him. A man of that calibre is an ornament to any parliament. ... "[1] Similar tributes were made to Coldwell subsequent to his defeat in the election of 1958. According to one report, a CBC commentator described his defeat as a national disaster while, some years later, in appointing him to the Privy Council, Liberal Prime Minister L. B. Pearson said,

Mr. Coldwell was ... an outstanding member of the Canadian House of Commons. A veteran of the first war, during the second his wisdom, industry and patriotism were an example of public and parliamentary service in the highest degree. I can think of no one who has better exemplified the standards that we hope to see embodied in the public and parliamentary life of our country.[2]

As these tributes indicate, the two leaders of the CCF had particularly distinguished careers as parliamentarians.

Successive CCF caucuses clearly established their position as a constructive opposition, supporting measures they felt to be good, opposing the bad, and consistently advocating their point of view. In addition, the vigorous and often passionate defence of the rights and liberties of others won for the CCF the admiration of many in and outside Parliament. Because they were few in number and because they represented a cause as well as a party, CCF members were diligent and diversified. They were diligent because they were, for the most part, motivated by their belief in the rightness of their cause and their recognition that their mistakes would be multiplied one hundredfold by an opposition that eagerly awaited socialist *faux pas*. They were diversified because their small number necessitated each member familiarizing himself with a number of topics to enable the party to make an impact in the House of Commons. The party never had more than 31 members; only in three parliaments, the 20th, 22nd and 23rd, were there more than 20 CCF members.

1 / *Hansard*, 1939, special session, 19.
2 / *Hansard*, 1964, 3972. The report on Coldwell's defeat is in *Hansard*, 1958, 43.

The CCF member was, as is the case in most political parties, a member of the party's elite. In a party-movement where there is not inconsiderable emphasis on the "struggle," the victor assumes a place of pre-eminence often denied elected members of parties more accustomed to victory than was the CCF. Accordingly, CCF members were more in the limelight in their own party and in the political world itself. The doctrinaires in the party read *Hansard* and were quick to note any departure from convention decisions or from the core doctrine itself. The elected members were expected to give leadership and yet remain within the limits of party policy as laid down by convention.

Because of the central position of the elected members, they were expected to "give their whole time to the movement";[3] to fulfil a limited number of speaking engagements during sessions of Parliament and to travel wherever they were needed when Parliament was not sitting. The fact that members had a railroad pass meant that they were able to travel widely at little expense to the party or to the local association sponsoring the meeting. In addition to speaking tours, members were expected to take part in the normal business of their constituency and provincial parties as well as to attend national conventions and meetings of the national council and executive if they were members. In 1940 members of the caucus agreed that elected members would contribute 5 per cent of their parliamentary indemnity to the party coffers.[4] This was usually increased to 10 per cent in election years.

To some extent the zeal of the CCF members can be attributed to the depression inheritance of the party. A not uncommon view among radicals in the thirties was that politicians were both rascals and parasites, who, by the mere act of standing for office, were assured an income and a sojourn amid the pleasures of Ottawa. By example the CCF members were expected to demonstrate their difference from the old party hacks. For the former, election to office was a responsibility to fulfil and it required energy and devotion beyond that demonstrated by even the more conscientious members of the old parties. Accordingly CCF members set out to demonstrate that they earned both their meagre parliamentary indemnity and the trust of their constituents. It was in keeping with this tradition of service that the CCF caucus opposed in 1954 the raising of the parliamentary indemnity – although it took four meetings to reach the decision.[5]

3 / From transcript of Douglas-Higginbotham interviews (1958–60), 139.
4 / Caucus Minutes, Nov. 27, 1940, CCFP, and Douglas-Higginbotham, 139.

5 / Caucus Minutes for Jan. 1954.

It remains to the credit of those who served in Parliament for the CCF that, on the whole, they acquitted themselves well. In the beginning and throughout the party's life, its members were supplied with ample ammunition for attacks on the government and for advancing, with a cogency often foreign to the House, their proposals for legislation. It is a characteristic of socialists that they are better read, indeed, more learned in the fields of their endeavour, than the greater part of their opposition. It was, as Woodsworth wrote, important that "Every CCF member ought to be able to give a reason for the faith that is in him."[6] The traditional emphasis of the left on education and discussion was, as has been discussed already, very much a characteristic of the CCF. The importance of debate and learned disquisition in ideological parties and movements is undeniable, particularly so in those with as direct an inheritance from the liberal-Fabian tradition as the CCF. Its members started with an appreciable advantage over their colleagues in the other parties: they had already done a considerable amount of talking and thinking about the problems of the nation and were expected to provide more than routine services for constituents and brute votes in the lobbies.

At the beginning of the party's official life in Parliament, the members of the LSR provided advice and detailed briefs. Frank Scott, Eugene Forsey, and Frank Underhill were no strangers to the CCF caucus in the thirties and early forties. They prepared briefs and memoranda on constitutional questions, economic matters, and questions of general social reform. *Social Planning for Canada* itself was a mine of material for the caucus. In 1940 Eugene Forsey and his wife spent the month of June devoting themselves to research as assigned by the caucus. In January 1943 the party established the post of Director of Research and the work previously performed for the caucus by the LSR was carried out by the research and education directors hired by the party, among whom were Lloyd Shaw, Stuart Jamieson, Lorne Ingle, and Donald MacDonald. Their work was supplemented by the material presented in *News Comment* and its successor, *Comment*. The preparation of material for *News Comment* was carried out by the research staff at Woodsworth House and by "correspondents" across the country, including Dorothy Steeves in British Columbia and Professor Carlyle King in Saskatchewan. Throughout his tenure as national secretary, David Lewis was a major source of advice and information for the caucus. In all it was a formidable apparatus that served the party and its members well. Further assistance, particularly in labour and economic

6 / Woodsworth, *Social Planning for Canada*, vi.

matters, was provided by the research section of the Canadian
Congress of Labour, directed by Eugene Forsey. The material
prepared by these people and published in *News Comment* was
of a consistently high level and remarkably free from any doctrinaire determination to twist facts or see problems where none
existed.

Because they were few in number and had to cover a variety
of topics, because they were devoted to their duties as parliamentarians, and because of the effectiveness of the CCF research
apparatus, CCF members had a familiarity with government and
politics that made them a highly effective opposition. It was often
said, particularly during the tenures of Manion, Hanson, Bracken,
and Graydon as leaders of the Conservative party in Parliament,
that the CCF was the real opposition in the House of Commons.
A random survey of the index to any session of the House of
Commons provides a clear indication of the extent of CCF participation in debates.[7] It was characteristic of the CCF that T. C.
Douglas should speak some sixty times during his first session as
an MP.[8] Equally characteristic was a comment made by the
Monetary Times and reprinted, with obvious pride, by *News
Comment*: "Best value for your money politically is the CCF.
Though the socialist crowd may be hard to take, at least give
them credit, they are an efficient and hard-hitting team. They'll
make it uncomfortable for the Liberals yet. And likely to steal
the headlines if not the leadership from the Conservatives ... "[9]

The management of a caucus normally as small as that of the
CCF would, in the context of traditional politics, present relatively
few problems. There was, however, an independence of spirit, a
proclivity for debate, and a whole-hearted acceptance of democratic procedures, that produced problems for the leader. Under
Woodsworth, the small caucus of seven (six after J. S. Taylor
withdrew in 1937) in the eighteenth Parliament suffered relatively few strains largely as a result of the respect each member
had for Woodsworth and their devotion to him as the embodiment of their movement. It was typical that throughout his tenure
as leader of the CCF in the House of Commons, Woodsworth
was referred to by his followers as "Mr. Woodsworth." Only
rarely did his colleagues call him "J. S."[10]

Woodsworth did not take advantage of his position. The

7 / In 1944, for example, CCF members spoke on more topics than
most back benchers, Stanley Knowles and M. J. Coldwell more than
most cabinet ministers.

8 / Douglas-Higginbotham interview, 1962, 145.

9 / Cited in *News Comment*, IV, no. 6 (June 1954), 7.

10 / Blair Fraser, "The Saintly Failure who Changed Canada," *Maclean's*, Nov. 1, 1951, 52.

caucus discussed with great thoroughness and freedom all the
issues before the house, vetting each member's speeches and
deciding the position the CCF group would take on each question.
It was not always Woodsworth's view that prevailed. Frequently
he would leave the decision entirely in the hands of the caucus
with the majority ruling. In 1937 he was invited by the government to go to the coronation of George VI as an empire parliamentary delegate. Heaps and Coldwell favoured his going, but
MacInnis, MacNeil, Douglas, and Woodsworth himself were
opposed on the grounds that it might provoke adverse criticism
of the group at a time when so many people in Canada were in
dire need. As a result he did not go.[11] The same year, the caucus
discussed the position the group should take on two Social Credit
resolutions proposing measures to increase purchasing power.
Woodsworth was inclined to oppose them, Coldwell and Douglas
to amend them, Heaps to support them, and MacInnis "to state
the socialist position and vote for the resolutions on their wording."[12] MacInnis' position prevailed and Coldwell was delegated
to speak for the resolutions supporting both within the context
of the socialist position.

The principle of full consultation and discussion of all matters
affecting the caucus was rigidly adhered to. In 1939 Mackenzie
King offered to allow Woodsworth as party leader to see despatches relating to the international situation. The offer was
conditional on Woodsworth treating such information as confidential. Woodsworth told the caucus that he did not care to see
these despatches if he was unable to consult with members of his
group. The caucus decided that he should accept the prime
minister's offer "making it perfectly clear that he intended to
consult members of the group, but would let the information go
no further."[13] The same position was taken by Coldwell throughout the war.

Typical of the extent to which the caucus as a group controlled
the activities of the CCF members in the House was the discussion
of the position the CCF would take in the foreign policy debate of
March 1939. The caucus met at some length on March 27, at
which time each member stated his position. Woodsworth and
Percy Rowe argued that "the olive branch should be held out to
the dictators, or perhaps more correctly, the CCF should place
the emphasis on the readjustment of the grievances of the dictatorship countries rather than on the restraining of the aggression of the dictators."[14] The other members of the caucus felt

11 / Caucus Minutes, Jan. 14, 1937, CCFP.
12 / *Ibid.*, Jan. 20, 1937; and see *Hansard*, 1937, 126 ff.
13 / *Ibid.*, March 15, 1939.   14 / *Ibid.*, March 27, 1939.

that "international order would have to be restored before international justice could be created."[15] The debate was carried over into the next meeting of the caucus two days later. At that time discussion centred around a private members' bill introduced by J. T. Thorson which would have its second reading March 31, in the midst of the foreign affairs debate.[16] Thorson's bill had been drafted by Frank Scott, Percy Corbett, J. B. Coyne, and "others" in Montreal, and was very brief: "Canada shall not assume the status of belligerent otherwise than by a declaration of war made by his majesty with specific reference to Canada and only on the advice of his majesty's government in Canada."[17]

The caucus agreed that Woodsworth should take part in the debate March 30, setting out "his own personal convictions on war as a means of settling international disputes." The others would speak in the debate after him, supporting Thorson's bill while, at the same time, outlining every aspect of the CCF position on foreign policy. Coldwell was to emphasize the need for "restraintive [sic] aggression and ... collective peace action"; Douglas the evils of private munitions industry; MacInnis the need for an embargo on arms and war material shipments; Grant MacNeil would demand conscription of wealth; and Percy Rowe was to "review the causes of the present international situation."[18] The procedure was effective, both the CCF and Woodsworth's stand being carefully enunciated – a considerable feat for a party of six members. The debate in the caucus showed clearly the division between Woodsworth and his followers and, to some extent, prepared the party for the painful split that came when Canada did enter the war.

The attitude of the caucus toward Woodsworth's position hardened once the division in the group had been publicly revealed. Following the speech from the throne opening the nineteenth Parliament, May 16, 1940, Woodsworth informed the caucus that he wished, in his speech on the address, to reiterate his stand on the war and challenge the government's attitude that "only the war matters."[19] He was vigorously opposed by all members. His followers felt that his position was already well known in the country and that a restatement would necessitate further restatement of the official CCF position. Woodsworth resisted because he "felt this was fundamentally an imperialist war, that the British Labour Party had deserted internationalism and that [his] own war position would be justified in three or

15 / *Ibid.*   16 / *Ibid.*, March 29, 1939.
17 / *Hansard*, Feb. 2, 1939, 539.
18 / Caucus Minutes, March 29, 1939, CCFP, and see *Hansard*, 1939, 2408 ff.
19 / Caucus Minutes, May 17, 1940.

four years." Opposed by all his followers in the House, he offered
to resign if retention of his post would embarass the group. He
had raised the same question at an earlier meeting; the decision
both times was that matters would be left until the CCF national
executive met. Woodsworth did not speak in the debate; illness
kept him from the House, as it did for most of the two years
remaining in his life. Coldwell was elected acting house leader at
the caucus meeting of November 6, 1940. The minutes of April
22, 1942 record his election as "leader of CCF members in the
House of Commons," which was the month after Woodsworth's
death.

Under Coldwell's leadership the nature of the caucus changed
somewhat. Coldwell's style was that of the chairman and con-
ciliator. He was not the charismatic leader of a movement that
Woodsworth was. He did not attempt to convince his colleagues;
he felt his role was that of finding the "sense of the meeting" and
acting accordingly. This is not to imply that he did not lead;
rather it is to emphasize his belief that the caucus had to act in
concert if it was to achieve its ends. Aware of the centripetal
forces in an ideological group, Coldwell was very conscious of
the need for unity. Typical of this is the entry in the caucus
minutes for March 8, 1937. The members were discussing their
position on the Foreign Enlistment Bill. Woodsworth favoured
supporting it even if the CCF amendments were not accepted.
MacInnis and MacNeil were opposed to it unless the amendments
were accepted; Coldwell expressed his concern that the group
should vote together. Before making any major speech in the
House he would prepare a detailed outline which would be
circulated in caucus, discussed, and then put into final form. The
advantages of the method, Coldwell felt, were that he spoke with
the full support of his caucus and had his speech enriched by the
discussion of his colleagues. He had on occasion to "shade his
own views somewhat," but never to the extent of any discom-
fort.[20] When the size of the caucus increased after 1945, the
leader's role became more difficult in the context Coldwell had
placed it; it required great patience and persistence to maintain
the policy of collective decision.

The increase in numbers from 11 to 28 meant that after 1945
caucus meetings were more formal and the caucus itself more
structured. Previously Coldwell had acted as chairman. After
1945 the caucus elected its own chairman and executive, of
which Coldwell was an *ex officio* member. Formal caucus committees were established to deal with the major areas and port-
folios of government. When members wished to propose a reso-

20 / Interview with M. J. Coldwell, Aug. 1963.

lution in the House or introduce a private member's bill, these
were normally referred to the appropriate caucus committee for
a report which would be discussed by the full caucus. Although
members of the group were agreed that the CCF should present
a unanimous front in the Commons, it was a caucus rule that
individual members had the right to express their opinions as
their consciences dictated, on the understanding that they would
first inform the caucus of their views. It was Coldwell's opinion
that where possible, differences should be aired and settled in
caucus rather than on the floor of the House.

The caucus imposed a remarkably stringent discipline on its
members. All requests for speeches outside the House were first
cleared by the caucus, and as a general rule members were seldom
given permission to be away during sittings of the House. They
were, on the other hand, expected to make themselves available
to the party for such organizational and propaganda activity as
could be carried on over the weekend. In keeping with the discipline, CCF members were forbidden to pair with other members.
They were not to be absent from the House during sittings and
if not in the chamber, were to be within call of the division bells.
Absence from the chamber without permission brought a rebuke
from the party whip. As a result the CCF record of attendance
at sittings of the House was far better than that of any other
party.

For the duration of each session, members of the CCF caucus
were immersed in the business of Parliament. In addition to
serving on two and sometimes three caucus committees, each
served on one or more Commons committees and reported regu-
larly to the caucus on the work of these bodies. The effectiveness
of the CCF in the House can be explained in part by the devotion
of these men to their job and to the fact that one of the products
of such devotion was a remarkably well-informed caucus. The
emphasis on discussion and group decision undoubtedly contributed as well to the solidarity of the group in the House of Commons. There were departures, such as those of J. S. Taylor and,
later, Ross Thatcher in April 1955, and there were occasional
splits in the party; but given the fact that the party was a minority,
and one of socialists at that, the degree of cohesion is impressive.
On the basis of the recorded divisions in the *Journals* of the
House of Commons, on only 48 divisions of a total of 970 in the
seven parliaments in which the CCF sat, did the party not vote
en bloc. In several instances the splits were on matters of procedure and in two cases on divorce bills. It is an impressive testimony to Coldwell's determination to maintain a united caucus

despite the fact that a united front was not as crucial for the CCF as it was for either the government or the official opposition.

This policy broke down most noticeably in 1955, although there had been occasions earlier when Coldwell had to inform the caucus that he could not support positions which the majority urged, though these tended frequently to revolve around matters of procedure. Coldwell was, in general, more inclined to facilitate the smooth operation of business in the House as long as this did not interfere with the presentation of the CCF point of view. This was an attitude which occasionally sat ill with some of his more fiery and rambunctious colleagues. In 1955 the division was deep enough to lead Coldwell to threaten to resign. The issue was German rearmament. The debate was on the motion to approve the Paris Agreements, signed by the existing members of NATO on October 23, 1954. The CCF had opposed German rearmament as early as 1951, a decision which was reconfirmed at the party's national convention in Edmonton in 1954. The national council met January 15, 1955, and reiterated the party's stand of "opposition to re-armanent of Western Germany at the present time."

The caucus found itself divided when on January 19, Coldwell read to the group the speech he planned to make in the debate. Initially Coldwell stood alone with Ross Thatcher on the issue, but subsequently four members of the caucus supported his position.[21] In his speech, Coldwell took the position that it was better for Germany to rearm under NATO control and supervision than to rearm "of her own volition and without supervision and control ... "[22] Stanley Knowles spoke for the majority of the caucus. He opposed the move because of his own deeply held convictions, because many Canadians were opposed to it, and because the national convention and the national council of the CCF had opposed it.[23] When the vote was taken in the House of Commons, 12 members of the CCF voted against the motion, the only members to do so, and 5 supported it. Five deliberately abstained as a gesture to Coldwell.

The debate in the caucus, at the best of times vigorous and direct, had been particularly acrimonious. Among those who opposed Coldwell's position were Colin Cameron, Herbert Herridge, and Harold Winch, formidable opponents under the most favourable circumstances. At the January 27 meeting of the caucus following the debate, Alistair Stewart suggested that

21 / Caucus Minutes, Jan. 17, 19, 1955, CCFP; interview with Alistair Stewart, Aug. 1962; *Comment*, v, no. 7 (1955), 7, 11.
22 / *Hansard*, 1955, 382.
23 / *Ibid.*, 393–4.

Coldwell might be reluctant to attend caucus in the absence of any general expression of support. With no debate the caucus unanimously passed a motion of confidence in his leadership.[24]

Coldwell maintained close and cordial relations with the national party although his view of the relationship of the parliamentary caucus to the party was not quite consistent with the national constitution. Article 7 of the party's constitution stated that the national convention was "the supreme governing body of the CCF, and shall have final authority in all matters of policy and program." Coldwell believed that the caucus should have the advice of the convention and the national council, but that it had to be free to make its own judgments and interpret party policy in the light of conditions as they arose.[25] In fact, there was seldom any occasion for this distinction to be exercised since there was a high degree of consensus between the parliamentary caucus and the leading figures in the party.

This consensus was ensured by the facts that the central apparatus of the party was in Ottawa, and that the key figures in the party bureaucracy were either in constant touch with the caucus or were members of the caucus themselves. Coldwell, Lewis, Scott, MacInnis, and Knowles were in constant contact on either or both of these bodies. In addition, the size of the caucus facilitated communication and provided for an easy interchange of views that enabled the party to present a united front on most issues. The processes of the party's conventions also lent themselves to the exercise of leadership by the parliamentary figures in the party who were able to sustain the consensus through their alliance with the other leading figures at the conventions and through their prominence as members.

The election programs on which members of the caucus campaigned were the work of the national executive and, where time permitted, the national council and national convention. Resolutions passed at party conventions frequently called upon the CCF caucus to state a particular point of view or else made a general statement of the CCF position. The key resolutions were those which either had the status of emergency resolutions – in which case they were prepared by the national executive and vetted by the council immediately before the convention – or they were resolutions which emanated from the executive and council in any case. After 1942, general resolutions from constituencies were passed through a resolutions committee which combined them into acceptable composites or rejected them,

24 / Caucus Minutes, Jan. 27, 1955 and National Executive Minutes, Feb. 12, 1955, CCFP.

25 / Interview with M. J. Coldwell, June 1966.

often as being inconsistent with views already stated by the CCF, which frequently meant by the parliamentary group. Because CCF membership in the House of Commons was small, unless the party members read *Hansard* assiduously it would have been difficult to ascertain whether or not the caucus had been following convention policy closely. Newspapers did not report all the speeches of the CCF group unless they caused a stir or were particularly apposite.

The first national council meeting of each year was traditionally the one at which the coming session of Parliament was discussed. Members of the council would engage in lengthy and far-reaching discussion of the major questions of the day, often armed with carefully prepared outlines and *précis* of essential material prepared by the party research staff. Members of Parliament who were not members of the council attended these sessions and took part in the discussion although they did not have a vote. If questions arose on which there was no general or specific party stand, the caucus conferred with either the executive or the council. Discussions of party foreign policy usually took place in this way. Typical of such a meeting was that held March 16, 1951. Coldwell reviewed the major issues which had come up in the House of Commons "and outlined the stand taken on them by the CCF group." The council then passed a motion that "the CCF at this time place the strongest possible emphasis on the necessity for lower prices for the essentials of life ... " Other matters, including transportation policy, were left in the hands of the caucus, "inasmuch as general national policy has already been laid down."[26] Eight of the thirteen members were at the meeting, four in their capacities as members of the council.

This kind of joint leadership on policy questions was of considerable value for caucus members. It enabled them to "pre-test" their arguments and gave them the benefit of the views of others not in Parliament and, on some matters, with more expertise and more time to do the necessary research. Committees of the national executive or council provided briefs or reports that were valuable sources of information. At a meeting of the national executive in 1945, the caucus members were provided with a comprehensive report on the Dumbarton Oaks proposals by a committee of Lewis, Scott, Coldwell, and George Grube.[27]

There was not always unanimity between the caucus and the party executive. On several occasions there was disagreement; on one, acute embarrassment as a result of the activities of some caucus members in the House of Commons. In one instance, the

26 / National Council Minutes, March 17, 1951, CCFP.
27 / National Executive Minutes, March 18, 1945, CCFP.

conscription crisis of 1942–4, the caucus led the party away from
its established position; on another, the Korean War, the caucus
through the party leader pre-empted the right of the convention
to make policy; and in a third instance, the statements of Harold
Winch and Erhart Regier in the House proved embarrassing to
the party in Quebec and to the national officers.

Conscription has been one of the major leavening agents in
Canadian political history. For the Liberal party it has meant
headlong descent into the maelstrom of racial antagonism, and
for the Conservative party a pavlovian response to the sirens of
empire. For the CCF it was initially a question of principle and
finally, one of politics. The National Resources Mobilisation Act
of 1940 gave the Liberal government sweeping power to mobilize
the nation's resources for war.[28] Throughout the debate on the
act, CCF members urged that there be conscription of wealth before conscription of manpower for military service, and that any
conscription of manpower be solely for home defence.[29] In Coldwell's view, the act was used "mainly to regiment labour, to
freeze agriculture and to conscript manpower for home defence
– but was not used to impose equal sacrifice on the privileged
and to harness industry and wealth to an all-out effort according
to a national war production plan and without strengthening the
hold of private monopoly over the life of Canada."[30]

The position the caucus took at this time was consistent with
the official position of the party. This position was reaffirmed at
a meeting of the national executive a year later by the passage of
a resolution calling for the conscription of wealth and opposing
conscription of men for overseas service.[31] Following the national
plebiscite of April 1942, which released the government from
any pledges made in the 1940 election not to introduce conscription for overseas service, Bill 80 was introduced in the House of
Commons. The bill repealed that section of the Mobilisation Act
which limited the use made of conscripted men. The bill provided that the government could impose overseas service on conscripted men by order-in-council without further reference to
Parliament.[32] The CCF had supported the plebiscite, on the
grounds that a "yes" vote would indicate support for conscription
of all the nation's resources, but opposed Bill 80. In the debate,

28 / *Hansard*, 1940, 863 ff.
29 / *Ibid.*, 888, 950.
30 / M. J. Coldwell, *Left Turn, Canada!* (New York 1945), 43.
31 / National Executive Minutes, Nov. 15, 1941, CCFP.
32 / The convoluted history of the conscription issue is told in several
places: J. W. Pickersgill, *The Mackenzie King Record*; C. G. Power, *A
Party Politician*, ed. by Norman Ward (Toronto 1966); and, a popular
account, Bruce Hutchison, *The Incredible Canadian* (Toronto 1952).

Coldwell pointed out that conscription was not the most important issue facing the country and that, in any case, his party did
not "propose to give the government a blank cheque to do by
order-in-council what this parliament alone should do."[33] He then
called again for the conscription of the nation's wealth as the
necessary prelude to any further conscription of manpower. The
national council endorsed this position and in 1943 passed a
resolution that the CCF should "stand fast by the position taken
when Bill 80 was before Parliament."[34]

In November 1944 the government passed an order-in-council
sending conscripted men overseas. The Prime Minister then introduced a motion of confidence in his government. A special
meeting of the national executive was called and the party's
position discussed. With some misgivings the executive – with the
caucus in attendance along with several members of the national
council as well – decided that the final decision on the party's
stand would be taken by the caucus but that the members would
repeat the demand for conscription of wealth and industry as
well as manpower and that "*in any case*, they should support
sending the Home Defence troops overseas as reinforcements
immediately."[35] The Quebec wing of the executive and council,
Scott, G. Desaulniers, F. Laroche, and O. Chartrand, opposed
the decision to support overseas service for the conscripts, not
on principle but because of the harm such support would do the
CCF cause in their province.

The position the CCF took in the debate was predicated on the
belief that the volunteers on active service were in need of reinforcement. Coldwell accordingly moved an amendment calling
for the "immediate removal of all distinctions between drafted
and volunteer personnel, thus making the entire home defence
army available for reinforcements overseas," and including the
standard plea, "and requires further the total mobilization of all
the resources of Canada, material and financial, as well as human, to ensure a total war effort ..."[36] Coldwell later wrote of the
event:

This stated the CCF policy which we had moved in every session of
Parliament since 1941, but with this difference, that we did not
make the sending overseas of conscripted men conditional upon the
conscription of industry and wealth. We were faced with a grave
decision and we made it according to the necessities of a situation
which we had not foreseen as a possibility from 1941, but which

33 / *Hansard*, 1942, 3259 ff.
34 / National Council Minutes, Sept. 5, 1943.
35 / National Executive Minutes, Nov. 24, 1944.
36 / *Hansard*, Nov. 27, 1944, 6625.

was not of our making. As realists, we could not do otherwise under
the circumstances.[37]

Scott thought otherwise. He had written to Coldwell earlier that
month pointing out that he was opposed to the policy "at this
stage of the war when victory is certain regardless of what Canadians do ..."[38] He thought that the cleavages it would produce in
Canada would preclude any careful discussion of the problems
of reconstruction which, in his view, were far more important at
that stage. At the time he wrote, Scott thought that Ralston's
resignation from the cabinet might precipitate an election.

The CCF amendment was ruled out of order but, by a shrewd
parliamentary move in which he had the collaboration of Stanley
Knowles, Coldwell moved an amendment to the main motion
which the Prime Minister accepted and which made possible CCF
and Social Credit support of the government. The amendment
converted a motion of confidence in the government's handling
of the war to a declaration of support for the war effort. Despite
this, the Conservative party, under the leadership of Gordon
Graydon, voted against the amended motion.[39]

The last act of the conscription crisis, as far as the CCF was
concerned, occurred at the national convention held November
29–December 1, 1944. The convention, "after lengthy discussion," passed a resolution introduced by the National Council
endorsing the caucus stand and followed this with another expressing "fullest confidence in National Leader M. J. Coldwell
and his colleagues in Parliament for the way they have inter-
preted the policy of the movement toward the war and Canada's
part in it."[40]

It is difficult to see what the party could have done other than
what it did for it had, to some extent, placed itself on a slippery
slope when it had decided to support the plebiscite in 1942. However vigorously it urged conscription of wealth and industry
while supporting the vote to free the parties of their pledge, it
came down on the side of opening the way for overseas service
for conscripts. By 1944, when the party was experiencing a
groundswell of support in all of Canada west of the Ottawa river,
there would be little inclination to stand by the principle. Not
having the same roots in Quebec as the Liberal party – indeed,
having few roots there at all – there was little that could demonstrate to Coldwell the importance of Quebec in this regard. It
could be added, however, that it probably would not have made

37 / Coldwell, *Left Turn*, 49.
38 / F. R. Scott to M. J. Coldwell, Nov. 2, 1944, CCFP.
39 / *Hansard*, 1944, 6935 ff.
40 / Report of the Eighth National Convention (1944).

much difference how the caucus voted. Speculation notwithstanding, by 1944 the leaders in the party were optimistic about
the party's future, were listening to the sounds of western Canada
and, not unnaturally, responding in a predictable way to some
of the more vicious propaganda attacks that their increased
strength had occasioned. It was necessary to do the right thing.

By 1950 the position of the party caucus on foreign affairs
was fairly orthodox, that is, it hewed closely to the line of the
British Labour party, which was itself quite orthodox. At this
juncture, CCF conventions were devoting increasing attention to
foreign policy and showing occasional signs of unorthodoxy. The
eleventh national convention was to be held in Vancouver, where
the leaders could rightly expect a fairly radical and heated convention because the west coast harboured a stern rump of left-
wing socialists such as Colin Cameron, Dorothy Steeves, and
E. E. Winch. The Korean War broke out between the final date
for the submission of resolutions and the opening of the convention, so it was an open issue. The question was resolved by
the national executive, which met in Vancouver two days before
the convention opened and decided that a resolution in support
of the UN action would be introduced at the convention.[41] Under
the constitution the matter was still open because the convention
had the power to refer resolutions back for redrafting under instructions. On the eve of the convention Coldwell made a public
statement endorsing the UN action.[42] When the convention
opened, the delegates had the choice of either repudiating the
party leader or supporting the executive resolution. In defence
of Coldwell's position it can be said that as the leader of a parliamentary group he had a right to make the statement he did and
it was in this capacity that he made it. The fact that he was also
national president and national leader gave his statement particular weight in the convention.

After the 1953 election it was fairly certain that the CCF was
not on the brink of power. There were ten additional seats to the
number the party had won in 1949 but the share of the popular
vote had declined. If this had any effect on the caucus it was to
make it more zealous and more outspoken and, in some respects,
more doctrinaire. The spirit of the movement prevailed when
the success of the party seemed more distant. In 1954 the national
executive chastised the caucus gently for its campaign to have
divorce cases removed from Parliament because "the impression
was being created that the CCF was in favor of easing the restric-

41 / National Executive Minutes, July 24, 1950, CCFP.
42 / Vancouver *Sun*, July 26, 1950, and see "The CCF Convention,"
Canadian Forum, xxx (Sept. 1950), 124.

tions on divorce." In fact it was quite likely that most members of the caucus were in favour of easing the restrictions. The executive suggested that "the CCF members, while continuing their campaign with all possible vigour, might consider ways and means of helping to correct this false impression."[43] The executive was concerned that the campaign was doing the party harm in Quebec.

Their concern was increased a few months later when speeches in the House of Commons by Erhart Regier, Harold Winch, and Angus MacInnis were construed as insulting to the French-speaking people of Quebec. The speeches were ill considered perhaps, but expressed a not uncommon point of view.[44] Leaders of the CCF Quebec section and the Quebec members of the national executive had threatened to resign as a result of the speeches. The executive was forced to issue a press release which said, in part, "Whenever any CCF member, whether English-speaking or French-speaking, says or does anything which is contrary to the policy outlined here [relating to Quebec language rights] he speaks and acts for himself alone and not for the CCF."[45]

The press release was not intended by the executive as an apology, although this was the interpretation of the newspapers which carried the Canadian Press story on the matter the following day. The Quebec provincial council accepted the statement as "an assurance to all French-speaking Canadians of the good faith of the CCF," but requested that the members concerned "retract, correct or clarify their statements in Parliament or else be censured by the National Council."[46] In addition they wanted Coldwell to dissociate the CCF from the views expressed by the members and to "reiterate the CCF policy on language, education and minority rights." The executive cleared Angus MacInnis of any guilt in the affair and asked Regier and Winch to correct the impression their speeches had left. There the matter rested.

In 1958 the parliamentary group was reduced to its pre-war level. Only 8 CCF members were left after the election. Half of these were comparative newcomers. The reduction was drastic because 25 had been elected in the year before. Missing from the House of Commons were the party leader, M. J. Coldwell, and his colleague of long standing, Stanley Knowles. The caucus met in Winnipeg April 23 and elected Hazen Argue house leader by

43 / National Executive Minutes, Nov. 28, 1954, CCFP.
44 / *Hansard*, Jan. 12, 1955, 118 ff.; Jan. 26, 1955, 556; Jan. 27, 1955, 596–7.
45 / National Executive Minutes, Feb. 12, 1955. The press release had been issued Feb. 1, 1955.
46 / National Council Minutes, *ibid*.

one vote over H. W. Herridge and Erhart Regier.[47] According to one account, this was the result which David Lewis, national chairman at the time, wanted and for which he lobbied.[48] At the party's national convention in Montreal later that year Coldwell was elected national leader although in his major address he had expressed a wish to retire.[49] The national executive, in the throes of establishing the new party, had decided that there was no advantage in electing a new national leader at a time when the CCF had only two or three years of life left.[50] There were positive disadvantages in that a "sitting" national leader of the CCF at the time of the formation of the new party would have a considerable advantage over his rivals, and that no one in the House of Commons at the time appealed to the party executive as a leader for their new party.

Relations between the caucus and the national executive after the 1958 election reflected a mutual lack of confidence and trust and, in the period between the last two national conventions, they steadily deteriorated. The national executive took few pains to hide its view that the caucus was second rate and that it was incompetent and lacked the discipline and intellectual rigour of previous caucuses. The caucus, for its part, felt that its interests were being sacrificed in the interest of the new party and, in any case, it was unwilling to accept any direction from either the party executive or defeated members, however long either group had served the CCF.

With the possible exception of Harold Winch, the post-1958 caucus contained no members of the CCF establishment. Only Winch could claim to be a long-standing member of the movement. Bert Herridge had always been a rebel who followed his own inclinations; Douglas Fisher, Arnold Peters, Frank Howard, and Murdo Martin were newcomers who had won their seats largely by their own efforts and were not indebted to the party establishment. Fisher had performed the seemingly impossible task of defeating C. D. Howe. Hazen Argue and Erhart Regier had slightly longer service records but neither was a member of that inner circle which had been the core of the CCF since its foundation.

With none of the old guard in the House of Commons there

47 / Caucus Minutes, April 23, 1958, CCFP.
48 / Douglas Fisher, "The Making of a Senator," Vancouver *Sun*, March 5, 1966. The discussion of caucus-executive relations which follows is based on the author's experience as a member of the national committee for the New Party, and on conversation and correspondence with a number of the principal actors.
49 / Report of the Fifteenth National Convention (1958).
50 / National Executive Minutes, July 11, 1958.

was no continuity between the founding fathers and the handful of troublesome offspring. The party establishment had a proprietary interest in the CCF and in the new party they had been instrumental in conceiving. They saw themselves as keepers of the faith, dedicated to the ideals of the CCF movement. Some of the members – Fisher, Howard, and Peters, for example – were not "movement men." They were young, independent, disinclined to defer to the party oligarchs and resentful of what they considered to be the patronizing attitude of some of the executive members. Others were plainly unnerved by their contact with the arch-priests of the CCF, felt inferior, and were belligerent as a result. The product of this almost classic confrontation of generations was a widening rift between executive and caucus, and a growing determination on the part of the caucus to emphasize those aspects of its behaviour that clearly were not the CCF norm.

Under Hazen Argue, the caucus was obstreperous, raucous, and, at times, perverse. Its approach to its job in Parliament was marked by an aggressiveness and a determination to be troublesome, decidedly not in the Coldwell-Knowles tradition, which sat ill with the party chieftains. The Howard-Peters divorce filibuster is one example of this approach. The members worked hard but were given little credit for their labours by their own party officers because their approach to their jobs was not in the CCF style. The fact that all were re-elected in 1963 offers some indication that they did serve their constituents. The members felt that the party machinery was being monopolized by the officers in the effort of building the New Party and that the caucus had to take second place. This did nothing to ease the tensions and helped foster a negative attitude toward the new venture. Matters were not helped when caucus members learned that Walter Pitman, elected as a New Party candidate in a by-election in 1960, had been advised by several of the party officers not to sit with the CCF caucus. They felt that his association with the parliamentary group might tarnish the image of the New Party. Pitman did join the caucus but there was nothing he could do to knit together the torn ligaments of the CCF.

The national executive was, as suspected, more concerned with the formation of the New Party than with the caucus. The national headquarters staff was heavily committed to new party business and the caucus did suffer as a result. Hazen Argue and Harold Winch were designated as the liaison between the national committee for the New Party and the caucus but were inadequate because neither man commanded enough respect to effect any reconciliation. It is doubtful that anyone else could have healed the split, but had the executive been more sensitive to the parliamentary situation it might have involved some of the younger members, their cockiness notwithstanding. However, it did not do so, and several of the newer members came to see their role as one of representing those elements in the CCF that were unhappy about the new relationship with labour and about the disappearance of the CCF. Paradoxically, Arnold Peters and Douglas Fisher became spokesmen for the rank-and-file that opposed any departure from the old. They stood up for the many party members who traditionally opposed "the brass" and defended the grass-roots tradition of the CCF.

Although he was House leader, Hazen Argue was more led than leading. He had been irritated by the decision in 1958 to re-elect Coldwell when it was clear Coldwell would not run for Parliament again. Argue was ambitious but unable to stand up to the combined weight of the CCF elite – particularly Lewis, Knowles, and Andrew Brewin. The architects of the new party did not want the CCF to go to the founding convention with an active national leader, and they particularly did not want Hazen Argue to be that leader. Their intention was to encourage T. C. Douglas to retire as premier of Saskatchewan in order to lead the new party. Lewis felt that Argue, tacitly at any rate, had accepted the views of the national committee concerning the leadership question.

Prior to the CCF's final national convention in 1960, Coldwell publicly announced his decision not to seek the leadership. The national council met before the opening of the convention to discuss the leadership question in the light of Coldwell's announcement and of the national committee's view that there should be no leader in the interim period.[51] At that meeting Douglas argued that the CCF could not function for a year as a "headless party." The national executive supported the national committee's view. To settle the question a committee was struck with instructions to draft a compromise. Argue was a member of the committee. It proposed that the post of "parliamentary leader" be created as something less than national leader yet more than House leader. The national council adopted this proposal with Hazen Argue assenting. Immediately after the council meeting, Fisher, Howard, and Peters told Argue that the caucus shared no part of the committee's views and that if he did not reverse his position, the caucus would reject him as House leader.[52] To the amazement of the national council, Argue announced to a cheering convention that the caucus unanimously rejected the council decision and that he was putting his name in

51 / Douglas-Higginbotham interviews, 1958–60, 581.
52 / Fisher, "The Making of a Senator."

nomination for the post of national leader. The convention followed the example of the caucus, turned down the council proposal, and elected Argue national leader.[53]

The rift between caucus and executive was now a chasm. Believing that Argue could not be trusted, the party officers increased their efforts to get Douglas to run for the leadership of the new party. Argue began to campaign in earnest for the same office. Making use of the party facilities at his disposal as national leader, he did his utmost to establish himself as a worthy successor to Coldwell and as a man of the rank and file who would not give way to the party "brass." The members of the executive resented Argue's use of his office to further his own political ambition, but there was little they could do to prevent him. The party headquarters' staff were in an awkward position as a result of the situation. Generally they aligned themselves with the officers, thereby exacerbating the alienation of the caucus. The work load occasioned by efforts to build the new party offered a convenient excuse for their inactivity on behalf of Argue and his supporters but it also served as another irritant.

When the founding convention of the new party opened in Ottawa in July 1961, the CCF was divided. The largest faction supported the party officers and their candidate, Tommy Douglas – who had managed to stay clear of the dispute. The other, which included most of the caucus, supported Argue and had cast itself as the defender of the true faith. It attracted those delegates who had misgivings about the new party, about organized labour, and about the exercise of legitimate authority. With the help of Douglas Fisher, his campaign manager, Argue put on a vigorous campaign, but, as everyone had expected, he was soundly defeated by Douglas. For one thing, the CCF executive had always emerged triumphant from struggles with the rank and file, and for another, Douglas, provincial premier and orator, was the CCF showpiece: for seventeen years head of the only socialist government in North America. Argue subsequently joined the Liberal party, lost his seat in Parliament, and was made a senator in 1966.

The internal politics of the CCF had little effect on its parliamentary reputation, although they provided the opportunity for occasional jibes from members on the opposite benches. The party's reputation in Parliament came, paradoxically, from the fact that it tended to behave most of the time as though it was the alternative to the party in power. Because it saw the two "old line" parties as essentially the same, the CCF saw itself as the real opposition and acted accordingly.

53 / National Council Minutes, Aug. 8, 1960, CCFP; Report of the Sixteenth National Convention (1960).

A party in the House of Commons which does not have any real opportunity of forming the government is frequently open to the charge of irresponsible behaviour. Critics whose allegiance is to the *status quo* have often argued that proximity to power breeds responsibility and that many of the things said by the CCF in and out of Parliament were said in the full knowledge that the party would not have to implement them or assume responsibility for them. It would be foolish to deny that there were occasions when the statements of CCF members warranted such criticism, but on balance it is unjust. Proof enough is the volume of legislation enacted by the Liberal and Conservative administrations that was first elucidated in the Commons by CCF members. Implicit in the criticism is the assumption that CCF members were little more than professional hell-raisers. This too is unjust and patently false in the light of the contributions made by the CCF group to Parliament and to the legislative process itself. The CCF's reputation as a parliamentary group was deservedly high, in part a tribute to Woodsworth, but more to Coldwell, who contributed a sense of balance and reasonableness to the parliamentary traditions of the party. He, more than his predecessor, accepted the rules of the parliamentary game. He was, more than Woodsworth, part of the institution, a confidant of Mackenzie King, a man at home with men of all parties, a conscientious legislator, and a trusted friend. It was not the role that Woodsworth played; it was one he could not play. To him Parliament was a vehicle for his crusade, whereas Coldwell saw it as something important in itself. He was, as Lewis and Scott wrote, "as perfectly suited to lead the CCF in its present stage of consolidation and strength as the social evangelist Woodsworth was in its earlier missionary stages."[54]

In 1932 Woodsworth moved the first of his annual resolutions calling for a co-operative commonwealth in Canada:

Whereas under our present economic arrangements large numbers of our people are unemployed and without the means of earning a livelihood for themselves and their dependents; and whereas the prevalence of the present depression throughout the world indicates fundamental defects in the existing economic system; be it therefore resolved: that in the opinion of this House the government should immediately take measures looking to the setting up of a co-operative commonwealth in which all the natural resources and the socially necessary machinery of production will be used in the interests of the people and not for the benefit of the few.[55]

54 / Lewis and Scott, *Make This* YOUR *Canada*, 130.
55 / *Hansard*, Feb. 19, 1932, 726 ff.

There was, of course, no hope of the resolution passing, but it was a public avowal of faith that Woodsworth made every year and one which provided the occasion for a swinging attack on capitalism and conservative institutions. In the period immediately after the formation of the CCF, the group in the House under Woodsworth's leadership supported many of the measures passed by Bennett's government, although they criticized the piecemeal approach he was taking. In the period 1932–5 they voted twelve times with the government. One of the major criticisms the group had of Bennett's "new deal" was its lack of constitutionality. A major plank in the CCF election address of 1935 was "The amendment of the B.N.A. Act ... so as to give the national government adequate powers to deal effectively with economic problems which are essentially national in scope."[56] The CCF joined with the Liberals on this point, arguments provided by F. R. Scott bolstering their position.

In the last years of the thirties, there was much to occupy the minds of the CCF members. Apart from the desperate situation of the unemployed and the particular problems of those in the relief camps, there were questions of civil liberty, concentrated particularly in section 98 of the Criminal Code of Canada, which was Arthur Meighen's contribution to the cause of liberty in 1919. The section denied jury trial to those charged with sedition or with the more vague crime of being "undesirable," the occasion for the section was the Winnipeg General Strike, in which Woodsworth had been active. In 1936 he had the satisfaction of seeing it repealed. Led by Woodsworth, the CCF group turned its attention to other similar problems such as the padlock law of Quebec's Premier Duplessis and the anti-Labour activities of Premier Hepburn of Ontario. No more lucid or passionate statements in defence of the liberties of Canadians can be found in *Hansard* than those made by members of the CCF caucus. They defended the rights of their enemies, the Communists, and attacked that most sacred of Canadian institutions, the RCMP, for its anti-labour activities, unwarranted interference with liberties, and undercover provocation.

How effective these attacks were is impossible to measure. Certainly the influence of the CCF in this period is clear in such areas as those mentioned and in that of labour legislation reform. The extent to which the Liberal government feared the persistence and accuracy of CCF attacks is, in some measure, demon-

56 / CCF Election Address, *C.C.F. Research Review*, Aug. 1935, 6–9. McNaught, *A Prophet*, provides a detailed discussion of the CCF in the House of Commons during this period; see esp. ch. 17.

strated by the threats and intimidation directed toward Grant MacNeil during the debate on the Bren gun scandal.

The scandal was first revealed in September 1938 in a magazine article by Col. George Drew, and concerned the government's decision to finance the rebuilding and tooling of a derelict factory of the John Inglis Company in order that the firm could make Bren guns.[57] As a result of the article, a Royal Commission was established to investigate the allegations. It sat for less than a month and in its report gave the government a clean bill of health insofar as the involvement of any government members in corrupt activities was concerned. However, it left open a number of questions about the procurement and production of armaments and the procedures followed by the government in letting defence contracts.

In his speech on the address, MacNeil urged that the House of Commons investigate the Bren gun case thoroughly.[58] Subsequently he moved that the whole matter be referred to the House Standing Committee on Public Accounts. The ensuing debate on the motion was one of the most heated of that Parliament. Ian Mackenzie, Minister of National Defence, having opened his speech on February 9 with the remark that he wanted to "discuss the issues as fairly, calmly and moderately as I can," went on to refer to the member for Mount Royal as a "splenetic dominie," to T. C. Douglas as a "quibbling romancer," to Coldwell as Douglas' "cynical colleague," and to the "Prussian mentality" of Mr. Homuth of Waterloo South.[59] It was not a distinguished speech but one which delineated the talents of the minister. MacNeil's speech was cool and logical by comparison. He said in part, "I should not be blamed by the Prime Minister and the Minister of National Defence if I hold vividly in recollection the memory of comrades who went gallantly to their deaths because they were furnished with faulty equipment by private manufacture resulting from a deal of this kind." He referred to the Ross rifle scandal of the First World War and chided the Minister of Defence for his pointless bluster. "All that I ask is a clean deal for men who may have to take arms in defence of the Country. But there is no clean, straightforward dealing when we have, as we have now, financial manipulation, bartering with company promoters and lack of faith in established Canadian industries."[60]

Prior to MacNeil's moving the resolution, and following his

57 / See Lt. Col. George Drew, "Canada's Armament Mystery," *Maclean's*, Sept. 7, 1938; and *Hansard*, 1939, 588 ff.
58 / *Hansard*, 1939, 345 ff.
59 / *Ibid.*, 794.
60 / *Ibid.*, 812 ff.

having given notice of it, A. A. Heaps, CCF whip, was visited by a clerk from the Liberal whip's office and informed by him that if MacNeil did not withdraw his motion to refer the Bren gun contract to the public accounts committee, "the old GWVA trouble would be brought up again."[61] The reference was to an investigation of some irregularity in the Great War Veterans' Association, of which MacNeil had been an administrative officer. In an ensuing investigation his activities had been vindicated. MacNeil raised the question in the House as one of privilege and received the assurance of the Prime Minister that if he did not move the resolution the government would.[62]

The tactics of the CCF in seizing upon an issue, finding the weakness in the government's armour, and pressing home the attack with a usually devastating array of carefully prepared material and skilful debate made it a formidable opposition. During the first year of the war the CCF caucus established itself as the major opposition to the government's war policy. In the 1940 session of the nineteenth Parliament the caucus attacked the manner of financing the war, the effects of the Defence of Canada Regulations on Civil Liberties, the government's failure to restrict the growth of monopoly through war contracts and, particularly, the extension of the Beauharnois Power Co. monopoly. The extent to which the constant CCF attack irritated Mackenzie King during the war can be seen from his diary. In 1943 he wrote, "It is significant that the C.C.F. were opposed to our participation in the war and have never given the war effort real support ... Their whole role has been contemptible from the point of view of true patriotism ..."[63] It is perhaps typical of King that he would forget that the CCF had supported Canadian participation in the war; only Woodsworth had opposed it finally. In any case, his pique tends to prove the effectiveness of CCF opposition.

The approach of the CCF group during the war was that laid down by the national convention in 1942: a total war effort committed to democratic ends. The party's basic criticism of the war effort in the House of Commons was that the war was being run as a big business affair. From the rescinding of the 5 per cent profit limitation in 1940 to the failure of the government to broaden participation in regulatory agencies to other than "dollar-a-year" men, the CCF, led by Coldwell, hammered incessantly on the failures of the Liberal administration. During the same period the party continued to press for better and more stable prices

61 / Caucus Minutes, Feb. 1, 1939, CCFP.
62 / *Hansard*, 1939, 519. The Bren Gun scandal is discussed in C. P. Stacey, *The Military Problems of Canada* (Toronto 1940).
63 / Pickersgill, *Mackenzie King Record*, I, 570.

for agricultural products and for guaranteed rights for organized labour. Toward the end of the war more attention was directed toward post-war planning, with particular attention to the government's stated intention to turn publicly financed war plants and equipment over to private interests. In private hands, the party argued, what the public had financed would not be used for public benefit.[64]

In the post-war period, a stronger CCF contingent was able to press the party's case with even more determination than before. Although over half the caucus of twenty-eight was from rural constituencies in Saskatchewan and Manitoba, the members displayed a good grasp of matters which were in no way connected with the endless plight of the prairie farmer. The policy of the party had been stated in broad terms by Coldwell in 1940 when he said that "enduring peace cannot be secured through the domination of one people by another or, in the narrower field of human relationships, through the domination of one man by another. This involves the elimination of exploitation both at home and abroad."[65] He returned to the same theme in his speech on the Address in the first session of the twentieth Parliament when he reminded the government of its election promises of jobs and prosperity and moved an amendment which urged that "immediate steps be taken to assure full employment, adequate purchasing power, and a large-scale housing programme ..."[66]

If there was any difference in the nature of the CCF attack in the post-war period as compared with the pre-war period, it was one consistent with the evolution of the party from the movement. Less emphasis was placed on the exposition of socialist philosophy from the forum of the House of Commons, and more was placed on the advocacy of measures leading to the welfare state. Planning became the key proposal and the inequities of an unplanned society the main targets of attack. In foreign policy the party moved toward an orthodox liberal position, support for the UN, for NATO, and for foreign aid and, generally, support for the rearmament that was necessary to meet the NATO commitment. The long-run effect of this softening of the CCF approach in Parliament was that the party's parliamentarians became more respectable.

One indication of the themes the party caucus saw as important is the amendment moved by Coldwell to the Address in Reply at the opening of each session of Parliament. The amendment

64 / See the address by M. J. Coldwell to the Eighth National Convention (1944).
65 / *Hansard*, 1940, 54.
66 / *Ibid.*, 1945, 42.

moved in 1946 is worth quoting in full because it represents the
view that was sustained throughout the following decade and
that was the post-war equivalent of Woodsworth's traditional
Co-operative Commonwealth resolution.

We respectfully submit, however, that in the opinion of this house,
Your Excellency's advisers in their reliance on private enterprise
have failed to propose the comprehensive national planning which
the present emergency demands;

We submit further that such planning is essential in order to
achieve full employment, provide for the adequate rehabilitation of
war veterans, assure the maintenance of stable and adequate farm
income, build urgently needed homes for the Canadian people, and
attain the high volume of both agricultural and industrial production
which alone will enable Canada to provide a rising standard of
living for our own people and contribute to the pressing needs of
war-ravaged countries in such a manner as to help lay the basis for
lasting peace.[67]

In 1947 the amendment criticized the government for failing to
control prices and allowing profits to soar; and in 1949 it called
for a national health plan and for the elimination of speculation
in and the orderly marketing of foodstuffs. In 1950 the same
criticism was advanced as well as a demand for the protection
of civil liberties. Indeed the statements of aim were largely ela-
borations on the ideas contained in that made in 1946. In 1953,
for example, the party emphasized the need for public control
of chartered banks and floor prices for cattle and hogs. In 1955
the need for a national fuel and power policy was a major issue.
Such a list as this, however, does not do justice to the CCF members for it implies that they were narrow in their scope, which is
far from the truth. These were major issues but not, to any extent,
the only ones. In the twenty-first Parliament, for example, over
thirty different matters of major concern were raised by the
group.

The question of the causal relationship between issues raised
and government policy will remain a moot one. There are several
instances which can be said, however, to demonstrate conclu-
sively the efficacy of the CCF as an advocate of reform. There are
others where it is difficult to establish beyond any doubt the role
played by the CCF in forcing a government to enact legislation.
As Coldwell pointed out in a radio address in 1953, "We have
seldom succeeded in achieving our full objective in any field. The
measures we have introduced and campaigned for have been
accepted reluctantly and half-heartedly by administrations that

67 / *Ibid.*, 1946, 59.

didn't really believe in them. In every case there are vast improvements still to be made."[68]

Among the major reforms for which the party took credit were unemployment insurance, first advocated by Woodsworth in 1922 and part of the Regina Manifesto and, in 1940, "after continuous pressure by the CCF," finally introduced by the Liberal government.[69] The introduction of the old age pension and the improvement of its provisions was claimed a CCF victory. In this case the role of Woodsworth in ensuring the passage of the first pension bill in 1926 is clearly established. The party also took credit for the hospital insurance program, family allowances, the establishment of the Wheat Board, and the inclusion of the marketing of oats and barley in the Board's jurisdiction. In each case the measure was first advocated by the CCF.

The methods the party used to achieve its success in this regard were best demonstrated by Stanley Knowles. His persistence and his familiarity and dexterity with parliamentary procedure enabled him to press the government constantly and with some success. In session after session he would move amendments, introduce bills, and, with his colleagues, continually press for reform when bills were in committee. Eight times in eight successive sessions in two Parliaments he introduced a bill to include the voluntary revocable check-off of union dues in the Industrial Disputes and Investigations Act. He saw this bill talked out, endorsed in committee, shelved by the government, and eventually defeated. He had given notice of introducing it again when he lost his seat in 1958.

The most successful demonstration of the technique of constant reiteration and the skilful use of the processes of Parliament was in Knowles's protracted battle to win back the pensions lost by striking CPR employees in the 1919 Winnipeg General Strike, and to protect the pension rights of all striking employees. Most of the participants in the Winnipeg strike who had lost their pensions had had them restored, including CNR employees, but not CPR employees, who had a non-contributory scheme. Knowles first raised the matter in 1944. By 1945, with the help of Alistair Stewart, member for Winnipeg North, and the railway brotherhoods, he had convinced the government of the importance of the matter to the extent that Harris Johnstone of the Department of Labour was instructed to investigate the employees' claims. Johnstone's report supported their position and called for a Royal Commission to investigate the entire situation, but the government did not act on the report.[70]

68 / Cited in *Comment*, Aug. 1956, 8.
69 / *Ibid.*, 9.   70 / See *Hansard*, 1947, March 10, 1213–16.

Knowles, in the meantime, had been introducing amendments to the Railways Act with unflagging persistence and on one occasion managed to refer the amendment to a standing committee. In the 1948 session the House had before it a government bill dealing with the amendment of the Industrial Disputes Investigations Act (Federal Labour Code). Knowles decided that it would be appropriate to move his pensions amendment to that bill for it would then apply to all employees under the jurisdiction of the Labour Code. In order to buttress his cause he wrote to Mackenzie King pointing out that since King had announced his retirement, it would be particularly fitting that he should right this wrong which had occurred in the year King had assumed the leadership of the Liberal party. In his reply King rejected Knowles's argument on behalf of the deprived CPR employees, pointing out that this was a private matter and outside the jurisdiction of the government. He made no mention of the protection of all striking workers.[71]

Knowles was subsequently called by the Minister of Transport, Lionel Chevrier, and told that King had asked Chevrier to deal with Knowles's request that legislative provision be made to protect strikers from loss of pension rights. Chevrier had been instructed to consult with the legal department of the CNR on the appropriate wording for such a measure. J. L. Ilsley, Minister of Justice, had also been asked by King to look into the matter. The Minister of Labour, Humphrey Mitchell, who was opposed to Knowles's bill, was not informed of these developments by King. Chevrier sent Knowles a draft amendment that differed little from Knowles's original proposal, apart from the CNR proviso that the strike had to be a legal strike. Knowles accepted the revision.

Chevrier then offered Knowles the privilege of moving the revised amendment during the committee stage of debate on the Labour Code. Aware that Mitchell had not been a party to these developments, Knowles declined, since he wisely thought that unnecessary irritation of the labour minister should be avoided. He also withdrew from the Commons order paper his private members' bill dealing with the same matter but as an amendment to the Railways Act because he feared that Mitchell might use the House rule prohibiting debate on the same topic under two separate items to kill the Chevrier amendment. During the committee stage Knowles moved his original amendment. Chevrier proposed the revised version and Knowles then withdrew his

71 / Interview with Stanley Knowles, Feb. 1967; S. H. Knowles to W. L. Mackenzie King, May 19, 1948; W. L. Mackenzie King to S. H. Knowles, June 7, 1948. Correspondence in Knowles' possession.

motion and the Chevrier amendment passed.[72] It was a major victory and a tribute to Knowles's persistence and political deftness.

These skills contributed significantly to a host of measures improving various pieces of government legislation ranging from the provision of eight statutory holidays in the Labour Code instead of seven, to extensions to the coverage of the Unemployment Insurance Act and the deduction of union dues from taxable income.[73] The method and tactics were typical of the CCF approach in the House of Commons. It would be inaccurate to see the CCF as having a monopoly in the House of Commons of the impetus to reform; however, the connection between legislation enacted, and the CCF advocacy of these issues seems too close to ignore. The causal relationship in most cases can only be inferred, however, not demonstrated beyond doubt.

What is certain is that the CCF in the House of Commons performed the tasks of opposition very well, better, in many respects, than the official opposition. The CCF was perhaps better suited to the role of opposition than the Conservative party because it stood at greater distance from the government. The Conservatives were not sufficiently different from the Liberals that their opposition meant much more than that they were sorry that they were not in power. Criticism from the CCF had about it a ring of true earnestness and was the product of that intense diligence that only ideological commitment can inspire. Because their opposition to the government was more fundamental, the CCF members were able to attack it with more telling effect than their Conservative colleagues on the opposition benches. If the "Tweedle-dum and Tweedle-dee" thesis has any validity, one of its effects is to vitiate the effectiveness of the official opposition.

The CCF in the House of Commons accepted the functions and the role of the opposition in Parliament and fulfilled them, but with one important difference. For the official opposition – which was the Conservative party for the better part of the CCF's career in Parliament – the major objective in directing the beams of the searchlight into the darker corners of government activity was to impress the electorate so that, in the next election, it would support them and not the party in power. For the CCF, which had not achieved that kind of proximity to power, the task was both simpler and more onerous. The socialist members had, on the one hand, to constantly advance and promote those reforms they

72 / *Hansard*, 1948, 5369 ff.; and see the *Winnipeg Citizen*, June 18, 1948.

73 / *Hansard*, 1951, 1815; *Comment*, Aug. 1956, 10–11; and see those issues of *Comment*, 1941–59 which review each session of Parliament.

believed in, while at the same time offering both support for and criticism of the government. There was little likelihood of their activities attracting enough public attention to win them the next election and when the reforms they supported were enacted, the Liberals or Conservatives got the credit for them.

The persistence of CCF members in introducing private members' bills in session after session may have gone unrewarded, but the party did take advantage of this procedure to demonstrate to its supporters and would-be supporters that the CCF was at least defending their interests. The regular bulletins of the Political Action Committee of the CCL and CLC contained many references to bills introduced by the CCF on behalf of labour, and similar information was provided the various farm organizations. There is no way of knowing how widely these bulletins were read and the House of Commons is not the most effective instrument for political education. For those who do not read *Hansard*, knowledge of what occurs in the House is provided only after it has been filtered through the prejudices of journalists and editors. Nevertheless the caucus did see its participation in Parliament as part of the party's propaganda function.

Flights of oratory for the sake of the press gallery were not uncommon to CCF members, but they seldom lost sight of their major aim: to influence the government. The approach was at times frontal assault, as in the obvious case of the pipeline debate of 1956, and at others more akin to the "sunny ways" of Laurier where the group hoped to win reform by supporting the government against the opposition, as in the case of the Fair Employment Practices Act of 1953.[74] During his tenure as leader of the CCF, Coldwell had much closer contact with the Liberals, particularly Mackenzie King, than he had with his opposition colleagues in the Conservative party.

Coldwell had much respect and affection for the House and the institution of Parliament and was acknowledged as a great parliamentarian. Norman Smith of the *Ottawa Journal* wrote, at the time of the pipeline debate, "He [Coldwell] is not a hot-blooded man and his respect for parliament has long been known to all men. When you hear him say parliament has become a farce it is time to search your soul rather than your prejudices."[75] He had a contemporary appreciation of the role of Parliament and, for the most part, his followers accepted it:

There was a time when ... the main function of this house was the

74 / See *Hansard*, 1953, 3766. In some sessions of Parliament CCF support for the government ran as high as 50 per cent of the recorded divisions. It averaged about 20 per cent.

75 / *Ottawa Journal*, June 4, 1956.

granting of supply and finding ways and means to give that supply
to the government. But times have changed and today this house has
the responsibility of supervising and inquiring into vast economic
undertakings and of assuming responsibility in a larger way than
ever before for social conditions and social legislation ... consequently members come here not only to supervise the expenditure of
money and to find ways and means of granting it to the crown, but
also to advance social policies now of permanent interest to the community and to inquire into the vast economic undertakings which
now belong properly to the government and will probably in future
years be extended.[76]

Because of the essentially reasonable approach of Coldwell and
his colleagues, the CCF did have "the ear of the house." Its arguments were not always accepted or acted upon but they were
listened to with respect. The hysterical accusations and inter-
jections that characterized the attitude of some parliamentarians
toward the CCF had, by the fifties, largely disappeared.

During the fifties the group in Parliament was the chief demonstration that the CCF was a viable national force because decline
had begun in the party at large. Initially the strategy of the CCF
had been broad. Parliament was only one battlefield or site for
its activities.[77] With the increasing emphasis on electoral organization and the importance of winning elections, more attention was focussed on Parliament. The effectiveness of CCF members was always a point of pride in the party; it became almost
a justification of the party during the lean years. The party caucus
provided the point of contact with the engine of government that
the CCF sought and it was natural and perhaps accurate to assume
that when the government finally did what the CCF members had
been saying it should do, it was because there *were* CCF members
in direct contact with government through Parliament. The aims
of the movement could be achieved piecemeal without the necessity of political power. And the rightness of the cause was demonstrated by the fact that the government had clearly been convinced by the argument presented by socialist members. Parliament was in many ways a demonstration and justification of
much that the CCF stood for. In theory it was the heart of democracy because it was a forum in which representatives of the
people legislated by process of rational argument. In fact it was
not, but the CCF treated it as such; there was not much else they
could do.

The relative success of the CCF in Parliament contributed to

76 / *Hansard*, 1942, 2759.
77 / See Robert Dahl, "Patterns of Opposition," in Dahl, *Political
Opposition in Western Democracies* (New Haven 1966).

the gradual weakening of the movement. For one thing, the
successes achieved by the party members were normative successes, that is, they were successes measured in specific reforms
here, amendments there, a better deal for labour, and so on. Although the members spoke often enough of the need to eliminate
the evils of competition and free enterprise, Parliament was not
constituted to bring about that kind of revolution in values. Its
role in the polity was, if anything, normative, and the CCF sought
to use it in this way. The measures they advocated – a bill of
rights, health insurance, improvements to existing laws relating
to unemployment insurance, agricultural marketing, and the like
– were measures of reform. They may have been generated by
the belief in the need for a revolution of values which motivated
some CCF members, but for an increasing number of people –
both members and supporters of the party – they came to represent what, for them, the CCF was all about: reform. The issues of
Comment which dealt with each session of Parliament as it
ended did not attack the government for failing to eradicate free
enterprise or modify competition; they attacked it for cutting the
price of No. 1 Northern wheat (June 1954); for failing to improve the housing situation (June 1953); and for refusing to increase family allowances (no. 12, 1956). The criticism expressed
in *Comment* was drawn largely from the speeches of CCF members in the House of Commons.

It would be difficult to avoid giving the CCF some general
credit for leading the arguments for reform in the Parliament of
Canada and for performing the tasks of the official opposition
often better than the official opposition itself was able to do. But
it is impossible to do more than this. In a democratic state the
government is, at any given moment on any particular policy
question, subject to many pressures, the least of which may be
those produced by the arguments of the members opposite in the
House of Commons. To suppose that a prime minister is responsive to his opposition critics, even over the long run, more than
he is to such pressure groups as are represented by his own
ministers and back-benchers and such external lobbies as the
labour congresses and chambers of commerce, is to misapprehend
the nature of Parliament. The CCF bill to provide for the voluntary revocable check-off for example, was shelved by the government because the two labour congresses could not agree on the
matter.[78] The constituency of any government is far wider than
Parliament – and even within that limited sphere, far wider than
the opposition, particularly a small fragment of that opposition
which has relatively little strength in the country. It may have

78 / *Hansard*, 1953, 4773.

been true that during and immediately after the war, Mackenzie
King responded to the goad of CCF argument because he feared
the rising strength of the party. He was, after all, a man for whom
leadership consisted in following the resultant of the parallelo-
gram of forces that is democratic politics. But, as Bruce Hutchison has laboriously pointed out,[79] King's sympathies did lie in
the direction of social betterment if *Industry and Humanity* is
any guide. It might be said that the CCF provided an excuse for
venting of the pent-up radicalism trapped in the soul of that
strange little man.

By emphasizing its parliamentary performance, the CCF was
accentuating the positive and demonstrating its undying faith in
the efficacy of rational argument. It was even possible to educate
Mackenzie King and Louis St. Laurent, although from time to
time it was clear that such pupils as these forgot their lessons
very quickly. It was with considerable pride that party leaders
pointed to measures adopted by the Liberal and Conservative
governments that were first advocated by the CCF, and with considerable pride that they saw newspapers and magazines hostile
to the party forced to admit the skill and efficacy of the CCF
group and of individual members in the House of Commons.[80]
The party leader's address before most conventions was a recita-
tion of the effectiveness of the CCF as an opposition group –
criticizing the government, ventilating issues, and advocating
reform.

However effective the CCF was in Parliament, it clearly did not
make much difference to the electorate. Frank Underhill's view
of the interest of Canadians in their legislature may be over-
stated, but it has some truth. It did not really matter how
hard CCF members worked, or how diligently they kept up their
attendance at sessions; they were not winning many extra votes.
As members of a party which was, in the general sense, un-
popular, they had little enough going for them except their
devotion to principle and duty, and their diligence. A socialist
minority in a capitalist system, even though in the position of
opposition in a parliamentary situation, is always on the defensive because its presence, its very right to be there, is suspect.
This puts the party front line on its mettle. Existing on sufferance,
as it were, it must demonstrate not only that it is composed of
honest men and that its cause is just, but that it is as respectable
as the capitalist; indeed, as defenders of Parliament and the
principles of liberal democracy, more respectable.

79 / Hutchison, *The Incredible Canadian, passim.*
80 / See, for example, the report of the national executive and council
to the Thirteenth National Convention (1954).

As the CCF moved toward the devastating experience of the 1958 election and the final tie with labour, its members moved further from the Woodsworthian tradition. The ringing resolutions calling for the institution of the co-operative commonwealth were no longer introduced. Amendments to the Address in Reply were practical, speeches were practical. The movement's chiliasm was muffled and gradually disappeared as socialists were socialized by the institution of Parliament, learned to play the game, to play it even better than the capitalist members for whom the institution was, after all, largely designed. In that sense it would not be true to say that all Canadians "don't give a damn about parliament." Most members of parliament do, and the CCF members certainly did.

9

9

THE CCF AND THE COMMUNIST PARTY

Again and again we have stated we have no
connection whatever with the Communist Party.

J. S. WOODSWORTH
House of Commons, 1934

Although the existence of communist parties has always posed a threat to right-wing parties, it has been a threat which united them, causing their ranks to close in defence of their beliefs. For democratic socialist parties the threat has been more serious tending to divide rather than unite them. The similarity between their policy and doctrine and that of the Communists has confused their members and resulted in divisions within their ranks. This similarity, even if only superficial, has meant that criticism of communist parties worked to the detriment of party unity within the democratic socialist movement. It is one thing to attack capitalism, but quite another to attack a party which ostensibly defends the rights of the working class and is even more vehement in its denunciation of capitalism than a democratic socialist party. To the unsophisticated, it seemed logical that two elements of what appears as a single movement – at least as far as explicit ends are concerned – should combine their efforts in advancing the cause of socialism.

The CCF faced this problem throughout its history. Although the Canadian Communist party – or Labour Progressive Party, as it was called from 1943 to 1960 – attacked the CCF, it also stressed the similarity of viewpoint between the two parties and urged co-operation, affiliation, and unity. At the same time it attempted to drive a wedge between CCF leaders and members. The CCF found it difficult to maintain a consistent opposition to the Communist party and its front organizations during the thirties and forties. The CCF leaders were clearly anti-Marxist and anti-Communist, but the rank and file were far from unanimity in their opposition to Communist organizations. The Communist party recognized this divergence and sought to capitalize on it in order to divide the national CCF executive from the rank and file. The use of front organizations such as the Canadian Labor Defense League, the League against War and Fascism, and the Peace Councils, facilitated this process, since if active co-operation with the Communist party was one thing, the signing of an anti-war petition or participation in a Labor Defense League parade on May Day was quite another for many CCF members.

The strict attitudes of Woodsworth and Coldwell at times exacerbated the situation. Though they remained within the framework of convention decisions, neither permitted the slightest deviation from the "party line" with respect to the Communist party. The suspicion of executive dictation, which seems to be a characteristic of democratic parties, worked to the advantage of the Communist party, which was always quick to point out that CCF opposition to their proposals for unity was simply evidence of the CCF leaders' betrayal of socialism and the needs of the working classes.

The internal problems created by Communist attacks and attempts to infiltrate were relatively minor in comparison with the damage done to the CCF image by the repeated flirtation of its left wing with the Communist party. This damage was compounded by confusion in the public mind between CCF and Communist policy. From the party's creation in 1932 there was a tendency on the part of the public at large and of the press to speak of the CCF and the Communist party in the same breath. The CCF suffered from guilt by association and, as a result, had to devote considerable attention to the business of establishing and maintaining a distinct and favourable public image. The task was further complicated by the readiness of the right-wing parties to link the CCF with the Communists for campaign purposes.

The CCF had to wage war on two fronts. Its limited resources were strained by the need to combat enemies within and to the left in addition to those on the right. Its ability to attack the capitalist parties was impaired as a result. The very need to wage war on the Communist party assisted its right-wing opponents immeasurably. It is utopian to expect the average voter to understand the distinction between communism and democratic socialism when both groups use much the same terminology, and both base much of their program on a class analysis of Canadian society. For the average person there was little difference between this statement:

We aim to replace the present capitalist system, with its inherent injustice and inhumanity, by a social order from which the domination and exploitation of one class by another will be eliminated, in which economic planning will supersede unregulated private enterprise and competition, and in which genuine democratic self-government based upon economic equality will be possible. The present order is marked by glaring inequalities of wealth and opportunity, by chaotic waste and instability; and in an age of plenty it condemns the great mass of the people to poverty and insecurity.[1]

and this paraphrase of the Communist Manifesto written by Tim Buck:

We shall replace the profit system, with its soulless exploitation of man by man, its classes and class antagonisms, by a system which expresses the social relations of economic, and thereby, political equals – a society in which, because of its collective ownership and

1 / The Regina Manifesto.

direction of the means of social production, the free development of each will be the condition for the free development of all. Such is the greater and richer Canada toward which we strive – a socialist Canada.[2]

It is perhaps asking too much to expect even the editorial writer to see the essential difference between the two parties.

The CCF hammered incessantly on the door of public sympathy, insisting that its socialism was brought by democratic means and was opposed to the violent revolution advocated by the Communist party. The door remained closed. The violence of CCF attacks on "big business" left some doubt in many minds as to how democratic the CCF would be once in power and opposed by the forces of capital. During the 1935 general election the Ontario CCF newspaper stated that the election "is a fight between those who stand for capitalism and those who are opposed to it."[3] The CCF slogans were not chosen to instil a sense of moderation or confidence in the minds of the electorate, calling as they did for CCF support in order to "Smash the big-shot monopoly" and "Smash the big-shot's slave camps and sweat shops." The New Commonwealth pointed out in 1936 that:

In no sense is the socialism of the C.C.F. mere reformism, mere gradualism, or compromise with capitalism of any kind. A C.C.F. government attaining power must proceed promptly, drastically, thoroughly to liquidate the power of capitalist forces and secure ... assurance that the capitalist interests could not sabotage, weaken or overthrow socialism.[4]

The consistency of CCF claims to democratic methods could be simply called to doubt and the parallel between communism and democratic socialism could be, and often was, easily drawn by opposition parties.

It was difficult for the populace to ignore the words of R. B. Bennett when he said, "What do these so-called groups of socialists and communists offer you? We know that throughout Canada this propaganda is being put forward by organizations from foreign lands that seek to destroy our institutions ..."[5] The Attorney-General of Ontario exhorted the churches to fight communism and "its partner, atheism," as represented by men like Woodsworth, Heaps, Bland, and A. E. Smith: "The CCF," he pointed out, is "probably directed from Moscow."[6] So common

2 / Tim Buck, Canada, The Communist Viewpoint (Toronto 1948), 36.
3 / New Commonwealth, July 20, 1935.
4 / New Commonwealth, April 18, 1936.
5 / Canadian Unionist, VI (Dec. 1932), 113.
6 / Toronto Star, Dec. 6, 1932.

was the feeling that the CCF was in fact a Communist organization that, "even the editor of the [*Winnipeg*] *Free Press*, as late
as 1938, believed David Lewis ... to be a communist."[7] Before
and after the war, the CCF was cast as a Communist or totalitarian
party by its opponents.

The members of the CCF were, it would seem, at pains to provide the proof required by their political opponents. At conventions a customary form of address was "comrade," and the fact
that the more articulate and vocal delegates were often from the
left wing of the party provided the opposition with abundant
evidence for proof of their assertions. In 1933 E. E. Winch supported a resolution at the Regina convention to delete the sentence "We do not believe in change by violence" from the Manifesto. The Toronto *Mail and Empire* gave this resolution some
prominence in its report of the convention.[8] In 1954 Rod Young,
of the British Columbia CCF, declared: "I'm proud to have people
tell me I'm a communist."[9] Hardly a newspaper in Canada missed the story.

But it would be inaccurate and unjust to argue that the weakness and vulnerability of the CCF in this respect were due entirely
to internal disease. The Communist party seized upon the weaknesses that existed and lost no opportunity to exploit them. At
the Sixth Congress of the Canadian Communist party, a declaration was passed which stated:

We accept and endorse the line of the Comintern letter on the Canadian Labor Party, and agree that in the present period it is not the
task of the Communist Party to build a Labor Party, but on the
contrary, our task is to combat the idea of a federated Labor Party
as an integral part of the struggle against social reformism, and to
intensify our struggle to bring those working class organizations that
are still affiliated to the C.L.P. under the direct and open leadership
of the Communist Party.[10]

According to J. B. Salsberg, one of the leading figures in the
Communist party until his resignation in 1956, the party in the
middle thirties looked upon the CCF as "one of the greatest
hindrances to the establishment of socialism in Canada."[11] The
technique adopted by the Communist party was the usual one of
co-operation and infiltration. It was a tactic that worked well

7 / McNaught, *A Prophet*, 269.
8 / Toronto *Mail and Empire*, July 20, 1933.
9 / Transcript of Proceedings, British Columbia CCF Convention, 1954,
CCFP. It turned out that he was.
10 / All Canadian Congress of Labour, *Labour Annual*, Sept. 2, 1929.
258   11 / J. B. Salsberg interview, 1962, Fox transcript.

because of the inevitable ideological confusion that prevails in democratic socialist movements and parties.

The Communist party initiated its long series of attempts at establishing a united front with the CCF in 1933. The leaders of the Communist party were in prison at the time, the work of the party being carried on by a "front" organization, the Canadian Labor Defense League, an organization which sought to "unite all forces willing to co-operate, into a broad national organization that will undertake to provide means for the defense and support of workers ... who are indicted and prosecuted on account of activity in the Labour Movement."[12]

The CLDL approached the Regina CCF convention in 1933 and requested the "formation of a broad united front to wage a struggle for the release of Tim Buck and the other seven leaders of the Communist Party ... and for the repeal of this infamous anti-working class section 98." The petition suggested a joint meeting of the CCF national council and the CLDL national committee to "agree upon joint mass meetings, delegations and demonstrations on this burning issue."[13] The Communist leaders had some hope of success because in the House of Commons Woodsworth and Heaps had vigorously protested the arrest of the Communist executive.[14] However, the CCF turned down the request in a reply which states clearly the official attitude of the CCF toward section 98 and toward union with the Communists:

We reiterate that the rights of freedom of speech and assembly be guaranteed to all workers, regardless of political affiliation; that section 98 of the Criminal Code, which has been used by a panic-stricken capitalist government, must be wiped off the statute books and political prisoners, who were imprisoned under it, be released. We believe these ends cannot be achieved except by securing control of the government. We believe in constitutional methods to attain this result. On that point there is fundamental cleavage between us and the leaders of your organization, who maintain civil strife is inevitable. This policy, in our opinion, would result in the intensification of political oppression. We, therefore, are unable to see that any useful purpose could be served by such joint mass meetings, delegations and demonstrations as you suggest.[15]

The course which the Communist party proposed to take failing their attempts to get any co-operation from the national CCF was

12 / "Application for Membership" card, Canadian Labour Defense League, 1933, CCFP.
13 / "A Call to the Rank and File of the CCF," Canadian Labour Defense League, 1933, CCFP.
14 / *Hansard*, 1932–3, 2096 ff.
15 / Copy of statement dated July 22, 1933, CCFP.

indicated in a letter from Becky Buhay, the secretary of the
Communist Party organization department, in which she stated:
"We have, therefore, no alternative but to appeal to your membership directly, and to build the united front within the rank and
file of the CCF through local action. We are confident that large
sections of your membership are ready and eager for united
activity on the issues we propose."[16] In October 1933, the Ontario provincial council passed a resolution prohibiting former
Communists from joining the CCF.[17]

The campaign to keep the CCF pure for democracy and socialism did not appeal to those in the party who could see more
similarity than difference between their party and the Communist
party, and whose practical natures rebelled at the waste and
division of labour involved in having two left-wing parties fight
separately the same enemy for what appeared to be the same
general ends. The federal structure of the CCF made it possible
for affiliated groups to adopt policies somewhat at variance with
official provincial or national policy. The Toronto Regional Labour Council refused to accept the Ontario provincial council's
membership provisos and stated: "We welcome in our ranks all
those who have honourable records of struggle against capitalism,
war and unemployment," further declaring itself opposed to the
general attitude of the provincial bodies toward Communists.[18]

The attitude of the Regional Labour Council was not atypical
at a time when many of the urban trade unions were either Com-
munist-dominated or sympathetically inclined toward communism. The influence of such unions as the International Fur and
Leather Workers, the United Electrical, Radio and Machine
Workers of America, the United Garment Workers, the Shipyard Workers, and the Vancouver Street Railwaymen's Union
meant that an urban labour council espoused an anti-Communist
attitude at its peril. At the same time many ordinary members
of the CCF found it difficult to accept the anti-Communist stric-
tures of the party executive. A. E. Smith records that "The
C.C.F. leaders could not stem the tide of United Front sentiment
in their own ranks" and that "C.C.F. clubs sent delegates to our
defense conferences in spite of the official ban."[19] Smith, a Com-

16 / Becky Buhay to J. S. Woodsworth, May 23, 1933, Woodsworth
Papers.
17 / Ontario Provincial Council Minutes, Oct. 1933, CCFP.
18 / Copy in the Loeb papers, cited in Caplan thesis, "Socialism and
anti-Socialism in Ontario, 1932–1945," 329. Caplan's study provides an
excellent picture of the activities of the Communist party *vis-à-vis* the
CCF in Ontario.
19 / A. E. Smith, *All My Life* (Toronto 1949), 163.

munist, is clearly not the least biased reporter, but subsequent events verify his statement.

In the early months of 1934 the CLDL appeals for a united front were at their height. Smith appeared at a Massey Hall rally and denounced J. S. Woodsworth and the CCF executive for their failure to defend labour's rights; he was joined on the platform and in his criticism by Wilfred Jones of the Toronto St. Paul's CCF club.[20] When the Ontario secretary of the CCF requested the expulsion of Jones, the club refused, and when the president of the Socialist party of Canada – affiliated with the Ontario CCF – moved to have the Communists expelled from the Socialist party, he was himself removed as president.[21] Woodsworth threatened expulsion of those who refused to accept party discipline[22] but, under the constitution, was unable to act himself, because only the provincial councils could recommend expulsion.

By 1934 the CLDL had enjoyed some success in establishing itself as the defender of labour's interests and what unity there had been in opposing it had largely dissolved. Consequently, decisions of the Ontario provincial executive and council urging non–co-operation and an anti-Communist attitude were ignored. The disintegration of the Ontario section and the withdrawal of the United Farmers of Ontario was a direct result of the conflict and confusion arising out of the role of the CCF in defence of the interests of labour. Despite the clear anti-Communist direction given by Woodsworth and the reorganization of the Ontario section to prevent further trouble, the Co-operative Commonwealth Youth Movement (CCYM), which was formed in the summer of 1934, adopted as its watchword "revolt" and insisted that its members address one another as "comrade." They co-operated jointly with the Communist party and the Women's League of Nations Society in sending a protest to Ottawa in connection with the treatment meted out to the Regina Trekkers.[23]

In October 1934 the Canadian Congress against War and Fascism came on the scene and attracted the attention and support of many in the CCF. At the first congress in Toronto greetings were received from several CCF clubs, and Alice Loeb, a prominent Toronto member of the CCF, was on the presiding committee.[24] In March 1935 a Toronto and District Conference against War and Fascism was held at which Frank Underhill

20 / M. Stewart and D. French, *Ask No Quarter* (Toronto 1959), 176.
21 / *Ibid.*
22 / *Toronto Star*, Feb. 14, 1934.
23 / Caplan thesis, 334.
24 / "Report of the First Canadian Congress against War and Fascism, Toronto, October 6 and 7, 1934," Woodsworth Papers.

spoke and George Grube took the chair.[25] In 1935 the Canadian
League against War and Fascism was formed and had as chairman A. A. Macleod, a member of the Communist party, and
T. C. Douglas as vice-chairman. Other members of the executive
were Salem Bland, William Irvine, Harold Winch, Ben Spence,
and Percy Rowe, MP, all members of the CCF; as well as Jacob
Penner and A. E. Smith of the Communist party.[26] The league
was in fact a "front," but there was at this point so much confusion among the various anti-fascist groups that it was difficult
for CCF members to know much more than that those who were
against war and fascism could not be bad allies. The national
council was told in November 1935 that the Saskatchewan youth
movement "was for all practical purposes, itself the League
Against War and Fascism."[27] The defence offered by several CCF
members to the November council meeting was that they were
simply acting as individuals, a position which Woodsworth rejected. He insisted there should be no co-operation with Communists at all.[28] In 1939 the name was changed to the Canadian
League for Peace and Democracy, such were the vicissitudes of
Soviet foreign policy. The CCF members had departed earlier.

It was difficult for many in the CCF to discern what kept the
two parties apart since there seemed to be so much agreement on
the issues of the day. In May 1935 the *New Commonwealth*
wrote of the "minor doctrinal differences" which separated the
parties.[29] In August the same year, the Mount Pleasant CCF unit
submitted the following resolution to the Ontario CCF council:
"Resolved that the National Convention of the C.C.F. delete all
clauses in its by-laws of constitution WHICH PROHIBITS unity of
action between the C.C.F. party and that of the Communist Party
[*sic*]."[30] The resolution died in committee but is indicative of the
confusion and the response in the constituencies to the Communist pressure.

The Communist party approached the CCF in 1935 with the
suggestion that the two groups co-operate in the general election
to ensure maximum use of pro-labour votes. Tim Buck and Sam
Carr, secretary and assistant secretary of the Communist party,
wrote to Woodsworth with the following proposal:

The Communist Election Committee, so far, proposes to contest only
sixteen seats of the total of 245 constituencies. The constituencies

25 / "Program," Toronto and District Conference against War and
Fascism, March 23–4, 1935, Woodsworth Papers.
26 / Letterhead in CCFP.
27 / National Council Minutes, Nov. 30, 1935, CCFP.
28 / *Ibid.*
29 / *New Commonwealth*, Oct. 12, 1935.
30 / Copy in CCFP.

were selected where the Communists have the greatest mass following. We are of the opinion that an agreement can be arrived at
between the Communist Election Committee and the CCF, making
possible an elimination of any possibilities for splits in the working
class vote and mutual support on the basis of a minimum program
of immediate needs for the toilers of Canada.[31]

The suggestion was rejected by the CCF.[32] Undeterred, the Communist party tried again in July with a slightly different approach.
The argument presented was that the Stevens Reconstruction
party was "the crystalization of a Fascist party in Canada under
a cloak of demagogic promises," and that "an agreement based
on the immediate needs of the people" was needed, "making
possible mutual support for the election of the greatest number
possible of anti-capitalist candidates."[33]

The aim of the Communists was not co-operation with the
CCF for the achievement of socialism, but the absorption of the
CCF by the Communist party. Despite the new approach adopted
by international communism after 1935, the Canadian Communists maintained the old tactic. The Communist party ad-
vertisements in the 1935 general election urged voters to elect
either a CCF or a Communist majority,[34] but the fact that the CCF
was also running candidates in all but two of the ridings contested by the Communist party would seem to indicate that Communist policy was more in line with the directive in the report of
the seventh session of the Communist party of Canada:

We must on no account allow the CCF to step forward as the working class alternative to the old parties, as it was able to do in the
provincial elections up to now. We must make such an application
of our revolutionary mass policy as to prevent the C.C.F. from
appearing in the eyes of the masses as the only alternative ...[35]

The CCF executive contributed to the confusion within the party
by campaigning on the slogan: "It is a fight between those who
stand for Capitalism and those who are opposed to it. That is the
only election issue ..."[36] Small wonder then that the rank and file
CCF members would feel few qualms about lending support to
the League against War and Fascism. And as the fascist menace
in Europe increased it was even more difficult for CCF members

31 / Tim Buck and Sam Carr to J. S. Woodsworth, April 4, 1935,
Woodsworth Papers.
32 / M. J. Coldwell to Tim Buck, April 10, 1935, CCFP.
33 / Sam Carr to M. J. Coldwell, July 12, 1935, CCFP.
34 / See the *Toronto Mail and Empire*, Oct. 5, 1935.
35 / Report of the seventh session of the Communist party of Canada,
Dec. 1934, as reported in the *New Commonwealth*, Oct. 12, 1935.
36 / *New Commonwealth*, July 20, 1935.

to stand aloof from the anti-fascist enthusiasms of the Communist party and its front organizations. Although many in the CCF were not pro-Communist, all were unquestionably anti-fascist.

The pressure for a united front increased in 1936, aided in no small measure by the apparent advantages of anti-fascist unity on the political left. It was in view of this pressure, which was growing within the CCF as well as being applied by the Communists from without, that the CCF parliamentary group and the national executive of the League for Social Reconstruction discussed the question of co-operation with the Communists at a confidential meeting. The strongest position against co-operation was taken by J. S. Woodsworth. He contended that "loyalty to the decisions of the CCF must be disciplined." He also pointed out "the difficulties involved with borderline organizations [and] suggested the better organization of CCF civil liberties leagues in the provinces." Woodsworth maintained this position throughout the discussions, insisting upon "the need for greater discipline and, if necessary, expulsion of disloyal members."[37]

However, the attitude of several others present at the meeting was more conciliatory. Coldwell thought "there were three possible attitudes regarding the united front: for, against, and those who believe a united front will come inevitably"; he pointed out the dangers both of co-operation and isolation. Lewis argued that although no local affiliation during elections should be tolerated, "the present policy of the C.P. had a definite appeal and that if it proved genuine, there should be a reconsideration of CCF policy." He was not entirely in favour of Woodsworthian discipline, preferring instead "investigation of activities of individuals" followed by "tactful requests that their first loyalty be to the CCF." Grant MacNeil underlined the implications of Lewis' statement when he pointed out that "the effect of anti-C.P. propaganda on members of the CCF is as dangerous as the effect on right wingers who will link the CCF with the C.P. if the CCF speaks on Communist platforms." The consensus was that united front affiliations at elections should be forbidden and that "the CCF as such should not affiliate with the League Against War and Fascism," but that "there is still a field – such as the Regina Trekkers – where some form of co-operation is unavoidable, but

37 / "Confidential Report: Summary of Discussions between CCF Parliamentary Group and L.S.R. National Executive," March 28, 1936, typewritten, CCFP. Those present at the meeting were: J. S. Woodsworth, A. A. Heaps, Angus MacInnis, M. J. Coldwell, J. S. Taylor, Grant MacNeil, T. C. Douglas, Grace MacInnis, F. M. Aykroyd, E. A. Forsey, J. King Gordon, J. C. Hemmeon, David Lewis, Carleton MacNaught, Helen Marsh, Leonard Marsh, George S. Mooney, F. R. Scott, R. B. Y. Scott, Graham Spry, F. H. Underhill.

that it is better not to deal with this in any statement to be issued."[38]

The very co-operation to which Woodsworth was opposed occurred in Ontario when a number of prominent CCF members participated in May Day celebrations in Toronto. A group of CCF members, led by Ben H. Spence, organized the celebrations and invited the support of the Communist party. As a result of this action the Ontario executive expelled three members, including Spence, and four CCF clubs. The individuals and the clubs were subsequently reinstated, but not before a bitter campaign had been waged against the Ontario and, by implication, the national executive, by an *ad hoc* committee struck to defend the expelled socialists. The incident illustrates the division that existed within the party on the question of co-operation with the Communists. In a letter to Woodsworth, Spence pointed out that a majority of the more prominent CCF members in the area, including Graham Spry and Carleton McNaught, had not been opposed to the idea of joint May Day celebrations under the auspices of the CCF.[39]

Although the CCF national executive was determined to stay in the "daily struggle," as Woodsworth called it, through their ancillary organizations such as the CCYM and the provincial civil liberty leagues, the party was nevertheless losing some leftist support as a result of its moderation. The moderation which characterized the pronouncements of the executive, coupled with the insistence upon party discipline and refusal to participate in any united front exercises, caused the CCF some harm and lent an air of credence to the Communist party attacks on the CCF executive. The vigour of the Communist onslaught gave the impression that it was the party most determined to fight for the rights of the worker. This weakened the CCF. It tended to alienate some members from the party leaders. And the Communist party scored easily from CCF reticence:

We [the C.P.] advocate that the Co-operative Commonwealth Federation should become a wide united front party. The Communist Party is prepared to affiliate to the CCF to work towards this objective promoting the widest unity of the workers, farmer and the middle class people who are being ruined by the capitalist crisis. The right wing leaders of the CCF oppose such a course. Pursuing a class-collaboration line of no struggle, preaching reliance on parliament, these leaders disperse the progressive masses who support the CCF, strive to narrow the CCF down to a skeleton election machine,

38 / "Confidential Report."
39 / Ben Spence to J. S. Woodsworth, May 24, 1936, CCFP.

and expel and disrupt CCF organizations which lead or participate
in the struggles of the day.[40]

The CCF national convention in 1936 reaffirmed the party's
determination to maintain its purity and independence. At the
same time it declared its readiness to co-operate and participate
in immediate struggles, indicating a recognition by the party
leaders of the need for some slight relaxation of discipline in the
interests of party cohesion. Significantly, decisions regarding co-
operation in the daily struggles – whatever they might be – were
to be left to the provincial councils.[41]

The resolution had been left vague deliberately because the
Saskatchewan section was in favour of leaving the way open for
co-operation with other groups short of organic union, the CCF
platform to be the basis of all co-operation. The Saskatchewan
section was anxious to prevent three and four-cornered fights in
provincial elections, but declared its unwillingness to compromise
its principles or policies, which it had modified considerably at
its 1936 convention, dropping the word "socialism" from the
provincial program.[42] The Saskatchewan decision led the Communist party to declare that a united front had been achieved in
Saskatchewan.[43] The Communist election committee in Winnipeg
stated in an election broadsheet that unity had been established
"despite the efforts of J. S. Woodsworth."[44] The theme of the
article in the broadsheet was that the members had triumphed
over Woodsworth and Coldwell, both of whom spoke against the
unity resolution at the Saskatchewan provincial convention.

The 1937 Saskatchewan convention reaffirmed "its belief in
the wisdom and necessity for cooperation between progressive
and democratic groups in the political field."[45] In a letter to the
presidents of the constituency associations in Saskatchewan, the
provincial leader, George Williams, underlined the fact that co-
operation was not fusion. He made it quite clear that any joint
candidacies would only harm the CCF by linking it with either
Social Credit or Communism, or with both. Yet, true to the
democratic nature of the CCF, he pointed out that individual
constituencies had the right to decide whether they were to
nominate or not and closed with the following statement:

40 / *What the Communist Party Stands For*, 3rd ed. (Toronto 1936),
88–9.
41 / Report of the Fourth National Convention (1936).
42 / Minutes of the Second Annual Saskatchewan CCF Convention,
1936, SAS.
43 / S. J. Farmer to G. H. Williams, Sept. 8, 1936, SAS.
44 / "The Winnipeg Voter," July 24, 1936, CCFP.
45 / Minutes of the Third Annual Saskatchewan CCF Convention, 1937,

This does not mean that there will be no co-operation, for although each Constituency has constituency autonomy in so far as nominating a CCF candidate or refraining from nominating, and although I would be disappointed if a CCF constituency failed to nominate a CCF candidate when they have a chance to elect him, I would also feel disappointed were any Constituency Committee to put a CCF candidate in the field merely to defeat a Social Credit candidate or Communist candidate. I believe that if the Social Credit and Communist Party will take the same position, it will be possible to prevent progressive candidates opposing each other.[46]

Although this position was welcomed by the Communists, it distressed the CCF national leaders. Woodsworth wrote to Williams pointing out that he was aware of the demand for a people's front and of the fact that the CCF was being put on the defensive by its attitude. He concluded: "But from the standpoint of *practical politics* alone, I'm convinced that the keeping of our hands free is the only way to win and keep the confidence of the electorate – you put it so well 'the policy of the CCF must be to run their own candidates on their own platforms.' I would add 'in every constituency possible.' "[47] Lewis had made this position clear a year earlier in an article in the *Canadian Forum* in which he said: "A fusion of the CCF, Communists, Social Crediters, Reconstructionists, and Left Liberals – which is what the Communists advocate – would under present Canadian conditions create confusion, compromise the socialist objective and the CCF as a party, and might even, by way of reaction, call forth a strengthening of the right forces."[48] In November 1938 the Saskatchewan provincial council disbanded the Meadow Lake constituency association because the association had nominated a "fusion" candidate.[49] Mrs. Dorise Neilsen resigned from the provincial council as a result and contested and won the 1940 federal election in North Battleford as a United Progressive. She was later active in the Labor Progressive Party. Tim Buck kept the unity pot boiling by urging co-operation on all fronts, pledging, for example, the support of the Communist party to the Herridge New Democracy movement.[50]

Despite the views he expressed in the *Canadian Forum*, Lewis

46 / G. H. Williams to Provincial Presidents and Campaign Managers, Oct. 4, 1937, mimeo., CCFP.
47 / J. S. Woodsworth to G. H. Williams, Oct. 19, 1937, SAS.
48 / D. Lewis, "The CCF Convention," *Canadian Forum*, XXVI (Sept. 1936), 7.
49 / "Memo to Meadow Lake Provincial Constituency and North Battleford Federal Constituency from G. H. Williams," Nov. 28, 1938, mimeo., CCFP.
50 / Regina *Leader Post*, April 24, 1939.

was himself carried away by the logic of the popular front idea. He recommended that the CCF candidate in the 1937 Ontario provincial election in St. Andrews riding be withdrawn in order that the labour vote not be split and result in the defeat of J. B. Salsberg, a Communist. Woodsworth was annoyed and wrote to Lewis pointing out that his action was inconsistent with his position and with the decisions of the national council and all the party conventions.[51] Salsberg was being backed by the Labour Representation League, a Communist front. Lewis replied that the labour vote would be split and said:

I believe that it is morally and politically wrong for the CCF to do an act which can bring no positive good to itself but may be the cause of defeating a labor candidate, even if he is a communist ... . What we have decided ... is that the CCF is to remain independent of the Communist Party or any other party. We did not decide that we must oppose or fight the Communist Party as a matter of principle.[52]

He concluded by stating that the unions would resent the CCF opposing the Labour Representation League. Woodsworth wrote back that the league did not represent the labour movement and that since the Conservative candidate was also pro-labour, did Lewis think that the CCF should not oppose the Conservatives?[53]

In 1939 Norman Freed, executive secretary of the Communist party, was reported in a Vancouver newspaper as having said that Communists should give their support to the King government in the approaching general election to forestall the fascism of a Conservative victory. Curiously enough, a CCF MP, Grant MacNeil, raised the matter with Tim Buck, thinking, apparently, that the Communist party should urge support for the CCF.[54] That MacNeil should feel obliged to write to Buck in complaint is indicative of the CCF's ambivalence toward the Communist party. There was acceptance of the doctrinal differences – although there was a wide variety of opinion on the kind or degree of difference that existed – and recognition of the threat posed to the CCF position as the left-wing party by Communist activity; thus the CCF would not co-operate with the Communist party. But the CCF seemed to think that the Communist party ought, at least, to support the CCF.

In his reply to MacNeil's letter Buck wrote that Freed had been misquoted but, in any case, better King than Manion for:

It is the concern of the Communist Party and the objective of our tactical line to prevent the unfolding of the plans of the reaction-

51 / J. S. Woodsworth to D. Lewis, Sept. 27, 1937, CCFP.
52 / D. Lewis to J. S. Woodsworth, Sept. 29, 1937, CCFP.
53 / J. S. Woodsworth to D. Lewis, Oct. 2, 1937, CCFP.
54 / Grant MacNeil to D. Lewis, March 14, 1939, CCFP.

aries and ensure that each change, no matter how small, shall be in the direction of progress. Therefore, as between the two old parties, we direct our attacks more directly against the Tories because the Tory party ... leads the fight for a reactionary change ... the King government ... has restored the conditions of bourgeois democracy that Bennett abrogated and which certainly would be endangered again if the Manion-Drew-Duplessis combination came to power.[55]

This qualified support for the Liberal party became outright support once the Communist "party line" had completed its circle from anti-fascist to anti-imperialist and back again, and the end sought changed from a people's peace to a people's victory.

The changing party line accounts for the Canadian Communist party's gyrations to a great extent, but not entirely. The facility with which it changed sides or supported both sides was due in no small way to the shrewd opportunism of its leaders. The Communists supported the CCF in the York South by-election in which Joe Noseworthy defeated Arthur Meighen. In this instance the editor of the official Communist organ, the *Clarion*, wrote to Lewis in December 1941, suggesting a meeting "to arrange to talk over the contribution the *Clarion* can make toward the success of Mr. Noseworthy."[56] The same newspaper had written earlier that the leaders of the CCF had betrayed the working class.[57] In January 1942 the *Canadian Tribune*, a Communist paper in all but name, applauded Coldwell for demanding conscription of material and financial resources in pursuing the war.[58] Less than two months later the same newspaper wrote: "It is a matter of deep concern that the C.C.F. leadership should advance the above slogan [conscription of wealth]. [It] is patently unrealisable as a practical measure of total war policy. Any fundamental challenging of the foundations of present-day Canadian society plays into the hands of Hitler ..."[59]

With the Soviet Union in the war and firmly on the allied side, the task of the CCF was increasingly difficult because it could not deal effectively with the Communist party – or Labour Progressive party as it became in 1943, the Communist party *per se* having been declared subversive under an order-in-council of November 16, 1939 – without incurring criticism for disloyalty to an ally in the fight against fascism. In February of 1940 the national executive of the CCF had criticized the Soviet Union for its attack on Finland. Despite the restiveness this caused within

55 / Tim Buck to Grant MacNeil, March 10, 1939, CCFP.
56 / R. Ballantyne to D. Lewis, Dec. 14, 1941, CCFP.
57 / *Clarion*, March 23, 1941.
58 / *Canadian Tribune*, Jan. 31, 1942.
59 / *Ibid.*, March 14, 1942.

the party, the national executive expressed its determination to
retain its right to criticize the Soviet Union. It was not until 1943
that serious division appeared in the party as a result of such
criticism. At this time Lewis was the centre of the storm occasioned by the Soviet government's execution of two Polish Socialist leaders, H. Erlich and Victor Alter.

Erlich and Alter were arrested by the Soviet government in
1941, charged with espionage and counter-revolution. When
news of the arrests reached North America protests were made
to Maxim Litvinoff, Soviet ambassador to the United States, and
later to Foreign Minister V. M. Molotov. The protests were made
independently and in concert by a number of Jewish organizations – Erlich and Alter were both Jews – and by such leaders
of the Jewish community and the trade union movement as
Albert Einstein, Clinton Golden of the Steelworkers, William
Green, president of the AF of L; Alvin Johnson of the New School,
Wendell Wilkie, and, from Canada, the CCF. Erlich was a member of the executive committee of the International Federation
of Trade Unions. The protests were in vain, for it was announced
by the Soviet foreign ministry in May 1943 that Erlich and Alter
had been executed shortly after their arrest in 1941. The Soviet
embassy and foreign ministry had received and acknowledged
the protests over the period of December 1941 to March 1943
without revealing what had in fact happened.

The national executive of the CCF passed a resolution stating:
"The National Executive regrets profoundly the execution by
the Soviet authorities of the two internationally known Jewish
socialist leaders, Erlich and Alter, and records its disappointment
at this recent evidence that dictatorship in the Soviet Union remains unchanged." The resolution did not concern the action of
the Soviet Union alone, but went on to attack Canadian Communists: "The executive condemns even more strongly the sordid
campaign carried on by local communists to vilify the characters
and past work of these two respected socialists."[60] But having
made this statement, the national executive urged the need for
continuing co-operation with the Soviet Union and therefore
decided that the resolution would not be made public.

Lewis wrote an article on the event which was published in
News Comment March 15, 1943. The provincial offices of the
CCF were contacted and the suggestion informally made that
consideration be given to reprinting the article in the provincial
party newspapers. The reception given the original article and
the suggestion that it be reprinted sheds some light on the atti-

tudes toward the Communist party, or LPP, that existed in the CCF during the war.

The article Lewis wrote stated the case for officially protesting the Soviet action clearly, without equivocation, and with remarkable objectivity. As Lewis himself explained:

It was extremely carefully and mildly done. The protest is couched more in sorrow than in anger. The need for unhampered co-operation with the Soviet Union is emphatically stated. I have no hesitation in suggesting that only those who have an unreasoning and un-scientific "yes" approach to everything Stalin does, could have taken any objection to it.[61]

At the centre, the official attitude was best expressed by Coldwell, then national leader, when he wrote to Lewis that whereas he favoured a protest he doubted that it would do any good.[62] The national executive unanimously agreed to protest; the national council split seven for and eight against protesting.[63] The most strenuous opposition was registered in British Columbia where the approach taken was essentially the same as that of the Communist groups and Communist press; namely that Erlich and Alter were Polish spies, agents of the Polish "fascist" government-in-exile – in other words, the official attitude of the Soviet Union. The Trail-Rossland and district CCF club expressed its view in a resolution sent to Lewis in June 1943: "We protest the stand taken by comrade Lewis, our National Secretary, in condemning the action taken by the USSR in executing the Two Polish Spies [sic]."[64] The West Kootenay CCF council passed a similar resolution and the Victoria district CCF council expressed its discontent in more mild tones, arguing that "The Soviet Union would not have executed those two men without very good reason."[65]

At a somewhat higher level the provincial executive of the British Columbia CCF passed a resolution regretting "the statement of the National Secretary on the execution of Erlich and Alter by the Soviet government and the subsequent actions of the National Executive and the Ontario and Quebec sections ... in making a public campaign of this issue at a time when such a campaign can only serve to discredit the Soviet Union and weaken the ties of the United Nations."[66] A letter to Lewis from Hilary Brown of the British Columbia executive pointed out that

61 / David Lewis to Frank McKenzie, May 28, 1943, CCFP.
62 / M. J. Coldwell to D. Lewis, March 23, 1943, CCFP.
63 / Taken from letters in the "Erlich and Alter" file, CCFP.
64 / Bert Shaw to D. Lewis, June 5, 1943, CCFP.
65 / M. E. Drew to D. Lewis, May 31, 1943, CCFP.
66 / Frank McKenzie to D. Lewis, May 14, 1943, CCFP.

the whole affair was a "typical Nazi propaganda yarn," adding
that the "rank and file and our voting support is overwhelmingly
pro-Soviet ... above all we realize the part that the U.S.S.R. will
play in the post-war world, and the nature of the opposition
which will then show itself." The letter concluded with the statement, "the overwhelming majority here will refuse to support
any action which might help stack the cards against Russia."[67]

In his reply to the resolution from the British Columbia executive and the letter from Brown, Lewis indicated that the CCF had
"done ever so much less than any other labour or socialist organization or party in Britain and the United States."[68] He went
on to point out that the mass meetings and other activities to
which British Columbia protested were chimerical:

This is just a communist lie and I am surprised what you people
swallow so unquestioningly. To my knowledge, the campaign consisted of a memorial meeting in the Jewish district in Montreal, a
memorial meeting in the Jewish district in Toronto and a resolution
before the Ontario convention, sent in by a local club ... There was
no "campaign" and what there was of it came from the communists
who showed themselves as dirty and unscrupulous in this instance as
in every other.[69]

Lewis was not entirely accurate, for the Quebec section of the
CCF did publish a resolution of protest and a "Special Manifesto
of Protest."[70]

That there was a campaign and that the strongest resolution
came from the CCF organization which was dominated by the
Communist-led Mine, Mill and Smelter Workers' Union add
credence to Lewis' statement. The Communist tactic was to play
up the issue to once again attempt to drive a wedge between the
left wing of the CCF and the party's national leadership. The issue
this time was not working-class rights, but patriotism and loyalty
to a great ally. The initial step in this campaign was taken by the
Canadian Tribune in its April 17 issue, in which it urged all
patriotic readers to "Smash the Anti-Soviet Plot inspired by
Lewis and Shane" – Bernard Shane being the Montreal manager
of the International Ladies Garment Workers Union, one of the
unions which vigorously protested both the arrest and the execution. The *Tribune* article continued:

For this work of disruption is Mr. Lewis' own, supported only by a
small group of professional anti-Soviet propagandists, and has noth-

67 / Hilary Brown to D. Lewis, May 14, 1943, CCFP.
68 / David Lewis to Hilary Brown, May 28, 1943, CCFP.
69 / *Ibid.*
70 / Copy in "Erlich and Alter" file, CCFP.

ing in common with the avowed policies of the CCF party or the views and aspirations of the masses of CCF members and supporters. We urge the CCF leaders and the CCF as a whole to repudiate and condemn this activity by a man who dares to speak in the name of the majority of Socialist-minded Canadians.[71]

The CCF was finding opposition from the Communist party in another direction, too. As Lewis and such leading figures in the trade union movement as Charles Millard tried to bring organized labour into a closer relationship with the CCF, they were opposed by Communists in the unions in both the TLC and the CCL. Graham Spry reported in 1937 that the Communist party was "capturing" many Toronto trade unions.[72] At a conference in 1939 Millard informed Lewis, MacInnis, and Jolliffe that there was more Communist influence in the labour movement than there was CCF influence.[73] Lewis discovered the extent of this influence when he attended the CCL convention in Hamilton in September 1941. In writing to MacInnis about the convention he reported that "the Communists came in terrific force" and that "they mustered a vote of about 175 out of a total vote of 359 and this was too damn close for comfort."[74] In the same letter he said that the Communists were attempting to gain control of the United Mineworkers in Nova Scotia and sever the ties with the CCF that existed there. At the CCL convention which endorsed the CCF as the "political arm of labour," the chief opposition to the endorsation came from the Communist party members in the CCL affiliates.[75]

Because the Communist party had members in many of the unions affiliated with the CCL, the leaders of the CCF in seeking local union affiliation had to contend with the problem of bringing Communists into the CCF in this way. The party officials were aware of the problem but found no satisfactory way of solving it.[76] Part of the difficulty came from the firm belief in political freedom held by the leaders of the CCF. They could not, for example, support the banning of members of the Communist party from the TLC in Halifax because, as Lewis pointed out, "we cannot be a party to action which would exclude people from full rights as members of a union, merely because of their political views, even when we are passionately opposed to those views."[77]

71 / *Canadian Tribune*, April 17, 1943.
72 / National Council Minutes, Jan. 30, 1932, CCFP.
73 / "Notes of conference with C. H. Millard," Feb. 11, 1939, typewritten, CCFP.
74 / D. Lewis to A. MacInnis, Sept. 16, 1941, CCFP.
75 / *Ibid.*, Sept. 21, 1943, CCFP.
76 / *Ibid.*, Sept. 18, 1943, CCFP.
77 / D. Lewis to L. Shaw, April 23, 1948, CCFP.

1937?

The solution Lewis proposed in the same letter was to educate
the union membership to greater participation in the affairs of
the council and prevent the election, by democratic means, of
Communists.

The position of the CCF was made awkward by the fact that it
professed to be the political arm of labour and sought labour
affiliation, but opposed any co-operation with the Communist
party, which also claimed to be the political arm of labour and,
in some unions, had a much larger following than the CCF. Both
the United Auto Workers and the United Steelworkers had
sizable Communist party membership in their ranks. George
Burt, president of the Auto Workers in Canada, was a frequent
speaker from Communist platforms. In 1943 the Ford Local of
the UAW wrote to the CCF provincial office in Ontario protesting
the presence of a CCF candidate on the hustings contesting the
St. Andrews provincial riding against J. B. Salsberg, the Communist candidate. The implication of the letter was that if the
CCF withdrew it would find more support for its candidates in
the Windsor area in which the Ford local was situated.[78] The
CCF did not withdraw and Salsberg won the seat. This approach
was also made in British Columbia. A Packinghouse Workers
Union representative suggested that, if the CCF would stay out
of ten ridings, the LPP would also stay out, leaving the field clear
in those ten for a "united labour candidate." He made the same
suggestion with respect to several urban and industrial ridings in
Regina and Saskatoon. The seats suggested were those in which
the CCF prospects were the best.[79] The CCF resisted these overtures and continued to work for closer ties with the trade unions.
It is likely that closer support would have been achieved much
sooner had there been no opposition from within the unions from
the Communists.

While the peripheral approaches were made to the CCF through
individuals and trade unions, the LPP continued to approach the
CCF in two ways, one being to maintain a constant barrage of
anti-CCF statements and the other to continue to plead for labour
unity. The anti-CCF diatribes in the *Canadian Tribune* were
balanced by the demands for unity made by the LPP and the
Dominion Communist Total War Committee, of which Tim Buck
was secretary. In December 1943 Buck wrote to Lewis insisting
that it was "necessary to unite the forces of progress in Canada
… and defeat the anti-socialist reactionaries."[80] He proposed that

78 / W. A. Muir to CCF Provincial Headquarters (Ontario), July 22,
1943, copy in CCFP.
79 / C. H. Millard to M. J. Coldwell and D. Lewis, May 13, 1947,
CCFP.
80 / Tim Buck to D. Lewis, Dec. 23, 1943, CCFP.

the CCF reconsider its position on the question of co-operation with the LPP: "we urge you to agree to at least that measure of co-operation which will eliminate the danger of Labour Progressive Party Candidates and CCF candidates contesting the same constituencies."[81] Lewis replied that "collaboration between our two parties is impossible and would create confusion rather than unity."[82]

Lewis' reply could not have surprised Buck for in September the almost annual request of the LPP for formal affiliation with the CCF had been rejected. It is an interesting insight into the LPP leaders' strategy to note that Buck's December request for electoral collaboration came only six months after a similar proposal had been made and rejected. On that occasion Michael Buhay and Evariste Dubé, campaign managers for Fred Rose in the Cartier federal by-election, had written to Frank Scott, Lewis' campaign manager, suggesting that Lewis withdraw in favour of Rose "in the interest of labour-unity."[83] Since Lewis had been nominated three weeks before Rose entered the field, the request was rejected as "ridiculous and insincere."[84] Rose won the by-election.[85] Buck presumably felt that by December Lewis would have learned his lesson and realized that co-operation was better than defeat. It was a remarkably naïve assumption on Buck's part if this was in fact his strategy.

The LPP, in the light of Justice Minister Lapointe's toleration of it, a creature of Liberal liberalism, did not, understandably, bite the hand that fed it. After the Teheran conference the swing to the right in the Communist party was obvious; the LPP dedicated itself to a government of national unity in a world of peaceful co-existence and attacked the CCF as disruptive and divisive.[86] In 1943 the CCF program was described by the *Canadian Tribune* as "a peculiar brand of petit bourgeois capitalism";[87] in 1944 the same paper quoted Tim Buck as saying that "the issue today is not socialism but social progress vs. reaction," and that the CCF policy of socialism was merely playing "into the hands of the reactionary forces" and dividing the country.[88] In a telegram to the CCF national convention in 1944, Buck attacked the "partisan

81 / *Ibid.*
82 / D. Lewis to Tim Buck, Jan. 3, 1944, CCFP.
83 / E. Dubé and M. Buhay to F. R. Scott, June 22, 1943, CCFP.
84 / F. R. Scott to E. Dubé and M. Buhay, July 4, 1943, CCFP.
85 / Rose was subsequently expelled from the House when convicted of espionage. The CCF caucus was asked by the LPP to testify as character witnesses on Rose's behalf at his trial! The caucus agreed to take no action. Caucus Minutes, June 5, 1946, CCFP.
86 / Tim Buck, *Thirty Years* (Toronto, n.d.), 194.
87 / *Canadian Tribune*, July 8, 1943.
88 / *Ibid.*, Feb. 19, 1944.

policy of Coldwell and the CCF parliamentary group [which]
aids the Tory conspiracy and is detrimental to the genuine interests of the working class." The telegram went on to urge the
CCF to reject the policies of Coldwell and "back up the King-
McNaughton reinforcement policies."[89]

The reversal was made complete when the *Canadian Tribune*,
in a remarkable feat of doctrinal distortion, described the Mackenzie King brand of liberalism as closely approaching "what used
to be known as Communism," while the CCF philosophy was
merely "a medieval form of Communism."[90] The objective of the
LPP was, it stated, the "resounding defeat of the C.C.F. at the
polls."[91] The Liberal-LPP alliance was most evident in the labour
movement, where both parties were much stronger than the CCF.
The unanimous election of Percy Bengough, a Liberal, as president of the Trades and Labour Congress and of Pat Sullivan, an
LPP member, as secretary treasurer, is indicative of the effect of
this alliance in the labour movement.[92] The swing of the LPP to
the right did have the effect of uniting the CCF ranks. Many who
were sympathetic to the aims of the Communist organization
when it was on the left were naturally extremely critical of it
when it became the advocate of King Liberalism. The 1944 CCF
national convention voted 470 to 2 against investigating the
possibilities of future co-operation with the LPP.[93]

The life and vigour which support from the Liberal party
brought to the LPP meant that it was very active throughout the
latter years of the war. The fruit of its labours was division and
confusion on the left wing in Canadian politics. In the 1943
Ontario provincial election, the LPP won only 2 seats and apart
from these had no effect on the success of the CCF anywhere else,
but 1945 was a different story. The LPP contested 37 seats, of
which 27 were held by the CCF. Only 5 of the CCF sitting members
did not face Communist opposition. In 5 seats, the absence of
LPP candidates would presumably have meant a CCF victory.
This would have made some difference to the CCF, for one of
these seats, York South, was the provincial leader's.[94] The total

89 / Tim Buck to CCF national convention, telegram, Nov. 29, 1944,
CCFP.
90 / *Canadian Tribune*, Aug. 31, 1944.
91 / *Ibid.*, Dec. 16, 1944.
92 / Proceedings, TLC convention, Aug. 1943; Caplan thesis, 753.
93 / *New Commonwealth*, April 27, 1944; and Report of the Eighth
National Convention (1944).
94 / Cochrane North, York South, Hamilton Centre, Niagara Falls,
and Toronto Bracondale. In this and subsequent calculations it is assumed
that most of the LPP vote would have gone to the CCF. Data from G. P.
Normandin, ed., *The Canadian Parliamentary Guide* (Ottawa), for the
relevant years.

LPP-CCF vote was greater than the CCF vote in 1943, and may
have included some who would have voted Liberal had there
been no LPP candidates. The CCF suffered at the hands of the
Communists in the federal election of 1945 as well. In that case
10 seats would have possibly been won by the CCF had they not
been also contested by the LPP.[95] Again this did not make the
difference between forming the government and defeat, but it
would have meant 38 seats for the CCF in Parliament, a boost in
party morale and, possibly, a more positive image.

In the 1948 provincial election in Ontario, the absence of LPP
candidates from all but 2 seats undoubtedly helped the CCF to
recoup some of its losses of the election before. In that election,
the party won 4 seats that it had lost in 1945 through Communist
intervention.[96] Had the LPP not contested St. Andrews and
Bellwoods, it is likely that these seats too would have fallen to
the CCF. In the 1951 provincial election it lost York South as a
result of an LPP candidate taking enough of the leftist vote to
defeat E. B. Jolliffe. After 1945 the electoral threat from the LPP
passed from the federal scene. The party was not a serious threat
in provincial politics outside the province of Ontario. Curiously
enough, it did not make any effort to contest provincial elections
in British Columbia although it did run in federal elections there.
In Manitoba it was usually successful in winning one seat in
multi-member Winnipeg North, and in 1949 Communists won
the provincial by-election in St. Clements and St. Andrews.

Despite the unity provided by the Communist apostasy, there
were some CCF members who would not give up their Communist
proclivities for either doctrinal or political reasons – or a combination of the two. The British Columbia section of the party
was perhaps the most consistently embarrassing one in this respect; its members flirted frequently and dangerously with the
Communist party and the LPP. It was a haven for the undiscip-
lined Communist and for the political man without a country, the
Trotskyite. The whole question of co-operation with the LPP was
investigated thoroughly by a special committee set up by the
British Columbia CCF in 1943. A resolution was passed at the
party's convention calling for a committee to "study the whole
question of the relations of the CCF to the Communist Party ...
and other progressive groups, and to consult with these to discover whether or not a basis for future co-operation ... may be

95 / Comox-Alberni, Kamloops, Nanaimo, New Westminster, Spring-
field, Toronto Trinity, Vancouver Burrard, Vancouver Centre, Vancouver
North, and Yukon.
96 / Hamilton Centre, Hamilton East, York South, Toronto Bracondale.

affected."[97] The verbatim report of the committee hearings is
interesting for the light it sheds on the opinions of some senior
CCF officials.

At the outset, Coldwell wrote that he felt the proposal contained in the resolution for meetings with Communist groups was
"the most reprehensible proposal that has been made by any
provincial organization for a number of years."[98] He continued:
"if such a meeting were held, with a view to coming to an understanding with the Communist Party, that provincial organization
would either be expelled from the movement, or your humble
servant would retire from the National Presidency ... that would
be my decision and nothing would persuade me to revise it."[99]
His sacrificial determination was hardly necessary since it had
been made quite clear that hearings would be held by the committee of CCF members before any decision was taken on the
advisability of contacting the LPP to invite them to make submission.

The hearings themselves were not well attended by senior CCF
personnel, but many made written submissions. Those on the
right, and this position included the national officers and most
of the senior MPs, supported the view of the LPP expressed by
Stanley Knowles, "I feel it is not too much to say that they are
our worst enemies."[100] Angus MacInnis expressed a similar
attitude:

Co-operation between the c.c.f. and the Communist Party would
open the door to intrigue and disruptive activities in which Communist party members are so well trained, and there would be no
check, no opposition within the movement once we had agreed to
co-operate, and instead of such co-operation helping to build democracy in Canada, it would destroy the c.c.f. completely in one
year ...[101]

Further to the left a curious sort of pragmatism was expressed
by George Grube, vice-president of the Ontario CCF, who wrote:

While it is true that, *if* the Communists greatly increase in strength
a crisis in the future may force co-operation of a temporary sort
upon us, we should not do anything to strengthen them at the moment and make such an unpleasant situation more likely ... On the
other hand, we must never allow ourselves to be manœuvred into a

97 / Frank McKenzie to D. Lewis, July 3, 1943, CCFP.
98 / M. J. Coldwell to Lloyd Shaw, July 16, 1943, CCFP.
99 / *Ibid.*
100 / Submission of Stanley Knowles, Transcript of Proceedings,
Special Committee on Relations with Other Political Groups, July 11,
1943, 27, CCFP.
101 / Submission of Angus MacInnis, Proceedings, 80.

position where we come to regard the Communists as *the* enemy. I would any time rather appear on a platform with Tim Buck than with George Drew, Hepburn or Mackenzie King.[102]

Colin Cameron, further left, opposed co-operation with the Communists, but for somewhat different reasons than those already cited. His main point was that the time had come for the CCF to adopt a militant attitude toward the Communist party since it was clearly a "dangerous reactionary organization."[103] Some sections of his submission present such a clear description of left-wing CCF thinking that they warrant extended quotation:

The C.C.F. has always advocated the transition to socialism by the easiest and most peaceful methods possible. This does not mean that anyone has assumed that the revolution will not be accompanied by violence. But we do maintain that the seizure of political power by existing parliamentary institutions is a necessary first step in any country in which the people have been accustomed to the exercise of democratic rights.

To effect a social revolution in Canada it is necessary to gain control of the state apparatus by recognized and accepted procdures both from the point of view of holding public support, and also from the point of view of resisting an onslaught from reaction. Without the power of the state in their hands first, the progressive forces cannot bring about or maintain a revolution.

In conclusion, I should like to remind the committee that I have for many years tried to establish harmonious relationships with the Communist party. So long as I felt that there was at least a reasonable doubt in favour of their being considered a genuine revolutionary party, I considered it essential to try to establish such relations ... Their recent slavish advocacy of everything the powers-that-be do to destroy the people's freedom, proves to me beyond a doubt that they are either prepared to see the working class movement destroyed in Canada ... or that they are now completely in the hands of the Mackenzie King government.[104]

Cameron went on to suggest that the Communists might have been under the thumb of the RCMP, as one section of the party had been through the activities of the police undercover agent, Sergeant J. Leopold.[105] Cameron concluded that no real measure of co-operation with the Communist party was possible.

102 / Submission of George Grube, Proceedings, 6–7, italics in original.
103 / Submission of Colin Cameron, Proceedings, 12.
104 / Proceedings, 14.
105 / As "Jack Esselwein," Leopold infiltrated the Communist party and was a key witness for the Crown in the trial of Tim Buck *et al.* in 1931. See W. Rodney, *Soldiers of the International* (Toronto 1968), 36, 45, 47 ff.

The British Columbia section of the CCF was not the only
section of the party to suffer internal difficulties from the Communist presence, although in that province the situation was more
chronic than in others. Brief mention has already been made of
the incidents in Ontario and Manitoba that involved the expulsion
of CCF members of the provincial legislatures for association
with, or endorsation of, the Communist point of view. In Ontario
the problem lay more with Communist activity in the trade unions
than in British Columbia. The expulsion of Robert Carlin in
1948 came about through his activities in the Communist-led
Mine, Mill and Smelter Workers' union. The problems in Manitoba that led to the disciplining of Richards and Johnson in 1945
were similar to the problem in British Columbia: the blurring of
the distinction on the left wing of the CCF between democratic
socialists and Communists. In April 1949 Berry Richards and
Wilbert Doneleyko, CCF MLAs in Manitoba, attacked NATO and
the European Recovery Program, repudiating the official CCF
position.[106] This resulted in considerable adverse publicity for
the party in the midst of the 1949 general election campaign.
The timing may have been coincidental.

In 1948 the LPP once more proclaimed its support for the CCF
and renewed the demands for unity on the left. In January Coldwell issued the following statement:

In the 1945 elections, Canada's communist party, the LPP, called on
the Canadian people to support Mackenzie King and the Liberals.
Today the party has switched its line again and is now declaring its
support for the CCF.

It is clear to me that the new switch in the Communist line is an
admission of the utter failure of the Labor Progressive Party to make
any progress in Canada and of its loss of support even in those
trade unions in which the Communists have had dominant control
hitherto. They are apparently trying to halt their party's decline by
seeking to identify themselves with the CCF. Naturally what Canadian Communists decide to do is entirely up to them. But I want to
make the position of the CCF crystal clear. That position has been
stated and re-stated by national and provincial conventions throughout the years.

The CCF will not collaborate with the Labour Progressive Party
in any way, direct or indirect. It will not enter into any electoral
arrangement with it or with any other party whether on a national,
provincial or constituency basis.[107]

Always willing to offer direct support, and always rebuffed by

106 / See the *Winnipeg Free Press*, May 13, 1949.
107 / National Executive Minutes, Feb. 15, 1948, CCFP.

the CCF, the LPP did not ignore the possibilities offered by indirect association. In 1948, through a front organization called the Housewives' and Consumers' League, the party organized a series of rallies to protest the rising cost of living. The tactic was to invite CCF members to speak at such rallies. It was difficult for the individuals invited to refuse since the subject was one which the CCF had raised on several occasions in the federal House and provincial legislatures. The experience of one CCF MP, John Probe, was typical: "The program was so arranged that even though Probe was the last speaker Burt was the main one. Burt spoke for well over an hour, leaving little time for Probe. The general impression Johnny got from the meeting was that it was not ours in tone or purpose."[108] The national executive found it difficult to lay down a strict policy apart from urging all CCF members to speak at such rallies only after determining that they were called by organizations or unions that were not under Communist influence or control.[109] The matter was complicated by the fact that for many in the CCF it was the issue that was important, and not the sponsors or the other occupants of the platform. The same problem arose in connection with the petitions and drives for peace and disarmament that flourished in the post-war period.

The establishment of the Canadian Peace Congress by the Communists and the creation of peace councils across the country in the post-war period once again raised the problem of party unity and discipline. The peace councils were organized under the aegis of Dr. James Endicott, a pro-Soviet, ex-United Church clergyman. The councils were designed to promote the signing of a petition being circulated in Canada by the Peace Congress of which Endicott was chairman. The petition called for the "unconditional banning by all countries of the atomic weapon as an instrument of aggression and mass extermination of people."[110] Coldwell refused to sign the petition, branding it a "cruel deception,"[111] and in January 1949 the CCF national newsletter *Across Canada* warned CCF members against signing the petition, pointing out that the congress and its spawn of councils were simply front organizations for the LPP and international communism.

The article provoked considerable response, most of it unfavourable. Donald C. MacDonald wrote to Grace MacInnis that "the reaction has reached proportions that cannot be ignored; we are disposed ... to return to the warning originally given and

108 / D. Lewis to M. Lazarus, Feb. 12, 1948, CCFP.
109 / National Executive Minutes, Feb. 15, 1948.
110 / Canadian Peace Congress Petition, copy in CCFP.
111 / M. J. Coldwell to Mary Jennison (Peace Congress secretary), Oct. 19, 1949, CCFP.

document the case for the benefit of the latest batch of CCF members who appear to have been drawn in."[112] The fact that E. E. Winch, Leo Nimsick, and Arthur Turner, CCF MLAs in British Columbia, had ignored the warning and signed the petition is indicative of the same division in party thinking that had existed in the pre-war period. The Peace Congress made much out of their support. For many in the CCF, opposition to a petition of this sort was tantamount to declaring in favour of war. The CCF national convention met in July 1950 and unanimously rejected the petition.[113] The national executive met in December 1951 and instructed the British Columbia party to take disciplinary action against the recalcitrant MLAs,[114] but the British Columbia section replied that the MLAs in question had simply forgotten about the convention resolution.[115]

The tide of anti-Soviet and anti-Communist sentiment which swept the western world after the war did have some effect as a moderating influence on the left wing of the CCF. Accordingly the task of wooing CCF members was increasingly difficult and the LPP was not noticeably successful. But left-wing sentiment dies hard and in British Columbia particularly so. The 1954 CCF provincial convention in Vancouver was shaken when former CCF member Rod Young declared that he was "proud to have people tell me I'm a communist." He continued, "I can personally introduce you to fifty former communists in the CCF."[116] Young's remarks were made in the course of a debate on a resolution submitted by the Sooke section which read: "Whereas the drive against Communism ... is merely a screen for the attack by big business on all working class organizations, bringing the threat of fascism, be it resolved that all members of the CCF be asked to refrain from assisting our class enemies by repeating their slanders on many fine class-conscious workers."[117] Byron Johnson, delegate to the convention from Sooke, admitted during the debate that he was a former member of the Communist party.

Although the convention was provincial, and the resolution came from Sooke, a small area known more for oysters than for political sagacity, the press gave the resolution and the ensuing debate full coverage. The *Ottawa Journal* wrote in a leading article: "Inevitably any consideration of the C.C.F. as a national

112 / D. C. MacDonald to Grace MacInnis, Feb. 17, 1944, CCFP.
113 / Report of the Eleventh National Convention (1950).
114 / Lorne Ingle to William Irvine, Dec. 22, 1951, CCFP. See also National Executive Minutes, Dec. 8, 1951, CCFP.
115 / National Executive Minutes, Feb. 29, 1952.
116 / Verbatim report of Proceedings, British Columbia CCF convention, July 11, 1954, typewritten, CCFP.

117 / *Ibid.*

political force is bound to be affected by anxiety over the possibility that the Communists boring from within might capture the
party itself and bind it to their will."[118] And the *Calgary Albertan*
insisted: "No such party can be trusted [for] the party is plugged
with muddle-headed theorists who are too blind to see the true
nature of today's Communism and who refuse to take sides in the
critical struggle between tyranny and freedom."[119] The situation
was not improved by the fact that in his campaign for the presidency of the British Columbia party, Young lost by only 35 votes.
A resolution calling for his dismissal from the party was defeated
52–55, and this despite the fact that Young had been expelled
twice before for "left-wing extremism." The implications of the
situation were not lost upon the press in Canada nor upon the
other political parties. The British Columbia executive was also
painfully aware of the situation and the wider implications for
the provincial party.

The British Columbia party was apparently becoming a haven
for the disenchanted Communist and the perpetually disenchanted Trotskyite. The situation was complicated by the fact that
sympathy for these people was such that there seemed little the
party could do in convention to rid itself of individuals who
caused more damage than good. A. B. Macdonald, vice-president
of the provincial party, wrote to Coldwell in June 1954: "The
B.C. movement does not have sufficient members willing to take
drastic action to clean up the situation which is getting worse ...
Many of the old Trotskyites and fellow travellers are flocking
back ..."[120] He concluded by suggesting that the CCF national
office help to solve this problem by instituting the vetting of
prospective candidates for suspicious colouration.

The attitude taken by the national office was to let British
Columbia handle the matter itself, although no doubt was left as
to what course ought to be followed: expel Young, following
suspension and trial.[121] There was a need for haste since Young
was to be a delegate to the national CCF convention in August
of that year. His appearance at the convention would undoubtedly lead to a debate on the matter to the intense embarrassment
of the party and its leader. Coldwell was particularly unhappy
about such a prospect.[122]

The matter was satisfactorily resolved on July 12. The British
Columbia executive suspended Young on the charge that he made
his statement at the convention "knowing that in doing so he

118 / *Ottawa Journal*, June 23, 1954.
119 / *Calgary Albertan*, June 21, 1954.
120 / A. B. Macdonald to M. J. Coldwell, June 14, 1954, CCFP.
121 / Lorne Ingle to Harold Thayer, July 5, 1954, CCFP.
122 / D. Lewis to Joseph Corsbie, July 5, 1954, CCFP.

would misrepresent the CCF and bring it into undeserved disrepute, contrary to his duty as a member ..."[123] Subsequent to his suspension he was to be tried on these charges. The day the suspension was announced Young resigned from the party. The relation of this incident to the party and the party's future was neatly summed up by Grace MacInnis: "the C.C.F. will never rise from its present level of small opposition until we can get rid of the see-sawing between doctrinaire Marxism and sensible democratic socialism."[124] In a democratic party such as the CCF, the need for discipline was paramount. Too frequently party members confused democracy with anarchy, feeling that membership in a democratic party enabled them to go whichever way they chose in as public a manner as their individual egos demanded – provided always that it was to the left. Socialist parties suffer from this misunderstanding of democracy and from the high number of outspoken and articulate members that they have.

In the years following 1955 the LPP was less and less a threat to the CCF, both internally and externally. The Communists suffered a decline in their membership and party unity as a result of the Hungarian revolution in 1956.[125] The party in Canada was less able to appear as either a viable working-class alternative to the CCF or as an agency of internal discord in the CCF. The leaders of the CCF remained alert to trouble from the far left but this was as much a reflex conditioned by many years of real danger as it was a response to genuine difficulties. In any case, by 1955 the damage had been done.

123 / Harold Thayer to Lorne Ingle, July 13, 1954, CCFP.
124 / Grace MacInnis to Lorne Ingle, July 11, 1954, CCFP.
125 / See Ivan Avakoumovitch, "Le Mouvement Communiste au Canada de la Destalinisation au Seizième Congrès (1956–1959)," *Est & Ouest*, Dec. 1, 1959.

10

CONCLUSION

10

For most of its history the role of the CCF has been
that of a voice crying in the wilderness, a conscience
informing, animating, goading old parties into some
overdue reforms.

ANDREW BREWIN (1943)

The CCF began in the West because it was there that the roots of protest had grown strong in the soil of discontent, that the isolation of the frontier, the malevolence of nature and eastern business were most keenly felt, driving the people to build their own organic society expressing values foreign to industrial capitalism. Chief among these values were co-operation and fellowship. It began in the West because many workers, isolated and alienated like the farmers, created their own societies either through their trade unions or through the simpler fellowship of learning and discussion.[1] And it was in the West that many immigrants settled, bringing to the plains the philosophy of the British Labour party and, from the United States, the populist and semi-socialist movements such as the Non-Partisan League. There was both cause and contact. A common link among these elements was their belief in fellowship; in some it was expressed by the social gospel, in some by the brotherhood of trade unions, and in others by the necessary unity of the working class.

The CCF was created by the bringing together of the politically active farm groups, the labour and socialist parties that had united in the Western Conference of Labour Political Parties, the Fabian intellectuals from eastern Canada, and the Ginger and Labour group from the House of Commons. If there was a catalyst it was James Shaver Woodsworth. The socialism the CCF espoused was the product of its Fabian element and meant different things to each of the groups that formed the party. Those who supported the CCF did so for various reasons, but reasons which, at that time, precluded support for the Liberal or Conservative parties.

The farmer supported the CCF because it offered him a means of overcoming the deficiencies of his situation. For the farmer's benefit the socialism of the CCF excluded public ownership of farms and, later, small businesses, was not too vehemently against profit or property if there was enough for all, and supported the idea that the farmer should be his own boss – free enterprise as opposed to private enterprise. In addition, the anti-establishment attitude of the CCF fitted well with the resentment and envy felt by the farmer toward the "fifty big-shots" and the eastern bosses.[2] The CCF offered to realize the frustrated ambitions of the farmer in a manner not inconsistent with either the Protestant ethic or free enterprise (on a small scale).[3] The Regina Manifesto was

1 / See ch. 7 above.
2 / See Daniel Bell, "Interpretations of American Politics," in D. Bell, ed., *The Radical Right* (New York 1963); and Peter Viereck, "The Revolt against the Elite," in the same volume.
3 / See Richard Hofstadter, "The Pseudo-Conservative Revolt," in Bell, *The Radical Right*, 70, 86.

one step further from the doctrines of the Progressives, a step for
which the failure of the Progressives had prepared the farmers.
The ideology and structure of the CCF were consistent with the
society they had built on the prairie.

The differences in the strength of the party in the three prairie
provinces was the result of a number of factors. In Manitoba its
strength was in the urban ridings; the rural population stayed
within the Liberal-Progressive tradition. The Manitoba Farmers
Union was never more than a lukewarm supporter of the CCF.
Winnipeg was a major urban centre, the home of the Grain Exchange, the major rail and stock yards. Manitoba was closer to
the rural Ontario tradition than Saskatchewan.

In Saskatchewan the farmers' organizations were actively involved in the formation of the CCF. There, more than in Alberta
and, certainly, more than in Manitoba, the one-crop economy
prevailed. There was, as well, a stronger infusion in Saskatchewan of immigrants with some European experience of socialism,
particularly the socialism of the British Labour party. Alberta
had been pre-empted by the United Farmers of Alberta before
the founding of the CCF, and when that party fell from power in
1935 and dwindled, it took the CCF down with it. Social Credit
answered the same needs there that the CCF answered in Saskatchewan, although with a more simplistic ideology. It nevertheless offered an explanation for the farmer's plight and proposed what seemed to be an adequate solution, that is, one consistent with the aims of the agrarian producer.

Outside the wheat belt the CCF could not count on the same
support because nowhere else was there as large or as homo-
geneous a group which shared similar economic and social conditions, attitudes, and geography. It had to rely for its membership on alienated groups in urban centres such as the immigrant
community in North Winnipeg and the working classes in Toronto and Vancouver. In Quebec and in the maritime provinces
the party failed to win a foothold because it was not indigenous
and consequently was seen as an alien force. It was opposed by
the Catholic church because it was seen as godless and as a threat
to private property, and by the liberals in Quebec because it was
Anglo-Saxon and centralist. In the maritime provinces, although
it had some slight success in Cape Breton in Nova Scotia, it con-
flicted with a rigid traditionalism in politics and an isolationism
that prevented any real progress despite the generally depressed
state of the economy.

The CCF lacked the pragmatism of approach and outlook
needed to cope with the variety of attitudes that existed in Canada. The image of the party was forged on the anvil of prairie

radicalism from iron supplied by Fabian intellectuals. Its approach was that of a movement, predicated on the assumption that there is universal agreement on the cause and cure of sin and that if such agreement is lacking it is the result of ignorance which education will remedy. The intellectual attitude prevalent in the CCF was, naturally enough, that socialism was the answer and that socialists knew the real truth. It followed from this that the one answer was as valid in Quebec as it was in Nova Scotia or Saskatchewan. Intellectually this was probably true, but politically it was false, and as a guide for a party, almost suicidal.

Most Canadians were unwilling to see business, profits, and competition as evils, and were unmoved by the educational activities of the CCF. Those who were victims of capitalism often viewed their misfortune as simply the luck of the game. The CCF assumed the existence of a Canadian working class. Objectively such a class existed, but the members of that class did not, for the most part, accept their position as such. Their aspirations and attitudes were middle class. They were not prepared to support a party that was not identified with the status to which they aspired. Democracy and the rags-to-riches philosophy were a part of the Canadian ethic. Those who accepted the major premise of unlimited upward mobility for those with energy and initiative could not support the CCF.

The kind of class consciousness that leads to concerted action to overthrow or radically alter existing institutions is often generated by confrontation with the blank wall of despair such as that faced by the single unemployed in 1935, which led to the Ottawa trek. Because of past experience and because of the dominant attitudes expressed by established political leaders and by the press, most Canadians were persuaded that things would get better. The CCF began by proposing ways of making things better, and as prosperity returned, argued that things would get worse and, finally, accepted implicitly the liberal assumption by basing its electoral appeal on equality of opportunity rather than on equality of condition. It was never able to arouse the unity of sentiment that true class consciousness implies because the working class did not see its position as static and hopeless.

Those who found themselves alienated from society could and did accept the socialist argument. Trade union leaders and activists were attracted to the CCF because they were outsiders like the farmers. Many were committed socialists and their support for the CCF was natural for this reason. But, unlike a large proportion of their followers, they felt most keenly the antipathy of society toward trade union activity. Despite their pre-eminence in their own union or in the Congress, society did not accord

them any status higher than that of their rank and file; indeed, in
some cases it was lower because they were seen as the co-ordina-
tors of disruption in a capitalist society. John Porter has pointed
out that such rights as trade unions have were granted as concessions.[4] It is not surprising that the men who represented trade
unionism would gravitate toward the CCF, nor is it surprising that
many of their union members, whose lack of interest in the trade
union *movement* is a notorious fact, would show little if any
interest in Canada's socialist party. For them the union was
merely one aspect of the acquisitive and competitive processes
of a capitalist society.

Throughout its history the CCF shared the general socialist
assumptions about the utility of education and about the purity
and altruism of the awakened proletariat. As a party it accepted
the liberal notions about the essential rationality of the citizen;
it was not until 1957 and 1958 that there was any indication in
the party's campaign literature that it recognized that lengthy
argument and documented prophecy of impending depression
had little impact on the electorate. The function of the party as
an educational movement between elections meant that the election campaigns themselves were fought on the same basis. Because of these beliefs and because of the immense amount of
energy devoted to spreading the CCF gospel, its leaders were prepared to wait, secure in the knowledge that the truth would win.

To hasten the process the advantages of socialism and the
deficiencies of capitalism were displayed through a constant barrage of criticism and analysis. Yet the voters the CCF had to woo
to win were part of the system, accepted it, and worked in it.
Socialism was seen by the press and much of the public as destructive and the CCF as an engine of chaos. Significantly, during
the war it was treated as fascist by its critics, and afterward as
communist;[5] it was always anti-capitalist, and to non-socialists
that meant anti-democratic. Only a modification of its ideology
and a muffling of radical members would have helped offset the
negative public image, but the requirements of the movement
prevented such action.

The CCF was not unacceptable to all Canadians at all times.
As the Gallup Poll figures showed, it "enjoyed" a remarkable
surge of support during the latter stages of the Second World
War when the social change and dislocation of the times and the
peace-time orientation of the party made it attractive. But it was

4 / Porter, *Vertical Mosaic*, 311.
5 / The Communist party gave credence to this criticism by its public
exclamations of support. In 1960 Tim Buck claimed that the Communists
had successfully infiltrated the New Party (NDP). Vancouver *Sun*, Aug.
31, 1960.

the movement that triumphed as Mackenzie King read the signs
and moved leftward. In any case it was not the socialism of the
CCF that appealed to that part of the electorate, roughly one-
quarter, that supported it, it was the image of the party as an
instrument of change.

Because it was a movement of protest the CCF attracted to its
ranks liberals, committed socialists, dedicated anti-capitalists of
various sorts, and those who were simply opposed to authority
in all its forms: anarchists, malcontents, and rebels. These elements made the CCF a fighting party, but by virtue of the strength
of their commitment, the more doctrinaire socialist and anarchist
elements were more dominant than their numbers warranted.
Unlike those who were solidly behind the party but not part of
the sub-movement of socialist ideologues, the doctrinaires were
prepared to give boundless time and energy to debate and criticism. They tended to be the activists in constituency organizations
and delegates to conventions. Their presence helped preserve the
movement and contributed to its critique of society. For some of
these elements the CCF provided an outlet for genuine social
protest founded on philosophical grounds; for a few it merely
institutionalized bitterness and provided a legitimate channel for
the expression of anti-authority neuroses. Most political parties
can tolerate a maverick or two, but the CCF seemed to attract more
than its share.

For the rest of the community the CCF came to be represented
by those who spoke the loudest and most often; and these tended
to be, at conventions at any rate, the rebels, those who deviated
most vehemently from middle-class mores, who were dedicated
to the destruction of the foundation of Canadian society – the
free market economy. Coldwell's calm, rational approach was
overlooked by people anxious to find a justification for their
fears about the CCF, and for the press, the behaviour of the
activists on the party's left wing provided much better copy than
anything the party leaders might say.

The presence of militants in the ranks was also an asset. Because it was a movement the CCF attracted only those who were
dedicated, and who gave freely of their time and money and
stayed with the party through defeat after defeat. Limited in
funds, the CCF depended on volunteer help in election campaigns,
and was able to command and receive prodigious effort from its
members, whose tireless canvassing succeeded in getting out the
socialist vote and, in more than one instance, winning the seat.

The militants opposed the development of the CCF as a political
party and made a fetish of their opposition to making ideological
sacrifices in order to win office. Success, they feared would trans-

form the CCF from a vehicle of protest into a disciplined party in
which there would be little room for the rebel. They preferred to
see the CCF remain as a perpetual gad-fly that bit the hide of the
establishment and goaded the "old line" parties into reform while
providing the outsiders of Canadian society with a platform and
a haven. By 1956 this attitude had become prevalent throughout
the party, even among those who, in many respects, were the
most anxious to make the CCF more a party. In his address to the
national convention in 1956 Lewis, then national chairman, said:

One of our major roles in Canada has always been and should
always be to be the conscience of the Canadian people in the political and social struggles of this country. And to be that conscience
we need not necessarily be in power. We can – if we are true to our
principles and our objectives, consistent in our determination to fight
the big interests in this country, determined to represent at all times
the interests of the Canadian people and of common people everywhere – we can continue to be as we have always been, the political
and social conscience of Canada, plaguing the unjust people, needling
the people who destroy democracy, demanding with untiring effort a
greater share of the goods of this life and the comforts of modern
existence for ever increasing numbers of our people.[6]

The CCF's structure was, in some ways, a hindrance to its
success as a party. Paradoxically it accepted the premises of
democracy within the party itself but rejected them within the
context of the Canadian political system. Within the party there
was debate, divergence, and compromise. There was room for
positive leadership, or "directed democracy" as it was described,
yet the necessity for compromise or for pragmatism within the
larger sphere of Canadian politics was never fully accepted. In
theory the party members set policy at the national conventions,
but in practice the leaders performed a function similar to that
of Rousseau's legislator. Although there is much evidence to
demonstrate the relevance to the CCF of Robert Michels' Iron
Law of Oligarchy, it is also true that the activities of the leaders
were limited by membership participation – enough at least to
make participation in the party battle more awkward than if their
control was absolute.

The position of the party's leaders was further limited by the
conditions of the times. When Woodsworth was leader, the CCF
was small, growing, and achieving many of its aims. The charismatic nature of his leadership provided great impetus whereas
his own inclinations kept the CCF from developing that side of it

that was party. Under Coldwell and Lewis, the party experienced both its greatest successes and its greatest strains, first during the early stages of the Second World War and then as the support generated by the dislocation of war evaporated in the prosperity of peace. The long decline after 1945 denied Coldwell the electoral successes a party leader needs to strengthen his hand. A succession of failures encourages independence and irresponsibility among the militants in a party. Perpetual failure tends to produce a membership dominated by the zealot who, in a democratic party, finds ample scope for his individuality. Coldwell's task became less that of leader and more one of grand arbiter in a house of all-sorts.

Despite these disabilities, which were largely the product of the conjunction of the roles of the movement and the party, the CCF altered the shape of the Canadian party system and provided an impetus for reform that was lacking in the Liberal government. It achieved this measure of success partly because its Members of Parliament learned to use that institution to great effect and, in so doing, demonstrated a competence to the leaders of the "old line" parties that was impressive; and partly because the CCF represented an alien force that stood for values seen as anathema by those same leaders. In some ways the Communist party was less feared because it was so obviously "outside." The CCF, on the other hand, was clearly working within the system, and working surprisingly well for its numbers, while steadfastly opposing some of the fundamental values of the system. It was a distinctly different political phenomenon.

Neither at the beginning nor at the end was the CCF like the other parties in Canadian national politics. It retained its unique character throughout the twenty-eight years of its existence. Starting as a confederation of radical parties and protest movements, it attracted and held as members and active politicians men and women of exceptional dedication and, in many cases, exceptional ability. When it became part of the New Democratic Party, it was no longer a confederation of movements and much less a movement than it had been in the forties. Most of those who had helped form the CCF in 1932 stayed with the party; some had been active in its councils throughout and helped to reshape it into a party and, finally, into the New Democratic Party.

What made the CCF unique was, first of all, that it was a socialist party which survived and remained a potential threat to the other parties on a continent in which socialist parties have a gloomy history of schism and failure. Some of the reasons for its success relative to similar parties in the United States have been debated elsewhere,[7] and there may be something in the composition of the Canadian "fragment" that is more conducive to the continued life of socialism – if at times by the merest thread – than in the United States. And, no doubt, the marriage of a federal state to a parliamentary system has played a part in generating the regional pressures that provide fertile ground for such parties as the CCF.[8] The "brokerage" thesis is also useful for the light it sheds on the success of the CCF – if staying alive can be so counted – because if this was the view held by such prime ministers as Mackenzie King, then clearly its impossibility contributed much to the strains which helped generate and nurture the CCF.[9]

These theories, all of which have an intellectual fascination, offer possible general explanations for the fact of the CCF. It began because, for various reasons, enough people were sufficiently dissatisfied with the *status quo* that they first created their own movements and parties and subsequently joined forces in the CCF. It came into being because the existing system was unable to satisfy these people or could not cope with them. In this respect, the system referred to was more than the party system; it was the sum total of the political, economic, and social systems that had failed in various ways to satisfy the expectations of these people or to cope with their demands. Their dissatisfaction came from the failure and remained to compel them to take action to remedy their own situation. The economic and social plight of the wheat farmer led him to protest; the inability of the existing political system to satisfy his demands compelled him to create his own party in order to express these demands and, ultimately, to bring about the changes he sought.

If the function of the party system is to "organize public opinion and link it to expert opinion for the purpose of finding a sound and acceptable definition of the national interest,"[10] then in the thirties, for a significant public opinion, it had failed to function. Its failure in this context could be traced to the rigidities of the parliamentary system that are inconsistent with fed-

7 / See G. Horowitz, "Conservatism, Liberalism and Socialism in Canada: An Interpretation," *CJEPS*, XXXII (May 1966).

8 / See S. M. Lipset, "Democracy in Alberta," *Canadian Forum* (Nov., Dec. 1954).

9 / See J. T. McLeod, "Party Structure and Party Reform," in A. Rotstein, ed., *The Prospect of Change* (Toronto 1965); and John Meisel, "The Stalled Omnibus: Canadian Parties in the Fifties," *Social Research*, XXX (1963). For a brilliant analysis of the relationship of the electoral system to the party system, with particular reference to the CCF, see Alan C. Cairns "The Electoral System and the Party System in Canada: 1921–1965," *Canadian Journal of Political Science*, March 1968.

10 / Meisel, "Omnibus," 367.

eralism and that demand a kind of superficial brokerage function of the major parties which they are ill-equipped to provide and Parliament ill-designed to enact. Its failure could equally well be attributed to the fact that the parties in the system were controlled by, or were fragments of, the "charter group" elite described by John Porter. Congealed by their origins, frozen in an attitude of obeisance to the elite and the value system espoused by that elite, the parties could not, of their own volition, make the adjustments required by the demands of the "protestant minority." It was assumed by the elite and its parties, that its position not only reflected the best interests of the country at large, but encompassed the views of all its citizens as well. In the absence of evidence to the contrary, it inevitably thought of itself as the embodiment of the Canadian consensus.

When the adjustments were made, they were only made under the threat of socialism as represented by the CCF. In the absence of a third party with a strident voice advocating values contradictory to those of the ruling elite, the parties of that elite could not justify, even within the context of the brokerage function, any legislative activity that interfered with the interests of the ruling group. With such a party on the scene, however, operating within the political system and therefore legitimate, the major parties had to respond to stave off the threat which this party constituted. Actions taken to meet this threat were justified by the nature of the challenge. When Mackenzie King wheeled his party to the left, he justified his action by pointing to the danger of the CCF. The old parties, in such circumstances, actually performed the brokerage function which they did not, in fact, perform before.[11]

In other words, before the twenties the two major parties mediated between the conflicting elements *within* the ruling group. There was no clash of values; there was only conflict of interest. But with a vocal minority threatening to destroy the system which the ruling elite had created for itself and which nurtured it, the major parties had to become brokers and seek to create a broader and more genuine national consensus in order to forestall the CCF. This was not a particularly difficult transition to effect since, as already mentioned, a majority of Canadians shared the values of the elite. The extension of the powers of the federal government and the widening of its authority during the

11 / Frank Underhill has argued the reverse, that "the old parties were too much under the control of one class group to function as honest brokers any more." (*In Search of Canadian Liberalism*, 198.) In fact, the old parties were always under the control of one class group and what brokerage they performed was within the context of the class group's interests.

war provided a demonstration of the inclusiveness of the government and gave the impression that it had a wider interest and was responding to the needs of all Canadians. This impression was accomplished, for the most part, with no major change in either the values or the structure of the party in power.

The extent to which the CCF was considered a threat can be seen by the lengths the press and business went to denigrate it and label it subversive. The degree of panic felt by the establishment can be measured by the extent to which it saw the CCF as constituting a root and branch attack on the institutions of capitalism, requiring a massive counter-attack in the form of elaborate and expensive propaganda campaigns. The CCF was not as revolutionary as it was seen to be, but the point is that it did appear as a threat and accommodations were made to avoid the danger of losing all in the maw of "state socialism." Business feared loss of property and power; the Liberal government feared loss of office as well.

Undoubtedly the existence of the CCF strengthened the hand of the Liberal party by enabling it to exact firmer and richer support from the business community. The lengths to which the Liberals were prepared to go in meeting the CCF challenge is indicated by their actions enabling the intervention of the Communist party (LPP) in the 1945 general election. Having defended the Communists' right to exist and resisted their poisonous advances, the CCF had the grim satisfaction of seeing Communists used by Liberals as a weapon in the defence of the capitalist establishment. There was as well some satisfaction to be derived from the fact that such movement to the left as occurred in Liberal policy was facilitated by the CCF threat, which was offered by King as an excuse and a reason to his party's right wing.[12]

The ignorance that is the foundation of faith in free enterprise extended to the nature of those agencies which, like the CCF, sought major reform but not revolution. Had the CCF formed the government there would have been significant changes because its leaders held different values and had a different perspective, but the extent of change was over-estimated. What the establishment feared was not the CCF party so much as the CCF movement and the image of that movement that their own propaganda had created.

12 / At a cabinet meeting June 22, 1944, Mackenzie King justified his opposition to J. L. Ilsley's budget proposals, claiming they "would be just fatal to the Government and play into the hands of the CCF ..." J. W. Pickersgill and D. F. Forster, *The Mackenzie King Record*, VII (Toronto 1968), 29. The extent to which the CCF loomed large in King's consideration during this period can be seen in this volume, e.g. pp. 30–2, 127, 137, 146.

The CCF, more successful than the Progressive party in influencing the system because it was a movement dedicated to more fundamental or value-oriented change than were the Progressives. The fact that the CCF was a movement meant that its participation in the party battle did not contaminate its goals so much that its influence in politics was lost. Its operation within the political system and its gradual acceptance of the rules of the game did bring about a dilution of its ideology in the programmatic sense, but did not significantly alter the party's goals. In a curious, paradoxical way, its strict adherence to the parliamentary rules of the game, its earnest profession of liberal values in defence of civil liberties, and its obvious honesty made it more acceptable to more people and, therefore, more of a threat. At times it seemed as though many commentators thought – if they did not say – "if only the CCF was not socialist." If it had not been socialist, it would not have been the CCF. It would not have remained a movement and, consequently, would have disappeared because it would have had no more reason for continuing to exist than had the Progressives.

There is a sense in which it may be said that all parties are ideological. Those which reflect the dominant values of the particular society have no need to express their ideology as a manifesto or declaration of principles. Political scientists who despair of finding a single coherent statement of the Liberal or Progressive Conservative "philosophy" have ignored the haystack in their search for a single needle. Liberalism and Progressive Conservatism are, in effect, what Liberals and Progressive Conservatives do when in office. Their behaviour reflects, by and large, the dominant values of Canadian society. The "ideological" party – that is, the one with a manifesto – is usually an agency for expressing dissatisfaction with the *status quo*. It is directed toward change, not maintenance.

It is almost invariably a movement as well as a party and can only attract people to its ranks by convincing them of the validity of its particular *weltanschauung*, something the "old line parties" do not need to do because they express the prevailing *weltanschauung*. To achieve its ends the "ideological" party must not only campaign, it must educate through whatever means are available to it. It must secure a reasonably permanent body of support among the electorate since its nature is to have a program of long-run goals that cannot be adequately achieved in one term of office. When it wins supporters, they tend to stay with it, as CCF/NDP voting history shows, because in so opting to oppose the *status quo* they have made a definite and identifiable commitment that is difficult to cast off. For one thing, the internal pressures of the party-movement they have espoused help them resist any return; for another, a return to the *status quo* would constitute an admission of error. To switch from Liberal to Conservative requires no great struggle with one's conscience since both parties reflect, with few real variations, the dominant values. One can switch allegiance from the Roughriders to the Argonauts without demonstrating any lack of faith in football. When the ideology is one that is as inconsistent with the *status quo* as was that of the CCF, then the need for education, for propaganda, is that much greater.[13] The party with an ideology is also a movement; its goals are more than the mere acquisition of power. The parties without such an ideology in this sense are mechanisms for achieving power; the party-movement is a mechanism for propagating and enacting beliefs through power.

A functional analysis would demonstrate that both kinds of parties perform functions which, in some respects, have little influence on the primary goals of each. Both provide focus and coherence for the electorate, offering a point of contact with the processes of government. They fulfil constitutional roles in the processes of electing leaders and nominating candidates. The list is long. There is one respect, however, in which the party-movement is functional to the democratic system and the "normal" party is not or, indeed, may even be dysfunctional. That is in the respect already discussed: the party-movement compels the traditional parties to perform functions which, in the absence of the threat the party-movement constitutes, would not be performed. Put succinctly, its presence demands the performance of leadership.[14] As with streams which meet no obstacles, which have no rapids, political parties grow placid, stagnant, and putrid in the absence of fundamental opposition. The two-party system predicated on the "ins and outs" thesis stagnates from the lack of the aerating qualities of robust ideological debate and vigorous local party activity.

The Canadian party system is unlike both the American and British party systems with which it is often compared. Many in the CCF chose to see it as a two-party system and hoped that the CCF would eventually replace the Liberal party as the party of

13 / Addressing the British Columbia NDP Convention in April 1968, T. C. Douglas said that the NDP was not interested in minor changes such as tariff reform and its like. "Our movement," he stated, "is fundamentally concerned with the basic structure of society itself." He characterised Canadian society as "a society of shabby values."

14 / The effect of the CCF on the Conservative party is described in J. L. Granatstein, *The Politics of Survival* (Toronto 1967), 69, 149–50, 166–7. Granatstein points out that "The CCF had ... forced the old parties to adjust their platforms and policies," 189.

the left.[15] Frank Underhill has described it as a multi-party system in disguise, more like the American than the British system.[16]
Certainly since 1922 third and fourth parties have been a part of
the system and a necessary part of the calculations of political
leaders, and in this sense alone it must be admitted that the party
system is "more multi than two." But it is not possible to say that
the Canadian party system is "more like" either one or the other
of the older systems. It suffers from the worst features of both,
compounded by the peculiarities of the Canadian constitution.

The parliamentary system exerts pressure toward the maintenance of a two-party system which in a federal state produces
strains that help create third and fourth parties. The parliamentary system also emphasizes strong central control of the parties,
an emphasis heightened in Canada by the wholly natural centralist attitude of federal politicians. Federalism exerts opposite
pressures, its nature demanding vigorous regional or provincial
party branches. The result of this network of tensions has been
central control of national parties with very weak provincial
branches and weak linkages between them, and strong provincial
parties which are either indigenous, as in the case of Social Credit
in Alberta, or independent of the national party, as was Hepburn's Ontario Liberal machine. There is no guarantee of easy
relations between a national prime minister and provincial pre-
miers of nominally the same party. They are more characteristically rivals than collaborators.

The local branches of national parties have no autonomy because they have no viable control over their Members of Parliament. They lack control because of the nature of the parliamentary system which requires cabinet or front-bench domination of
the parliamentary party. In the national context, local politicians
are beholden to Ottawa and not, as is the case in the United
States, the centre more beholden to the branches. There is nothing to tie the national party – branches and centre – together,
so what articulation there is in the structure is very weak. Between federal elections the provincial branches of the national
parties are dormant, dependent almost entirely on the centre for
stimulus and direction.

The provincial parties, by comparison, are both more active
and more independent. They represent provincial interests and
tend to act in competition with the centralist tendencies of the
national parties. The fact that the national Liberal party had to

15 / See for example, Donald MacDonald, "The Three P's and Political
Trends," *Canadian Forum*, XXVI (Dec. 1946).
16 / "The Party System in Canada," "The Canadian Party System in
Transition," and "Concerning Mr. King," in *In Search of Canadian
Liberalism*.

establish a separate organization to fight the 1965 federal election in Saskatchewan, campaign support having been effectively denied it by Ross Thatcher's provincial Liberal party, offers a recent and perhaps extreme example of this phenomenon. Although they share personnel, the national and provincial parties tend to maintain a separate and often divergent existence.

Given the existence of weak and dormant local units and consequently of relatively little local input through the national party machinery, the direction of the national party is handled entirely by and from the centre with little feedback. The fact that the formal headquarters apparatus of the major national parties is traditionally small is indicative of the tight "in-group" control of these parties and of the irrelevance of feedback from the provincial branches. The growing reliance on professional advertising men for high campaign strategy has offset whatever trend there has been toward the broadening of the base of these parties. Major party decisions are traditionally taken by a small caucus or inner circle, and are based on its assessment of the national political scene and the advice of professional public relations firms.

Consequently there is a built-in propensity toward stagnation in the absence of viable or seemingly viable third and fourth parties. These minor parties, struggling to achieve major status, have provided the inputs which the major parties lack. Starting from a regional or class base, they have represented and consequently brought to the attention of the major parties the particular attitudes or grievances of sections of the country that the major parties have ignored or failed to deal with. By providing as well the kind of ideological confrontation which is typically absent in contests between the two major parties, they have served to stimulate the older parties and reactivate their previously dormant philosophies. The multi-party system in the setting of parliamentary federalism functions to prevent the stagnation which a pure two-party system necessarily produces. Two parties alone cannot successfully represent all the interests or act as a broker – honest or otherwise. Attempts to represent a national consensus have been usually based on the assessment of a few with limited access to the attitudes of the whole. The result has been that the national consensus has in fact been the view of the most dominant voices in the old parties. And these are the voices at the centre; historically, the voices of the elite or the establishment.

The CCF's ideology and structure, which was a product of the ideology, helped to offset the fissiparous effects of parliamentary federalism. Unlike the two major parties, which had no specific ideology as a reference point, the CCF had democratic socialism as elucidated in the Regina Manifesto. It provided a single body of doctrine valid federally and provincially. It was the tie that bound the party together into a national unit. The CCF was not immune to the pressures that divide parties; there was, as has been discussed, a high degree of independence within provincial CCF parties. But the separation was not as great as in the two old parties. National CCF leaders played a more active part in provincial politics on behalf of their provincial sections than was ever the case with the Liberal or Conservative parties.

Pure autonomy was not possible because all sections of the CCF were part of a single movement. Agreement on basic goals superseded differences over policy. Because the movement sought to educate, it relied on the central office for information, material, and direction. Because it was surrounded not so much by an opposition as by enemies, it bound itself together with biennial conventions, newsletters, and the adulation of a leader. Its structure was highly articulated; democracy and socialism made it so.

A clearly defined ideology also strengthens the central control since the goals of the ideology transcend the goal of power for its own sake. The preservation and elaboration of the ideology enhances the centre and increases the dependence of the branches on the central leadership. The ideology and the structure which follows from it integrate the party, increase its strength, and act as a powerful preservative. There is always the danger of internal division on ideological questions – the history of the British Labour party bears this out – but finally the splits heal because in one way the dissidents have nowhere else to go, and in another the basic consensus with respect to the long-range goals of the movement usually remains.

The success of the CCF as a movement was the extent to which the CCF as a party performed an input function, as measured by legislation enacted by the Liberal government which reflected the ideas, if not the ideology, of the CCF. The relationship between the CCF *qua* movement and the CCF *qua* party was close and interdependent. The movement succeeded to the extent it did because the party was able, at one point at least, to pose a threat to the established order through legitimate channels – it could not be suppressed as was the Communist party because the CCF accepted the rules of the game, although there were those in the CCF who felt this was an act of treachery. Thanks to the British Labour party which, like the eldest child in the family, broke a trail for those that followed, democratic socialism was accepted within the parliamentary tradition. The movement and party aspects intermeshed, one aiding the development and aims of the

other while at the same time hindering its development and
distorting its aims.

As the argument is pursued it is increasingly difficult to disentangle one from the other because, of course, the CCF was a
party-movement. Speculation about what would have happened
had the CCF cast off its ideological raiment and met the other
parties on their own ground, or if it had hewn to a more consistently doctrinaire position than it did, is idle. The argument
of this book is simply that to understand the CCF and the role it
played, it is necessary to see it as both a party and a movement,
and to see the crucial interaction of these two aspects of the single
organism that was the Co-operative Commonwealth Federation
in Canada.

APPENDIX A

CALGARY PROGRAMME, 1932

What is the Co-operative Commonwealth Federation?

1 A Federation of organizations whose purpose is the establishment in Canada of a Co-operative Commonwealth in which the basic principle regulating production, distribution and exchange, will be the supplying of human needs instead of the making of profits.

2 The object of the Federation shall be to promote co-operation between the member organizations and to correlate their political activities.

3 We endorse the general viewpoint and program involved in the socialization of our economic life, as these have already been outlined and accepted by the Labor, Farmer and Socialist groups affiliating.

4 Organization

(a) A Provincial Council in each Province composed of representatives of each member organization.

(b) A Dominion Council composed of a President and a Secretary appointed by the Annual Convention, and a delegate appointed by each member organization.

5 We recommend that an annual affiliation fee of twenty-five dollars ($25.00) be paid by each member organization and that a national appeal be made for voluntary subscriptions.

6 The name of the Federation shall be "THE CO-OPERATIVE COMMON-WEALTH FEDERATION (Farmer, Labor, Socialist)."

Provisional Program of the Federation

1 The establishment of a planned system of social economy for the production, distribution and exchange of all goods and services.

2 Socialization of the banking, credit and financial system of the country, together with the social ownership, development, operation and control of utilities and natural resources.

3 Security of tenure for the farmer on his use-land and for the worker in his own home. ("Use-land" – land used for productive purposes: by implication no such guarantee is given to the land speculator.)

4 The retention and extension of all existing social legislation and facilities, with adequate provision for insurance against crop failure, illness, accident, old age and unemployment during the transition to the socialist state.

5 Equal economic and social opportunity without distinction of sex, nationality or religion.

6 Encouragement of all co-operative enterprises which are steps to the attainment of the Co-operative Commonwealth.

7 Socialization of all health services.

8 Federal Government should accept responsibility for unemployment and tender suitable work or adequate maintenance.

NOTE: The above program was adopted provisionally by the Calgary Conference in August 1932, pending the first Annual Convention of the Federation to be held in Regina in July 1933. At this forthcoming Convention, to be attended by representatives of all member organizations, consideration of the program will be one of the chief tasks of the delegates.

REGINA MANIFESTO

(Programme of the Co-operative Commonwealth Federation, adopted at First National Convention held at Regina, Sask., July 1933)

The C.C.F. is a federation of organizations whose purpose is the establishment in Canada of a Co-operative Commonwealth in which the principle regulating production, distribution and exchange will be the supplying of human needs and not the making of profits.

We aim to replace the present capitalist system, with its inherent injustice and inhumanity, by a social order from which the domination and exploitation of one class by another will be eliminated, in which economic planning will supersede unregulated private enterprise and competition, and in which genuine democratic self-government, based upon economic equality will be possible. The present order is marked by glaring inequalities of wealth and opportunity, by chaotic waste and instability; and in an age of plenty it condemns the great mass of the people to poverty and insecurity. Power has become more and more concentrated into the hands of a small irresponsible minority of financiers and industrialists and to their predatory interests the majority are habitually sacrificed. When private profit is the main stimulus to economic effort, our society oscillates between periods of feverish prosperity in which the main benefits go to speculators and profiteers, and of catastrophic depression, in which the common man's normal state of insecurity and hardship is accentuated. We believe that these evils can be removed only in a planned and socialized economy in which our natural resources and the principal means of production and distribution are owned, controlled and operated by the people.

The new social order at which we aim is not one in which individuality will be crushed out by a system of regimentation. Nor shall we interfere with cultural rights of racial or religious minorities.

What we seek is a proper collective organization of our economic resources such as will make possible a much greater degree of leisure and a much richer individual life for every citizen.

This social and economic transformation can be brought about by political action, through the election of a government inspired by the ideal of a Co-operative Commonwealth and supported by a majority of the people. We do not believe in change by violence. We consider that both the old parties in Canada are the instruments of capitalist interests and cannot serve as agents of social reconstruction, and that whatever the superficial differences between them, they are bound to carry on government in accordance with the dictates of the big business interests who finance them. The C.C.F. aims at political power in order to put an end to this capitalist domination of our political life. It is a democratic movement, a federation of farmer, labor and socialist organizations, financed by its own members and seeking to achieve its ends solely by constitutional methods. It appeals for support to all who believe that the time has come for a far-reaching reconstruction of our economic and political institutions and who are willing to work together for the carrying out of the following policies:

1 *Planning*

THE ESTABLISHMENT OF A PLANNED, SOCIALIZED ECONOMIC ORDER, IN ORDER TO MAKE POSSIBLE THE MOST EFFICIENT DEVELOPMENT OF THE NATIONAL RESOURCES AND THE MOST EQUITABLE DISTRIBUTION OF THE NATIONAL INCOME.

The first step in this direction will be the setting up of a National Planning Commission consisting of a small body of economists, engineers and statisticians assisted by an appropriate technical staff.

The task of the Commission will be to plan for the production, distribution and exchange of all goods and services necessary to the efficient functioning of the economy; to co-ordinate the activities of the socialized industries; to provide for a satisfactory balance between the producing and consuming power; and to carry on continuous research into all branches of the national economy in order to acquire the detailed information necessary to efficient planning.

The Commission will be responsible to the Cabinet and will work in co-operation with the Managing Boards of the Socialized Industries.

It is now certain that in every industrial country some form of planning will replace the disintegrating capitalist system. The C.C.F. will provide that in Canada the planning shall be done, not by a small group of capitalist magnates in their own interests, but by public servants acting in the public interest and responsible to the people as a whole.

2 *Socialization of Finance*

SOCIALIZATION OF ALL FINANCIAL MACHINERY – BANKING, CURRENCY, CREDIT, AND INSURANCE, TO MAKE POSSIBLE THE EFFECTIVE CONTROL OF CURRENCY, CREDIT AND PRICES, AND THE SUPPLYING OF NEW PRODUCTIVE EQUIPMENT FOR SOCIALLY DESIRABLE PURPOSES.

Planning by itself will be of little use if the public authority has not the power to carry its plans into effect. Such power will require the

control of finance and of all those vital industries and services which,
if they remain in private hands, can be used to thwart or corrupt the
will of the public authority. Control of finance is the first step in the
control of the whole economy. The chartered banks must be socialized and removed from the control of private profit-seeking interests;
and the national banking system thus established must have at its
head a Central Bank to control the flow of credit and the general
price level, and to regulate foreign exchange operations. A National
Investment Board must also be set up, working in co-operation with
the socialized banking system to mobilize and direct the unused
surpluses of production for socially desired purposes as determined
by the Planning Commission.

Insurance Companies, which provide one of the main channels
for the investment of individual savings and which, under their
present competitive organization, charge needlessly high premiums
for the social services that they render, must also be socialized.

3 Social Ownership

SOCIALIZATION (DOMINION, PROVINCIAL OR MUNICIPAL) OF TRANS-
PORTATION, COMMUNICATIONS, ELECTRIC POWER AND ALL OTHER IN-
DUSTRIES AND SERVICES ESSENTIAL TO SOCIAL PLANNING, AND THEIR
OPERATION UNDER THE GENERAL DIRECTION OF THE PLANNING COM-
MISSION BY COMPETENT MANAGEMENTS FREED FROM DAY TO DAY
POLITICAL INTERFERENCE.

Public utilities must be operated for the public benefit and not for
the private profit of a small group of owners or financial manipu-
lators. Our natural resources must be developed by the same methods.
Such a programme means the continuance and extension of the
public ownership enterprises in which most governments in Canada
have already gone some distance. Only by such public ownership,
operated on a planned economy, can our main industries be saved
from the wasteful competition of the ruinous over-development and
over-capitalization which are the inevitable outcome of capitalism.
Only in a regime of public ownership and operation will the full
benefits accruing from centralized control and mass production be
passed on to the consuming public.

Transportation, communications and electric power must come
first in a list of industries to be socialized. Others, such as mining,
pulp and paper and the distribution of milk, bread, coal and gasoline,
in which exploitation, waste, or financial malpractices are particularly
prominent must next be brought under social ownership and operation.

In restoring to the community its natural resources and in taking
over industrial enterprises from private into public control we do not
propose any policy of outright confiscation. What we desire is the
most stable and equitable transition to the Co-operative Commonwealth. It is impossible to decide the policies to be followed in particular cases in an uncertain future, but we insist upon certain broad
principles. The welfare of the community must take supremacy over
the claims of private wealth. In times of war, human life has been
conscripted. Should economic circumstances call for it, conscription
of wealth would be more justifiable. We recognize the need for compensation in the case of individuals and institutions which must

receive adequate maintenance during the transitional period before the planned economy becomes fully operative. But a c.c.f. government will not play the role of rescuing bankrupt private concerns for the benefit of promoters and of stock and bond holders. It will not pile up a deadweight burden of unremunerative debt which represents claims upon the public treasury of a functionless owner class.

The management of publicly owned enterprises will be vested in boards who will be appointed for their competence in the industry and will conduct each particular enterprise on efficient economic lines. The machinery of management may well vary from industry to industry, but the rigidity of Civil Service rules should be avoided and likewise the evils of the patronage system as exemplified in so many departments of the Government today. Workers in these public industries must be free to organize in trade unions and must be given the right to participate in the management of the industry.

4 *Agriculture*

SECURITY OF TENURE FOR THE FARMER UPON HIS FARM ON CONDITIONS TO BE LAID DOWN BY INDIVIDUAL PROVINCES; INSURANCE AGAINST UNAVOIDABLE CROP FAILURE; REMOVAL OF THE TARIFF BURDEN FROM THE OPERATIONS OF AGRICULTURE; ENCOURAGEMENT OF PRODUCERS' AND CONSUMERS' CO-OPERATIVES; THE RESTORATION AND MAINTENANCE OF AN EQUITABLE RELATIONSHIP BETWEEN PRICES OF AGRICULTURAL PRODUCTS AND THOSE OF OTHER COMMODITIES AND SERVICES; AND IMPROVING THE EFFICIENCY OF EXPORT TRADE IN FARM PRODUCTS.

The security of tenure for the farmer upon his farm which is imperilled by the present disastrous situation of the whole industry, together with adequate social insurance, ought to be guaranteed under equitable conditions.

The prosperity of agriculture, the greatest Canadian industry, depends upon a rising volume of purchasing power of the masses in Canada for all farm goods consumed at home, and upon the maintenance of large scale exports of the stable commodities at satisfactory prices or equitable commodity exchange.

The intense depression in agriculture today is a consequence of the general world crisis caused by the normal workings of the capitalistic system resulting in: 1 Economic nationalism expressing itself in tariff barriers and other restrictions of world trade; 2 The decreased purchasing power of unemployed and under-employed workers and of the Canadian people in general; 3 the exploitation of both primary producers and consumers by monopolistic corporations who absorb a great proportion of the selling price of farm products. (This last is true, for example, of the distribution of milk and dairy products, the packing industry, and milling.)

The immediate cause of agricultural depression is the catastrophic fall in the world prices of foodstuffs as compared with other prices, this fall being due in large measure to the deflation of currency and credit. To counteract the worst effect of this, the internal price level should be raised so that the farmers' purchasing power may be restored.

We propose therefore:

1 The improvement of the position of the farmer by the increase of purchasing power made possible by the social control of the financial system. This control must be directed towards the increase of employment as laid down elsewhere and towards raising the prices of farm commodities by appropriate credit and foreign policies.

2 Whilst the family farm is the accepted basis for agricultural production in Canada the position of the farmer may be much improved by:

(a) The extension of consumers' co-operatives for the purchase of farm supplies and domestic requirements; and

(b) The extension of co-operative institutions for the processing and marketing of farm products.

Both of the foregoing to have suitable state encouragement and assistance.

3 The adoption of a planned system of agricultural development based upon scientific soil surveys directed towards better land utilization, and a scientific policy of agricultural development for the whole of Canada.

4 The substitution for the present system of foreign trade, of a system of import and export boards to improve the efficiency of overseas marketing, to control prices, and to integrate the foreign trade policy with the requirements of the national economic plan.

5 External Trade

THE REGULATION IN ACCORDANCE WITH THE NATIONAL PLAN OF EXTERNAL TRADE THROUGH IMPORT AND EXPORT BOARDS.

Canada is dependent on external sources of supply for many of her essential requirements of raw materials and manufactured products. These she can obtain only by large exports of the goods she is best fitted to produce. The strangling of our export trade by insane protectionist policies must be brought to an end. But the old controversies between free traders and protectionists are now largely obsolete. In a world of nationally organized economies Canada must organize the buying and selling of her main imports and exports under public boards, and take steps to regulate the flow of less important commodities by a system of licenses. By so doing she will be enabled to make the best trade agreements possible with foreign countries, put a stop to the exploitation of both primary producer and ultimate consumer, make possible the co-ordination of internal processing, transportation, and marketing of farm products, and facilitate the establishment of stable prices for such export commodities.

6 Co-operative Institutions

THE ENCOURAGEMENT BY THE PUBLIC AUTHORITY OF BOTH PRODUCERS' AND CONSUMERS' CO-OPERATIVE INSTITUTIONS.

In agriculture, as already mentioned, the primary producer can receive a larger net revenue through co-operative organization of purchases and marketing. Similarly in retail distribution of staple commodities such as milk, there is room for development both of public municipal operation and of consumers' co-operatives, and such co-operative organization can be extended into wholesale distribution and into manufacturing. Co-operative enterprises should be assisted by the state through appropriate legislation and through the provision of adequate credit facilities.

7 *Labor Code*

A NATIONAL LABOR CODE TO SECURE FOR THE WORKER MAXIMUM INCOME AND LEISURE, INSURANCE COVERING ILLNESS, ACCIDENT, OLD AGE, AND UNEMPLOYMENT, FREEDOM OF ASSOCIATION AND EFFECTIVE PARTICIPATION IN THE MANAGEMENT OF HIS INDUSTRY OR PROFESSION. The spectre of poverty and insecurity which still haunts every worker, though technological developments have made possible a high standard of living for everyone, is a disgrace which must be removed from our civilization. The community must organize its resources to effect progressive reduction of the hours of work in accordance with technological development and to provide a constantly rising standard of life to everyone who is willing to work. A labor code must be developed which will include state regulation of wages, equal reward and equal opportunity of advancement for equal services, irrespective of sex; measures to guarantee the right to work or the right to maintenance through stabilization of employment and through employment insurance; social insurance to protect workers and their families against the hazards of sickness, death, industrial accident and old age; limitation of hours of work and protection of health and safety in industry. Both wages and insurance benefits should be varied in accordance with family needs.

In addition workers must be guaranteed the undisputed right to freedom of association, and should be encouraged and assisted by the state to organize themselves in trade unions. By means of collective agreements and participation in works councils, the workers can achieve fair working rules and share in the control of industry and profession; and their organizations will be indispensable elements in a system of genuine industrial democracy.

The labor code should be uniform throughout the country. But the achievement of this end is difficult so long as jurisdiction over labor legislation under the B.N.A. Act is mainly in the hands of the provinces. It is urgently necessary, therefore, that the B.N.A. Act be amended to make such a national labor code possible.

8 *Socialized Health Services*

PUBLICLY ORGANIZED HEALTH, HOSPITAL AND MEDICAL SERVICES. With the advance of medical science the maintenance of a healthy population has become a function for which every civilized community should undertake responsibility. Health services should be made at least as freely available as are educational services today. But under a system which is still mainly one of private enterprise the costs of proper medical care, such as the wealthier members of society can easily afford, are at present prohibitive for great masses of the people. A properly organized system of public health services including medical and dental care, which would stress the prevention rather than the cure of illness should be extended to all our people   **309** in both rural and urban areas. This is an enterprise in which Dominion, Provincial and Municipal authorities, as well as the medical and dental professions, can co-operate.

9 B.N.A. Act

THE AMENDMENT OF THE CANADIAN CONSTITUTION, WITHOUT INFRINGING UPON RACIAL OR RELIGIOUS MINORITY RIGHTS OR UPON LEGITIMATE PROVINCIAL CLAIMS TO AUTONOMY, SO AS TO GIVE THE DOMINION GOVERNMENT ADEQUATE POWERS TO DEAL EFFECTIVELY WITH URGENT ECONOMIC PROBLEMS WHICH ARE ESSENTIALLY NATIONAL IN SCOPE; THE ABOLITION OF THE CANADIAN SENATE.

We propose that the necessary amendments to the B.N.A. Act shall be obtained as speedily as required, safeguards being inserted to ensure that the existing rights of racial and religious minorities shall not be changed without their own consent. What is chiefly needed today is the placing in the hands of the national government of more power to control national economic development. In a rapidly changing economic environment our political constitution must be reasonably flexible. The present division of powers between Dominion and Provinces reflects the conditions of a pioneer, mainly agricultural, community in 1867. Our constitution must be brought into line with the increasing industrialization of the country and the consequent centralization of economic and financial power – which has taken place in the last two generations. The principle laid down in the Quebec Resolution of the Fathers of Confederation should be applied to the conditions of 1933, that "there be a general government charged with matters of common interest to the whole country and local governments for each of the provinces charged with the control of local matters in their respective sections."

The Canadian Senate, which was originally created to protect provincial rights, but has failed even in this function, has developed into a bulwark of capitalist interests, as is illustrated by the large number of company directorships held by its aged members. In its peculiar composition of a fixed number of members appointed for life it is one of the most reactionary assemblies in the civilized world. It is a standing obstacle to all progressive legislation, and the only permanently satisfactory method of dealing with the constitutional difficulties it creates is to abolish it.

10 External Relations

A FOREIGN POLICY DESIGNED TO OBTAIN INTERNATIONAL ECONOMIC CO-OPERATION AND TO PROMOTE DISARMAMENT AND WORLD PEACE. Canada has a vital interest in world peace. We propose, therefore, to do everything in our power to advance the idea of international co-operation as represented by the League of Nations and the International Labor Organization. We would extend our diplomatic machinery for keeping in touch with the main centres of world interest. But we believe that genuine international co-operation is incompatible with the capitalist regime which is in force in most countries, and that strenuous efforts are needed to rescue the League from its present conditions of being mainly a League of capitalist Great Powers. We stand resolutely against all participation in imperialist wars. Within the British Commonwealth, Canada must maintain her autonomy as a completely self-governing nation. We must resist all attempts to build up a new economic British Empire in place of the old political one, since such attempts readily lend themselves to the purposes of capitalist exploitation and may easily lead to further world wars. Canada must refuse to be entangled in any more wars fought to make the world safe for capitalism.

11 *Taxation and Public Finance*

A NEW TAXATION POLICY DESIGNED NOT ONLY TO RAISE PUBLIC REVENUES BUT ALSO TO LESSEN THE GLARING INEQUALITIES OF INCOME AND TO PROVIDE FUNDS FOR SOCIAL SERVICES AND THE SOCIALIZATION OF INDUSTRY: THE CESSATION OF THE DEBT CREATING SYSTEM OF PUBLIC FINANCE.

In the type of economy that we envisage, the need for taxation, as we now understand it, will have largely disappeared. It will nevertheless be essential during the transition period, to use the taxing powers, along with the other methods proposed elsewhere, as a means of providing for the socialization of industry, and for extending the benefits of increased Social Services.

At the present time capitalist governments in Canada raise a large proportion of their revenues from such levies as customs duties and sales taxes, the main burden of which falls upon the masses. In place of such taxes upon articles of general consumption, we propose a drastic extension of income, corporation and inheritance taxes, steeply graduated according to ability to pay. Full publicity must be given to income tax payments and our tax collection system must be brought up to the English standard of efficiency.

We also believe in the necessity for an immediate revision of the basis of Dominion and Provincial sources of revenue, so as to produce a co-ordinated and equitable system of taxation throughout Canada.

An inevitable effect of the capitalist system is the debt creating character of public financing. All public debts have enormously increased, and the fixed interest charges paid thereon now amount to the largest single item of so-called uncontrollable public expenditures. The CCF proposes that in future no public financing shall be permitted which facilitates the perpetuation of the parasitic interest-receiving class; that capital shall be provided through the medium of the National Investment Board and free from perpetual interest charges.

We propose that all Public Works, as directed by the Planning Commission, shall be financed by the issuance of credit, as suggested, based upon the National Wealth of Canada.

12 *Freedom*

FREEDOM OF SPEECH AND ASSEMBLY FOR ALL; REPEAL OF SECTION 98 OF THE CRIMINAL CODE; AMENDMENT OF THE IMMIGRATION ACT TO PREVENT THE PRESENT INHUMAN POLICY OF DEPORTATION; EQUAL TREATMENT BEFORE THE LAW OF ALL RESIDENTS OF CANADA IRRESPECTIVE OF RACE, NATIONALITY OR RELIGIOUS OR POLITICAL BELIEFS.

In recent years, Canada has seen an alarming growth of Fascist tendencies among all governmental authorities. The most elementary rights of freedom of speech and assembly have been arbitrarily denied to workers and to all whose political and social views do not meet with the approval of those in power. The lawless and brutal conduct of the police in certain centres in preventing public meetings and in dealing with political prisoners must cease. Section 98 of the Criminal Code which has been used as a weapon of political oppression by a panic-stricken capitalist government, must be wiped off the statute book and those who have been imprisoned under it must be released. An end must be put to the inhuman practice of deporting immigrants who were brought to this country by immigration propaganda and now, through no fault of their own, to find themselves victims of an executive department against whom there is no appeal to the courts of the land. We stand for full economic, political and religious liberty for all.

13 *Social Justice*

THE ESTABLISHMENT OF A COMMISSION COMPOSED OF PSYCHIATRISTS, PSYCHOLOGISTS, SOCIALLY-MINDED JURISTS AND SOCIAL WORKERS, TO DEAL WITH ALL MATTERS PERTAINING TO CRIME AND PUNISHMENT AND THE GENERAL ADMINISTRATION OF LAW, IN ORDER TO HUMANIZE THE LAW AND TO BRING IT INTO HARMONY WITH THE NEEDS OF THE PEOPLE.

While the removal of economic inequality will do much to overcome the most glaring injustices in the treatment of those who come into conflict with the law, our present archaic system must be changed and brought into accordance with a modern concept of human relationships. The new system must not be based, as is the present one, upon vengeance and fear, but upon an understanding of human behaviour. For this reason its planning and control cannot be left in the hands of those steeped in the outworn legal tradition; and therefore it is proposed that there shall be established a national commission composed of psychiatrists, psychologists, socially-minded jurists and social workers whose duty it shall be to devise a system of prevention and correction consistent with other features of a new social order.

14 *An Emergency Programme*

THE ASSUMPTION BY THE DOMINION GOVERNMENT OF DIRECT RESPONSIBILITY FOR DEALING WITH THE PRESENT CRITICAL UNEMPLOYMENT SITUATION AND FOR TENDERING SUITABLE WORK OR ADEQUATE MAINTENANCE; THE ADOPTION OF MEASURES TO RELIEVE THE EXTREMITY OF THE CRISIS AS A PROGRAMME OF PUBLIC SPENDING ON HOUSING, AND OTHER ENTERPRISES THAT WILL INCREASE THE REAL WEALTH OF CANADA, TO BE FINANCED BY THE ISSUE OF CREDIT BASED ON THE NATIONAL WEALTH.

The extent of unemployment and the widespread suffering which it has caused, creates a situation with which provincial and municipal governments have long been unable to cope and forces upon the Dominion government direct responsibility for dealing with the crisis as the only authority with financial resources adequate to meet

the situation. Unemployed workers must be secured in the tenure   Appendix A
of their homes, and the scale and methods of relief, at present altogether inadequate, must be such as to preserve decent human
standards of living.

It is recognized that even after a Co-operative Commonwealth
Federation Government has come into power, a certain period of
time must elapse before the planned economy can be fully worked
out. During this brief transitional period, we propose to provide
work and purchasing power for those now unemployed by a far-
reaching programme of public expenditure on housing, slum clearance, hospitals, libraries, schools, community halls, parks, recreational
projects, reforestation, rural electrification, the elimination of grade
crossings, and other similar projects in both town and country. This
programme, which would be financed by the issuance of credit based
on the national wealth, would serve the double purpose of creating
employment and meeting recognized social needs. Any steps which
the Government takes, under this emergency programme, which may
assist private business, must include guarantees of adequate wages
and reasonable hours of work, and must be designed to further the
advance towards the complete Co-operative Commonwealth.

Emergency measures, however, are of only temporary value, for
the present depression is a sign of the mortal sickness of the whole
capitalist system, and this sickness cannot be cured by the application
of salves. These leave untouched the cancer which is eating at the
heart of our society, namely, the economic system in which our
natural resources and our principal means of production and distribution are owned, controlled and operated for the private profit of
a small proportion of our population.

No c.c.f. Government will rest content until it has eradicated
capitalism and put into operation the full programme of socialized
planning which will lead to the establishment in Canada of the Co-
operative Commonwealth.

1956 WINNIPEG DECLARATION OF PRINCIPLES OF THE CO-OPERATIVE COMMONWEALTH FEDERATION (PART I SOCIAL DEMOCRATIQUE DU CANADA)

The aim of the Co-operative Commonwealth Federation is the establishment in Canada by democratic means of a co-operative commonwealth in which the supplying of human needs and enrichment
of human life shall be the primary purpose of our society. Private
profit and corporate power must be subordinated to social planning
designed to achieve equality of opportunity and the highest possible
living standards for all Canadians.

This is, and always has been, the aim of the ccf. The Regina
Manifesto, proclaimed by the founders of the movement in 1933,
has had a profound influence on Canada's social system. Many of the
improvements it recommended have been wrung out of unwilling
governments by the growing strength of our movement and the
growing political maturity of the Canadian people. Canada is a

better place than it was a generation ago, not least because of the cry
for justice sounded in the Regina Manifesto and the devoted efforts
of CCF members and supporters since that time.

Canada Still Ridden by Inequalities

In spite of great economic expansion, large sections of our people
do not benefit adequately from the increased wealth produced.
Greater wealth and economic power continue to be concentrated in
the hands of a relatively few private corporations. The gap between
those at the bottom and those at the top of the economic scale has
widened.

Thousands still live in want and insecurity. Slums and inadequate
housing condemn many Canadian families to a cheerless life. Older
citizens exist on pensions far too low for health and dignity. Many
too young to qualify for pensions are rejected by industry as too old
for employment, and face the future without hope. Many in serious
ill-health cannot afford the hospital and medical care they need.
Educational institutions have been starved for funds and, even in
days of prosperity, only a small proportion of young men and women who could benefit from technical and higher education can
afford it.

In short, Canada is still characterized by glaring inequalities of
wealth and opportunity and by the domination of one group over
another. The growing concentration of corporate wealth has resulted
in a virtual economic dictatorship by a privileged few. This threatens
our political democracy which will attain its full meaning only when
our people have a voice in the management of their economic affairs
and effective control over the means by which they live.

The Folly of Wasted Resources

Furthermore, even during a time of high employment, Canada's
productive capacity is not fully utilized. Its use is governed by the
dictates of private economic power and by considerations of private
profit. Similarly, the scramble for profit has wasted and despoiled our
rich resources of soil, water, forest and minerals.

This lack of social planning results in a waste of our human as well
as our natural resources. Our human resources are wasted through
social and economic conditions which stunt human growth, through
unemployment and through our failure to provide adequate education.

The Challenge of New Horizons

The CCF believes that Canada needs a program for the wise development and conservation of its natural resources. Our industry can and
should be so operated as to enable our people to use fully their talents
and skills. Such an economy will yield the maximum opportunities
for individual development and the maximum of goods and services
for the satisfaction of human needs at home and abroad.

Unprecedented scientific and technological advances have brought
us to the threshold of a second industrial revolution. Opportunities
for enriching the standard of life in Canada and elsewhere are greater

than ever. However, unless careful study is given to the many problems which will arise and unless there is intelligent planning to meet them, the evils of the past will be multiplied in the future. The technological changes will produce even greater concentrations of wealth and power and will cause widespread distress through unemployment and the displacement of population.

The challenge facing Canadians today is whether future development will continue to perpetuate the inequalities of the past or whether it will be based on principles of social justice.

Capitalism Basically Immoral

Economic expansion accompanied by widespread suffering and injustice is not desirable social progress. A society motivated by the drive for private gain and special privilege is basically immoral.

The CCF reaffirms its belief that our society must have a moral purpose and must build a new relationship among men – a relationship based on mutual respect and on equality of opportunity. In such a society everyone will have a sense of worth and belonging, and will be enabled to develop his capacities to the full.

Social Planning For a Just Society

Such a society cannot be built without the application of social planning. Investment of available funds must be channelled into socially desirable projects; financial and credit resources must be used to help maintain full employment and to control inflation and deflation.

In the co-operative commonwealth there will be an important role for public, private and co-operative enterprise working together in the people's interest.

The CCF has always recognized public ownership as the most effective means of breaking the stranglehold of private monopolies on the life of the nation and of facilitating the social planning necessary for economic security and advance. The CCF will, therefore, extend public ownership wherever it is necessary for the achievement of these objectives.

At the same time, the CCF also recognizes that in many fields there will be need for private enterprise which can make a useful contribution to the development of our economy. The co-operative commonwealth will, therefore, provide appropriate opportunities for private business as well as publicly-owned industry.

The CCF will protect and make more widespread the ownership of family farms by those who till them, of homes by those who live in them, and of all personal possessions necessary for the well-being of the Canadian people.

In many fields the best means of ensuring justice to producers and consumers is the co-operative form of ownership. In such fields, every assistance will be given to form co-operatives and credit unions and to strengthen those already in existence.

Building a Living Democracy

The CCF welcomes the growth of labour unions, farm and other organizations of the people. Through them, and through associations   315 for the promotion of art and culture, the fabric of a living democracy is being created in Canada. These organizations must have the fullest opportunity for further growth and participation in building our nation's future.

In the present world struggle for men's minds and loyalties, democratic nations have a greater responsibility than ever to erase every obstacle to freedom and every vestige of racial, religious or political discrimination. Legislation alone cannot do this, but effective legislation is a necessary safeguard for basic rights and a sound foundation for further social and educational progress.

Therefore, the CCF proposes the enactment of a Bill of Rights guaranteeing freedom of speech and of expression, the right of lawful assembly, association and organization, equal treatment before the law, freedom to worship according to one's own conscience and the enjoyment of all rights without distinction of race, sex, religion or language.

Basis for Peace

The solution of the problems facing Canada depends, in large part, on removing the international dangers which threaten the future of all mankind. Therefore no task is more urgent than that of building peace and of forging international policies which will banish from the earth the oppressive fear of nuclear destruction. Only if there is a determined will to peace and if every part of the world is free from the fear of aggression and domination, can progress be made toward a lasting settlement of outstanding differences.

Throughout the years the CCF has maintained that there has been too much reliance on defence expenditures to meet the threat of communist expansion. One of the urgent needs for building a peaceful world and for extending the influence and power of democracy is generous support of international agencies to provide assistance to under-developed countries on a vast scale.

The hungry, oppressed and underprivileged of the world must know democracy not as a smug slogan but as a dynamic way of life which sees the world as one whole, and which recognizes the right of every nation to independence and of every people to the highest available standard of living.

Support of UN

The CCF reaffirms full support for the United Nations and its development into an effective organization of international co-operation and government. The world must achieve a large measure of international disarmament without delay and evolve a system of effective international control and inspection to enable the prohibition of nuclear weapons.

The CCF believes in full international co-operation which alone can bring lasting peace. The practices of imperialism, whether of the old style or the new totalitarian brand, must disappear. The CCF strives for a world society based on the rule of law and on freedom, on the right to independence of all peoples, on greater equality among nations and on genuine universal brotherhood.

The CCF has confidence in Canada and its people who have come from many lands in search of freedom, security and opportunity. It is proud of our country's origins in the British and French traditions which have produced our present parliamentary and judicial systems.

The CCF believes in Canada's federal system. Properly applied in a spirit of national unity, it can safeguard our national well-being and at the same time protect the traditions and constitutional rights of the provinces. Within the framework of the federal system the CCF will equalize opportunities for the citizens of every province in Canada. True national unity will be achieved only when every person from the Atlantic to the Pacific is able to enjoy an adequate standard of living.

Socialism on the March

In less than a generation since the CCF was formed, democratic socialism has achieved a place in the world which its founders could hardly have envisaged. Many labour and socialist parties have administered or participated in the governments of their countries. As one of these democratic socialist parties, the CCF recognizes that the great issue of our time is whether mankind shall move toward totalitarian oppression or toward a wider democracy within nations and among nations.

The CCF will not rest content until every person in this land and in all other lands is able to enjoy equality and freedom, a sense of human dignity, and an opportunity to live a rich and meaningful life as a citizen of a free and peaceful world. This is the Co-operative Commonwealth which the CCF invites the people of Canada to build with imagination and pride.

APPENDIX B

TABLE I ELECTION RESULTS 1935–62

		B.C.	ALTA.	SASK.	MAN.	ONT.	QUE.	N.S.	N.B./P.E.I. NEWF.	TOTAL
1935	votes	97,015	30,921	73,505	54,491	127,927	7,326	—	—	391,185
	%	33.6	13.0	21.3	19.4	8.0	0.6	—	—	8.9
	seats	3	—	2	2	—	—	—	—	7
1940	votes	103,181	35,082	106,267	61,448	61,166	7,610	17,715	761	393,230
	%	28.4	13.0	28.6	19.4	3.8	0.6	6.3	0.4	8.5
	seats	1	—	5	1	—	—	1	—	8
1945	votes	125,945	57,077	167,233	101,892	260,502	33,450	51,892	17,684	816,259
	%	29.4	18.4	44.4	31.6	14.4	2.4	16.7	.06	15.6
	seats	4	—	18	5	—	—	1	—	28
1949	votes	145,442	31,329	152,399	83,176	306,551	17,767	33,333	11,173	782,410*
	%	31.5	9.3	40.9	25.9	15.2	1.1	9.9	.02	13.4
	seats	3	—	5	3	1	—	1	—	13
1953	votes	125,487	23,573	156,406	64,402	212,224	23,833	22,357	8,028	636,310
	%	26.6	6.9	44.2	23.6	11.1	1.5	6.7	.02	11.3
	seats	7	—	11	3	1	—	1	—	23
1957	votes	131,873	27,127	140,293	82,398	274,069	31,780	17,117	3,002	707,659
	%	22.3	6.3	36	23.6	12.1	1.8	4.4	—	10.7
	seats	7	—	10	5	3	—	1	—	25
1958	votes	153,405	19,666	112,800	74,906	262,120	45,594	18,911	4,996	692,398
	%	24.5	4.4	28.4	19.6	10.5	2.3	4.5	.01	9.5
	seats	4	—	1	3	3	—	—	—	8
1962†	votes	212,035	42,305	93,444	76,514	456,459	91,795	39,689	51,081	1,045,853
	%	30	8.5	22.4	20.2	17.5	4.5	9.9	5	13.5
	seats	10	—	—	2	6	—	1	—	19

*Includes Yukon-Mackenzie River
†The first election contested by the NDP.
Source: H. Scarrow, *Canada Votes* (New Orleans 1963); Ottawa, *Reports of the Chief Electoral Officer.*

TABLE II GALLUP POLL RESULTS 1942–61

Year	CCF	Liberal	Conservative
1942	21	39	23
1943	29	28	28
1944	24	36	27
1945	19	40	27
1949	15	54	28
1950	13	51	33
1953	11	53	29
1954	12	50	29
1955	13	46	32
1956	10	50	31
1957	9	49	34
1958	9	32	57
1959	10	37	46
1960	8	49	36
1961	7	47	39

Source: Compiled from poll results published in *Public Opinion Quarterly* 1946–51; Zakuta, *A Protest Movement Becalmed*; Alford, *Party and Society*; and reports of the Canadian Institute of Public Opinion. Figures are per cent of national sample.

TABLE III CCF MEMBERSHIP 1947–60*

Year	Membership	Year	Membership
1947	29,820	1956	24,771
1948	38,782	1957	27,586
1949	32,330	1958	24,852
1950	20,238	1959	23,022
1951	24,121	1960	29,097
1952	24,204		
1953	25,046		
1954	18,273		
1955	19,351		

Source: National Secretary's Reports to the National Conventions.

*No national membership records were kept prior to the introduction of the national membership fee in 1946. In his reports to the relevant national conventions, the national secretary estimated party membership at slightly more than 20,000 in 1938, less than 30,000 in 1942, and over 90,000 in 1944. Provincial records were not much more accurate and were kept only on a monthly basis. It is known, for example, that there were almost 26,000 members in Saskatchewan and 10,216 in Ontario in 1944. The national secretary's estimate for that year must be considered slightly inflated.

INDEX

Aberhart, William, 159
Abrams, M., 188 n., 190
Across Canada, 125, 150, 166, 281
Acton, Lord, 58
Affiliated groups, 143
Agrarian protest, 14
Akroyd, F. M., 264 n.
Alberta Labour News, 17 n., 24 n., 27 n., 141
Alford, R. R., 206
Alienation, 35–6
All-Canadian Congress of Labour, 41, 77, 82
Alter, Victor, 270–2
Anti-CCF propaganda, 202 ff.
Anti-intellectualism, 70
Argue, Hazen, 133, 167, 169 n., 172, 213, 235; elected house leader, 234–5; as house leader, 236; and NDP leadership, 237; as national leader, 238; becomes Liberal, appointed to Senate, 238
Armstrong, Myrtle, 86, 112, 122
Avakoumovitch, Ivan, 284 n.

Ballantyne, Murray G., 211 n., 212 and n.
Ballantyne, R., 269 n.
Barnes, S. H., 214 n.
Barrett, Silby, 80, 82
Bartlett, W. J., 26
Beck, M., 188 n.
Bell, Daniel, 58, 64, 160, 287 n.
Bellamy, Edward, 33, 54, 62
Bengough, Percy, 276
Bennett, R. B., 257; and New Deal, 240
Beveridge Report, 109
Bland, Salem, 16 n., 262
Blatchford, Robert, 21, 33, 40, 41
Bloc Populaire, 212, 214

Boothe, Jack, 202, 203
Borgford, Inge, 104
Bracken, J., 222
Bren gun scandal, 241–2
Brewin, F. Andrew, 117 n., 122, 130 and n., 133, 168, 169 n., 170, 172, 237
British Columbia provincial executive, 271
Brown, Hilary, 271
Bruce, John, 79 n.
Bryce, William, 110
Bryden, Kenneth, 182
Buck, Tim, 65, 256, 259; and CCF, 262, 274–5; and Liberal party, 268–9, 275–6; and NDP, 290 n.
Buhay, Becky, 260
Buhay, Michael, 275
Burt, George, 122, 209, 274, 281
Burton, Joseph, 110

Calgary Albertan, 283
Calgary convention, 43 ff.
Calgary program, 43
Campbell, M. N., 29 n.
Cameron, Colin, 103, 132, 192, 194, 195, 227, 233; on small business, 114; on CCF philosophy, 128; on Communist party, 279
Canadian Brotherhood of Railway Employees (CBRE), 142
Canadian Catholic Congress of Labour, 214
Canadian Congress of Labour (CCL), 222; and CCF, 82–6, 273; and union with Trades and Labour Congress (TLC), 131
Canadian Forum, 32, 127, 199
Canadian Labour Congress, 132–3; *see also* Canadian Congress of Labour

321

Canadian Labour Defense League, 144, 255, 259 ff., 261
Canadian Labour party, 23, 24, 25, 33, 41, 145
Canadian League against War and Fascism, 261, 262
Canadian League for Peace and Democracy, 262
Canadian Peace Congress, 281
Canadian Socialist League, 23
Canadian Register, 212
Canadian Tribune, 269, 272, 274–5
Canadian Unionist, 77, 83, 99, 134
Caplan, Gerald, 29 n., 260 n.
Carr, Sam, 262
Casgrain, Thérèse, 167, 168, 169 n.
Cassidy, Harry, 43
Carlin, Robert H., 195, 280
Carter, G., 13 n.
Champagne, Father A., 213
Charbonneau, Archbishop, 211
Chartrand, Omer, 127 and n., 173, 231
Chevrier, Lionel, 246–7
Citizen and Country, 24
Clarion, 24, 269
Coldwell, M. J.: on CCF as movement, 10; member of Progressive party, 15; Regina alderman, 21; forms ILP, 21; elected president of Farmer-Labour party, 22; compared with Woodsworth, 28, 57, 160, 163, 239; on party philosophy, 49 n., 61, 62, 66, 128; as teacher, 51; on private property, 62–3, 107; on monopolies, 63 n.; on profiteering, 65; on conscientious objection, 91; and war, 92, 94–5, 106; as leader, 99, 162–3, 168; on socialism, 120; on redefinition of philosophy, 126, 170; and NDP, 134; on cencohesion, 147 n.; on democratic parties, 154; on policy-making, 154; compared with David Lewis, 163; and foreign policy, 224; and tralization of party, 147; on party CCF caucus, 224 ff., 232; and German re-armament, 227–8; and national party, 228; and conscription, 230–2; and Korean War, 233; defeated in 1958, 234; and Quebec, 234; and party leadership in 1960, 237; as parliamentarian, 239, 248–9; and Bren gun scandal, 241; on co-operative commonwealth, 243–4; and post-war reconstruction, 243; on CCF influence, 244–5; contact with Liberals, 248; and Communist party, 255, 278 and n.;

on united front, 264; attacked by Communist party, 266; on Communist and Liberal parties, 280; on Peace Councils, 281
Comment, 221, 250; *and see News Comment*
Commonwealth party, 30
Communist party (Labour Progressive Party, LPP), 8, 27, 121, 144, 191, 240, 296; and TLC, 77; opposition to CCF in unions, 83; attitude toward CCF, 255 ff.; overtures to CCF, 262 ff.; criticism of CCF, 265–6; and Saskatchewan CCF, 266; and Liberal party, 275–7; and electoral effect on CCF, 276–7
Conferences of Western Labour Political Parties, 5, 21, 24 ff., 41, 287
Congress of Industrial Organizations (CIO), 78, 82
Connell, Rev. Robert, 191
Conquergood, H., 131
Conroy, Pat, 82, 84, 85, 122
Conscription, 230–2
Conservative party, 3, 15, 52, 139, 141, 144, 156, 187, 191, 197, 222, 232, 247
Coote, G. G., 29 n., 44, 47, 48, 51
Co-operative Commonwealth: UFA definition of, 18–19
Co-operative Commonwealth Federation (CCF)
founding and growth: Calgary conference, 13; pedigree, 16; impetus for formation of, 24; purpose of, 41–2; immediate program (1934), 50; growth by 1944, 111–12; post-war decline, 139; failure, 177
goals, 58, 66–7; as "educational crusade," 50–2; as movement, 59; commitment to, 57
as movement and party, 6, 9, 290 ff.; as movement, 3, 22–3, 136–7, 209; as urban party, 13, 33, 86
platform, 116–17, 134–5, 300–1; defined as socialist party, 61; and capitalism, 72–3; and welfare state, 109; and small business, 113–14; and socialization, 123–4; revision of philosophy, 126–7; and Communist party, 256–7, 259, 277, 282–4, 276–7; and civil liberties, 65; and trade unions, 77–8, 82–7, 89, 121–2, 130–4; and farmers, 90
membership, 150–1, 183–5, 187; clubs, 142–3, 145; leaders, 167;

membership-activists, 185–7; Ontario expulsions, 191
organization and structure, 139, 180–2; convention procedure, 112–13; policy-making, 116, 153–5; constitution, 141; centralization of, 148–9; campaign literature, 88–9, 125 n.; appeal to the people, 196 ff.
support, 98, 209–10; in eastern Canada, 33; in Quebec, 210; and Roman Catholic church, 210 ff.
parliament: reputation of, 190; contribution to parliament, 239 ff.; influence of, 245 ff.; as opposition, 247–8; effect of parliamentary activity on movement, 249–50
attitude to war, 90 ff.; effect of war upon, 97–9; and conscription, 106; and Korean War, 233; and war effort, 242–3
ccf caucus, 11, 222 ff.; and party, 228 ff., 238; and conscription, 230–2; and leadership after 1958, 235; and foreign policy, 233
CCF News, 213
CCF Research Review, 49, 73
Co-operative Commonwealth Youth Movement (ccym), 261, 265
Co-operative movement, 49
Co-operative Press Association, 53
Corbett, Percy, 224
Cotterill, M., 122
Coyne, J. B., 224
Crerar, T. A., 29
Criminal Code (Section 98), 240

Dawes, Norman, 204 n.
Debs, Eugene, 54
Democracy Needs Socialism, 70
Democratic structure, 141
Depression, 18 ff., 74
Desaulniers, G., 231
Diefenbaker, John, 9
Dixon, Fred, 16 n., 23
Dodge, Bill, 133
Dominion Labour party, 23, 33; at Lethbridge, 25
Dominion Communist Total War Committee, 274
Doneleyko, Wilbert, 280
Dooley, D. J., 188 n.
Douglas, Major C. H., 41, 49
Douglas, T. C., 159; forms Weyburn Labor Association, 21; on public ownership, 62; on war, 92 n., 95; on Winnipeg Declaration, 130; and ndp leadership, 237, 238

Dowd, N., 85
Dowling, Fred, 80, 84, 85, 99, 209
Drew, Lt. Col. George, 190; and Bren gun scandal, 241
Dubé, Evariste, 275
Duncan, J. S., 204 n.
Duplessis, Maurice, 211, 214, 240
Duverger, M., 151, 183

Economic Reconstruction Clubs, 145
Edmonton Trades and Labour council, 25
Eight-point program, 42, 48
Einstein, Albert, 270
Elliot, P., 29 n.
Endicott, Dr. James, 281
Engelmann, Fred, 154, 164, 183
Erlich, H., 270–2
"Esselwein, Jack", *see* Leopold, Sgt. J.

Fabianism, 288
Fabian Socialism, 36, 40
Fabian Society, 30, 31, 50, 54, 76
Farmer, S. J., 23, 266 n.
Farmer-labour: co-operation, 18; antagonism, 33
Farmer-Labour Party, 21, 23; in Saskatchewan, 143
Farmers: alienation, 73–4; and Regina Manifesto 47–8; and socialism, 73–4
Farmers Political Association, 15, 20, 21; merges with Saskatchewan ILP, 21
Farmers Union, 20
Federal Labour party, 23
Federated Labour party, 23
Federationist, The, 24, 115
Fines, Clarence, 25, 51
First Term Program, 123–4
Fisher, Douglas, 235, 236; and ndp leadership, 237
Forke, Robert, 29
Forsey, Eugene, 44, 69 and n., 70 n., 71, 72, 79 n., 96, 97, 221, 222, 264 n.
Forster, D. F., 8 n., 296 n.
Fourteen-point program (1932), 42
Frankfurt Declaration, 170
Freed, Norman, 268
Freudian revolution, 179
Fulford, Robert, 52 and n.

Gadsby, H. F., 74 n.
Gaitskell, Hugh, 134
Galbraith, J. K., 186
Gallup Poll, 110, 125, 182, 200, 290
Gardiner, Robert, 19, 29 n., 30, 41;

Index

succeeds H. W. Wood, 18
Gargrave, Herbert, 93, 96, 192, 198
Garland, E. J., 29 n., 44, 57, 93, 105 and n., 147 and n.
Gauthier, Mgr. Georges, 211
General Relations Services Ltd., 203
German re-armament, 227–8
Gillis, Clarence, 85, 172
Ginger Group, 14, 18, 29, 287; role in formation of CCF, 29; and co-operation with Woodsworth's labour group, 30
Golden, Clinton, 270
Good, W. C., 29 and n., 47, 48
Gordon, King, 32, 44, 51, 69 and n., 70 n., 72, 79, 90, 264 n.
Gouldner, A., 160
Grain Growers Association, 20
Grain Growers' Guide, 14
Granatstein, J. L., 298 n.
Grange, 51
Graydon, Gordon, 222, 232
Green, William, 270
Grube, G. M. A., 31 n., 106, 167–8, 169 n., 170, 229, 262, 279; on Communist party, 278

Halifax Trades and Labour council, 273
Hamilton, Carl, 133, 168, 169 n.
Hanson, Richard, 222
Hayek, F., 204
Heaps, A. A., 23, 76 n., 93, 223, 242, 259, 264 n.
Heberle, R., 4 n., 157 n.
Hemmeon, J. C., 264 n.
Henderson, H., 157 n.
Hepburn, Mitchell, 240, 299
Herridge, Herbert, 128, 227, 235
Herridge, W. D., 165
Housewives' and Consumers' League, 281
Howard, Frank, 235, 236, 237
Hutchison, Bruce, 157, 251

Identity, 34–5
Ideology, 39; and parties, 297–8
Ilsley, J. L., 246, 296 n.
Image, 188–91
Independent Labour party (ILP), 21, 26, 30, 33, 192; in Saskatchewan, 15, 20, 21, 22, 27, 40, 43, 143; in Manitoba, 23, 24, 25, 33, 43
Industry and Humanity, 8, 251
Ingle, Lorne, 127 and n., 168, 172, 173, 182, 200, 221, 283 n.
Inglis, John, 241
International Fur and Leather Workers Union, 260

International Ladies Garment Workers Union, 272
International Socialist Conference, 170
International Woodworkers of America, 83
Iron Law of Oligarchy, 140
Irvine, William, 16 n., 23, 29, 30, 34 and n., 42, 51, 113, 128, 150, 157, 262
Ivens, William, 23, 51

James, M. E., 56 n.
Jamieson, Stuart, 203, 221
Jewish *Verbund*, 81
Jodoin, Claude, 132
Johnson, Alvin, 270
Johnson, Byron, 282
Johnson, D. L., 195, 280
Johnstone, Harris, 245
Jolliffe, E. B., 79 n., 87, 94, 109, 117, 118, 203, 277
Jones, Wilfred, 261

Kennedy, D. M., 29 n.
King, Carlyle, 127, 221
King, Jack G., 49 n., 179
King, William Lyon Mackenzie, 11, 29, 88, 190, 239, 240, 246, 251, 294, 295, 296 n.; and CCF, 8, 251, 291 ff., 242; and J. S. Woodsworth, 8, 219, 223; *Industry and Humanity*, 8, 251
Knowles, Stanley, H.: asked to be speaker, 9; and NDP as "movement," 10; on war, 93; and party leadership, 237; and CPR pensions, 245–7; and Industrial Disputes Investigations Act, 246; on Communist party, 278

Labour party (British), 54, 76, 81, 105, 126, 132, 133, 135, 143, 170, 224, 233, 287, 288; as movement, 3 n.
Labour Progressive Party, *see* Communist party
Labour Representation League, 23, 268
L'Action Catholique, 212, 213
Lane, Robert, 189
Langer, H. E., 79 n.
Lapointe, Ernest, 89 n., 275
La Presse, 213
Laroche, F., 172, 231
Latham, George, 41
Latham, Mrs. George, 42
Lazarus, Morden, 127 and n., 173, 200
Leacock, Stephen, 204 n.

Leadership, 155 ff.
League against War and Fascism, 255; and CCF, 264
League for Industrial Democracy, 31
League for Social Reconstruction (LSR), 30, 36, 41, 43, 44, 49, 51, 69, 71, 72, 73, 75, 134, 146, 210; first meeting of, 31; manifesto of, 31; and CCF, 31, 32, 70, 71, 221; Toronto branch, 32; socialism of, 40; and Regina Manifesto, 43; and agrarian radicalism, 73
Levens, Bert, 79 n.
Lebourdais, D. N., 145 n.
Le Devoir, 212
Left Turn Canada, 125
Leopold, Sgt. J., 279
Lewis, David: as national secretary, 55, 148; on CCF goals, 56–7, 61, 66, 128, 292; on socialism, 56–7, 81, 115–16, 128; on profits, 63; as socialist, 75, 81 n.; on farmers in CCF, 76; and trade unions, 77–8, 84–5; and war, 92, 93, 95, 96, 104; political career, 97 and n.; on needs of CCF, 98–100; 111–12, 201; on small businessmen, 114–16; criticism of, 118; as orator, 124; and party leadership, 127 n., 150, 162, 167, 235, 237; and NDP, 133, 134; and Sas-katchewan, government, 148 n., 166 n.; on recruiting members, 150–1; on activism, 152; domi-nance of, 163 ff.; central position of, 163 ff., 168–9; on leadership, 166; on role of caucus, 168 n., 221, 229; and party discipline, 192–3; on campaign material, 195, 198; on co-operation with Communist party, 264, 267, 268; and Erlich and Alter case, 270–3; and Communist party and trade unions, 273; and Cartier by-election, 275
Liberal party, 3, 8, 31, 47, 52, 64, 88, 122, 139, 141, 144, 156, 177, 187, 191, 197, 205–6, 207, 208, 214, 230, 232, 240–1, 247, 269, 276, 296–7, 299
Lipset, S. M., 53 n., 60, 86, 151, 162, 184, 211
Litvinov, Maxim, 270
Loeb, Alice, 261
Lucas, Louise, 42
Lyman House, 204 n.

MacAuley, A. J., 26
MacAuslane, A. A., 84

Maclean's Magazine, 109
Macdonald, A. B., 283
MacDonald, Donald C., 10, 112, 150, 172, 182, 209 n., 221, 281, 282
McGuigan, Archbishop, 212
MacInnis, Angus: first elected, 32; on war, 93, 96, 103; resigns from National Council, 95; on Com-munist party, 121, 278; on CCF clubs, 185; on pragmatism, 199; and caucus, 223–5; and Quebec, 234
McInnis, Edgar, 44
McLarty, N., 85
MacInnis, Grace, 27 n., 160, 167, 172, 264 n., 284
McKenzie, Frank, 162
Mackenzie, Ian, 241
Macleod, A. A., 262
McNaught, Carleton, 264 n., 265
McNaught, K. W., 13, 92 n., 157, 159, 240 n.
MacNeil, C. Grant, 51, 76 n., 91, 93, 103, 106, 150, 169 n., 192, 223, 224, 225, 241–2, 264 and n., 268
Macphail, Agnes, 29 and n., 30, 76 n.
Macpherson, C. B., 16 n., 62, 72, 206, 208 n.
Mahan, Archbishop P. J., 213
Make This YOUR Canada, 125
Mallory, J. R., 66 n.
Manion, Dr. R. J., 222
Manitoba: agrarian liberalism in, 16
Manitoba Farmers Union, 288
Manitoba Free Press, 5, 24, 26
Marsh, Helen, 264 n.
Marsh, Leonard, 49 n., 69 n., 70 n., 264 n.
Martin, Murdo, 235
Marx, Karl, 41, 45, 54
Mather, Barry, 198
Meighen, Arthur, 106, 204 n., 240; and York South by-election, 269
Meisel, John, 207 n.
Membership, 124, 142 ff., 151–3
Michels, Robert, 150, 156, 162 n., 167–8; on oligarchy, 140, 167, 292
Millard, Charles, 79 n., 80, 82, 83, 122, 191, 209, 273
Mine, Mill and Smelter Workers Union, 83, 195, 272, 280
Mitchell, Humphrey, 246
Mitchell, John, 78, 79 n.
Molotov, V. M., 270
Mooney, George S., 264
Moore, Tom, 84

Index

Morton, W. L., 14, 27
Mosca, Gaetano, 138, 139
Mosher, A. R., 41, 42, 76, 80, 82, 83, 84, 85, 99
Movements, 39, 52, 73; defined, 3–5; and parties, 6–7, 11; membership in, 35
Murdoch, J. Y., 204 n.
Murray, Gladstone, 117, 202, 204

National Committee for the New Party, 133
National conventions, 154–5
National Council, 146, 149; and leadership, 237–8; on Erlich and Alter, 271
National Executive, 146–7, 169; and Quebec, 234; and leadership, 237–8; attitude toward USSR, 269; on Erlich and Alter, 270
National Farmers Union, 85
National Labour College (U. K.), 40
National membership fee, 149
Neilsen, Dorise, 267
New Commonwealth, 262
New Democracy, 267
New Democratic Party (NDP), 10, 60, 75, 121 n., 132–4, 170, 175, 177, 178, 216, 236, 293
New Party, *see* NDP
New Party Clubs, 133
New Statement of Principles, 172–3
News Comment, 104, 105, 109 and n., 110, 125, 126, 134, 150, 166, 221, 222
Nicholson, A. M., 108
Nimsick, Leo, 282
Non-Partisan League, 180, 287; philosophy of, 16–17
NATO, 243
Noseworthy, Joe, 106, 172, 269

Oligarchy, 167–8, 170, 174–5
One Big Union, 83
Ontario campaign (1945), 118
Ontario expulsions, 144–5
Ontario provincial council; and Communists, 260
Ontario Labour Conference, 143
Ontario Trade Union Committee, 85
Orliffe, H., 79 and n.
Ostrogorski, M., 35 n., 170, 185
Ottawa *Journal*, 202
Outlook, 204

Park, Eamon, 80, 180
Parkinson, J. F., 44, 49 n., 69 and n., 70 n.
Partridge, E. A., 51
Parties, *see* political parties

Parties, *see* political parties
Peace Congress, 282
Peace councils, 255, 281
Pearson, L. B., 219
Penner, Jacob, 262
Peters, Arnold, 235–7
Philpott, Elmore, 44, 145
Pitman, Walter, 236
Planning for Freedom, 125
Plumptre, A. F. W., 44
Political Action Committee (PAC), CCL, CLC, 83, 120, 208–9, 209 n., 248
Political parties, 140–1; functions of, 3–4; and movements, 3–5, 40; brokerage function of, 39; ideology, 39, 297 ff.; discipline, 149; leadership, 162 ff.; and the party system, 293 ff.
Patrons of Industry, 51
Porter, John, 290, 295
Price, John, 24
Priestley, Norman, 42, 44
Pritchard, F., 51
Probe, John, 281
Progressive party (and Progressive movement), 13, 14, 21, 29, 31, 34, 39, 54, 67, 71, 100, 288, 296; tradition of, 6; and the CCF, 14, 15; as "crypto-liberals," 14; legacy of, 15; nature of, 15; and populism, 15; and UFA, 17
Public Informational Association, 202
Puritanism, 73
Puttee, A. W., 23

Quebec: and CCF, 210 ff.
Queen, John, 21, 42

Reconstruction party, 263
Redl, Fritz, 161
Regenstreif, Peter, 185, 186, 208
Regier, Erhart, 213, 230, 234, 235
Regina convention, 44
Regina Manifesto, 9, 13, 19, 31, 34, 39, 40, 42 n., 44 ff., 63, 69, 87, 111, 124, 137, 146, 170, 171, 173, 256 n., 287–8, 300; compared with Calgary program, 43; revision of, 125–7
Regina Trades and Labour council, 25
Regina Trekkers, 261, 264
Reid, Escott, 43
Responsible Enterprise Ltd., 204
Richards, Berry, 195, 280
Road to Serfdom, 204
Roman Catholic church (and CCF), 210 ff.

Ronning, Chester, 93
Roper, E., 51
Rose, Fred, 275 and n.
Ross, Sinclair, 159
Rowe, Percy, 223, 224, 262
RCMP, 240, 279

St. Laurent, Louis, 251
Salsberg, J. B., 258, 268, 274
Saskatchewan, immigrants and radicalism, 16; CCF victory in 1944, 109
Saskatchewan French-Canadian Catholic Association, 213
Scott, F. R.: and LSR, 31–2, 69 ff.; on Regina Manifesto, 43; on profits, 63; on business, 64; influence on CCF through LSR, 71; on war, 93; on welfare socialism, 109; provincial policy conference, 110–11; on CCF decline, 119; on revising Regina Manifesto, 126, 170, 171; on tactics and theory, 128; and NDP, 134; on Woodsworth, 160–1; collaboration with David Lewis, 165; on CCF in Quebec, 213–15; and caucus, 229, 240; Cartier by-election, 275
Scott, R. B. Y., 264 n.
Shane, Bernard, 272
Sharp, P. F., 15
Shaw, Lloyd, 194, 221
Shaw, J. T., 29 n.
Sheelty, "Alb.," 79 n.
Shipyard workers, 260
Sidaway, John, 24
Skinner, Robert, 24
Small, W. E., 26
Smith, A. E., 144, 145, 260, 261, 262
Smith, Norman, 248
Smith, Ralph, 23
Smith, Vernon, 17
Social Constructives, 191
Social Credit party, 3 ,6, 13, 15, 33, 34, 36, 52, 62, 88, 232, 267, 288, 299
Social Gospel, 34, 158
Socialism, 40, 41, 53–4, 61, 76
Socialists and movements, 3
Socialist candidates, 23
Socialist parties: as movements, 4
Socialist Party of Canada, 23, 30, 261; in B.C., 41, 145
Social Planning for Canada, 44, 70, 221
Social Reconstruction Clubs, 145
Social Suicide, 203
Speakman, Alfred, 47, 48
Spence, Ben, 262, 265
Spencer, H. E., 29 n., 34
Spry, Graham, 44, 49 n., 70 n., 145, 264 n., 265, 273
Stand Up and Be Counted, 203

Stewart, Alistair, 227, 245
Steeves, Dorothy, 93, 103, 170, 192, 221, 233
Stevens Royal Commission on Price Spreads, 72
Sullivan, Pat, 276

Taylor, J. S., 76 n., 222, 226, 264 n.
Thatcher, Ross, 226, 227, 299
Thomas, Norman, 54, 121
Thorson, J. T., 224
Toqueville, Alexis de, 185
Toronto Regional Labour Council, 260
Toronto *Star*, 257 n.
Trade union, and CCF, 79–80
Trade union committees, 120
Trades and Labor Congress, 23, 77, 78–9, 84, 86, 89, 273, 276; union with CCL, 130–1
Trail-Rossland and district CCF club, 271
Trestrail, B. A., 117, 200, 202, 203, 204
Trotskyites, 195
Trudeau, P. E., 214
Turner, Arthur, 282

Underhill, Frank H.: on origin of CCF, 13 n.; and LSR, 31, 32, 69 ff.; and 1932 program, 42; principal author of Regina Manifesto, 42 n., 54, 43; CCF as movement, 58; on war, 93; on centralization of CCF, 148; party strategy, 196, 198; on party system, 295 n., 298
Union Nationale, 214
United Auto Workers Union, 83; and Communist party, 274
United Electrical, Radio and Machine Workers, 83
United Electrical, Radio and Machine Workers of America, 260
United Electrical Workers Union, 260
United Farmers of Alberta (UFA), 14, 16–19, 27, 33, 41, 43, 48, 62, 99, 145, 288
United Farmers of Canada (Saskatchewan Section), 5, 20, 21–2, 26, 41, 43
United Farmers of Manitoba, 33, 43
United Farmers of Ontario (UFO), 16, 41, 48, 99, 144, 261
United Garment Workers of America, 260
United Mine Workers of America, 81, 83, 104, 274
United Nations, 243
United Packinghouse Workers Union, 80, 274
United Progressive party, 267

Index United Steelworkers of America, 80, 87, 274

Vancouver Street Railwayman's Union, 260
Vancouver Trades and Labour council, 25
Victoria district CCF council, 271
Villeneuve, Cardinal, 211, 212, 213
Von Pilis, F., 200

Wallas, Graham, 179 and n., 188
Ward, W. J., 29 n.
Weber, Max, 157
West Kootenay CCF council, 271
Western Labour News, 24
Wheat Pools, 48
White, Fred J., 25, 33 n.
Who Owns Canada?, 125
Wilkie, Wendell, 270
Williams, George, H., 20, 22, 42, 51 and n., 62 and n., 90, 91 and n., 92, 94, 95, 103, 191, 266–7
Winch, E. E., 47 n., 50 n., 55 n., 173, 174, 179, 191, 233, 258, 282
Winch, Harold, 57 n., 60 n., 71 and n., 79, 81 n., 113, 133, 169 n., 187, 193, 194, 212, 213, 227, 230, 234, 235, 236, 262
Winnipeg Declaration of Principles (1956), 31, 40, 65, 66, 117, 127–30, 134, 137, 170, 172–4; preparation of, 172–3
Winnipeg Convention (1934), 50
Winnipeg General Strike, 14, 240
Women's League of Nations Society, 261
Wood, Henry Wise, 16–18, 28, 46, 142
Woodsworth, Grace, *see* MacInnis, Grace
Woodsworth, J. S.: and old age pension, 8; and aims of CCF, 9, 58; on centralization, 10, 147;

and Non-Partisan League, 16; elected MP (1921), 23; Conferences of Western Labour Political Parties, 25–7; compared with Henry Wise Wood, 28; and Social Gospel, 28; and socialism, 28, 45, 53–4; and Ginger Group, 29, 30; and Commonwealth party, 30; as leader, 28, 57, 95, 156 ff., 168, 292; and LSR, 31; CCF president, 42; on making converts, 50, 56, 180; as pedagogue, 51; on public ownership, 61–2; on monopolies, 65; as urban socialist, 75; as labour man, 76; and Criminal Code (Section 98), 89; as pacifist, 92 ff., 224 ff.; on CCF structure, 141–2, 143, 144; on membership, 142; on CCF clubs, 143; on CCF as movement, 147 n.; on electoral politics, 178–9, 178 n.; on idealism, 186; as parliamentarian, 219, 239, 240; as caucus leader, 222 ff.; annual resolution for co-operative commonwealth, 239–40; and civil liberties, 240; and unemployment insurance, 245; on Communist party, 255; and defence of Communist party executive, 259; and Ontario CCF and Communist party, 261; on united front, 264, 267 and n.; attacked by Communist party, 266; on Labour Representation League, 268; as catalyst, 287

York South by-election, 269
Young, Rodney, 191, 258; expulsion of, 282–4

Zakuta, Leo, 116, 151, 164
Zaplitny, Fred, 152, 200

This book

was designed by

ALLAN FLEMING

with the assistance of

ANTJE LINGNER

and was printed by

University of

Toronto

Press